Tackling John Elway

The Definitive Collectors Guide

By: Jared Kraus

FIRST & GOAL PUBLISHING

ISBN: 979-8-218-99777-9
First Edition

Tackling John Elway
The Definitive Collectors Guide

By: Jared Kraus

For my son, Adam.

May his heroes be champions in their field, too.

YOU SHOULD BE IN HIS SHOES.

February 1985
Jared Kraus and John Elway
Greybull, Wyoming.

YOU SHOULD BE IN HIS SHOES.

I had to have it. It was 1983, I was 12 and in a sporting goods store in Casper, Wyoming. I offered to buy it, but the salesman refused to sell. It was his last one, on a pillar behind the register. I was disappointed, but a few minutes later as I was leaving the store, he told me to wait, climbed a small ladder, pulled it down, rolled it up, and handed it to me. It had tack holes and was torn and taped, but it didn't matter, my John Elway collection started that day. It would be months before his rookie card came out of a pack of cards I bought with money from my 13th birthday.

Begun in 1983, this project endured 16 seasons, 148 wins, and Super Bowls both lost and won. Then took an additional 21 years to complete.

The digital version started in 2004, the same year Elway was inducted into the Pro Football Hall of Fame. It has survived two desktops, five laptops, two operating systems, nine CD's, several flash drives, two software applications, and two external hard drives. It was finally completed November 20, 2024.

Its been a great run!

This book is dedicated to anyone who ever tried "Tackling John Elway."

Jared Kraus

1975-78

At Lincoln Junior High in Pullman, Washington, John Elway directed a single-wing offense for the freshman team. Following the school year, he and his family moved to Los Angeles, and John and his sisters Jana, and Lee Ann were enrolled at Granada Hills High School. It was there that Elway was introduced to the West Coast Offense by one of its originators, Head Football Coach, Jack Neumeier.

Playing sparingly as a sophomore, Elway threw for 835 yards, and 5 touchdowns.

As a junior his star began to shine as he threw for 3039 yards, and 25 touchdowns.

A knee injury sidelined him for the second half of his senior season, but in the five games he played, Elway threw for 1837 yards, and 19 touchdowns.

Named the Southern California Athlete of the Year by Citizen Savings, Elway was the top rated prep quarterback, and the highest recruited high school player in the nation.

He was selected to the *Parade, Football News, Scholastic Coach, National Coaches Association,* and *Joe Namath Magazine* All-American Teams.

1979

A two-sport star, Elway was 4-2 as a pitcher with a 1.03 ERA, and a .491 batting average. He hit .692 in the city playoffs, was named the tournament MVP, and was drafted by the Kansas City Royals.

1979 MLB Amateur Baseball Draft

RD	#	Name	Team
1	1	Al Chambers	Seattle Mariners
1	6	Andy Van Slyke	St. Louis Cardinals
2	44	Chris Brown	San Francisco Giants
4	99	Dan Marino	Kansas City Royals
6	144	Harold Reynolds	San Diego Padres
17	440	Orel Hershiser	Los Angeles Dodgers
19	463	John Elway	Kansas City Royals
19	493	Don Mattingly	New York Yankees
27	676	Joe Carter	Chicago Cubs

July 21, 1979
Shrine Bowl - All-Star Game
In leading the North past the South, 35-15, Elway, in his final prep football appearance, completed 23/37 passes for 363 yards, and four touchdowns.

LIFE

Republicans Rush for the Presidency

For Music's Top Stars Home Is a Fancy Bus

The Case of the Clumsy Spies

October 1979 $1.50

Singer Dolly Parton tours by bus

October 1979

A source of pride to his football-coach father, spoiled utterly by his mother and two sisters and admired by his Granada Hills High (Calif.) classmates, quarterback John Elway graduated with a 3.7 average and was named to five all-American teams, courted by colleges from coast to coast and drafted 18th by the Kansas City Royals for his pitching arm and fielding abilities. John admits, "I have a tendency to be a bad sport. I don't like to lose." He found it impossible to choose between football and baseball and decided that "at this time I couldn't give up one for the other." So he accepted Stanford's offer of a full scholarship.

Stanford Head Coach Bill Walsh resigned in January, and was replaced by Rod Dowhower who had beeen coaching quarterbacks and receivers. Elway impressed enough during summer camp that Babe Laughenberg and Grayson Rodgers transferred to other schools.

The Cardinal was ranked #13 going into the first game, a 33-10 loss to Tulane. They would finish 5-5-1.

Elway, platooning with Turk Schonert, played in 9 games. He completed 50/96 passes for 544 yards, and six touchdowns.

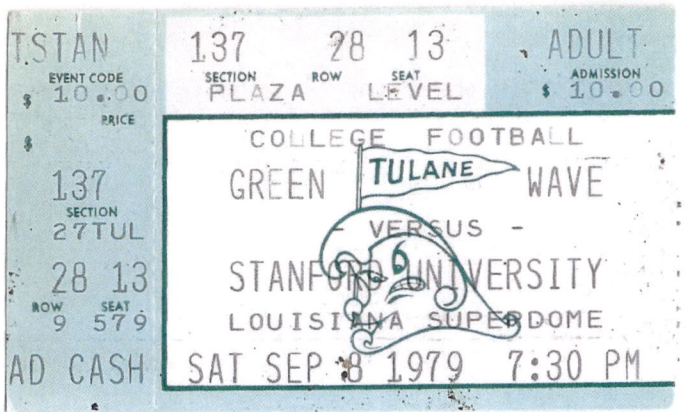

September 8, 1979
In a 31-10 loss to Tulane, Elway made his NCAA debut. Late in the game Elway replaced Turk Schonert and completed 2/8 passes for 21 yards.

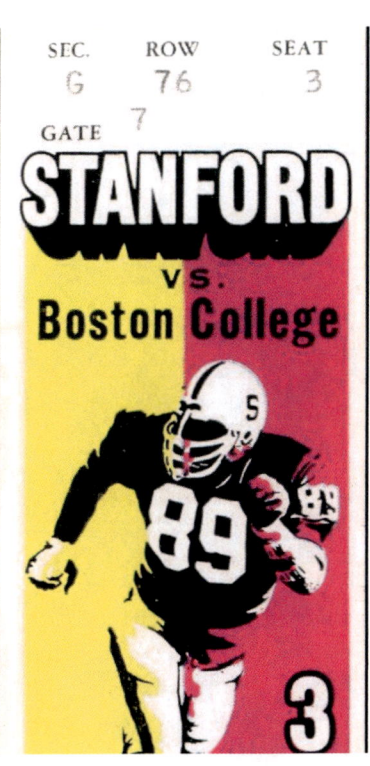

September 29, 1979
A 33-14 win against Boston College, Elway completed his first NCAA touchdown pass to Ken Margerum.

October 6, 1979
A 27-24 win against UCLA, alternating with Turk Schonert, John Elway led the no-huddle offense and connected on 16 of 23 passes for 178 yards, and a touchdown. He was also the placeholder for the 56-yard, game winning, field goal.

1980

The Stanford Baseball Team was 29-24.

Elway hit .269 with 1 home run, and 18 RBI.

Paul Wiggin replaced Rod Dowhower as Head Coach, and Stanford was ranked #15 in the pre-season polls. They would begin the season 5-1 which included a win over #4 Oklahoma. They would be ranked as high as #11, but faded down the stretch. Losing four of their final six games, eliminated them from bowl contention.

Elway played all 11 games, completed 248/379 passes for 2889 yards, and 27 touchdowns. He also rushed for 50 yards, and 4 touchdowns.

Elway led the Pac-10 in attempts, completions, yards, and touchdowns.
He was the Pac-10's Player of the Year for 1980.

September 6, 1980
John Elway starts his first NCAA game, a 35-25 win over Oregon. He completed 17/26 passes for 250 yards, and touchdowns of 41 yards to Ken Margerum, and 11-yards to Andre Tyler.

September 27, 1980
A 31-14 Cardinal win, Oklahoma was ranked #4, but fell behind 31-0 before finding the endzone. Elway completed 20/34 passes for 237 yards, and three touchdowns. He also had 18 carries for 95 yards rushing, and an additional score.

November 1, 1980

Against Oregon State, a 54-13 Stanford win, Elway throws 6 touchdown passes setting a new PAC 10 single-game record. He threw 4 in the second quarter, also a record.

STANFORD UNIVERSITY

7 JOHN ELWAY
QB 6-3 180 SOPH.
NORTHRIDGE, CA

1980 Stanford Team Issued Photo

1980 Stanford Team Issued Photo

November 8, 1980

Officially it was a 46 yard touchdown pass, in a 34-9 Stanford loss, to the #4 ranked USC Trojans. But what a throw! The ball was placed at the USC 46-yard line, upon the snap Elway took a seven step drop, and was at the Stanford 45 when the pocket collapsed. With the USC defense closing in, Elway retreated to the Stanford 30 before twisting and turning back toward the line of scrimmage. He had run nearly to the USC sideline before unloading the ball at the Stanford 40, (16 yards behind the line of scrimmage). Ken Margerum had gotten behind USC safety Ronnie Lott and was in the middle of the field...Elway's pass hit Margerum in the numbers three yards deep in the middle of the end-zone. The ball had travelled over 70 yards in the air.

1981

Stanford was 43-22 and advanced to the Austin Regionals in the NCAA Tournament.

Elway hit .361 with 9 home runs, and 50 RBI.

He was selected in the second round of the amateur draft by the New York Yankees.

June 8, 1981
1981 Amateur Baseball Draft

Round	#	YR		Team	POS
1	1	JR	Mike Moore	Seattle Mariners	P
1	2	JR	Joe Carter	Chicago Cubs	OF
1	6	JR	Kevin McReynolds	San Diego Padres	OF
1	9	JR	Ron Darling	Texas Rangers	P
2	52	JR	John Elway	New York Yankees	OF
3	58	JR	Tony Gwynn	San Diego Padres	OF
8	199	JR	Mark McGwire	Montreal Expos	P-1B
9	233	JR	Fred McGriff	New York Yankees	1B
12	289	JR	Roger Clemens	New York Mets	P
20	513	JR	Vince Coleman	Philadelphia Phillies	OF

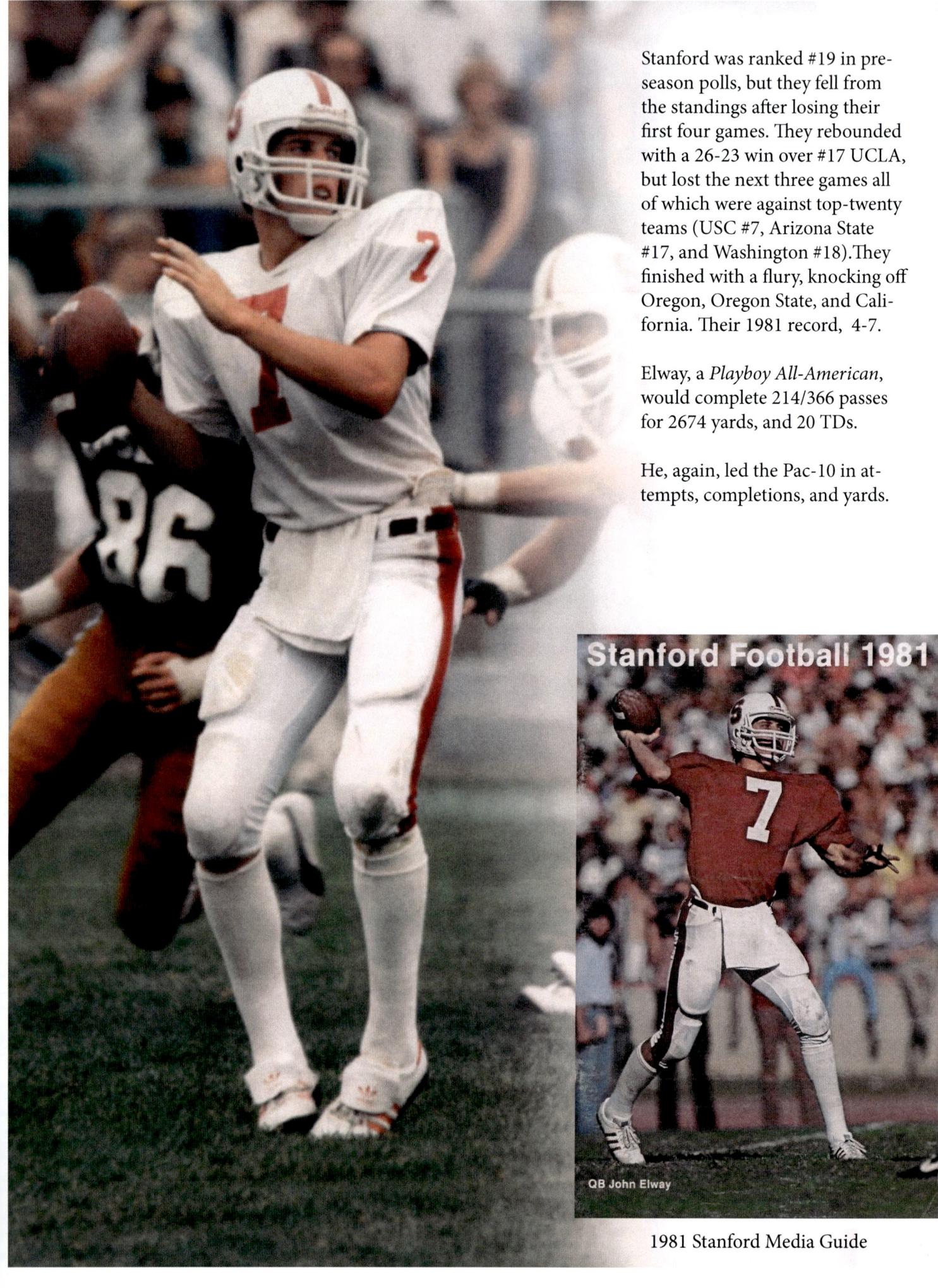

Stanford was ranked #19 in preseason polls, but they fell from the standings after losing their first four games. They rebounded with a 26-23 win over #17 UCLA, but lost the next three games all of which were against top-twenty teams (USC #7, Arizona State #17, and Washington #18). They finished with a flurry, knocking off Oregon, Oregon State, and California. Their 1981 record, 4-7.

Elway, a *Playboy All-American*, would complete 214/366 passes for 2674 yards, and 20 TDs.

He, again, led the Pac-10 in attempts, completions, and yards.

Stanford Football 1981

QB John Elway

1981 Stanford Media Guide

STANFORD UNIVERSITY

7 JOHN ELWAY QB
6-4 202 JR.

31 DARRIN NELSON HB
5-9 185 SR.

25 ANDRE TYLER SE
6-1 175 SR.

66 JOHN MACAULAY C
6-3 242 SR.

88 CHRIS DRESSEL TE
6-4 225 JR.

62 CHRIS ROSE OG
6-5 255 JR.

26 MIKE TOLLIVER FL
6-0 175 JR.

8 MARK HARMON K
5-9 165 SO.

1981 Stanford Team Sheet

OFFENSE

Left to right, top to bottom: John Elway, quarterback, Stanford; Kurt Becker, lineman, Michigan; Terry Tausch, linem
Texas; Brad Edelman, center, Missouri; Dwayne Crutchfield, runner, Iowa State; Tim Wrightman, tight end, UCLA; Cha
Pell, Coach of the Year, Florida; Anthony Carter, receiver, Michigan; Ed Muransky, lineman, Michigan; Roy Foster, linem
Southern California; Herschel Walker, runner, Georgia; Darrin Nelson, runner, Stanford; Steve Fehr, kicker, Na

PLAYBOY'S 1981 PREV

DEFENSE

Playboy August 1981

eft to right, top to bottom: David Galloway, lineman, Florida; Johnie Cooks, linebacker, Mississippi State; Robert Abraham, nebacker, North Carolina State; Jim Bob Harris, back, Alabama; Lester Williams, lineman, Miami, Florida; Rohn Stark, punter, lorida State; Darrell Songy, back, Oklahoma; Tim Wilbur, back, Indiana; Mike Richardson, back, Arizona State; Chip anks, linebacker, Southern Cal; Irv Eatman, lineman, University of California at Los Angeles; Kenneth Sims, lineman, Texas.

V ALL-AMERICA TEAM

STANFORD UNIVERSITY

7 JOHN ELWAY
QB 6-4 202 Jr.
Heisman Trophy Candidate
Northridge, Calif.

1981 Stanford Team Issued Photo

Jack and John Elway

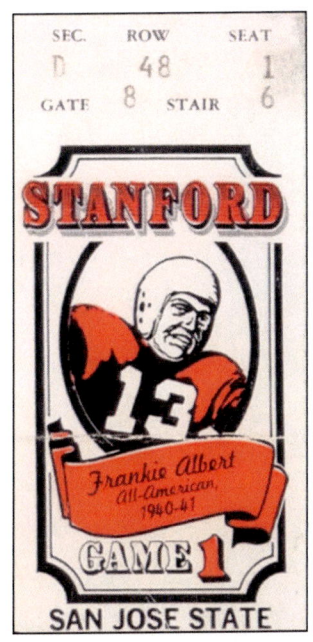

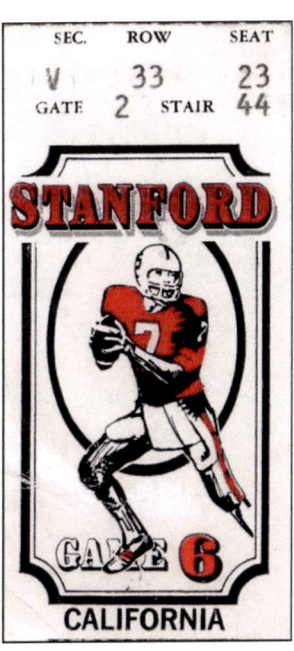

September 19, 1981
Playing against San Jose State, and Head Coach, Jack Elway, John had the worst day of his collegiate career. Hampered by an ankle sprain, Elway was sacked seven times, and threw 5 second half interceptions. He completed 6/24 passes for 72 yards. Stanford fell 28-6.

October 10, 1981
The Cardinal was 0-4 when they faced #17 UCLA. Stanford humbled the Bruins 26-23 before a home crowd of 70,103. Elway completed 19/32 passes for 201 yards, and a touchdown.

November 21, 1981
Elway was featured on the ticket for "The Big Game" against California. 84,563 were in attendance to witness Elway lead the Cardinal to a 42-21 win. He completed 18/27 passes for 245 yards, and 3 touchdowns,

1982

The 1982 Oneonta Yankees finished first in the New York-Penn League with a record of 43-33. They lost 2-1 to Niagara Falls in the NY-PENN Championship Series.

Elway spent six weeks with the Yankees. A left-handed hitting outfielder, he played 42 games and batted .318 over 151 at bats. He had 48 hits with 6 doubles, 2 triples, and 4 home runs. He also had 13 stolen bases, 25 RBI, and 26 runs scored.

Defensively he had 69 putouts, 8 assists, and one double play.

JOHN ELWAY   OF

1982 TCMA Oneonta Yankees #13

1982 Oneonta Yankees pay-stub (Endorsed on the reverse John A Elway Jr.)

JOHN ELWAY

Outfielder . . . 6-4, 202, 22 years old, Yankees 1st pick in June '81 . . . playing this summer at Oneonta . . . bats left, throws right . . . attends Stanford where he plays baseball and was All-American quarterback on football team.

1982 New York Yankees
Official Yearbook Bio

NAME	John Albert Elway Jr.				SIGNED	K/EXT	TERM	BONUS DUE	CHECK#	AMOUNT	DATE
					3/24/82	5 yr. Pymt.			22258	$5.00	3-24
DATE	TRANSFERRED TO:										

	PAYMENT BASIS		PAYMENTS		CASH			PICS		COMMENTS	
	SER/CARD	SUDATE	GIFT		DATE	AMT.	NO.	H	A		
19						$					
19						$					
19						$					
19						$					
19						$					
19						$					
19						$					
19						$					
19						$					
19						$					

NAME	ELWAY, JR., JOHN ALBERT	YEARS REMAINING								
		1	2	3	4	5	6	7	8	9

Topps signed Elway for the use of his likeness on their baseball cards. A similar file was kept for every player under a Topps contract. His information card from the Topps company.

Sports Illustrated

NOVEMBER 8, 1982 $1.50

BOMBS AWAY!

Stanford's John Elway Demolishes Washington

STANFORD UNIVERSITY

88 CHRIS DRESSEL TE
6-4 225 SR

7 JOHN ELWAY QB
6-4 202 SR

67 BRIAN HOLLOWAY OT
6-7 270 SR

66 JOHN MACAULAY C
6-3 242 SR

28 KEN MARGERUM FL
6-1 175 SR

10 KEN NABER K-P
6-4 175 SR

31 DARRIN NELSON RB
5-9 185 SR

25 ANDRE TYLER SE
6-1 175 SR

1982 Stanford Team Sheet

1982

The Stanford Cardinal would not have a national ranking at any time during the 1982 season. Their 3-1 start included an impressive win over #13 Ohio State, their loss, 35-31 to Jack Elway and San Jose St. They'd lose the following two, at #11 Arizona, and home to #14 USC, before beating Washington State and #2 Washington. At 5-3 the season was still promising, but but losses to Arizona and at #12 UCLA jepordized that. A "Big Game" win at Cal would secure the season and a bowl bid for the Cardinal.

In 11 games Elway completed 262/405 passes for 3242 yards, and 24 touchdowns. He was named 1982 Pac-10 Player of the Year, awarded the Sammy Baugh Trophy, finished second in the Heisman Trophy balloting, and was a Consensus All-American.

October 30, 1982
Unranked Stanford defeated the #2 ranked Washington Huskies 43-31. Elway completed 20/30 passes for 265 yards and two touchdowns.

STANFORD UNIVERSITY

JOHN ELWAY
6-4, 202, Senior, Quarterback
1982 Heisman Trophy Nominee

1982 Stanford Team Issued Photo

1982 Stanford Cardinal Pocket Schedule

Sept 23, 1982

Entering the game, Ohio State was ranked #13. Elway threw the winning score, an 18-yard touchdown pass, to Emile Harry with :35 seconds remaining -Stanford 23 - OSU 20.

Elway was 35/63 passing for 411 yards, and 2 touchdowns.

1982 Heisman Trophy Brochure

Heisman Trophy Candidate
John Elway

Has there ever been a better college quarterback?

Berkley, California; Cal's Kevin Moen (26) leaps with the ball in the air after scoring Cal's winning touchdown, while the Stanford band runs to get out of his way.

November 20, 1979

Cal had a 19-17 lead late in the fourth, but Elway had driven the Cardinal into field goal range. Mark Harmon converted the 35-yard kick and Stanford had a 20-19 lead. With :04 remaining, Stanford kicked to Cal. During the return, the ball was lateralled 5 times before Kevin Moen caught it, weaved through the Stanford band - which had mistakenly stormed the field - and scored, spiking the ball off trombone player Gary Tyrrell.

The result was a Cal 25-20 victory.

The following is a transcript of Cal announcer Joe Starkey's - KGO-AM 810 radio - famous call.

"All right, here we go with the kickoff. Harmon will probably try to squib it and he does. Ball comes loose and the Bears have to get out of bounds. Rodgers, along the sideline, another one... they're still in deep trouble at midfield, they tried to do a couple of – the ball is still loose, as they get it to Rodgers! They get it back now to the 30, they're down to the 20... Oh, the band is out on the field! He's gonna go into the end zone! He got into the end zone!

Will it count? The Bears have scored, but the bands are out on the field! There were flags all over the place. Wait and see what happens; we don't know who won the game. There are flags on the field. We have to see whether or not the flags are against Stanford or Cal. The Bears may have made some illegal laterals. It could be that it won't count. The Bears, believe it or not, took it all the way into the end zone. If the penalty is against Stanford, California would win the game. If it is not, the game is over and Stanford has won.

We've heard no decision yet. Everybody is milling around on the (conferencing officials now finally signal a touchdown) field! And the Bears! The Bears have won! The Bears have won! Oh, my God! The most amazing, sensational, dramatic, heart-rending... exciting, thrilling finish in the history of college football! California has won the Big Game over Stanford! Oh, excuse me for my voice, but I have never, never seen anything like it in the history of I have ever seen any game in my life! The Bears have won it! There will be no extra point!"

1982 Adidas Stanford Sports Poster

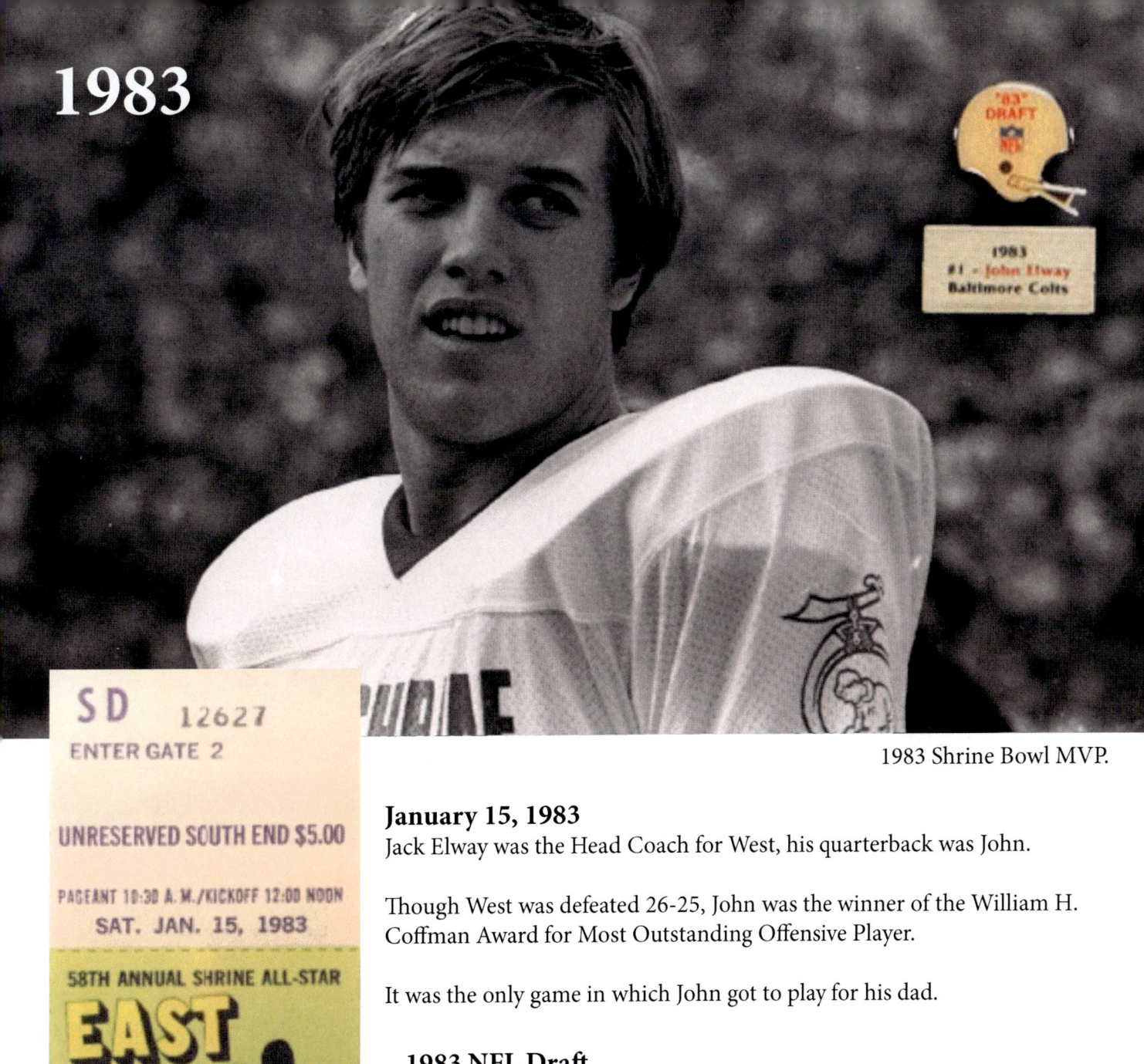

1983

1983 Shrine Bowl MVP.

SD 12627

ENTER GATE 2

UNRESERVED SOUTH END $5.00

PAGEANT 10:30 A. M./KICKOFF 12:00 NOON

SAT. JAN. 15, 1983

58TH ANNUAL SHRINE ALL-STAR

EAST WEST

FOOTBALL GAME AND PAGEANT

26

STANFORD STADIUM

BENEFIT SHRINERS
HOSPITAL FOR CRIPPLED CHILDREN
AND BURNS CENTERS

ENTER GATE 2

SD 12627

January 15, 1983

Jack Elway was the Head Coach for West, his quarterback was John.

Though West was defeated 26-25, John was the winner of the William H. Coffman Award for Most Outstanding Offensive Player.

It was the only game in which John got to play for his dad.

1983 NFL Draft

April 26, 1983

PIck	Team	Name	Pos	School
1	Baltimore	John Elway*	QB	Stanford
2	Los Angleles	Eric Dickerson*	RB	SMU
4	Denver	Chris Hinton	G	Northwestern
6	Chicago	Jimbo Covert*	T	Pitt
9	Houston	Bruce Mathews*	T	USC
14	Buffalo	Jim Kelly*	QB	Miami
27	Miami	Dan Marino*	QB	Pitt
28	Washington	Darrell Green*	CB	TX A&M Kingsville
203	Chicago	Richard Dent*	DE	Tenn St.

Hinton was packaged by Denver and traded to Baltimore for John Elway.
* Elected to the Hall of Fame.

Sports Illustrated

AUGUST 15, 1983 $1.75

LOOKING LIKE A MILLION

Denver's John Elway Makes A Dazzling NFL Debut

Riddell

May 02, 1983

The Baltimore Colts trade John Elway to the Denver Broncos. The Colts receive Denver's 1983 first round pick, Tackle Chris Hinton, reserve Quarterback, Mark Hermann, and Denver's 1984 first round pick. (The Colts selected Ron Solt, Guard, University of Maryland.)

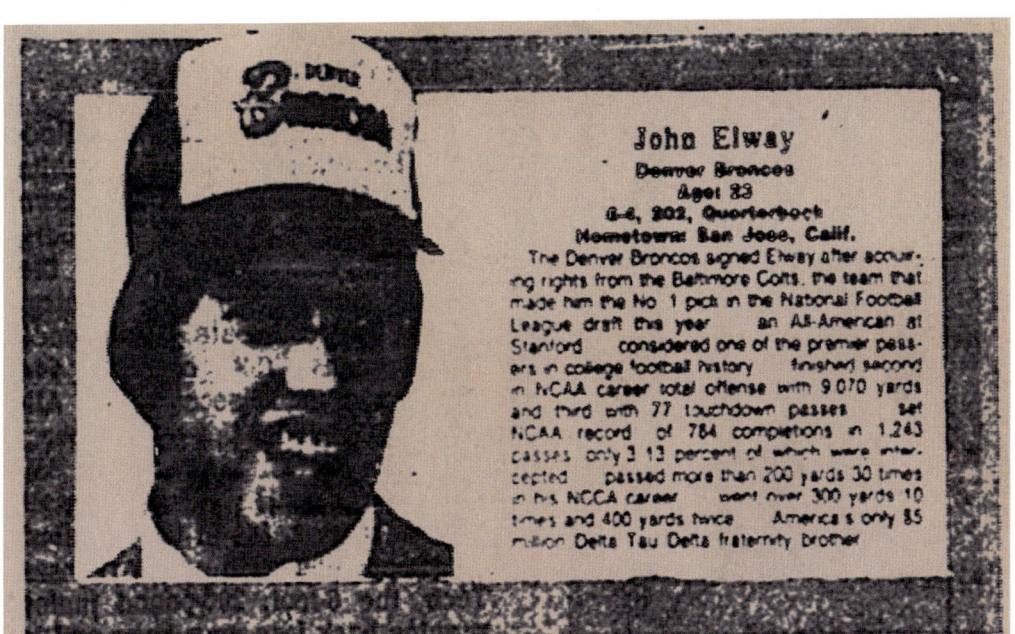

Wichita Eagle-Beacon, Bubblegum-less card September 19, 1983

1983 NFLTV Slide

Elway started the first five games, but struggled. Though Denver won the first two, they were trailing both when Elway was replaced by Steve DeBerg. John was given a chance to watch and learn for the next four games, all Bronco wins. Elway was "ready" when Steve Deberg was injured in week 10. Elway started for the remainder of the season. Denver finished 9-7, third in the AFC West, and good enough to qualify for the playoffs. A healthy Steve DeBerg returned for the playoff game, a 31-7 loss to the Seattle Seahawks.

For the season, Elway completed 123/259 passes for 1663 yards and 7 touchdowns. He would add 28 carries for 148 yards, and a touchdown.

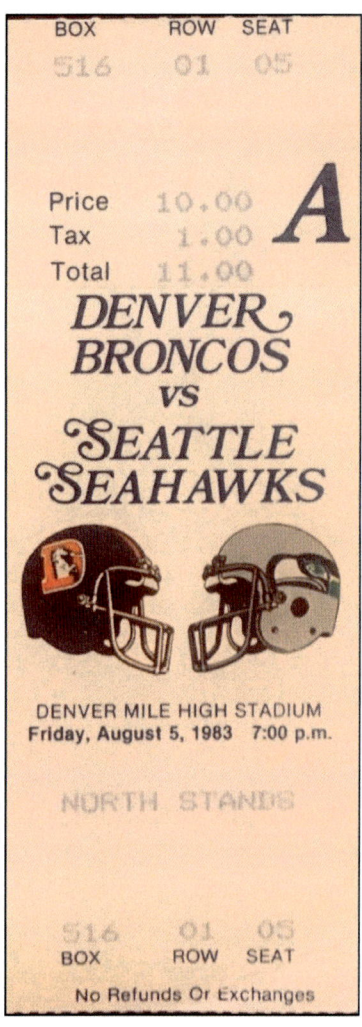

BOX ROW SEAT
516 01 05
Price 10.00
Tax 1.00
Total 11.00
A
DENVER BRONCOS
VS
SEATTLE SEAHAWKS
DENVER MILE HIGH STADIUM
Friday, August 5, 1983 7:00 p.m.
NORTH STANDS
516 01 05
BOX ROW SEAT
No Refunds Or Exchanges

August 5, 1983

Professional Debut: Elway, playing the second half, was 10/15. He connected on 6/9 during the final 75-yard drive.

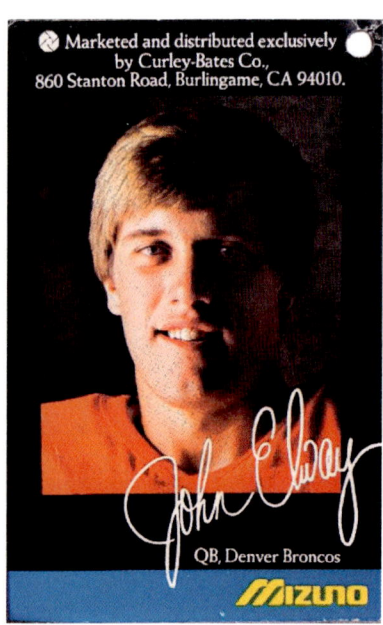

Marketed and distributed exclusively by Curley-Bates Co., 860 Stanton Road, Burlingame, CA 94010.
John Elway
QB, Denver Broncos
MIZUNO

1983 Mizuno Shoe Tag

GO BRONCOS
Courtesy of
Joslins
7
John Elway

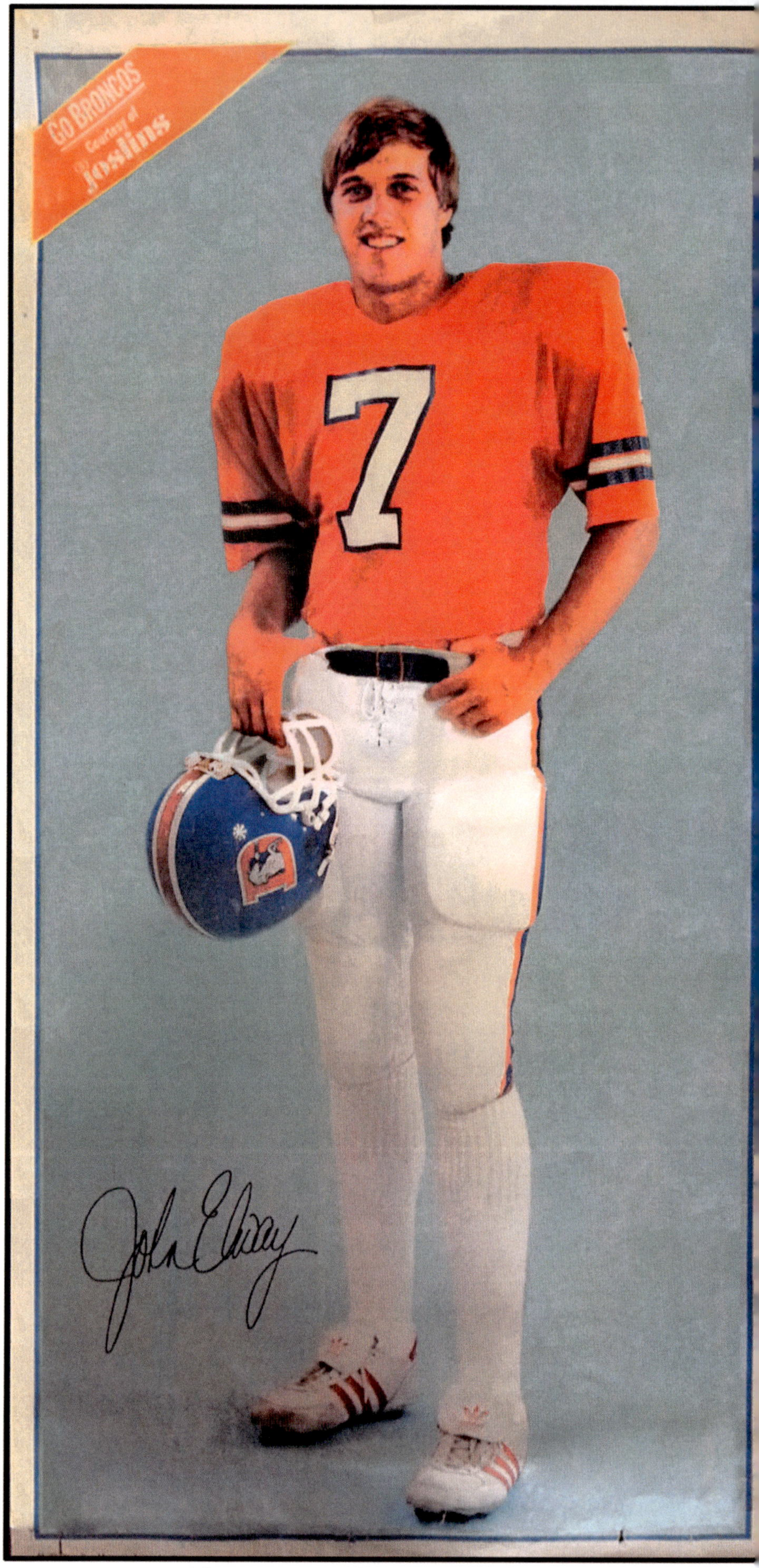

The Denver Post Magazine Joslins Poster Insert
August 21, 1983

RICH McCABE

1983 Kellogg's Sticker

September 4, 1983
Official NFL Debut: Elway was 1/8 for 14 yards.

Rich McCabe was the defensive secondary coach who died Jan 4, 1983. The Broncos wore this patch in memorandum in their week one game against Pittsburgh a 14-10 win.

September 18, 1983

Against the Philadelphia Eagles at Mile High Stadium, a 13-10 Denver loss, Elway threw a 33-yard touchdown pass to running back Rick Parros. It came in the fourth quarter with 1:43 left. It was his first NFL touchdown pass. He was 18/33 for 193 yards.

JOHN ELWAY   QB   DENVER BRONCOS

1983 Team Issued Photo

December 1, 1983

The Baltimore Colts led the Broncos 19-0 after three quarters. But the fourth quarter belonged to Elway who threw three touchdown passes giving Denver a 21-19 win. It was his first come from behind victory. He'd finish 23/44 for 345 yards.

1984

The Broncos finished 13-3, first in the AFC West. They hosted the Pittsburgh Steelers in the Divisional Round of the playoffs, but lost 24-17.

Elway started 14 games, completed 214/380 passes for 2598 yards, and 18 touchdowns. He rushed 56 times for 237 yards, and a touchdown.

All original AFL teams celebrated their 25th anniversaries. Denver wore this commorative patch.

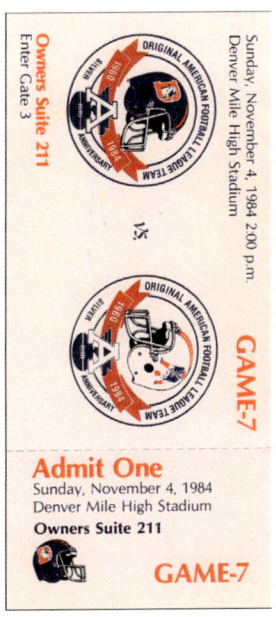

November 4, 1984

Elway was NFL Player of the Week in a 26-19 victory over the New England Pariots. He completed 26/40 passes for 315 yards, and 3 touchdowns.

1984 Mizuno Fan Card 5x7

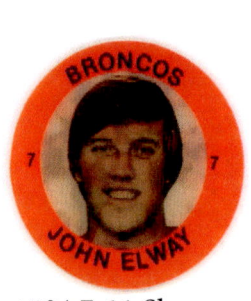

1984 7-11 Slurpee
Disc #W17

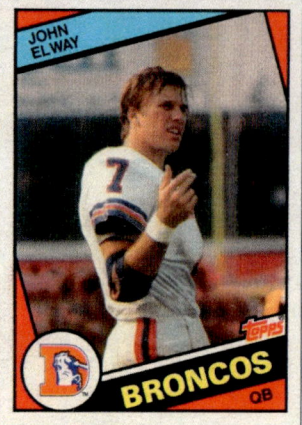

1984 Topps #63

1984 Topps Sticker #179

November 18, 1984

Elway was 16/19 for 218 yards, and 5 touchdowns. The only 5 touchdown game of his career, a 42-21 victory over Minnesota.

1984 NFLTV Slide

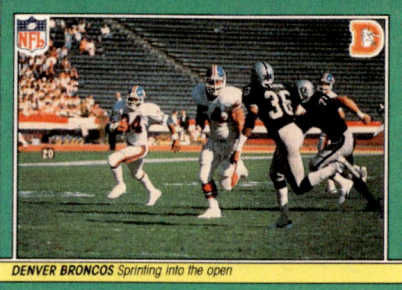

1984 Fleer #88

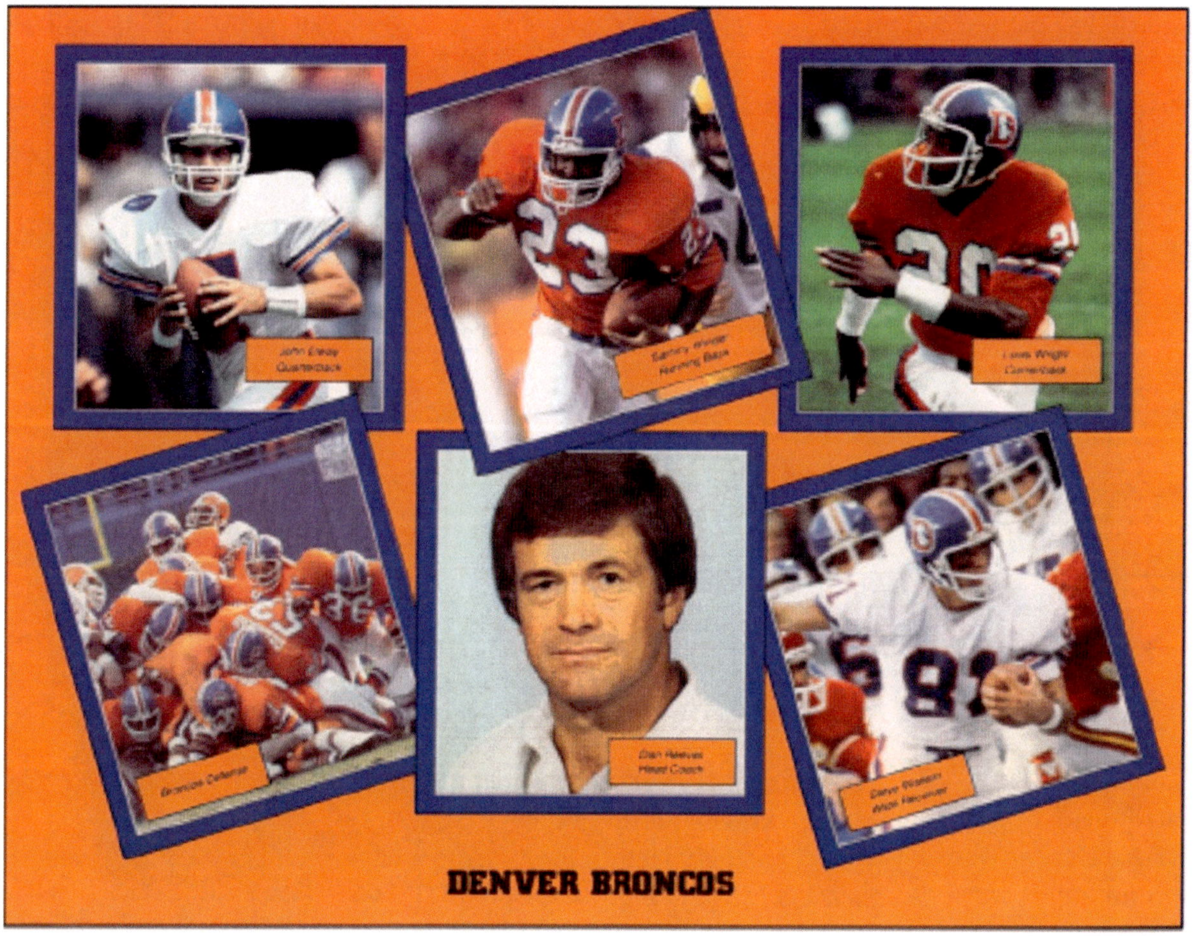

1984 NFL Super-Pro Club Team Sheet

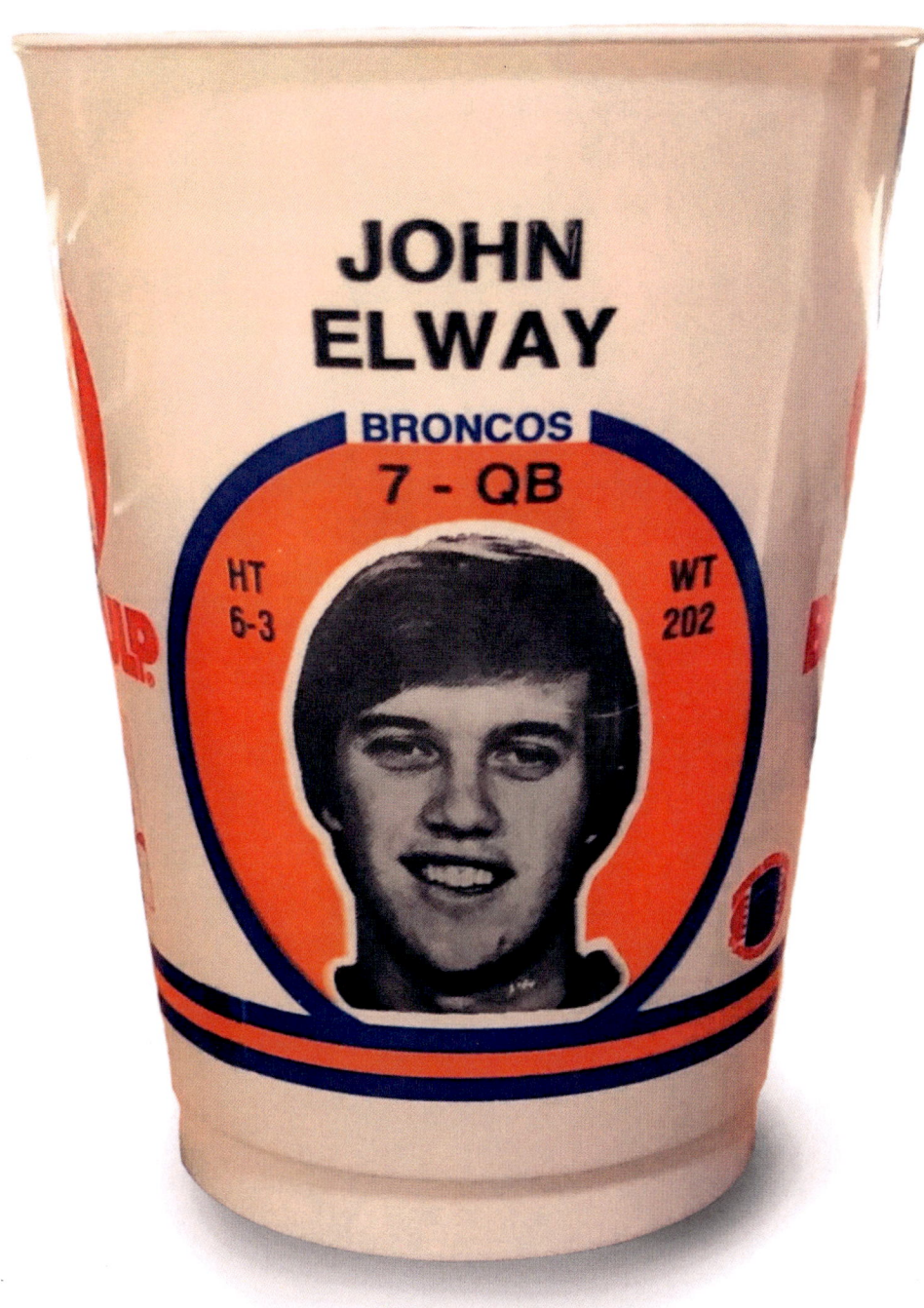

JOHN
ELWAY

BRONCOS

7 - QB

HT
6-3

WT
202

1984 7-Eleven Cup

1984 Denver Broncos Magazine Pull-Out Poster

BRONCOS

December 30, 1984

The 13-3 Broncos were the second seed in the AFC. They faced the #3 Pittsburgh Steelers in the divisional playoff round.

Elway threw for 184 yards and two scores, but was sacked four times, and intercepted twice. Pittsburgh won 24-17.

Injured in the first half, Elway played the second half with his right leg bandaged from his thigh to his hip.

"If anybody had any doubts about his courage under fire, he answered everybody's questions. He wasn't forced to stay in the game, he wanted to play"

Tom Jackson

1985

A pre-season Super Bowl favorite, Denver finished 11-5 and was the second in the AFC West. Due to a tie-breaker with the New England Partiots (record among common opponents) they failed to make the playoffs, and became the first team to win 11 games and not qualify for the post-season.

Elway started all 16 games. He led the League with 605 passing attempts. He completed 327 for 3891 yards, and 23 touchdowns He rushed for 231 yards on 53 carries.

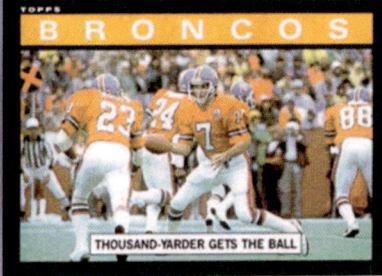

1985 Topps #235

1985 Topps #238

1985 Topps Glossy #3   1985 Topps Sticker #24   Reverse   Coming Soon

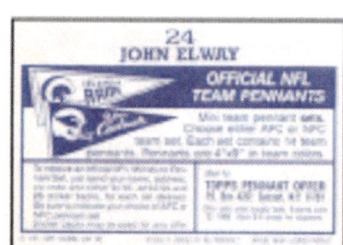

DENVER BRONCOS

1985 NFL Super-Pro Club Team Sheet

1986

After an 8-1 start Denver stumbled to an 11-5 record. They won the AFC West, and hosted the New England Patriots in the divisional round of the playoffs, a 22-17 win.

Elway completed 280/504 passes for 3485 yards, and 19 touchdowns. He added 257 yards on 52 carries with one touchdown, and was selected to his first Pro-Bowl.

1986 Fleer #19

1986 Topps #112

1986 Topps Sticker #176

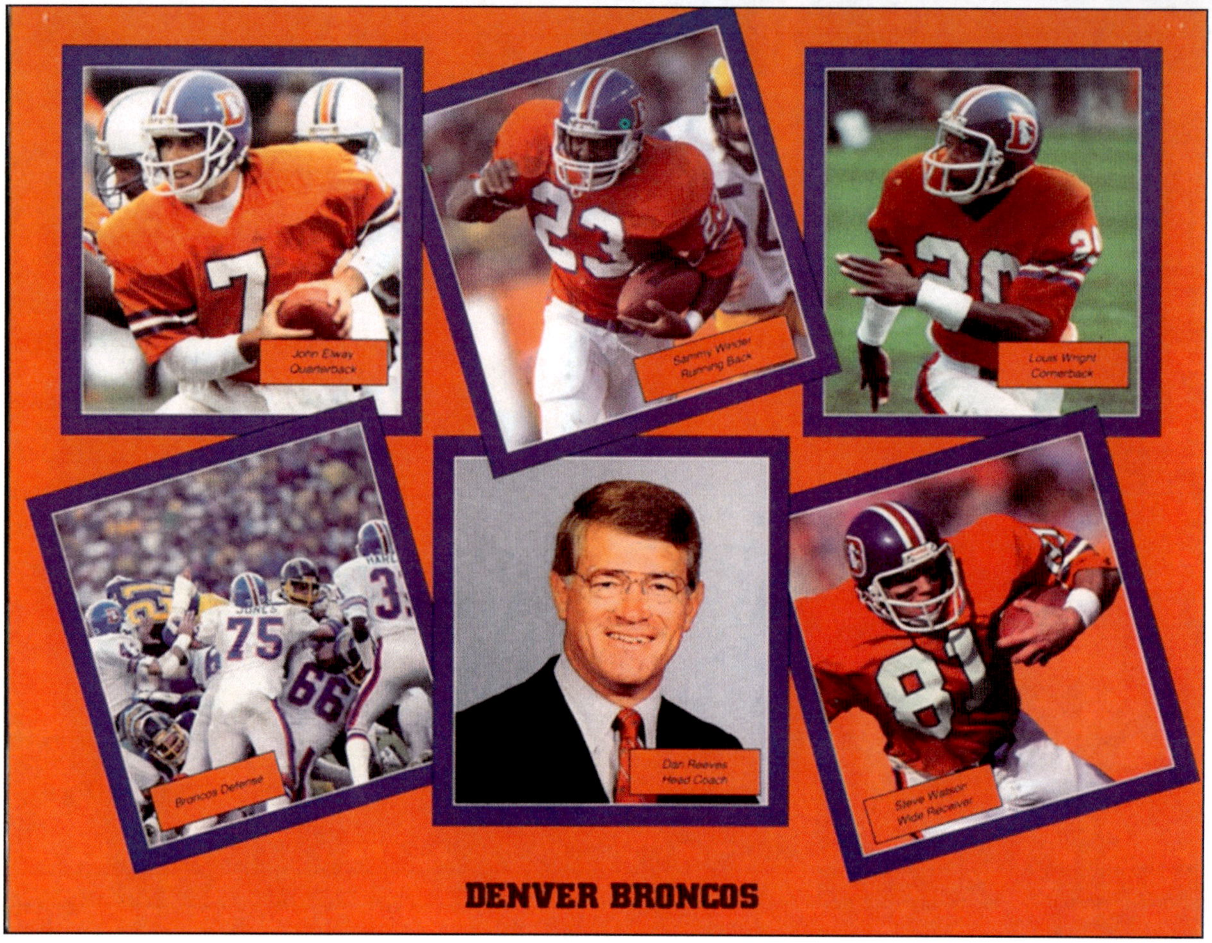

DENVER BRONCOS

1986 NFL Super-Pro Club Team Sheet

1986 NFL TV Slide

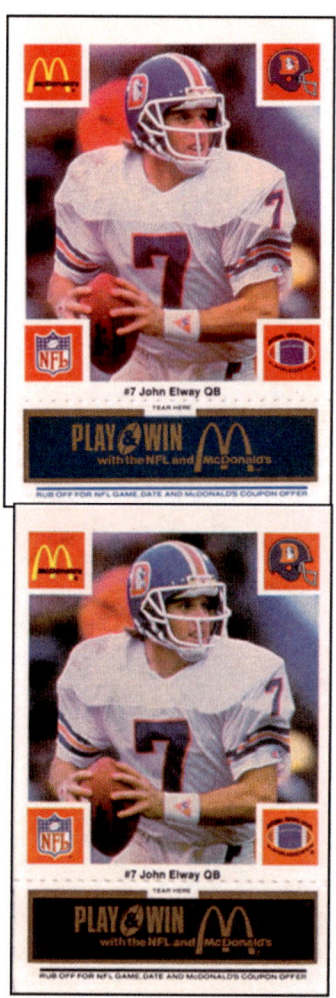

1986 McDonalds
Rocky Mountain News Coupon

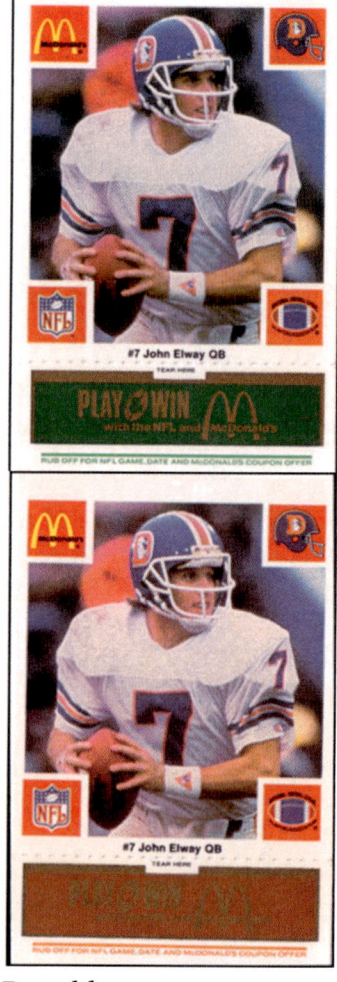

1986 McDonalds

1986 McDonalds Cup

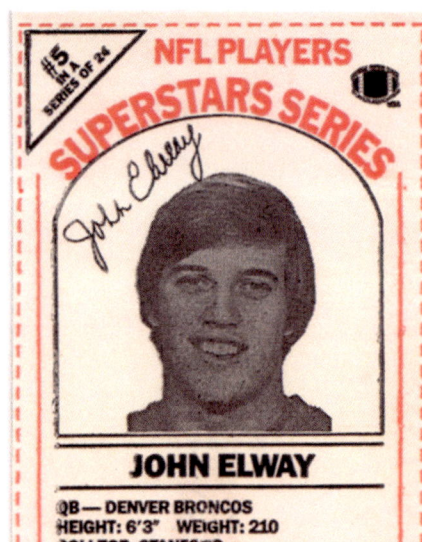

NFL PLAYERS
SUPERSTARS SERIES
#5 IN A SERIES OF 24

JOHN ELWAY

QB — DENVER BRONCOS
HEIGHT: 6'3"   WEIGHT: 210
COLLEGE: STANFORD
YEARS IN NFL: 4

NFL PLAYERS
SUPERSTARS SERIES
#5 IN A SERIES OF 24

JOHN ELWAY

QB — DENVER BRONCOS
HEIGHT: 6'3"   WEIGHT: 210
COLLEGE: STANFORD
YEARS IN NFL: 4

NFL PLAYERS
SUPERSTARS SERIES
#5 IN A SERIES OF 24

JOHN ELWAY

QB — DENVER BRONCOS
HEIGHT: 6'3"   WEIGHT: 210
COLLEGE: STANFORD
YEARS IN NFL: 4

NFL PLAYERS
SUPERSTARS SERIES
#5 IN A SERIES OF 24

JOHN ELWAY

QB — DENVER BRONCOS
HEIGHT: 6'3"   WEIGHT: 210
COLLEGE: STANFORD
YEARS IN NFL: 4

NFL PLAYERS
SUPERSTARS SERIES
#5 IN A SERIES OF 24

JOHN ELWAY

QB — DENVER BRONCOS
HEIGHT: 6'3"   WEIGHT: 210
COLLEGE: STANFORD
YEARS IN NFL: 4

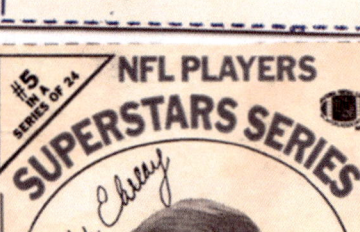

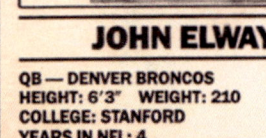

NFL PLAYERS
SUPERSTARS SERIES
#5 IN A SERIES OF 24

JOHN ELWAY

QB — DENVER BRONCOS
HEIGHT: 6'3"   WEIGHT: 210
COLLEGE: STANFORD
YEARS IN NFL: 4

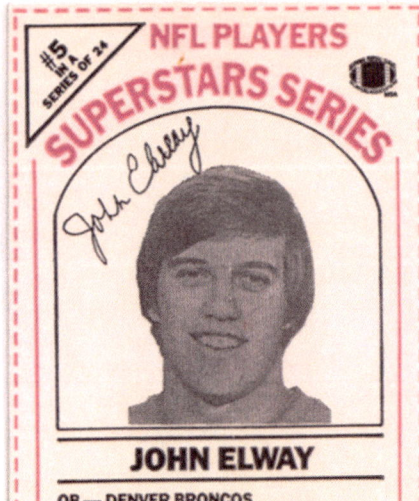

NFL PLAYERS
SUPERSTARS SERIES
#5 IN A SERIES OF 24

JOHN ELWAY

QB — DENVER BRONCOS
HEIGHT: 6'3"   WEIGHT: 210
COLLEGE: STANFORD
YEARS IN NFL: 4

NFL PLAYERS
SUPERSTARS SERIES
#5 IN A SERIES OF 24

JOHN ELWAY

QB — DENVER BRONCOS
HEIGHT: 6'3"   WEIGHT: 210
COLLEGE: STANFORD
YEARS IN NFL: 4

NFL PLAYERS
SUPERSTARS SERIES
#5 IN A SERIES OF 24

JOHN ELWAY

QB — DENVER BRONCOS
HEIGHT: 6'3"   WEIGHT: 210
COLLEGE: STANFORD
YEARS IN NFL: 4

1986 DairyPak #5

1986 Napco Pencil #3

Sports Illustrated

OCTOBER 13, 1986 $2.25

DENVER IS UNDEFEATED

ELWAY AND EVERY WHICH WAY

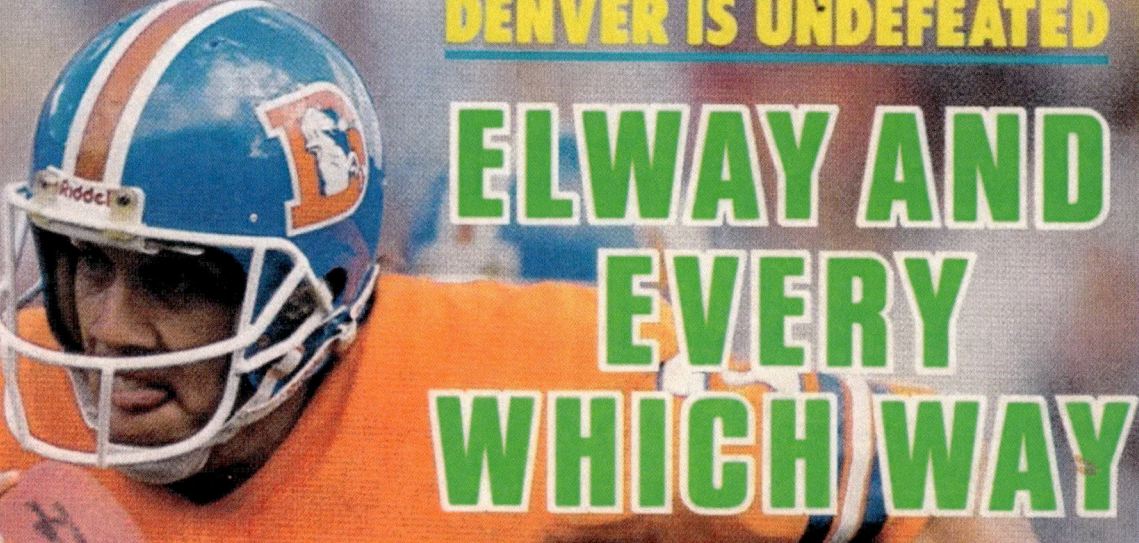

1986 Jenos #48

1986 A Question of
Sport #2

October 5, 1986

Elway was 12/24 for 200 yards and 3 touchdowns. He added 19 yards on 3 carries.

The Denver defense intercepted Steve Pelluer three times and held Herschell Walker to 34 yards rushing. Denver prevailed 29-14 over Dallas, and remained undefeated with a 5-0 record.

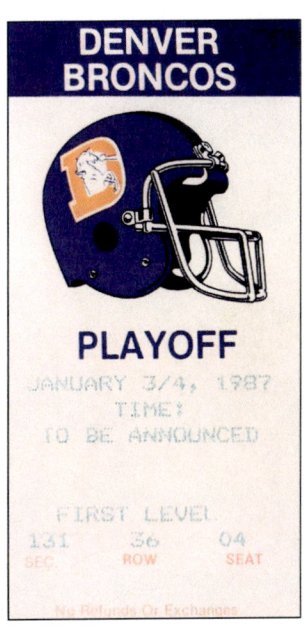

October 26, 1986

A 20-13 victory over the Seattle Seahawks, Elway was named NFL Player of the Week. He completed 18/32 passes for 321 yards, and one touchdown.

November 30, 1986

A 34-28 victory over the Cincinnati Bengals, Elway was NFL Player of the Week. He completed 22/34 passes for 228 yards, and 3 touchdowns.

January 4, 1987

A 22-17 win over the New England Patriots, Elway completed 13/32 passes for 257 yards, and a touchdown. He scored Denver's first touchdown on a 22-yard run.

It was his first playoff win.

Denver would face the Cleveland Browns at Municipal Stadium for the AFC Championship.

150-PIECE JIGSAW PUZZLE

NFL Officially Licensed Product

John Elway
QUARTERBACK

DENVER BRONCOS

AFC Championship
January 11, 1987

Tied at 13 through much of the fourth quarter, Bernie Kosar threw a 48 yard touchdown pass to Brian Brennan to take a 20-13 lead. Denver's Ken Bell mishandled the kickoff, eventually falling on it at the Denver two yard line. With 5:32 remaining, Denver had the ball, first down and 98 yards to go. In what would become the signature moment of his career, Elway began what has become known simply as "The Drive."

1986 AFC Championship Ring

"The Drive"

1. – First down and 10, Denver 2-yard line. Sammy Winder 5-yard pass from Elway.

2. – Second down and 5, Denver 7-yard line. Winder 3-yard run.

3. – Third down and 2, Denver 10-yard line. Winder 2-yard run.

4. – First down and 10, Denver 12-yard line. Winder 3-yard run.

5. – Second down and 7, Denver 15-yard line. Elway 11-yard run.

6. – First down and 10, Denver 26-yard line. Steve Sewell 22-yard pass from Elway.

7. – First down and 10, Denver 48-yard line. Steve Watson 12-yard pass from Elway.

Two-minute warning

8. – First down and 10, Cleveland 40-yard line (1:59 remaining). Incomplete pass by Elway, intended for Vance Johnson.

9. – Second down and 10, Cleveland 40-yard line (1:52 remaining). Dave Puzzilli sack of Elway, 8-yard loss.

10. – Third down and 18, Cleveland 48-yard line (1:47 remaining). Mark Jackson 20-yard pass from Elway.

11. – First down and 10, Cleveland 28-yard line (1:19 remaining). Incomplete pass by Elway, intended for Watson.

12. – Second down and 10, Cleveland 28-yard line (1:10 remaining). Steve Sewell 14-yard pass from Elway.

13. – First down and 10, Cleveland 14-yard line (:57 remaining). Incomplete pass by Elway, intended for Watson.

14. – Second down and 10, Cleveland 14-yard line (:42 remaining). John Elway 9-yard run (scramble).

15. – Third down and 1, Cleveland 5-yard line (:39 remaining). Mark Jackson 5-yard pass from Elway for the touchdown.

Rich Karlis hits the game winning 33-yard field goal in overtime. The win sets up a showdown with the New York Giants in Super Bowl XXI.

Elway was 22/38 for 244 yards, and a touchdown. He added 56 yards rushing.

SUPER BOWL XXI
January 25, 1987
Denver was defeated 39-20 by the NFC Champion New York Giants, Elway was 23/37 passing for 304 yards and 1 touchdown. He also was Denver's leading rusher with 27 yards on 6 carries with 1 touchdown.

AFC-NFC Pro Bowl
February 1, 1987

In his first Pro-Bowl, Elway was 6/12 for 90 yards and the only touchdown, a 10-yard pass to Los Angeles tight end, Todd Christiansen. The AFC won 10-6.

1987 Pro Bowl Watch

Wilson

Wilson
Celebrating 75 years as Brand of the Pros

1987

Denver started 1987 1-0-1, then the players went on strike. Week three was cancelled, games during weeks four, five, and six were played using replacement players. Denver went 2-1 with replacements and finished 10-4-1, first in the AFC West. They hosted the Houston Oilers who they defeated 34-10 in the divisional round, and then had an AFC Championship rematch with Cleveland at Mile High Stadium.

They would face the NFC Champion Washington Redskins in Super Bowl XXII.

Elway completed 224/410 passes for 3198 yards, and 19 touchdowns. He had 66 carries for 304 yards and 4 touchdowns.

Selected to his second Pro-Bowl, Elway was AFC Offensive Player of the Year. Sporting News Player of the Year, and Associated Press NFL MVP. He was a First Team All-Pro selection from The Newspaper Enterprise Associated, The Sporting News, College and Pro Football Newsweekly, Gannett News Service's Joel Buchsbaum, and National Sports Daily.

1987 United Way Pocket Schedule

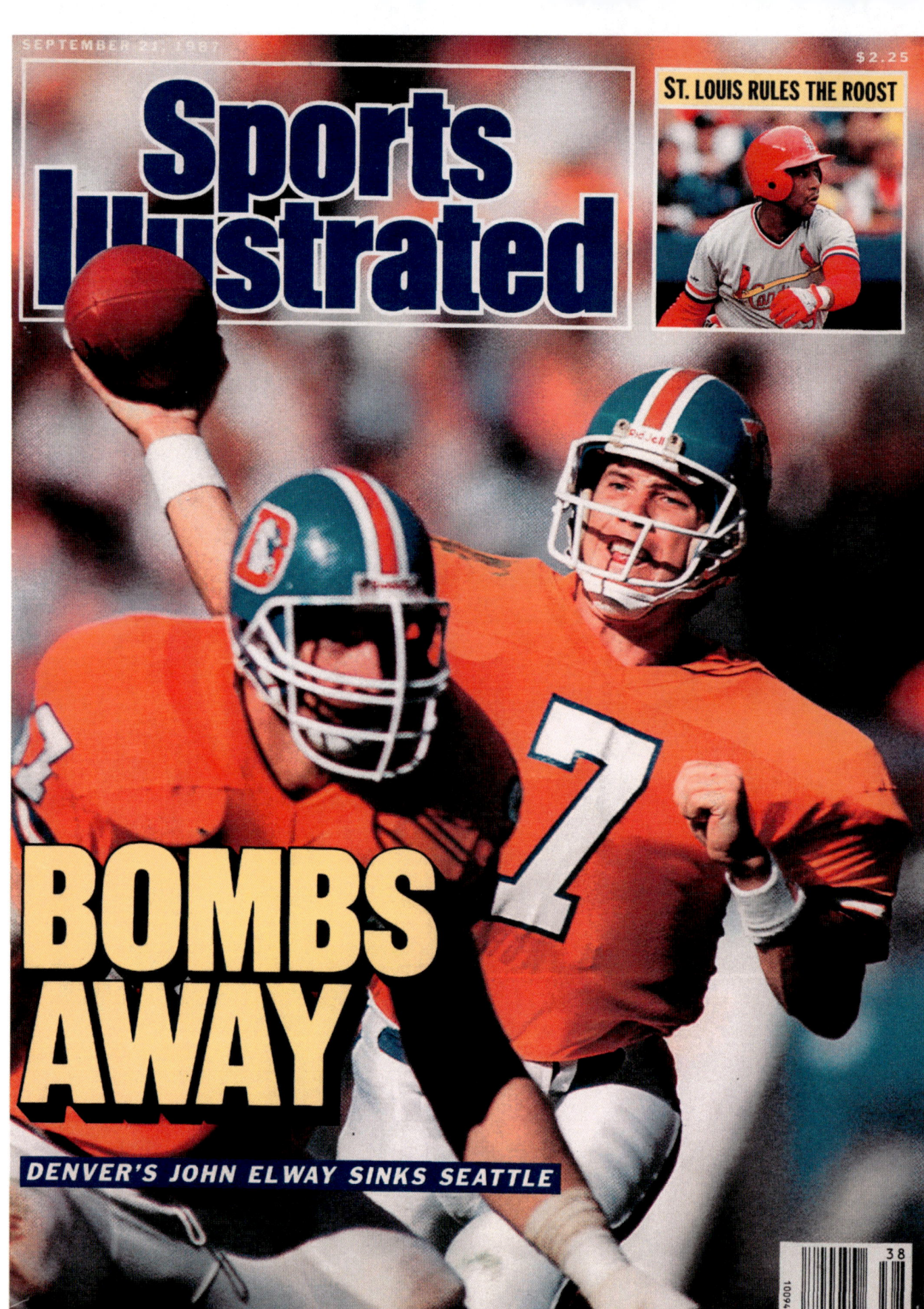

SEPTEMBER 21, 1987

$2.25

Sports Illustrated

ST. LOUIS RULES THE ROOST

BOMBS AWAY

DENVER'S JOHN ELWAY SINKS SEATTLE

38

10094

0 724454 6

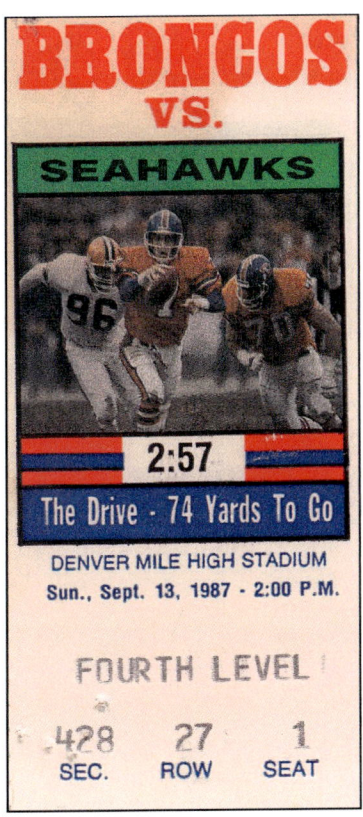

Sept 13, 1987

Elway was NFL Player of the Week against the Seattle Seahawks a 40-17 a week 1 win. He completed 22/32 passes for 338 yards and 4 TD's.

1987 Broncos Team Deck

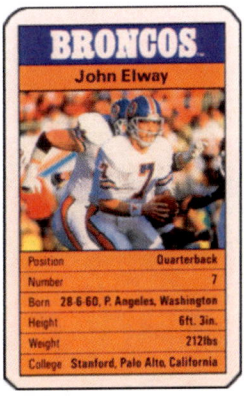 

1987 Ace Fact Pack   1987 NFLTV Slide

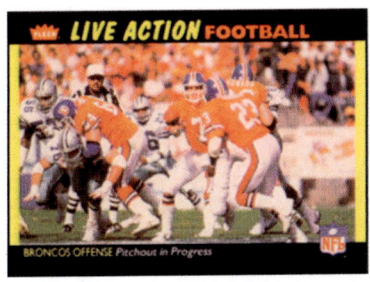  

1987 Fleer #13   1987 Fleer #87   1987 Topps Team Leader #30

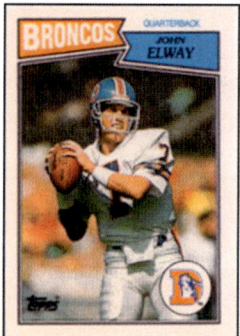

1987 Topps UK #6

1987 Topps UK William 'Refrigerator'
Perry Puzzle Reverse

1987 Topps Sticker #174

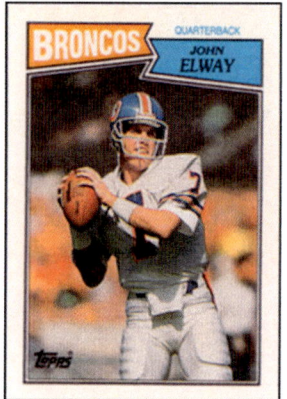

1987 Topps #34

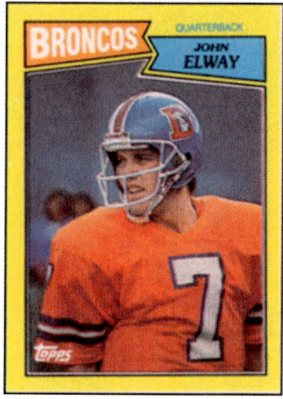

1987 Topps Box Bottom #D

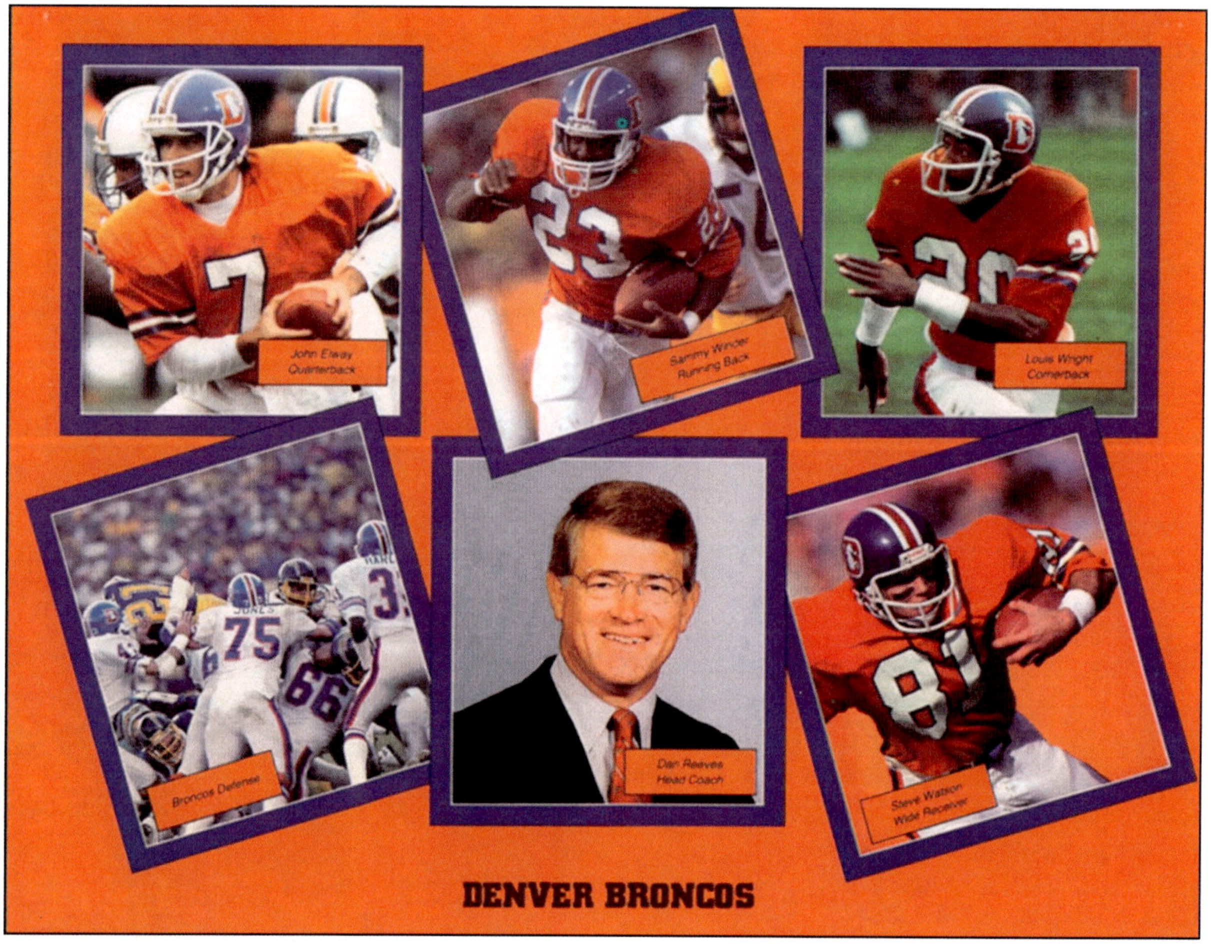

1987 NFL Super-Pro Club Team Sheet

1987 Marketcom/SI #18

1987 Wheaties Mini Poster #22

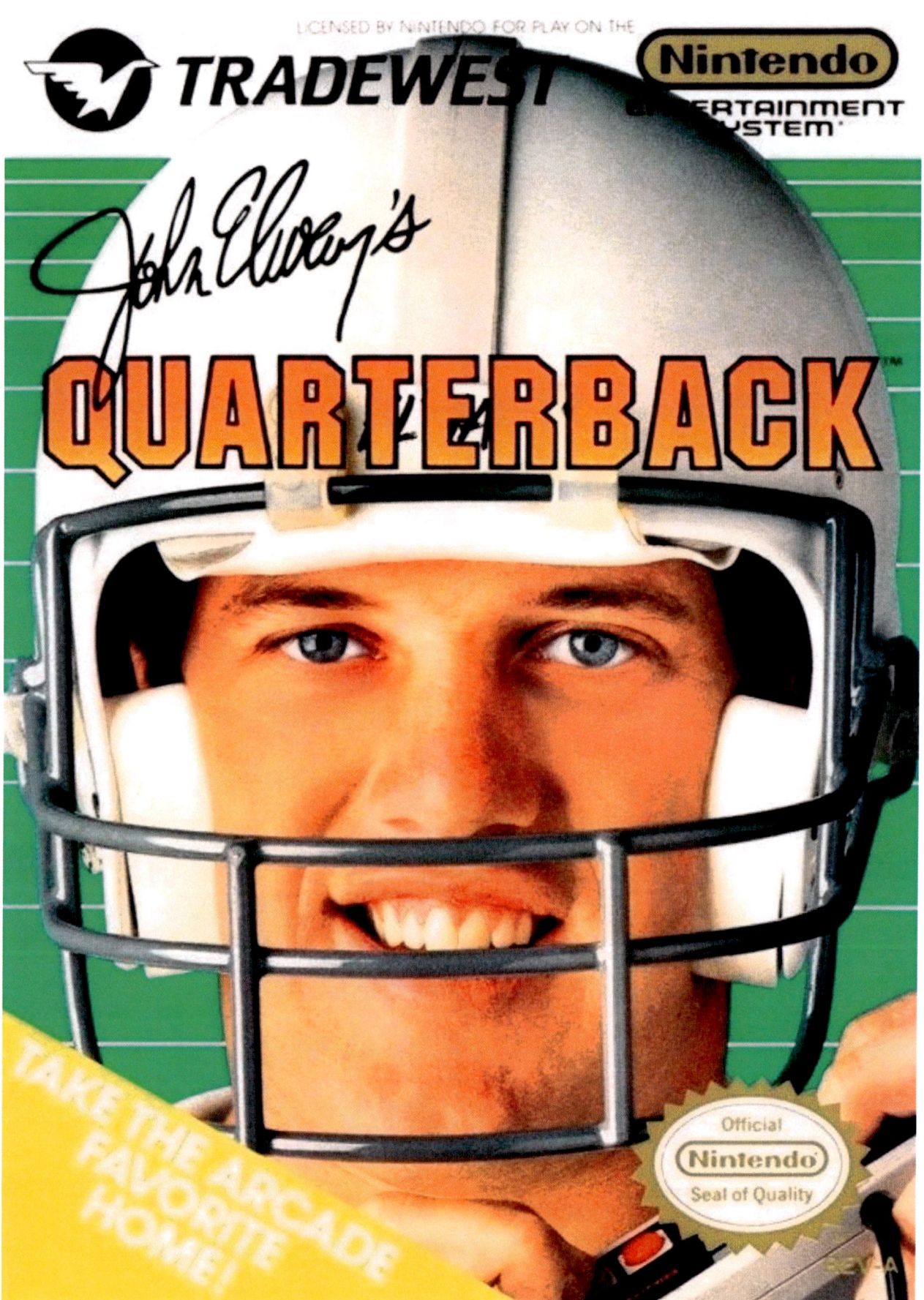

1987 John Elway's Quarterback Challenge Debuts.

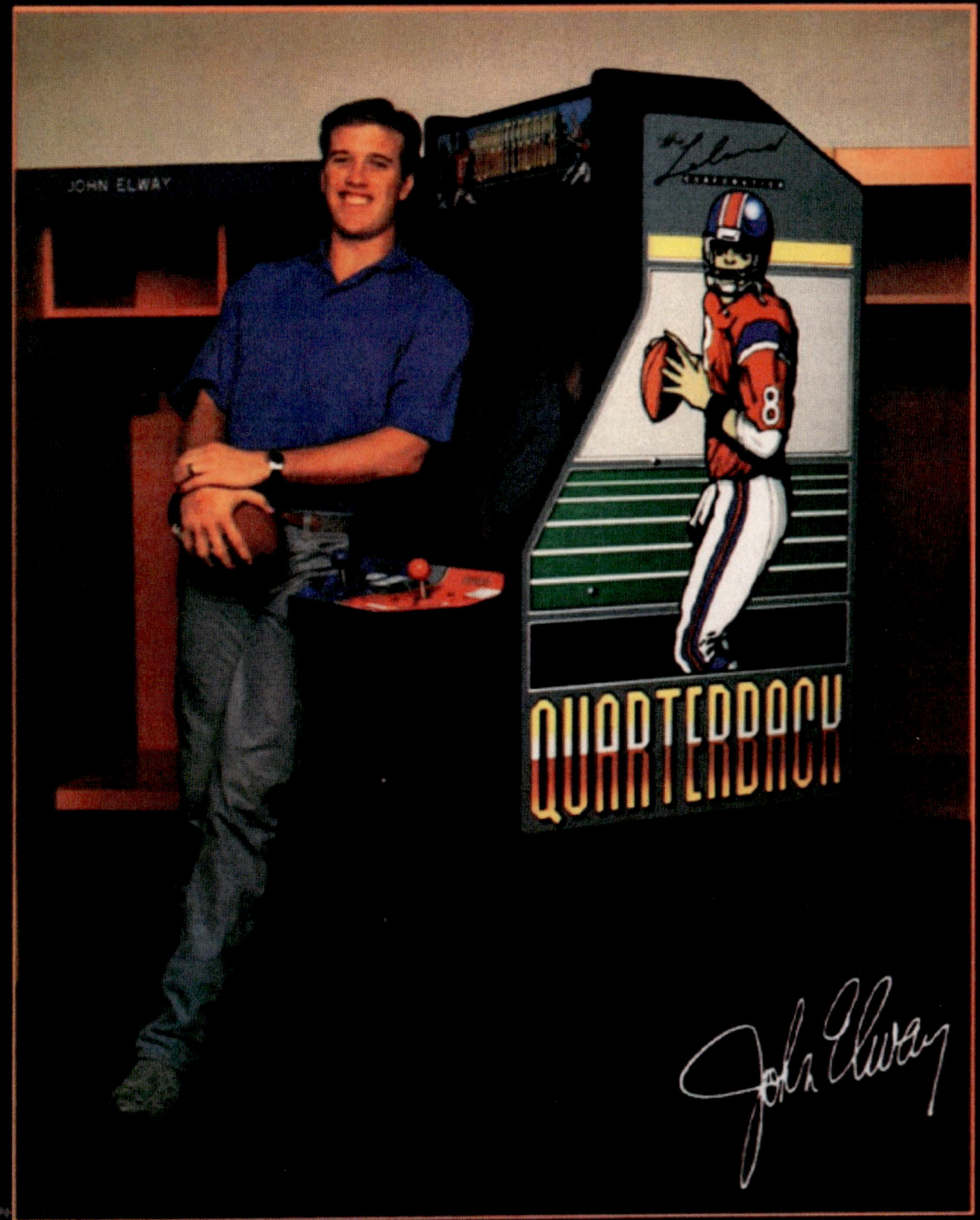

YOU CAN TELL A LOT ABOUT A GAME
BY THE PEOPLE WHO PLAY IT.

QUARTERBACK

1987 Football Pin-Ups Magazine

JOHN ELWAY

Denver Broncos

QUARTERBACK SNEAKS.

Mizuno
ATHLETIC FOOTWEAR

Team Issued Glossy Photo (Facsimile)

PARTNERS IN EXCELLENCE

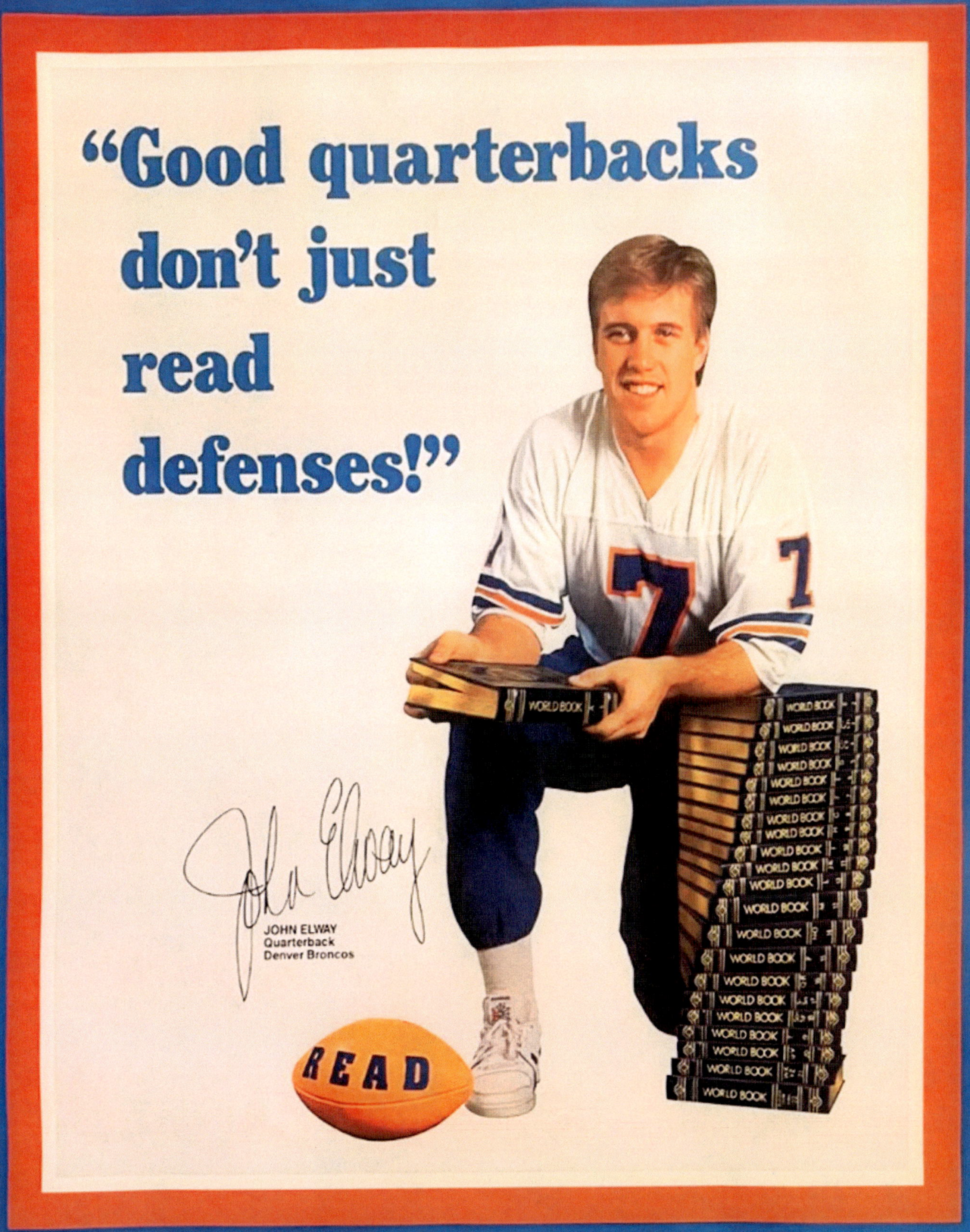

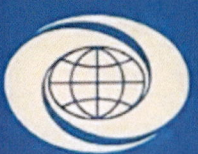

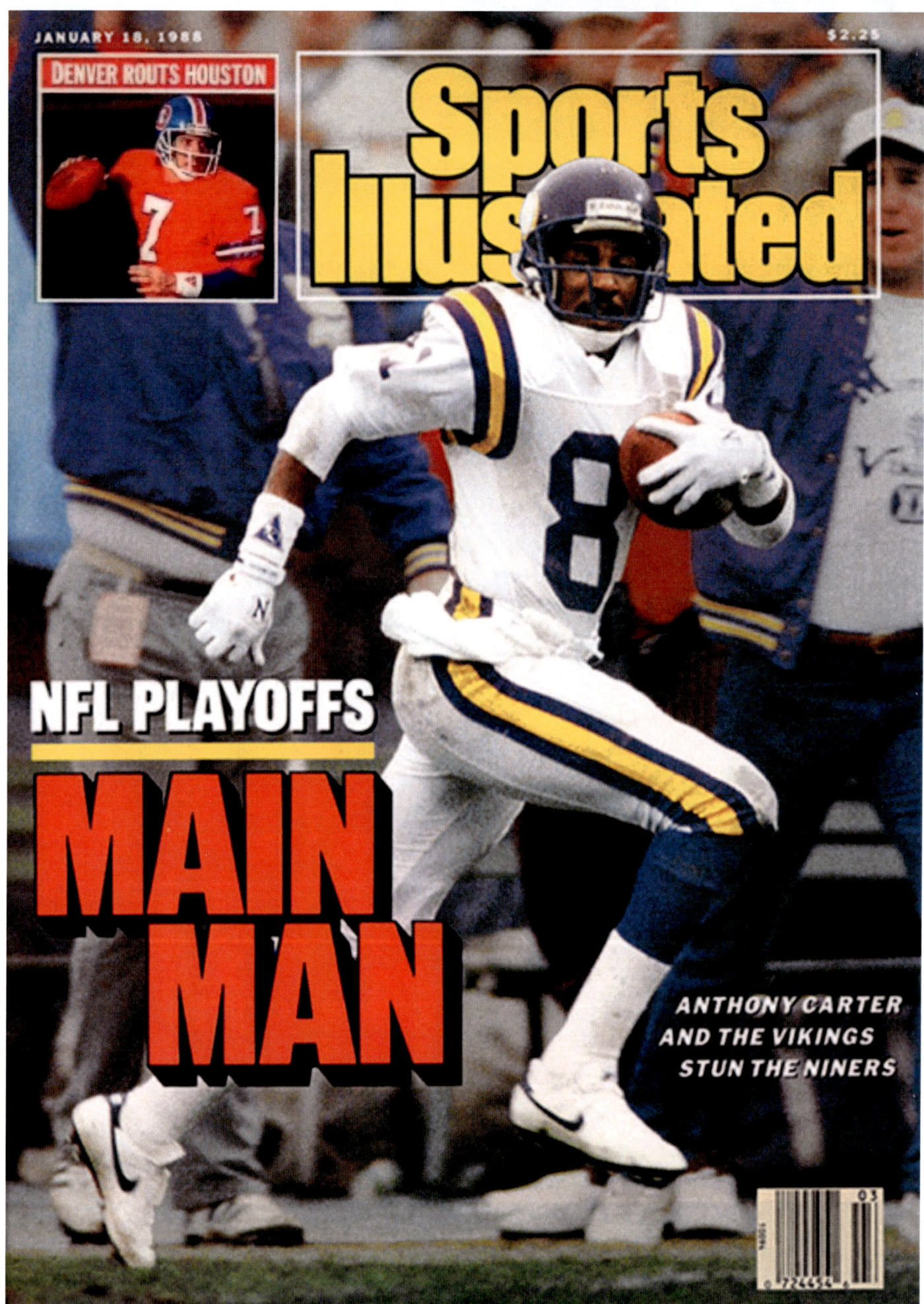

JANUARY 18, 1988

$2.25

DENVER ROUTS HOUSTON

Sports Illustrated

NFL PLAYOFFS

MAIN MAN

ANTHONY CARTER
AND THE VIKINGS
STUN THE NINERS

AFC Divisional Playoff
January 10, 1988
The Broncos defeated the Houston Oilers in the divisional round of the playoffs, 34–10. Capitalizing on two early turnovers, Denver jumped to a 14–0 lead in first quarter. They were up 24-3 at half, then traded scores in the third and fourth quarters.

Elway was 14/25 for 259 yards, and two touchdowns.

DENVER
BRONCOS

NFL

AMERICAN
FOOTBALL CONFERENCE
PLAYOFF

D

TIME AND DATE
TO BE ANNOUNCED

FIRST LEVEL
131   36   8
SEC.   ROW   SEAT

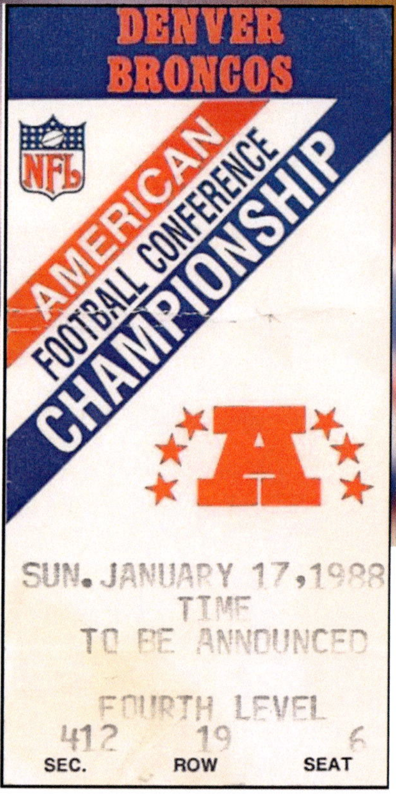

AFC Championship
January 17, 1988

Denver once held a 21-3 lead, but quarterback Bernie Kosar led the Browns back to tie 31-31. Denver scored, and with 1:12 remaining was leading 38-31. Kosar brought Cleveland back again, and from the 8-yard line had a first and goal. Running back Ernest Byner, took the ensuing handoff and rushed for six yards before being stripped of the ball. Denver cornerback, Jeremiah Castille recovered at the two-yard line. The Broncos then gave an intentional safety, and were able to hang on for a 38-33 win.

Elway was 14/26 for 281 yards, and 3 touchdowns.

1987 AFC Chamoionship Ring

JANUARY 25, 1988
$2.25
Sports Illustrated
JOHN ELWAY
SUPER BOWL BOUND!
IT'S THE BRONCOS
AGAINST THE REDSKINS

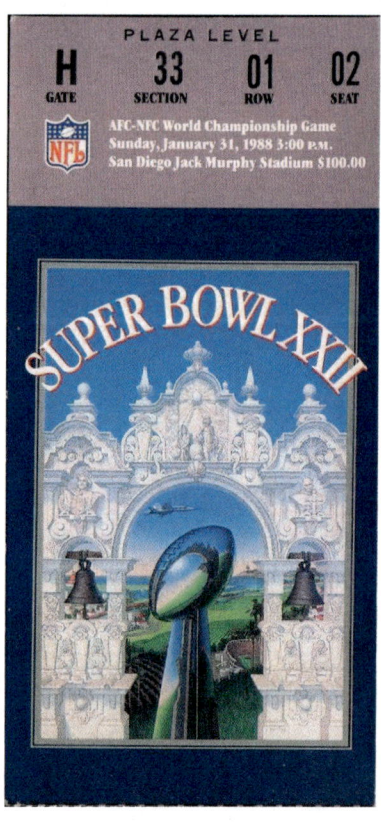

SUPER BOWL XXII
January 31, 1988

Making their second consecutive Super Bowl appearance, Denver was a pregame 3-point favorite. The Broncos forced Washington to punt on their first posession. Then on Denver's first offensive play, Elway threw a 56-yard touch-down pass to Ricky Nattiel. The Broncos would lead 10-0 at the end of the first quarter. Washington scored 35 points in the second quarter, and had a 35-10 hafltime lead. Denver couldn't counterpunch and was shutout the rest of the way. Elway was intercepted 3 times. Washington scored again in the fourth quarter, and the Broncos fell 42-10.

Elway was 14/38 for 257 yards, and 1 touchdown.

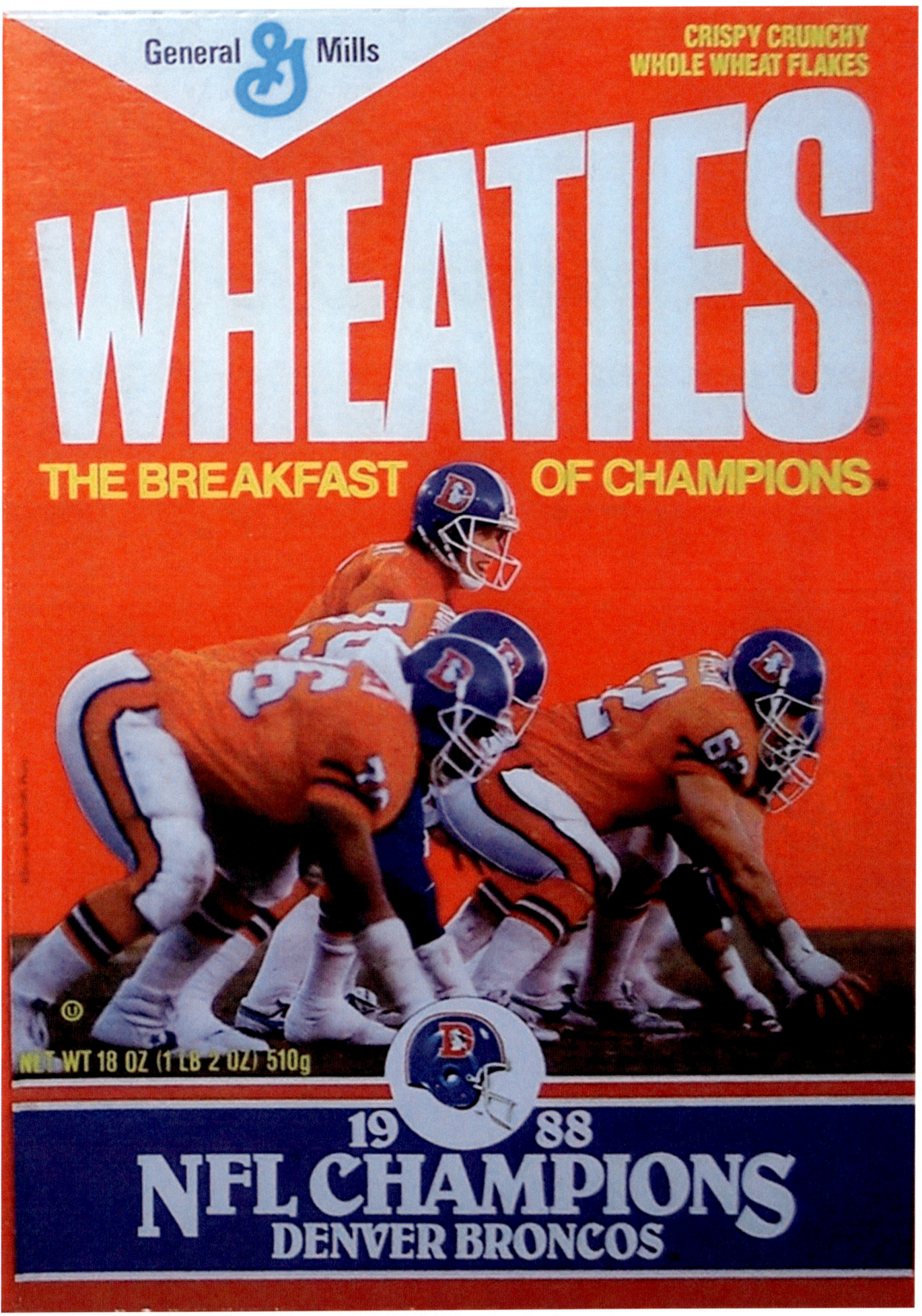

1988 Phantom Wheaties Box

1988

Coming off their Super Bowl loss, the 1988 Broncos never could get it together. By mid-season they were 4-4, and though they were second in the AFC West with an 8-8 record, they did not qualify for postseason play.

Elway started 15 games. He was 274/496 for 3309 yards, and 17 touchdowns. He rushed for 234 yards on 54 carries, and scored one touchdown.

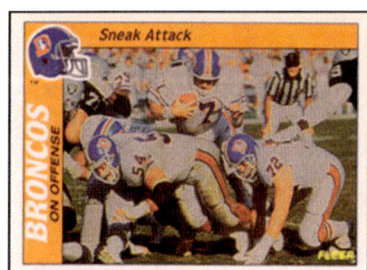
1988 Fleer #5

1988 Fleer #59

1988 Fleer #69

1988 Napco Pencil

1988 Heros Sticker #7

1988 Panini Sticker #53

1988 Starting Lineup

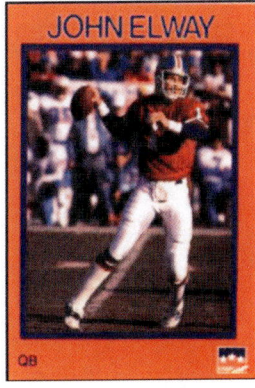

1988 Starline Promo

1988 Topps #23

1988 Topps Sticker #175

1988 Topps Sticker Foil #147

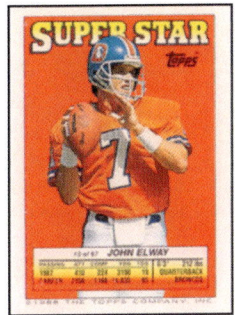

1988 Topps Super
Star Mini #3

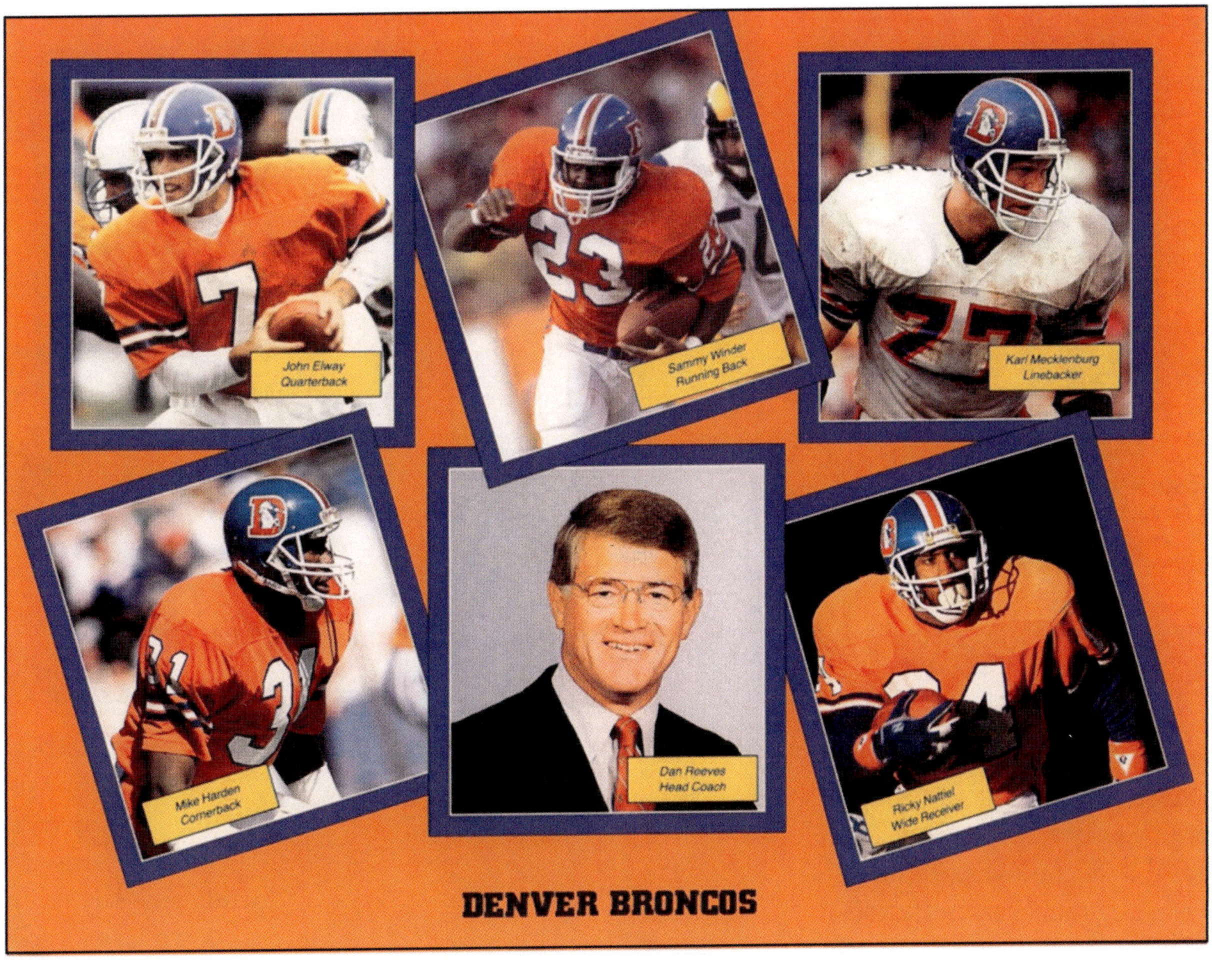

1988 NFL Super-Pro Club Team Sheet

1988 Ace Fact Pack

1988 Wagon Wheels #6

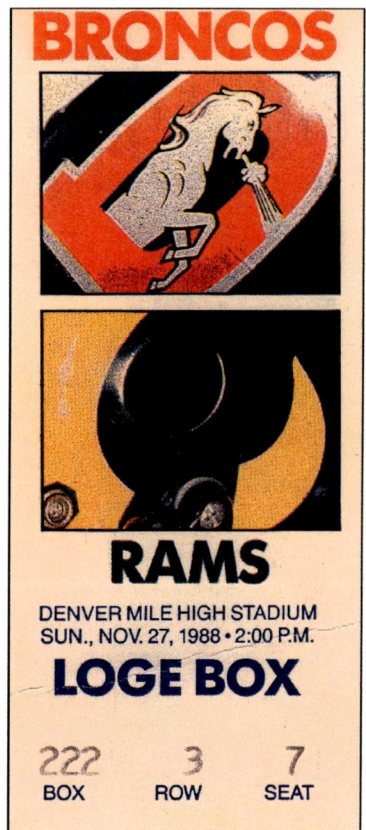

1988 Gentry Original
(my brother made it for me!)

November 27, 1988

a 35-24 victory over the Los Angeles Rams, Elway was 21/36 for 252 yards and 3 touchdowns. He also had a rushing touchdown. He was named NFL Player of the Week.

December 4, 1988

A 27-28 loss to the Los Angeles Raiders. Elway completed 29/49 for 324 yards and two touchdowns. His second touchdown was 4 yards to Clarence Kay, it was Elway's 100th career touchdown pass.

1988 IPCO Milk
1/2 Pint School Lunch Size

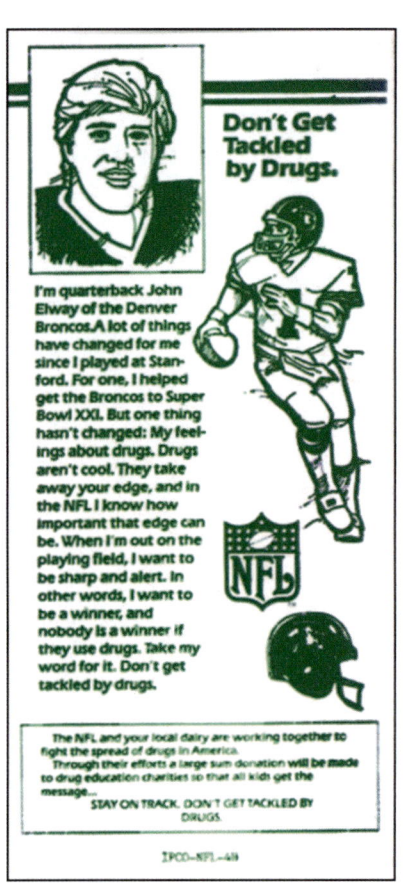

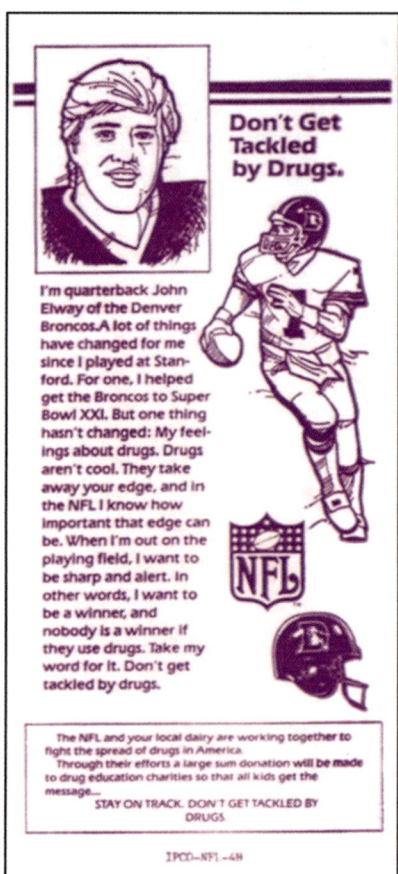

1988 Bridgemans IPCO Milk
1/2 Gallon Cartons

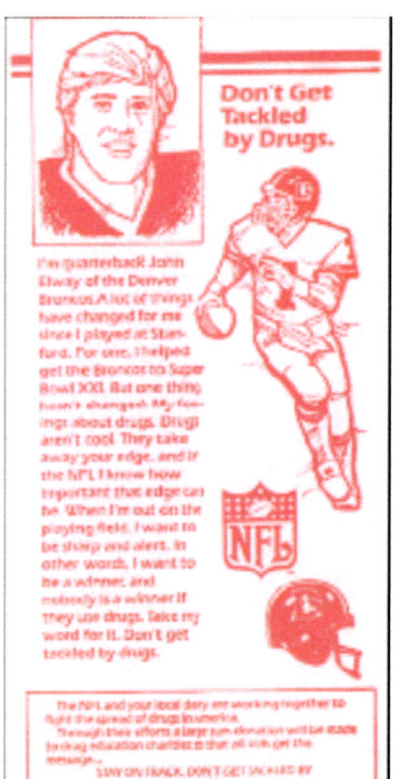
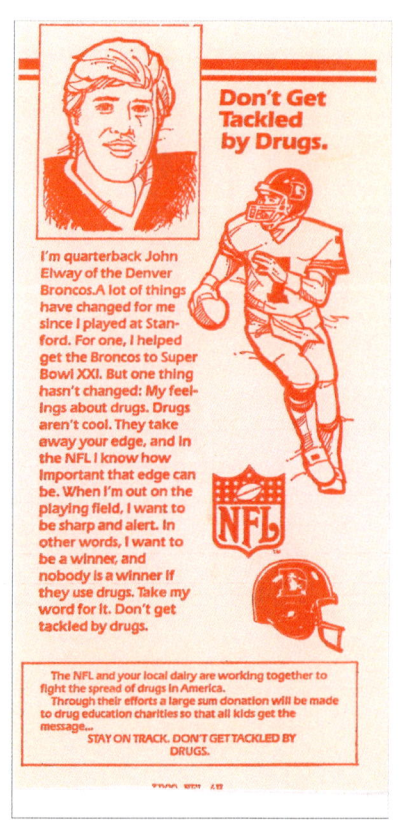
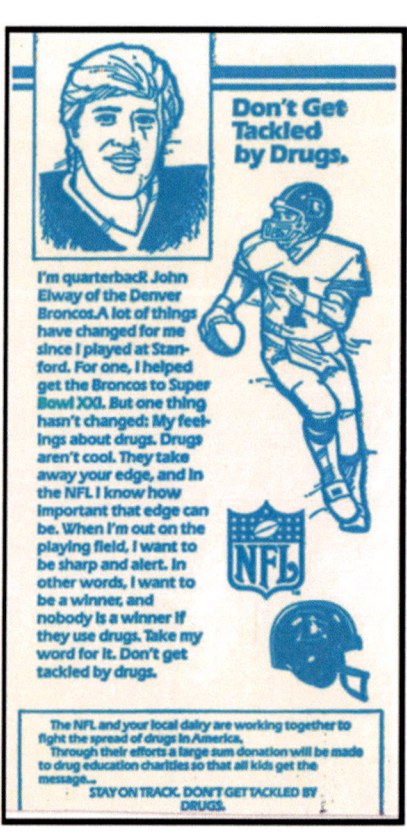

**n't Get
ckled
Drugs!**

en you get tackled by
FL defender, you get
up again and go on
g. But when you get
ed by drugs, your
e life can be ruined.
s why this dairy and
NFL are working togeth-
help stop the spread of
s in America. Through
awareness programs,
work, and donations
ti-drug education char-
all of us can come out
ers in this fight."

*John Elway
Quarterback
Denver Broncos*

**Special
NFL Team
Cap Offer!**

an officially licensed team cap for your favorite NFL
—a $12.00 retail value for only $4.75. Caps are white
twill with team name and helmet embroidered on front;
able, one size fits all. To order, include:
r name and complete mailing address; 2. Your choice of
s); 3. A check or money order made out to NFL Cap Offer
.75 plus $1.75 postage and handling per cap.
: NFL Cap Offer, P.O. Box 5515, Maple Plain, MN 55348.
e allow 6-8 weeks for delivery.

$1.00 donation per cap ordered will be made to
FL Charities for its anti-drug education programs.

NFL-J.E.-CA88-1

**Don't Get
Tackled
By Drugs!**

"When you get tackled by
an NFL defender, you get
back up again and go on
playing. But when you get
tackled by drugs, your
whole life can be ruined.
That's why this dairy and
the NFL are working together to help stop the spread of
drugs in America. Through
drug awareness programs,
hard work, and donations
to anti-drug education charities, all of us can come out
winners in this fight."

*John Elway
Quarterback
Denver Broncos*

**Special
NFL Team
Cap Offer!**

Order an officially licensed team cap for your favorite NFL
team—a $12.00 retail value for only $4.75. Caps are white
cotton twill with team name and helmet embroidered on front;
adjustable, one size fits all. To order, include:
1. Your name and complete mailing address; 2. Your choice of
team(s); 3. A check or money order made out to NFL Cap Offer
for $4.75 plus $1.75 postage and handling per cap.
Send to: NFL Cap Offer, P.O. Box 5515, Maple Plain, MN 55348.
Please allow 6-8 weeks for delivery.

A $1.00 donation per cap ordered will be made to
NFL Charities for its anti-drug education programs.

NFL-J.E.-CA88-1

**Don't Get
Tackled
By Drugs!**

"When you get tackled by
an NFL defender, you get
back up again and go on
playing. But when you get
tackled by drugs, your
whole life can be ruined.
That's why this dairy and
the NFL are working together to help stop the spread of
drugs in America. Through
drug awareness programs,
hard work, and donations
to anti-drug education charities, all of us can come out
winners in this fight."

*John Elway
Quarterback
Denver Broncos*

**Special
NFL Team
Cap Offer!**

Order an officially licensed team cap for your favorite NFL
team—a $12.00 retail value for only $4.75. Caps are white
cotton twill with team name and helmet embroidered on front;
adjustable, one size fits all. To order, include:
1. Your name and complete mailing address; 2. Your choice of
team(s); 3. A check or money order made out to NFL Cap Offer
for $4.75 plus $1.75 postage and handling per cap.
Send to: NFL Cap Offer, P.O. Box 5515, Maple Plain, MN 55348.
Please allow 6-8 weeks for delivery.

A $1.00 donation per cap ordered will be made to
NFL Charities for its anti-drug education programs.

NFL-J.E.-CA88-1

1988-89 IPCO PSA 1/2 Gallon Cartons

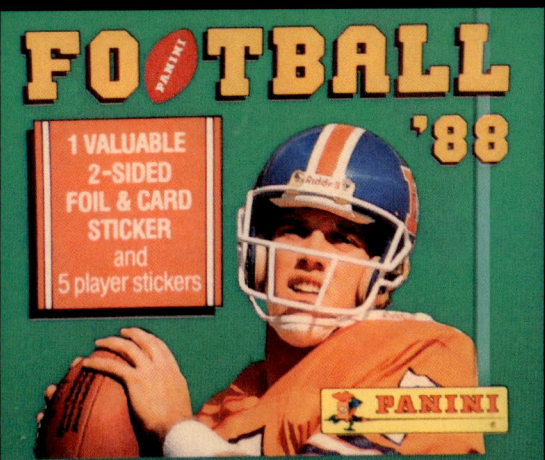

1988 Panini Sticker Package

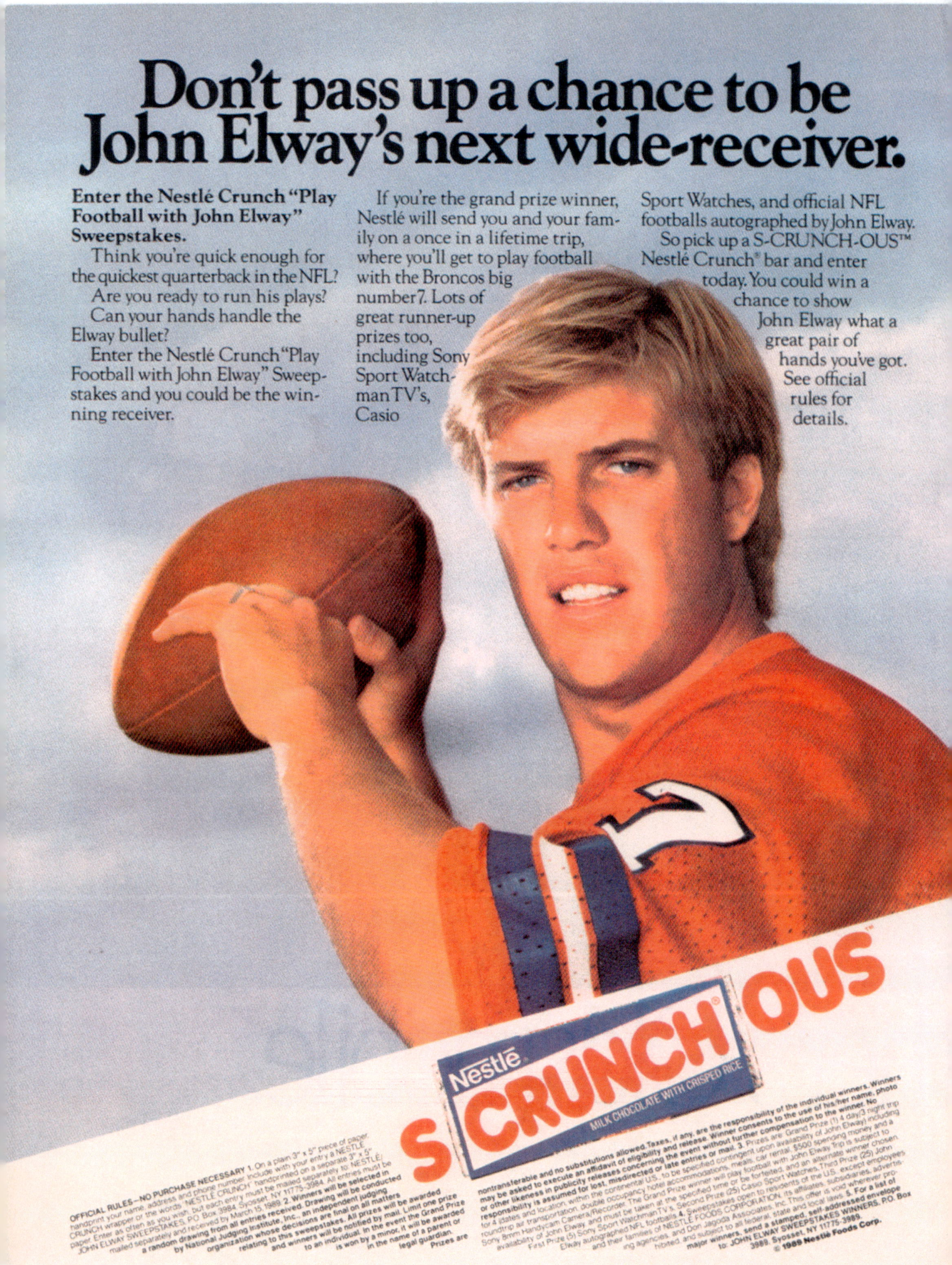

Don't pass up a chance to be John Elway's next wide-receiver.
Enter the Nestlé Crunch "Play Football with John Elway" Sweepstakes.
Think you're quick enough for the quickest quarterback in the NFL? Are you ready to run his plays? Can your hands handle the Elway bullet? Enter the Nestlé Crunch "Play Football with John Elway" Sweepstakes and you could be the winning receiver.
If you're the grand prize winner, Nestlé will send you and your family on a once in a lifetime trip, where you'll get to play football with the Broncos big number 7. Lots of great runner-up prizes too, including Sony Sport Watchman TV's, Casio Sport Watches, and official NFL footballs autographed by John Elway.
So pick up a S-CRUNCH-OUS™ Nestlé Crunch® bar and enter today. You could win a chance to show John Elway what a great pair of hands you've got. See official rules for details.
S CRUNCH OUS™
Nestlé
CRUNCH®
MILK CHOCOLATE WITH CRISPED RICE
OFFICIAL RULES—NO PURCHASE NECESSARY 1. On a plain 3" x 5" piece of paper handprint your name, address and phone number. Include with your entry a NESTLÉ CRUNCH wrapper or the words "NESTLÉ CRUNCH" handprinted on a separate 3" x 5" paper. Enter as often as you wish, but each entry must be mailed separately to: NESTLÉ/JOHN ELWAY SWEEPSTAKES, P.O. Box 3984, Syosset, NY 11775-3984. All entries must be mailed separately and received by March 15, 1989. 2. Winners will be selected in a random drawing from all entries received. Drawing will be conducted by National Judging Institute, Inc., an independent judging organization whose decisions are final on all matters relating to this sweepstakes. All prizes will be awarded and winners will be notified by mail. Limit one prize to an individual. In the event the Grand Prize is won by a minor, it will be awarded in the name of a parent or legal guardian. Prizes are nontransferable and no substitutions allowed. Taxes, if any, are the responsibility of the individual winners. Winners may be asked to execute an affidavit of eligibility and release. Winner consents to the use of his/her name, photo or other likeness in publicity releases concerning the event without further compensation to the winner. No responsibility is assumed for lost, misdirected or late entries or mail. 3. Prizes are: Grand Prize (1) 4 day/3 night trip for 4 (dates and location within the continental U.S., to be specified contingent upon availability of John Elway) including roundtrip air transportation, double occupancy hotel accommodations, meals, car rental, $500 spending money and a Sony 8mm Handycam Camera/Recorder. The Grand Prize winner will play football with John Elway. Trip is subject to availability of John Elway, and must be taken at the specified time or be forfeited, and an alternate winner chosen. First Prize (5) Sony Sport Watchman TV's. Second Prize (25) Casio Sport Watches. Third Prize (25) John Elway autographed NFL footballs. 4. Sweepstakes open to residents of the U.S., except employees and their families of NESTLÉ FOODS CORPORATION, its affiliates, subsidiaries, advertising agencies, and Don Jagoda Associates, Inc. This offer is void wherever prohibited, and subject to all federal, state and local laws. 5. For a list of major winners, send a stamped, self-addressed envelope to: JOHN ELWAY SWEEPSTAKES WINNERS, P.O. Box 3989, Syosset, NY 11775-3989.
© 1989 Nestlé Foods Corp.

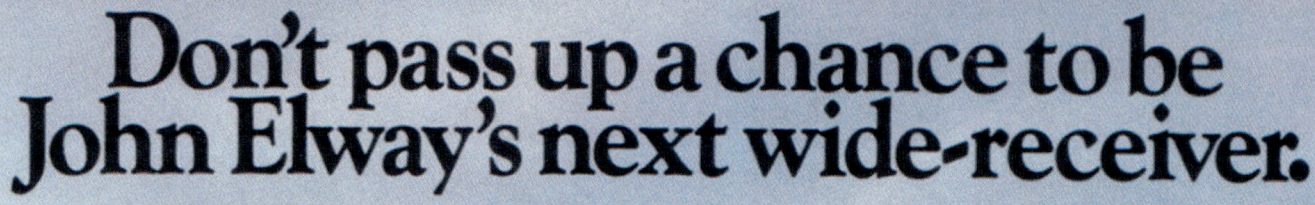

MIZUNO

1989 Mizuno Advisory Staff Photo

1989

The Broncos rebounded and won the AFC West with a record of 11-5. They hosted the Pittsburgh Steelers in the divisional round of the playoffs, a 24-23 win, then met the Cleveland Browns, for the third time in four years, to decide the American Football Conference Championship. Denver would prevail 37-21.

Super Bowl XXIV would put the Broncos against the defending champion San Francisco 49ers.

For the season, Elway was 223/416 for 3051 yards, and 18 touchdowns. He also rushed for 244 yards on 48 carries, and scored three touchdowns.

He was selected to his third Pro-Bowl.

1989 Pacific
Steve Largent #70

1989 Panini Sticker
#263

Reverse

UK #263

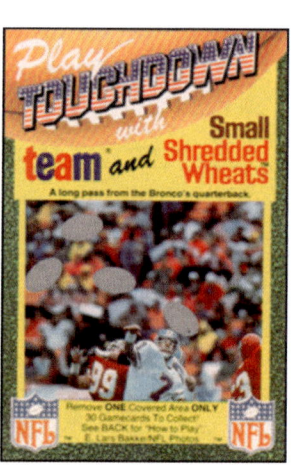

1989 Play Touchdown
UK #28

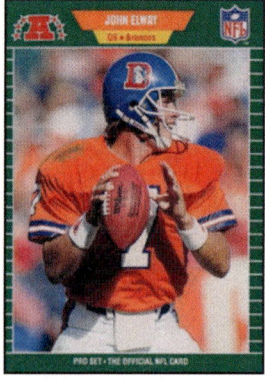

1989 Pro Set #100

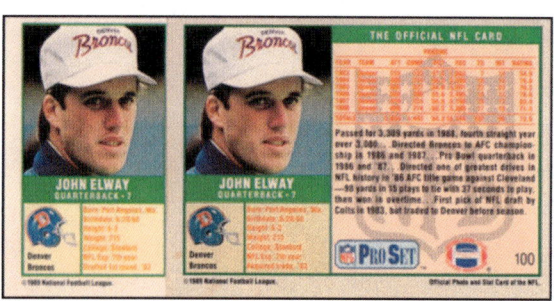

1989 Pro Set A-Draft & B-Trade Reverse

1989 Pro Set
Super Bowl #100

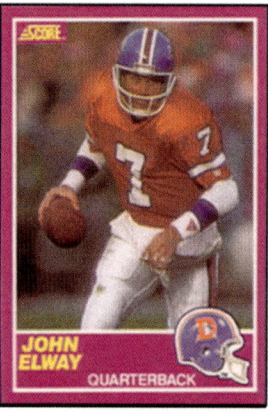

1989 Score
Supplemental #339S

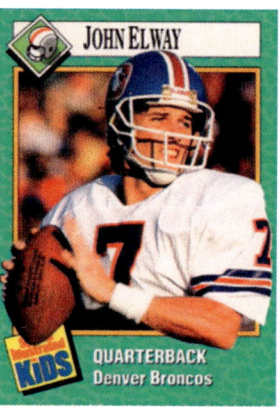

1989 SIFK #103

1989 Starting Lineup

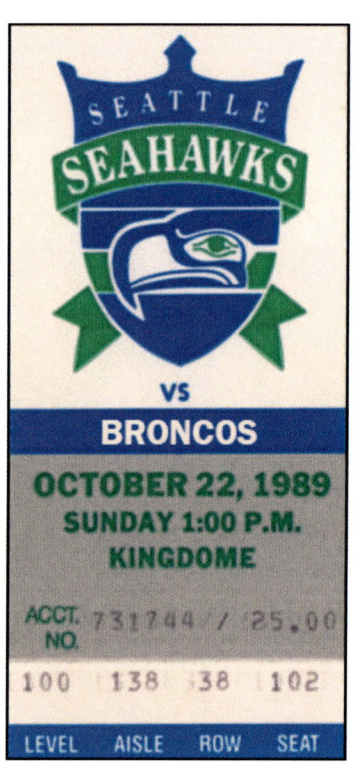

October 22, 1989
A 24-21 win at Seattle,
Elway completed 18/35
passes for 344 yards and 2
touchdowns. He was the
NFL Player of the Week.

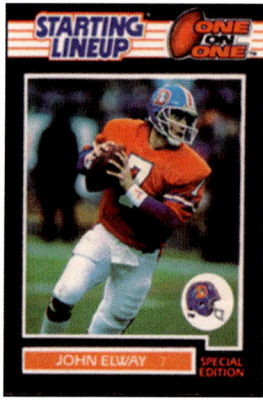

1989 Starting Lineup
One on One

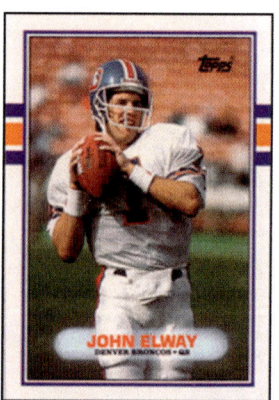

1989 Topps #241

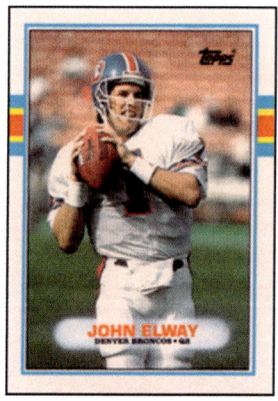

1989 Topps UK #4

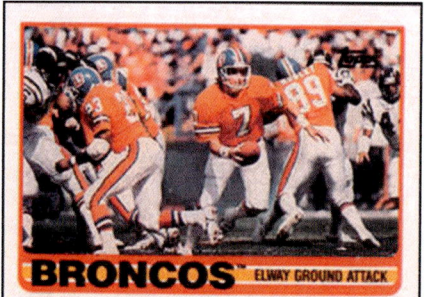

1989 Topps #238

1989 TV4 NFLQB #19

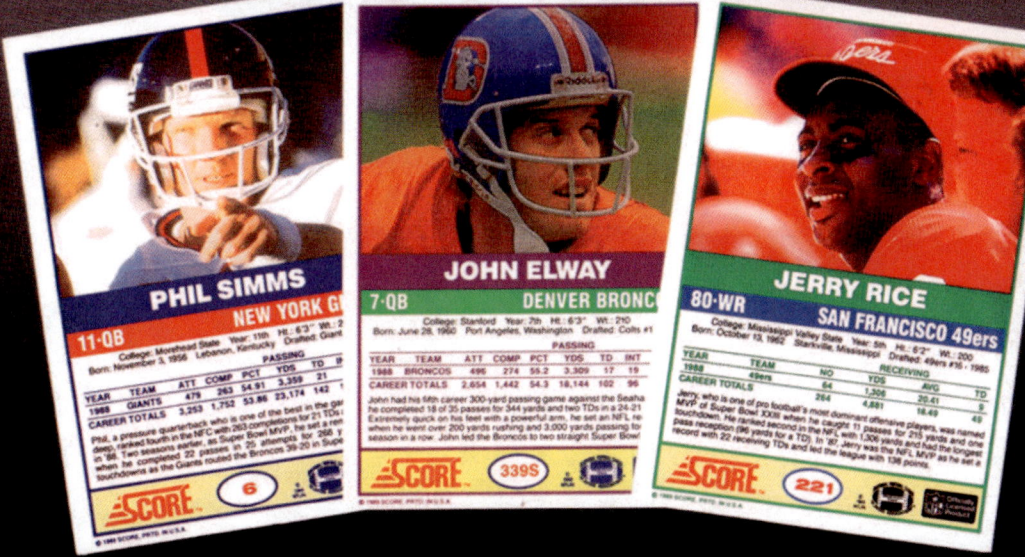

JOHN ELWAY

1989 Starline NFLPA Birthday Card

1989 MacGreggor Game Cards

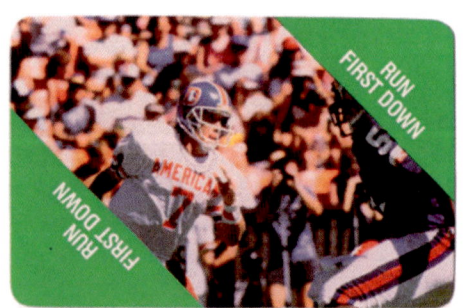

SPLIT-SECOND VICTORIES

00:37

1 9 8 6 A F C
CHAMPIONSHIP GAME
D E N V E R 23
C L E V E L A N D 20

Down 20-13, John Elway and the Broncos got the ball on their own 2 with 5:32 left in the game. On the ensuing 15-play drive, Elway (7, above) ran twice for 20 yards and completed six passes, including a low five-yarder to Mark Jackson with 37 seconds left that sent the game into overtime. In the overtime, Elway engineered another drive, of 60 yards, capped by Rich Karlis's game-winning 33-yard field goal.

SPECIAL OFFER: SUPER BOWL XXIV WATCH!

Here's your chance to get a special-edition Super Bowl XXIV digital calendar watch for only $2.99! To order send (1) your name and complete mailing address, (2) check or money order for $2.99 (includes postage and handling) made out to Starline, Inc., and (3) name of dairy on whose milk carton this offer appears to:

Split-Second Victories, Starline, Inc., 19-10 Hazen Street, East Elmhurst, New York 11370

No purchase is necessary. Please allow 6-8 weeks for delivery. No orders will be accepted after February 15, 1990. OFFER VOID WHERE PROHIBITED BY LAW.

1989 Split Second Victories Milk Panel

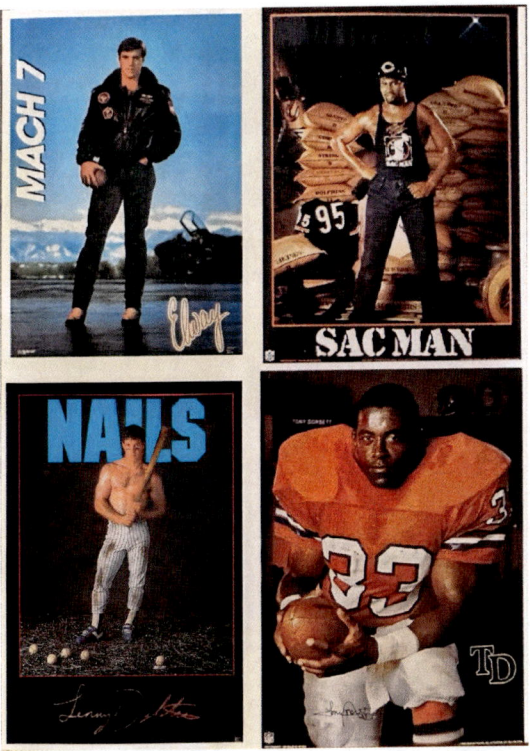

1989 Making Waves Poster Promo Postcard

1989 Denver Broncos Fan Club Card

Photo Mike Powell ALLSPORT USA

John Elway

AFC Championship
January 14, 1990

In one of his finer post-season games, Elway completed 20/36 passes for 385 yards, and three touchdowns. He also gained 39 yards on five rushing attempts.

Dominant in all phases of the game, Denver defeated Cleveland 37-21, and advanced to Super Bowl XXIV. Waiting for them was the defending champion San Francisco 49ers, who at 14-2, had the best record in the League, and had outscored their playoff opponents 71-16.

1989 AFC Championship Ring

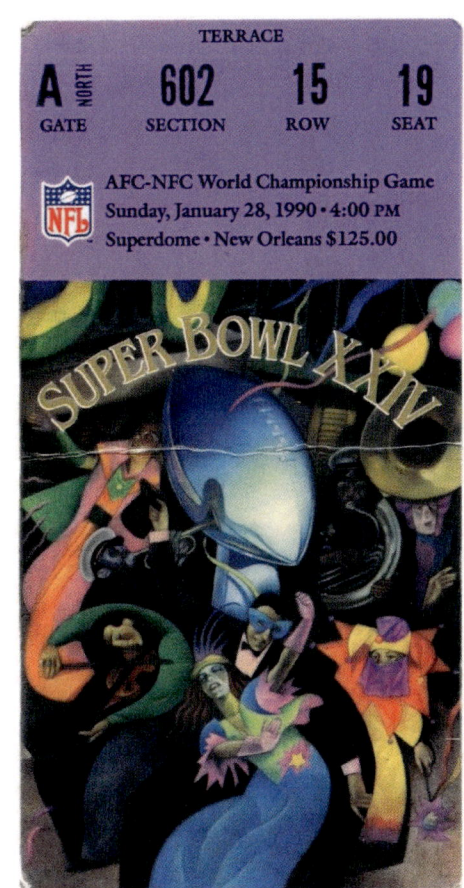

SUPER BOWL XXIV
January 28, 1990

On his way to MVP honors Joe Montana would pass for 297 yards and 5 touchdowns. Tom Rathman and Brent Jones each caught a touchdown, Jerry Rice caught three,

Denver turned the ball over 4 times, and was outgained by nearly 300 yards, 461 to 167. It was the most lopsided Super Bowl loss in history; final score 55-10.

Elway was 10/26 for 108 yards.

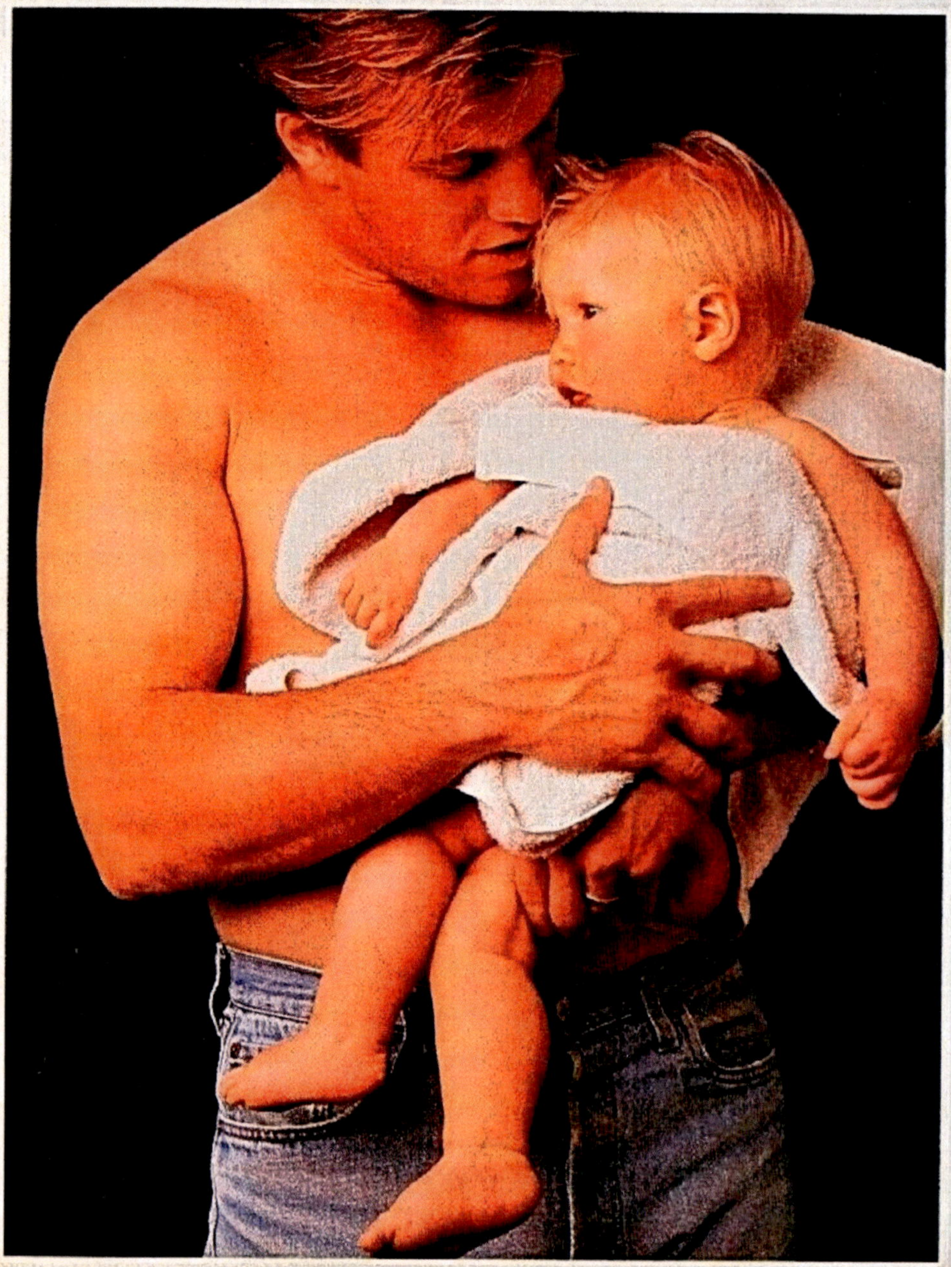

John Elway. Cardmember since 1984.

Membership Has Its Privileges.℠

Don't leave home without it.®

Call 1-800-THE CARD to apply.

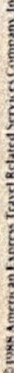

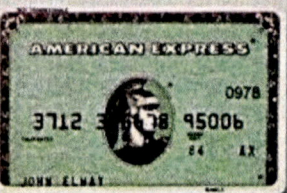

1990

The blowout loss in the previous Super Bowl might have had a hangover effect. Denver finished 5th in the AFC West with a 5-11 record. Six of the losses were by a combined 18 points. They failed to make the post-season.

Elway completed 294/502 passes for 3526 yards, with 15 touchdowns. He rushed for 258 yards, on 50 carries, and scored 3 touchdowns.

DENVER BRONCOS 1990

85 KOA NEWSRADIO

1990 KOA Pocket Schedule

1990 Action Packed # 63

1990 BP Gas #1

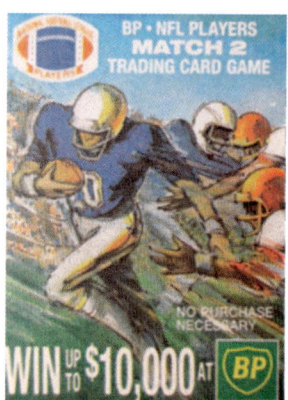

1990 BP Gas #1
Reverse A

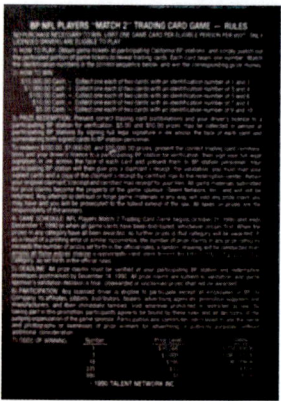

1990 BP Gas #1
Reverse B

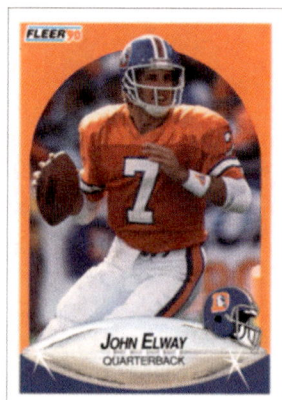

1990 Fleer #21

1990 Fleer #21 Reverse A & B

1990 Football Card
News #11

1990 Legends Magazine
WNT-90

1990 Little Big
Leaguers

1990 Panini
Sticker #53

Reverse #53

UK Reverse #53

1990 Panini Sticker #395

UK #395

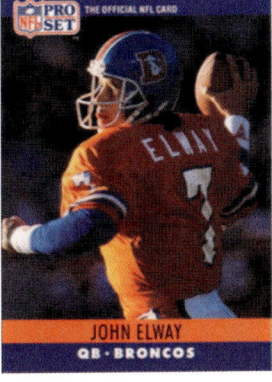

1990 Pro Set # 88

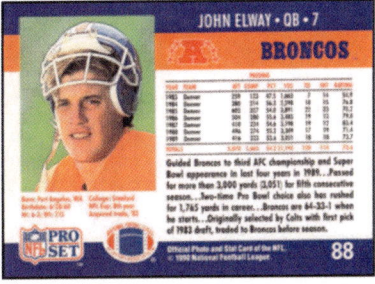

Reverse

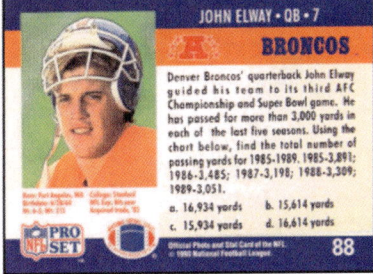

1990 Pro Set FACT #88 Reverse

1990 Pro Set #789 Reverse

1990 Pro Set
Collect A Book #15

1990 Score
MVP Pin #19

1990 Score #25

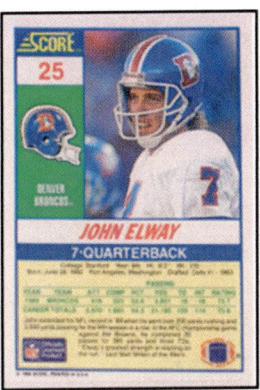

Reverse

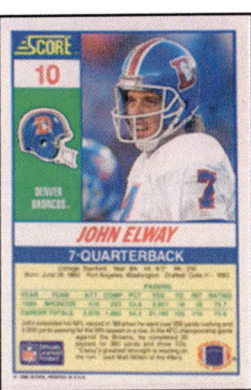

1990 Score Hot 100
#10 Reverse

1990 Score #564

1990 Pro Set Super Bowl
Lamar Hunt Trophy Reverse

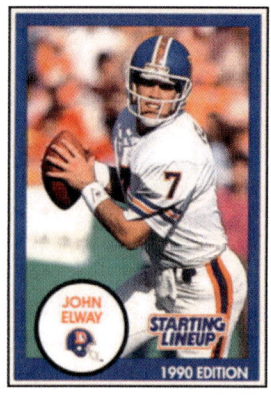

1990 Starting Lineup

1990 Starting Lineup Rookie

1990 Star Cal Decal
Prototype

1990 Star Cal #23A

1990 Star Cal #23B

1990's McDonalds Cup

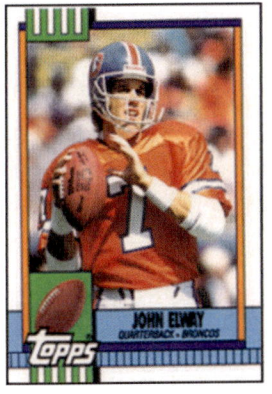
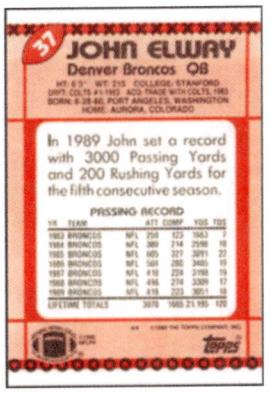

1990 Topps Tiffany #37   Reverse

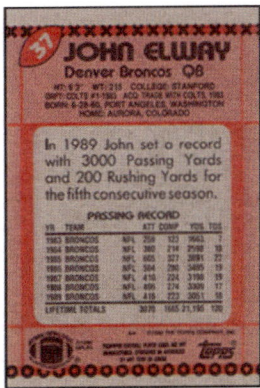

1990 Topps # 37   Reverse A   Reverse B
                     (Non Disclaimer)   (Disclaimer)

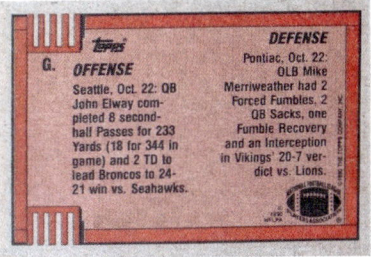
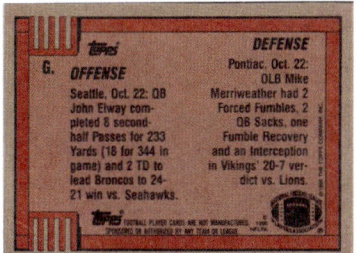

1990 Topps Box Bottom #G   Reverse A   Reverse B
                            (Non Disclaimer)   (Disclaimer)

JOHN ELWAY

1991

The Broncos finished the 1991 season 12-4 which put them first in the AFC West, their third division crown in five years. A first round bye, and the Broncos hosted the Houston Oilers in the divisional playoffs.

For the season, Elway was 242/451 with 3252 yards, and 13 touchdowns. Selected to his fourth Pro-Bowl, he had 255 yards rushing on 55 attempts, with 6 touchdowns.

1991 Action Packed #63

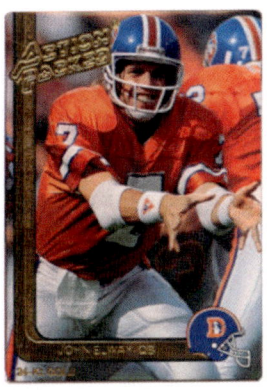

1991 Action Packed 24G #14G

1991 Bowman #127

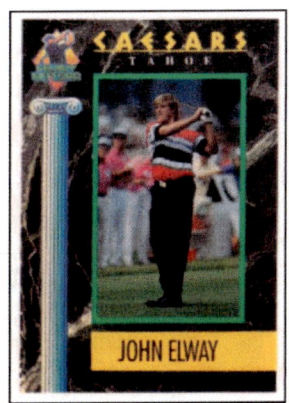

1991 Caesars Palace Heavy Hitters #5

1991 Fleer Special Edition Sheet

1991 Dominos QB #7

1991 FACT Pro Set
#138 Reverse

1991 Fleer #45

1991 Stars and
Stripes #16

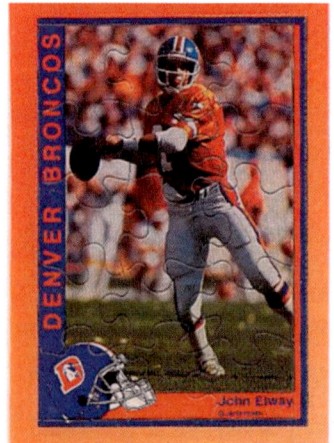

1991 Green Leaf
Puzzle Post Card

1991 Pacific #115

1991 Pacific Flash Card #34

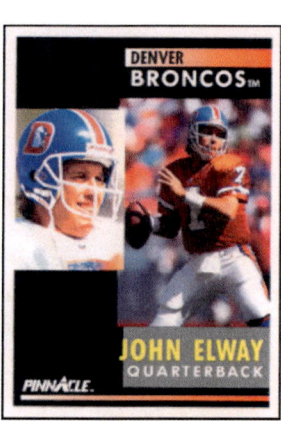

1991 Pinnacle #7

1993 SIFK Pullout Poster

JOHN ELWAY

FREE IN *Today*

No. 1: THE QUARTERBACKS COLLECTION

1991 ProSet Today Promo Panel UK #1

1991 ProSet Platinum #28

1991 ProSet Spanish #57

1991 NFL Experience #23

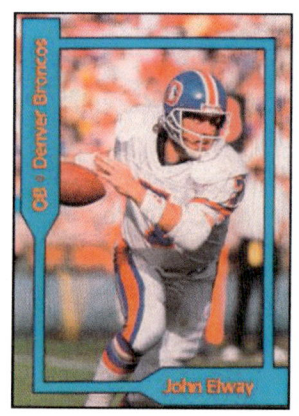

1991 SCD Pocket Guide #57

1991 Score #410

1991 Stanford
All-Centruy #20

1991 Stadium Club #294

1991 Pro Line Sample #21

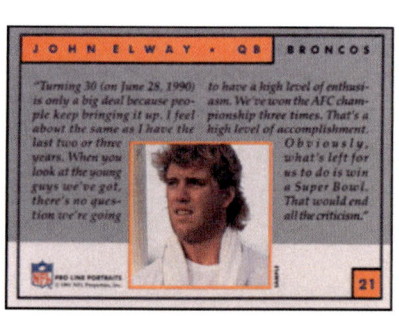

1991 Pro Line Sample #21
Reverse

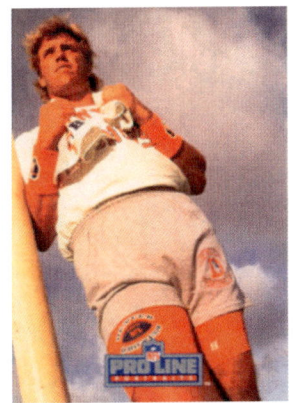

1991 Pro Line Portrait #257

1991 Pro Line National
Convention #257

1991 Pro Line
Punt Pass & Kick #PPK4

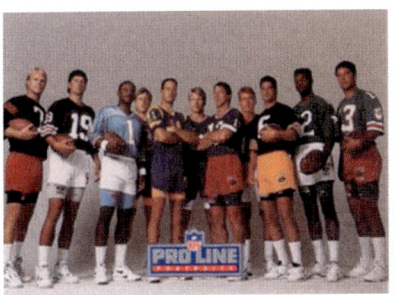

1991 Pro Line
Punt Pass & Kick Checklist

1991 Pro Line Auto #68

1991 ProSet #138

1991 ProSet #326

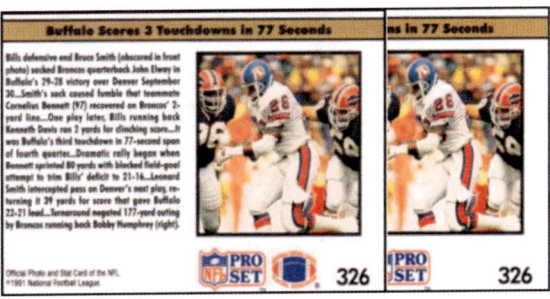

1991 ProSet #326
Reverse A & B

1991 ProSet #345

1991 Elway Foundation Card

1991 NFLPA Foto Wristband

1991 Topps #554

1991 Ultra #35

1991 Upper Deck #75

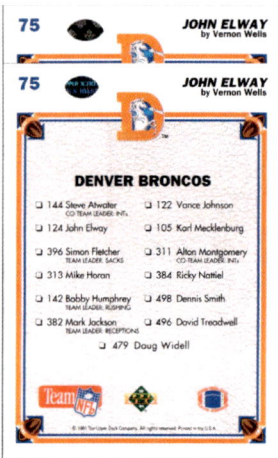

1991 Upper Deck #75
Reverse A & B

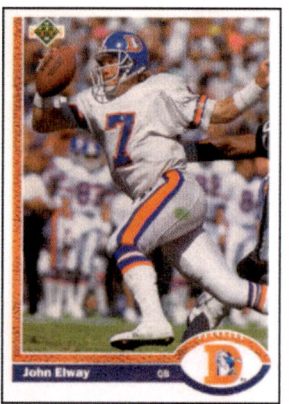

1991 Upper Deck #124

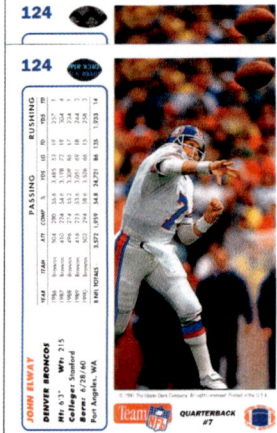

1991 Upper Deck #124
Reverse A & B

1991 Wild Card #4

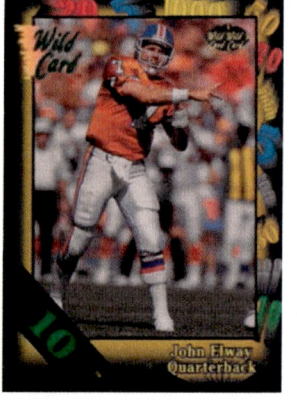

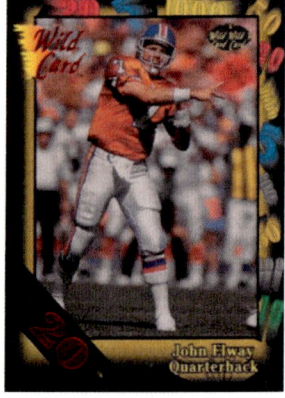

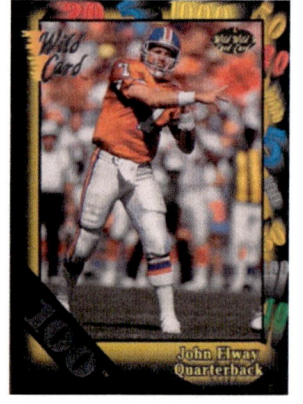

Wilson.
WILSON SPORTING GOODS CO.

John Elway
PROFESSIONAL
ADVISORY STAFF MEMBER

1991 Wilson Advisory Staff Photo

January 4, 1992
AFC Divisional Playoffs

A 26-24 Denver victory over Houston. The Oilers had finished a game behind Denver at 11-5, and were the third seed in the AFC. They had defeated the New York Jets in the wildcard round. Denver struggled to contain the passing of QB Warren Moon and found itself down 21-6 after Houston's first three posessions, and it remained so until halftime. The second half was different as Denver's defense tightned, while the offense chipped away at the lead. A one-yard touchdown by Greg Lewis followed by a David Treadwell field goal had closed the gap to 21-16. The Denver defense would yeild a field goal early in the fourth quarter, giving Houston a 24-16 lead. The ensuing posession was an 80 yard Denver drive capped by another Greg Lewis one-yard run, and the score was 24-23. The Denver defense was able to stop Moon and the Oilers on their next drive. On fourth down punter Greg Montgomery pinned the Broncos deep in their own territory. His punt was downed at the Denver two. There was 2:07 remaining.

Elway completed 19/33 passes for 257 yards and a touchdown. He also added 39 yards on 6 carries.

THE DRIVE II

1. - First down and 10, Denver 2-yard line Michael Young 22 yard pass. 2:07 remaining.

2. - First Down and 10, Denver 24-yard line, **pass incomplete.**

3. - Second Down and 10, Denver 24-yard line, **pass incomplete.**

4.- Third Down and 10, Rickey Nattiel 4-yard pass from Elway 1:43 remaining (10 second runoff).

5.- Fourth and six, Denver 28- yard line, Elway 7-yard run. 1:17 remaining.

6. - First Down, Denver 35-yard line, **pass incomplete.**

7. - Second Down and 10, Denver 35-yard line, incomplete pass intended for Derek Russell. 1:08 remaining.

8. - Third Down and 10, Denver 35-yard line, incomplete pass inteded for Vance johnson. :59 remaining.

9-Fourth Down and 10, Denver 35-yard line, Vance Johnson 44 yard pass from Elway. :50 seconds remaining.

10. - First down and 10, Houston 21-yard line, Steve Sewell 10 yard run. :23 seconds remaining.

11. - First down and 10, Houston 11-yard line, Elway incomplete pass (downs the ball.) :20 seconds remaining.

12. - Second down and 10, Houston 11-yard line, David Treadwell 28-yard FG :16 to play.

The following week, Denver would face the Buffalo Bills in the AFC Championship.

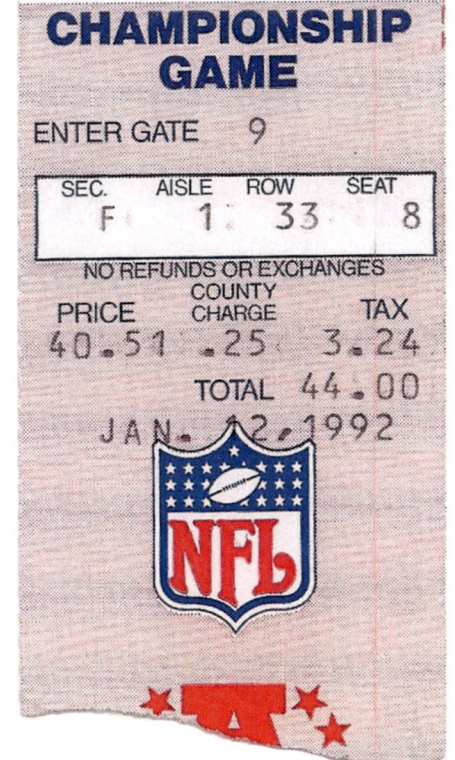

January 12, 1992
AFC Championship
Buffalo 10 - Denver 7.
Denver had three first-half posessions end in missed field goals attempts, and the halftime score was 0-0.

Elway injured his thigh at the beginning of the third quarter which limited his mobility. Facing second and 10 from their own 19, Elway threw a middle screen pass to Steve Sewell which was tipped by Bills Nose Tackle Jeff Wright. Linebacker Carlton Bailey intercepted the ball and returned it 11 yards for the lone Buffalo touchdown.

Scott Norwood added a 44-yard field goal later making the score 10-0.

Elway's injury worsened, and in the 4th quarter he was replaced by Gary Kubiak, who led an 8 play, 85-yard drive for Denver's only score.

Elway was 11/21 for 121 yards.

The Bills were defeated 37-24 by the Washington Redskins in Super Bowl XXVI.

1992

1992 Action Packed #14

1992 Action Packed 24K #2G

1992 Action Packed Mint

After a 7-3 start, Elway suffered a shoulder injury and the 1992 Denver Broncos went 1-5 to end the season. At a disappionting 8-8, they finished third in the AFC West. Following the season, Head Coach Dan Reeves was fired.

Due to the injury, Elway was limited to 12 starts. He completed 174/316 passes for 2242 yards, and 10 touchdowns. He added 94 yards on 34 rushing attempts, with 2 touchdowns.

Elway was selected as the NFL's 1992 Walter Payton Man of the Year.

1992 All World #88

1992 Bowman #280

1992 Bowman Foil #28

1992 Classic NFL Game #16

1992 Collectors Edge #37

1992 Collectors Edge #37 Reverse

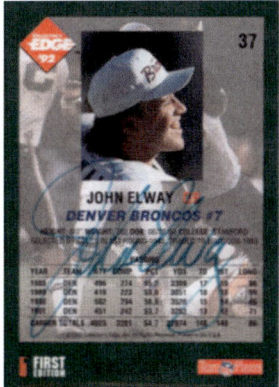

1992 Collectors Edge #37 Autograph

September 6, 1992

A 17-13 Denver victory over Los Angeles, Elway completed 10/24 passes for 171 yards, and a touchdown. He was named NFL Player of the Week.

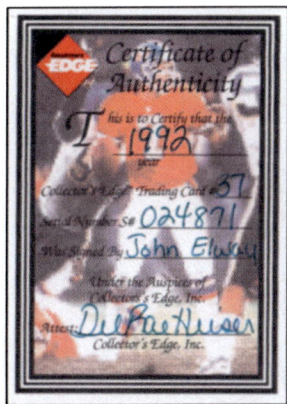

1992 Collectors Edge #37 Auto COA

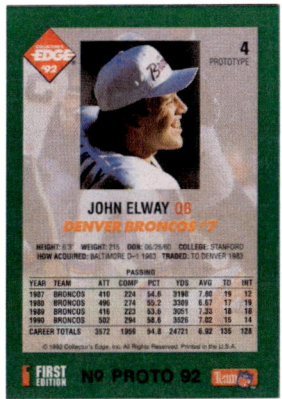

1992 Collectors Edge Prototype #4

1992 Collectors Edge Prototype Blank Back

1992 Collectors Edge Prototype Protective Backing

Auto

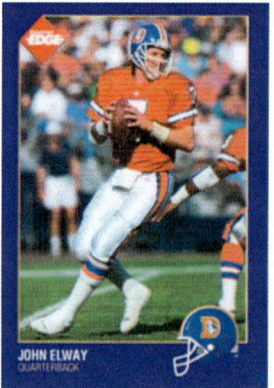

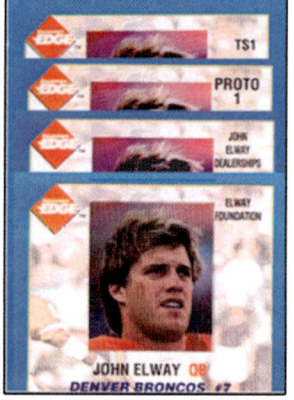

1992 Collectors Edge Promos

1992 Diamond
Sticker #18

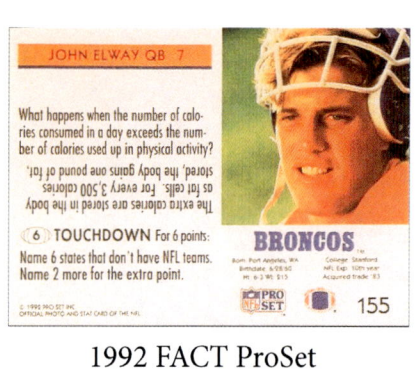

1992 FACT ProSet
Mobile #155

1992 Dog Tag #43

1992 Topps Finest #6

October 5, 1992

Elway threw two touchdown passes in the final 1:55 to give
Denver a 20-19 victory over Kansas City. He completed 23/38
passes for 311 yards. He was named NFL Player of the Week.

1992 Fleer #94

1992 Fleer # 471

1992 Fleer Team
Leaders # 16

1992 GameDay
GameBreaker #3

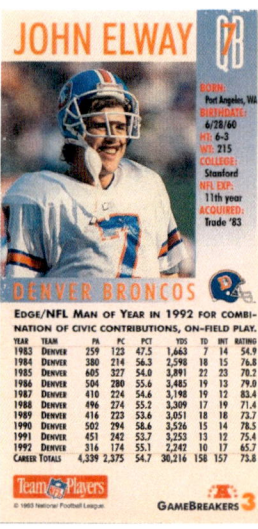

1992 GameDay
GameBreaker #3
Reverse

1992 GameDay #23

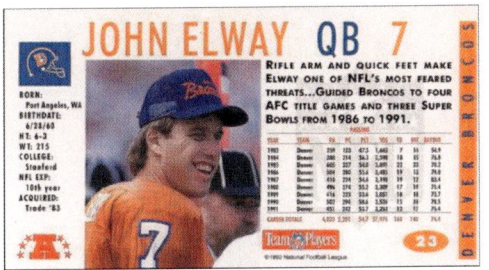

1992 GameDay #23 Reverse

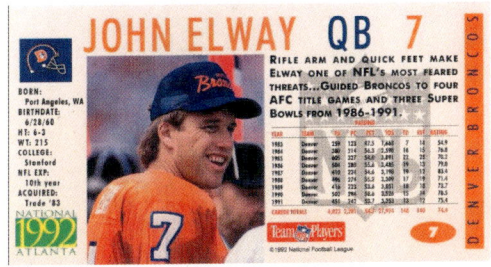

1992 GameDay National Promo #7 Reverse

1992 Intimidator Bio Sheet #7

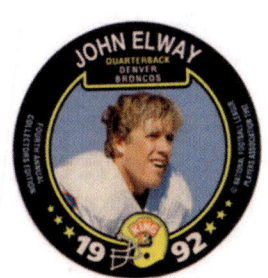

1992 King Bee #11

1992 Heze Sports China

1992 New Sport

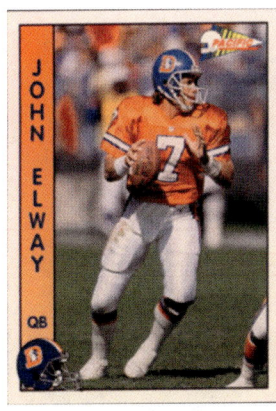

1992 Pacific #75

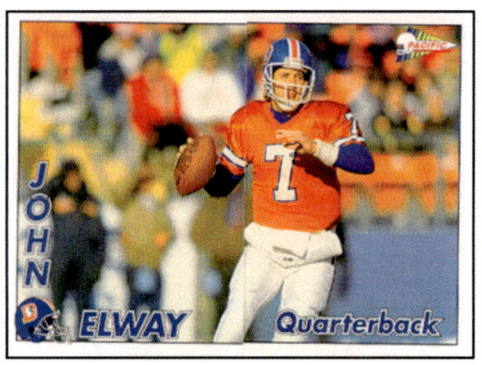

1992 Pacific Triple Folder

1992 Pinnacle #212

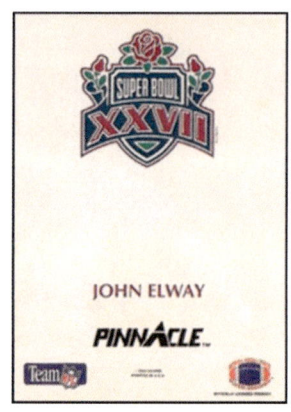

1992 Pinnacle Super Bowl
Promo Reverse

1992 Pinnacle Super Bowl Promo Sheet

1992 Pinnacle #353

1992 Playoff #77

1992 Playoff Promo #2

1992 ProSet Power #7

1992 ProSet #25

1992 ProSet #155

1992 ProSet MVP #4

1992 GE QB Greats #4

1992 Score #413

1992 SkyBox
Impact #10

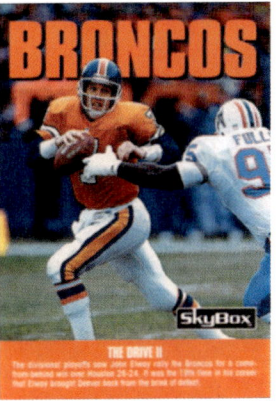

1992 SkyBox
Impact #283

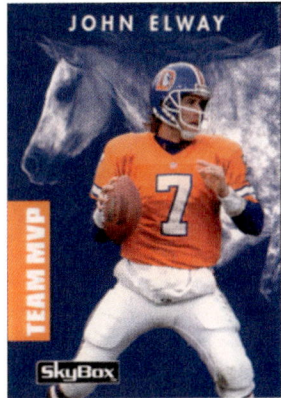

1992 SkyBox
Prime Time #257

1992 SkyBox Prime
Time #257 Reverse

1992 SkyBox PT
Promo Reverse

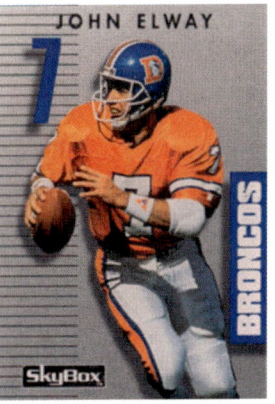

1992 SkyBox
Prime Time #50

1992 Sports Deck
#12 D

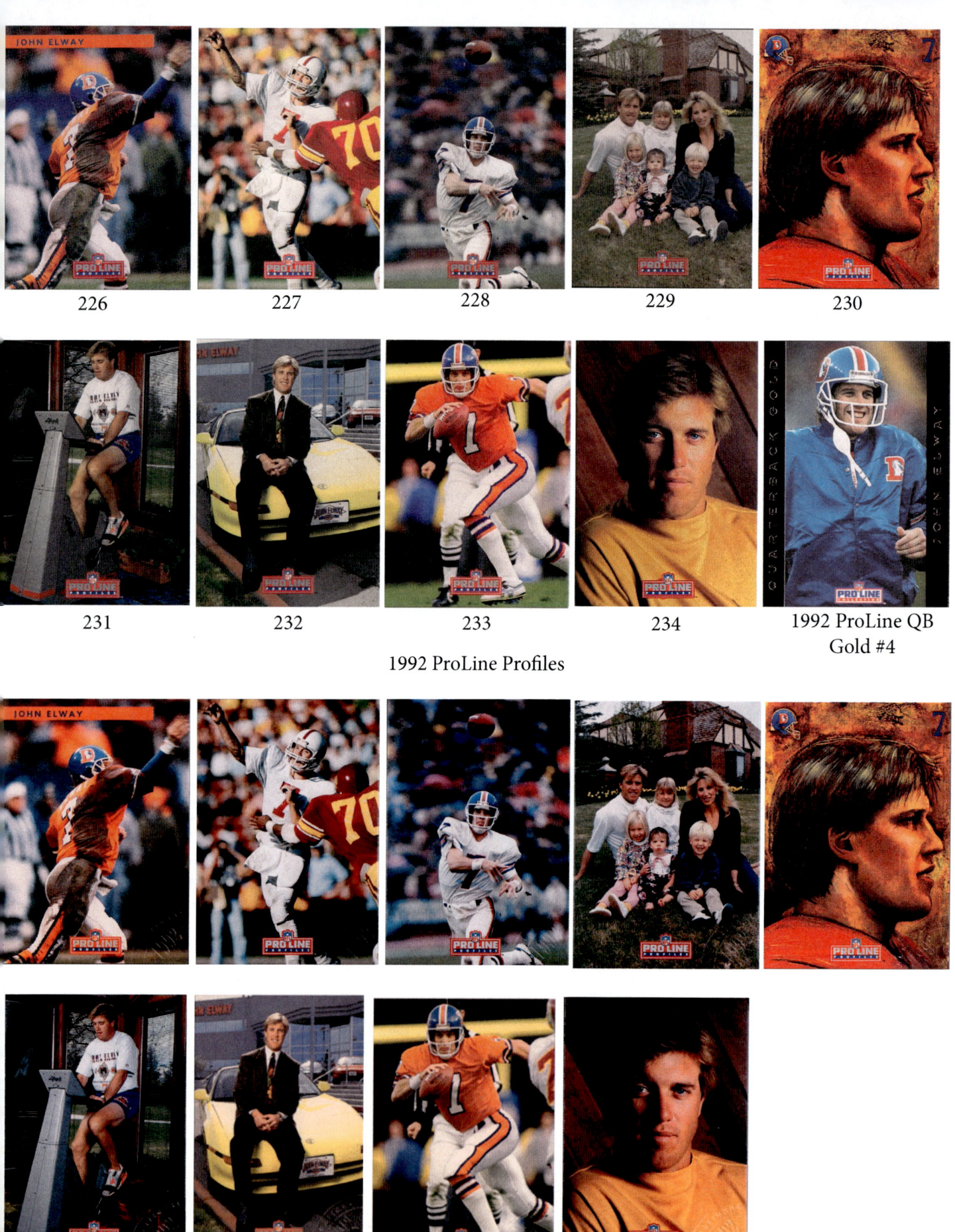

226 227 228 229 230

231 232 233 234 1992 ProLine QB
Gold #4

1992 ProLine Profiles

1992 ProLine Profiles National Convention

  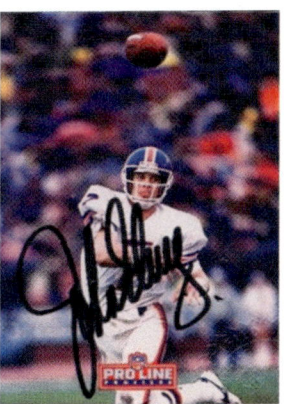 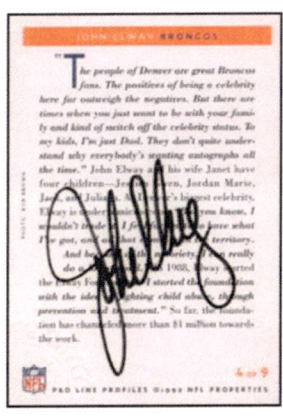 

  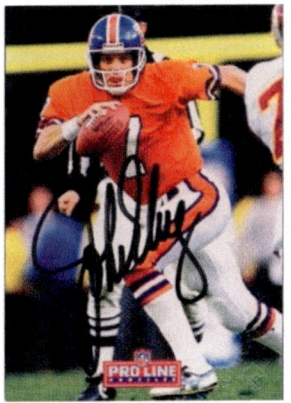  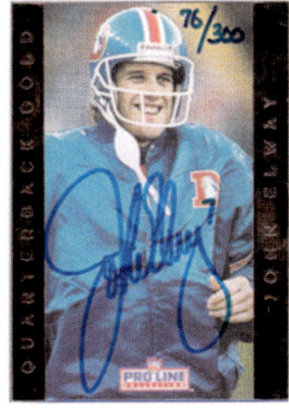

1992 ProLine Profiles Autographs

1992 ProLine
Quarterback Gold
Auto

1992 Sports Cards
Magazine #40

1992 Stadium Club #110

1992 Sports Illustrated
For Kids #437

1992 Topps #125

  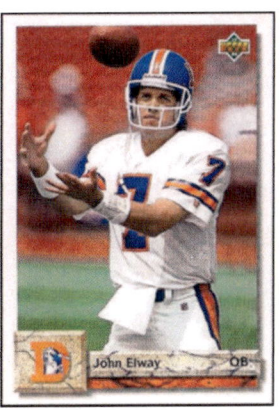 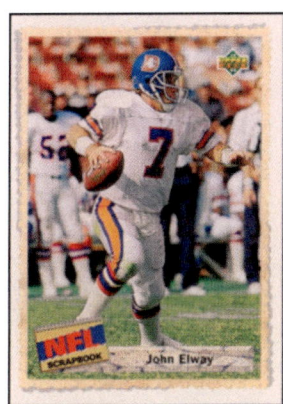

1992 Topps Gold #125

1992 Ultra #97

1992 Upper Deck #200

1992 Upper Deck #514

1992 Post Card

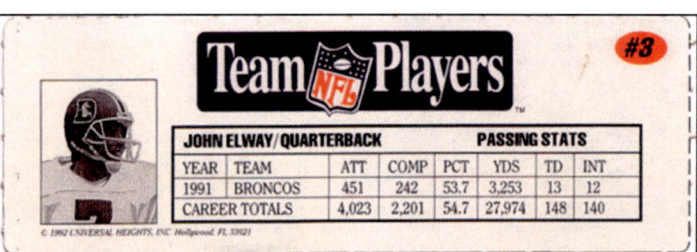

1992 Universal Heights #3 Super Silhouette

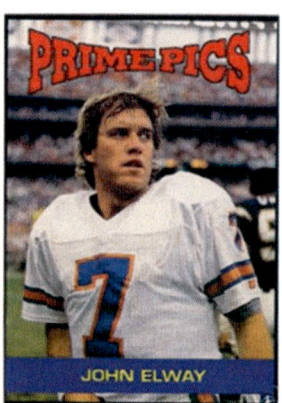

1992 Prime Pics

1992 Mini Helmet Sticker

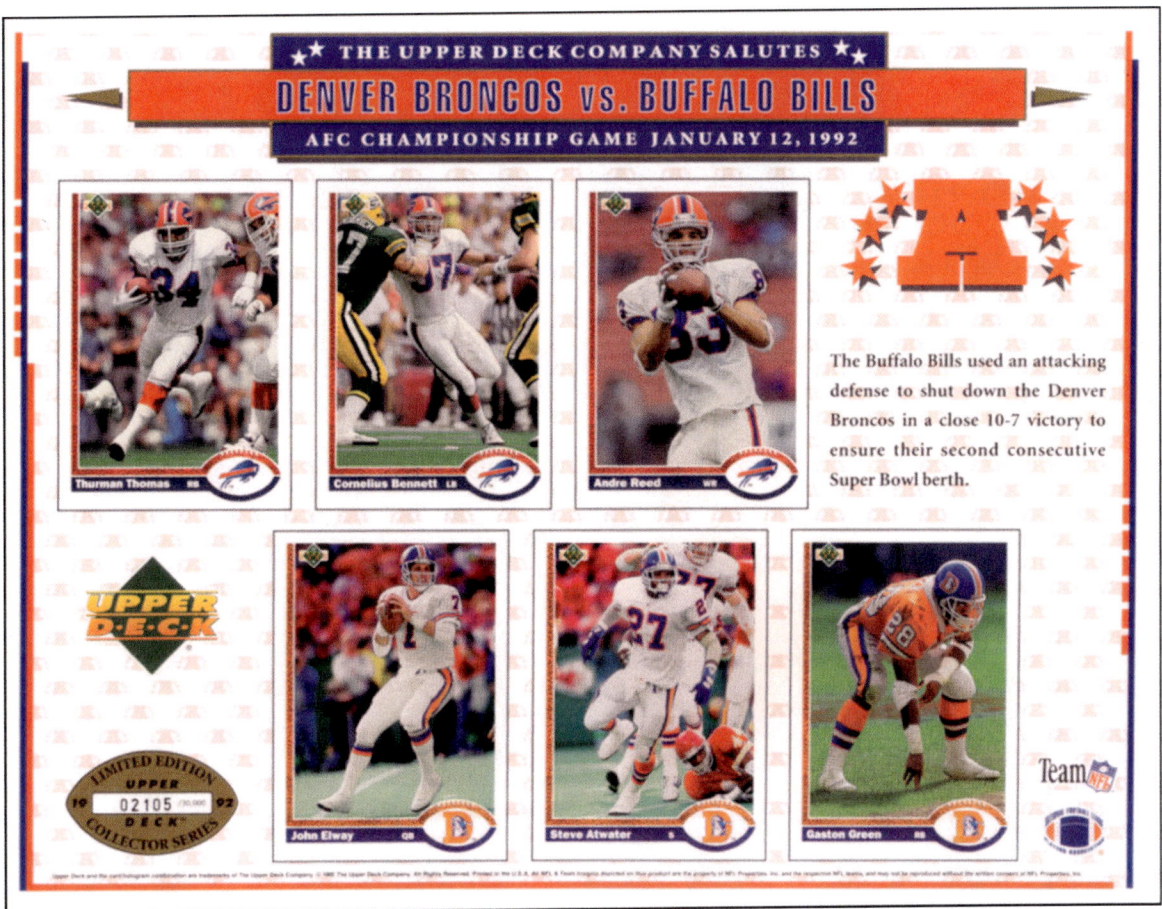

1992 Upper Deck NFL Sheet #1

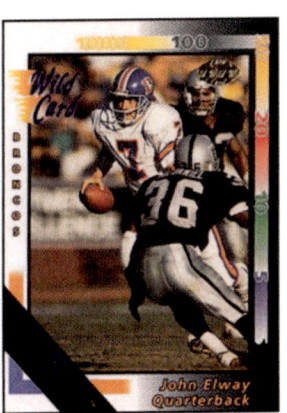
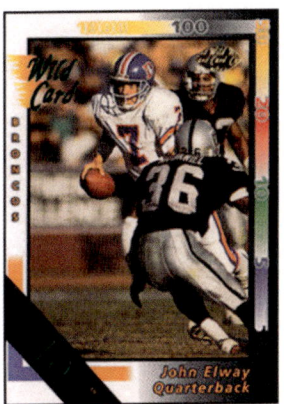
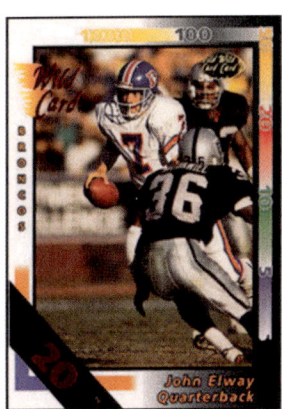

1992 Wild Card #117

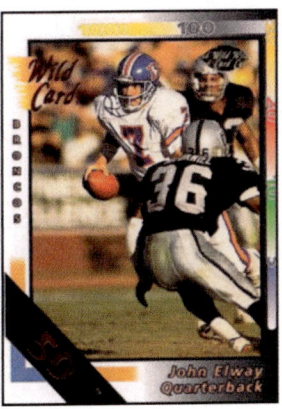
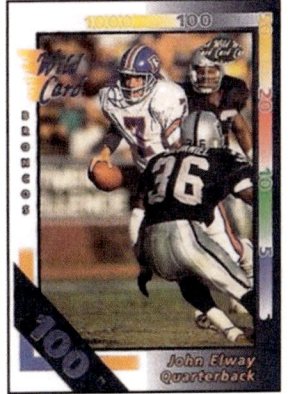

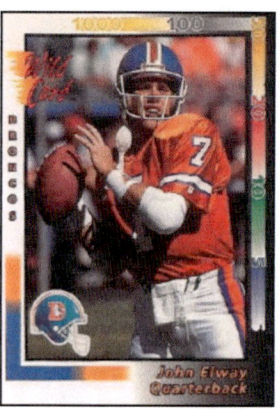

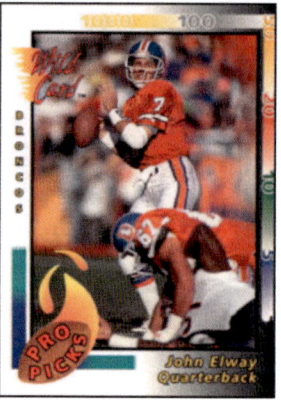

1992 Wild Card
Prototype #P9

1992 Wild Card
Pro Pic #6

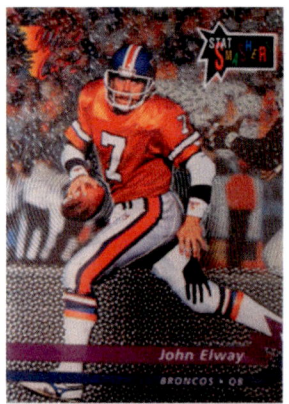

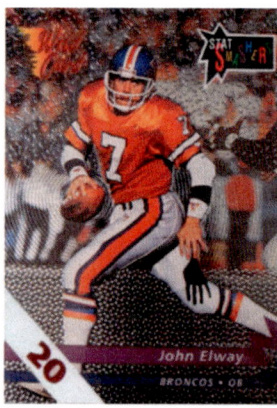

1992 Wild Card
Stat Smasher #4

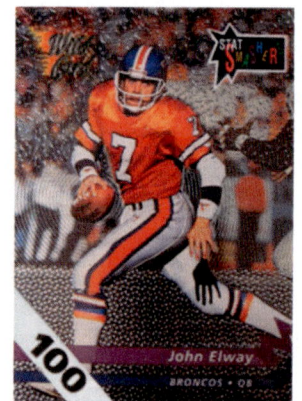

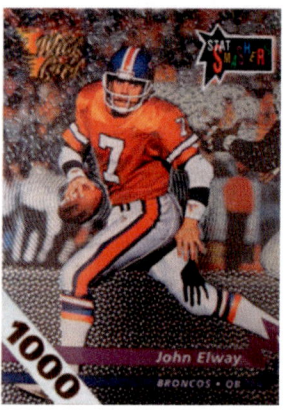

1992 Wild Card
Field Force #5

1992 Wild Card
Field Force Silver #5

1992 Wild Card
Field Force Gold #5

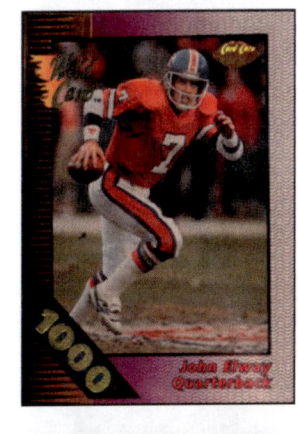

1992 PM Silver

1992 PM Platinum

1992 PM Gold

1993

1993 Action Packed #14

1993 Action Packed
QB Club #QB3

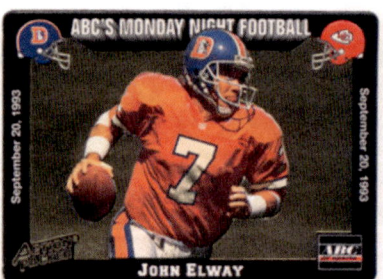

1993 Action Pakced
Monday Night Football #10

1993 Action Packed Monday Night
Football Mint Parallel #10

Wade Phillips replaced the departed Dan Reeves as Head Coach. The 9-7 Broncos finished third in the AFC West and made the post-season. They were defeated by the Los Angeles Raiders 42-24 in the wildcard playoff.

Elway led the NFL with 551 attempts, 348 completions, and 4030 yards. His 25 touchdowns were second to Steve Young's 29. He added 153 rushing yards on 44 carries.

Elway was AFC Offensive Player of the Year, was voted to the Pro-Bowl for the fifth time, and was named First Team All-Pro by *Pro Football Weekly* and *UPI*.

AUGUST 2, 1993 • $2.95 (CAN. $3.95)

Sports Illustrated

Good Riddance   Grow Up

John Elway
is ecstatic
that he's still
in Denver
and his
nemesis
Dan Reeves
is now in
New York

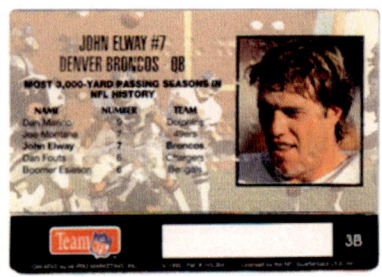

1993 Action Packed
QB Club Braille #3B

1993 Bowman #400

1993 Collectors Edge Jumbo #2

1993 Action Packed
QB Club #3

1993 Classic Tonx #37

1993 Classic Gold Tonx #QB4

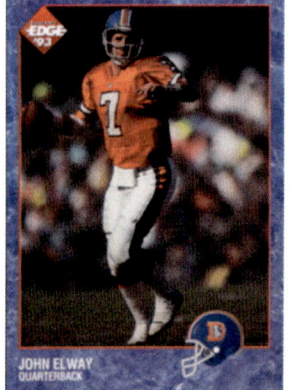

1993 Collectors
Edge #59

1993 Collector's Edge
Prototype #PRO1

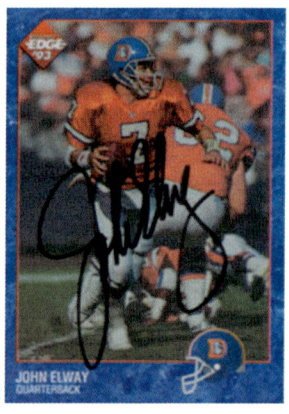

1993 Collector's Edge
Prototype #PRO1
Black Auto

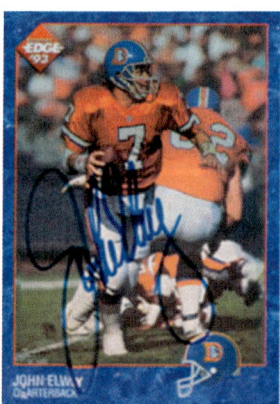

1993 Collector's Edge
Prototype #PRO1
Blue Auto

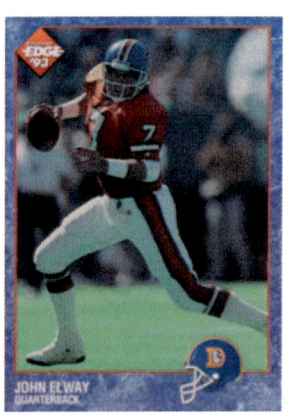

1993 Collector's
Edge #301

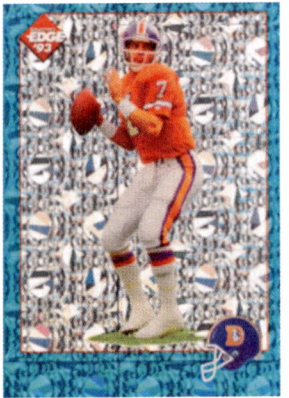

1993 Collectors
Edge #E1

1993 Collectors
Edge #E2

1993 Collectors
Edge #E3

1993 Collectors
Edge #E4

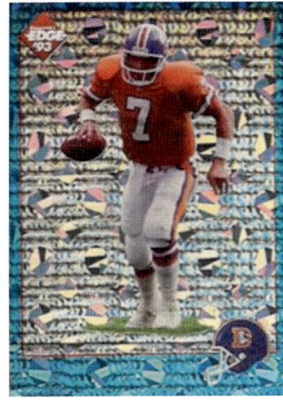

1993 Collectors
Edge #E5

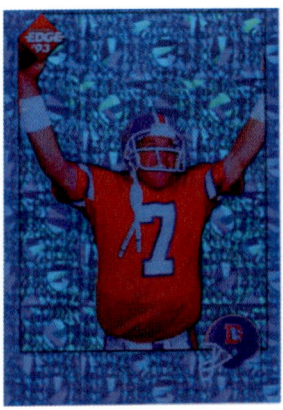

1993 Collectors
Edge #S1

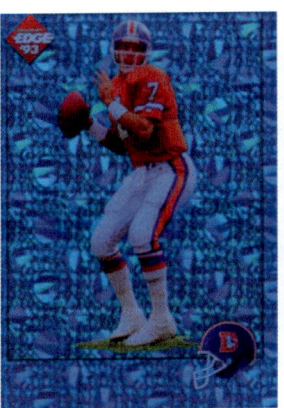

1993 Collectors
Edge #S2

1993 Collectors
Edge #S3

1993 Collectors
Edge #S4

1993 Collectors
Edge #S5

1993 Collectors
Edge #E1

1993 Collectors
Edge #E2

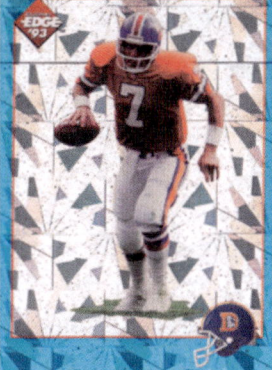

1993 Collectors
Edge #E3

1993 Collectors
Edge #E4

1993 Collectors
Edge #E5

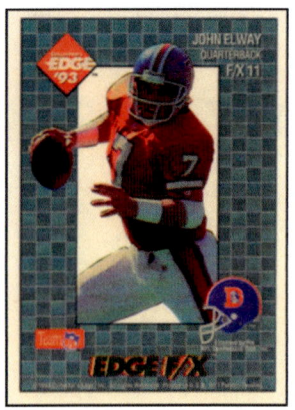

1993 Collectors Edge
FX #11

1993 Collectors Edge
FX Gold #11

1993 Collectors Edge #53

1993 Dog Tag #54

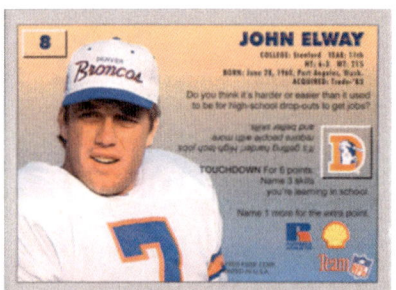

1993 Fact Fleer Shell #8

1993 Fleer #91

1993 Fleer #237

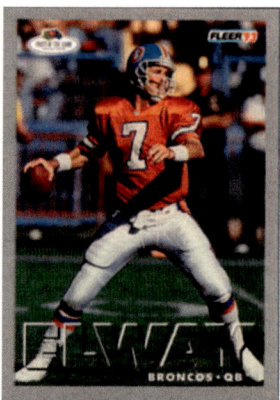

1993 Fleer Fruit
of the Loom #7

November 7, 1993
A 29-14 victory over
Cleveland, Elway com-
pleted 17/23 passes
for 244 yards, and 3
touchdowns. He was
named NFL Player of
the Week.

November 21, 1993
A 37-13 victory over
Pittsburgh, Elway com-
pleted 18/25 passes for
276 yards, and 1 touch-
down. He was named
NFL Player of the Week.

1993 Fleer
Team Leaders #4

1993 Game Day #10

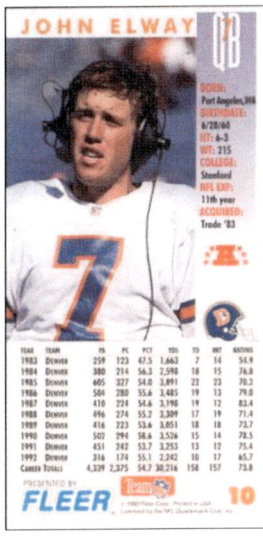

1993 Game Day #10
Reverse

1993 McDonalds
Game Day #22

1993 McDonalds
Game Day #1

1993 Pacific #352

1993 Pacific Prism #23

1993 Highland Mint
Bronze

1993 Highland Mint
Silver

1993 Pacific #103

1993 Pinnacle Men
of Autumn #7

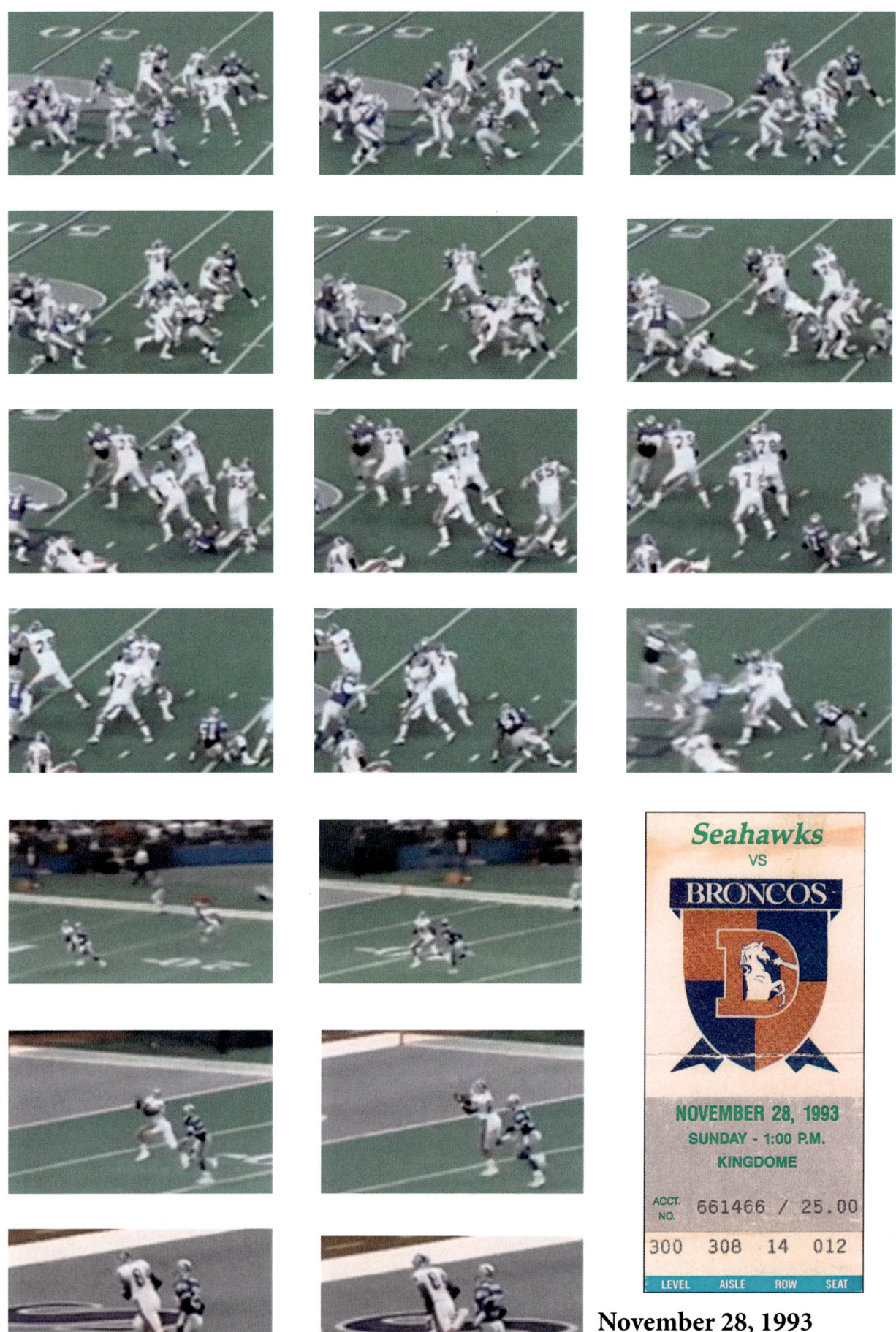

November 28, 1993
a 17-9 win over the Seattle Seahawks,
Elway completed 20/37 for 226 yards,
and THE touchdown.

1993 Playoff #102

1993 Playoff
Contenders #89

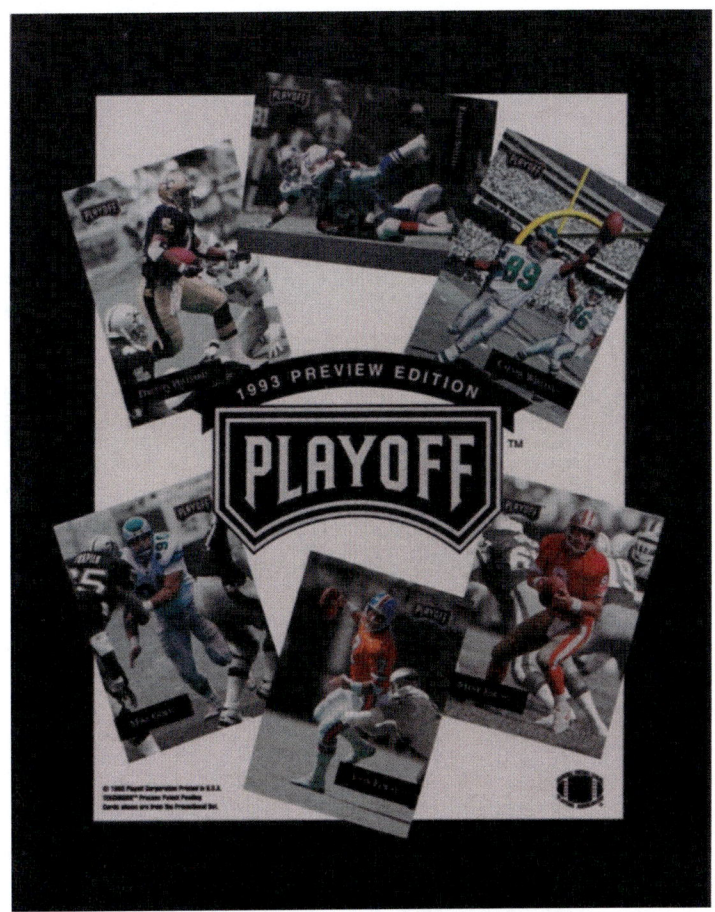

1993 Playoff Preview Promo 8x10

1993 SkyBox Impact
Color #83

1993 SkyBox Impact #83

1993 Power #7

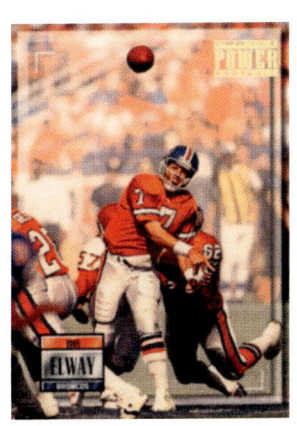

1993 Power Gold #7

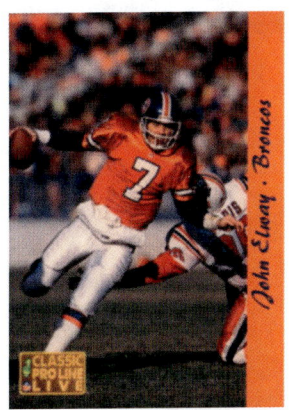

1993 Pro Line Live #69

1993 Pro Set #3

1993 Pro Set #123

1993 SCD Pocket Guide #95

1993 Score #40

1993 Score Franchise #7

1993 Score Ore-Ida
Quarterback Club #QB1

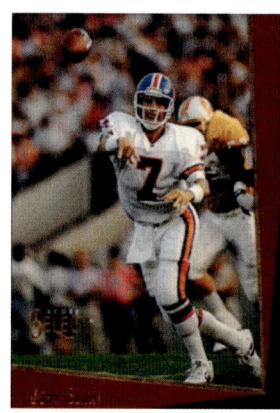

1993 Select #34

1993 Select
Grid Skills #4

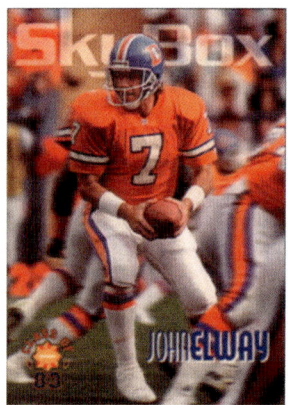

1993 Sky Box
Impact #341

1993 Sky Box
Impact Color #341

1993 Sky Box
Premium #139

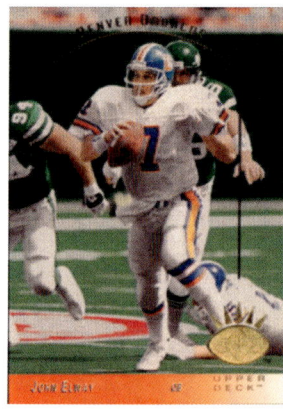

1993 SP #76

1993 Stadium Club #70

1993 Stadium Club First
Day Production #70

1993 Stadium Club
Members Only #70

1993 Stadium Club
Members Only
Super Bowl #70

1993 Stadium Club #241

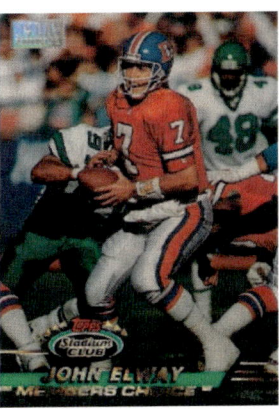

1993 Stadium Club
First Day Production
#241

1993 Stadium Club
Members Only #241

1993 Stadium Club
Members Only
Super Bowl #241

1993 Stadium Club Super
Team #4

1993 Stadium Club Super Team
Members Only #4

1993 Starting Lineup

1993 Starting Lineup
Aerial Artist

1993 Topps #100

1993 Topps #264

1993 Topps
FantaSports #7

1993 Topps Gold #100

1993 Topps Gold #264

1993 Ultra #111

1993 Upper Deck #357

1993 Upper Deck
Team MVP #4

1993 Upper Deck
Magazine Hologram

1993 Upper Deck Miller #3

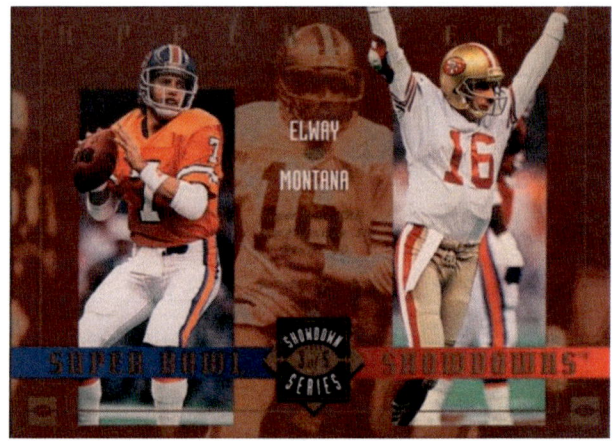

1993 Upper Deck Miller #4

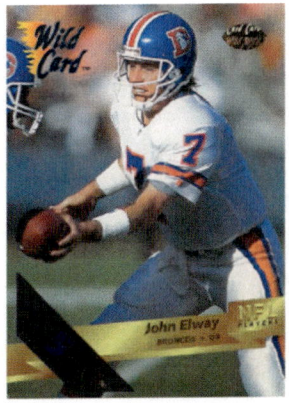

1993 Wild Card #33

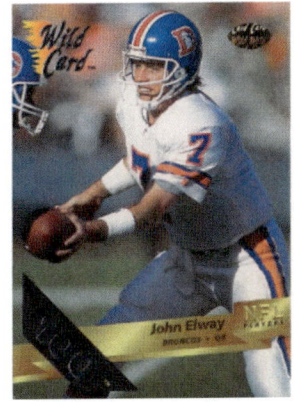
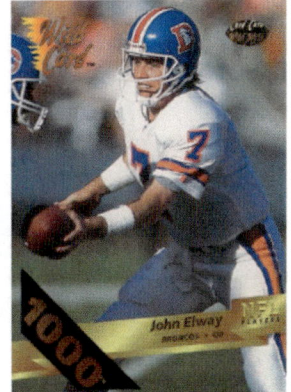

1993 Wild Card
Chrome #33

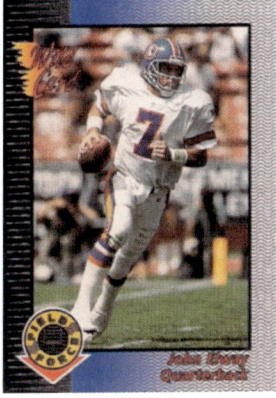

1993 Wild Card
Field Force #38

1993 Wild Card
Field Force Gold #38

1993 Wild Card
Field Force Silver #38

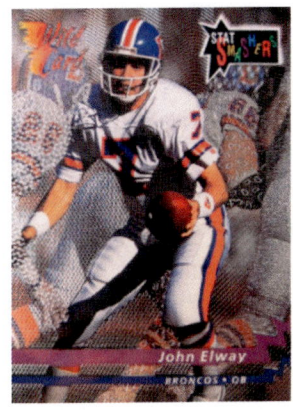

1993 Wild Card
Stat Smasher Gold #57

1993 Wild Card
Stat Smasher Silver #57

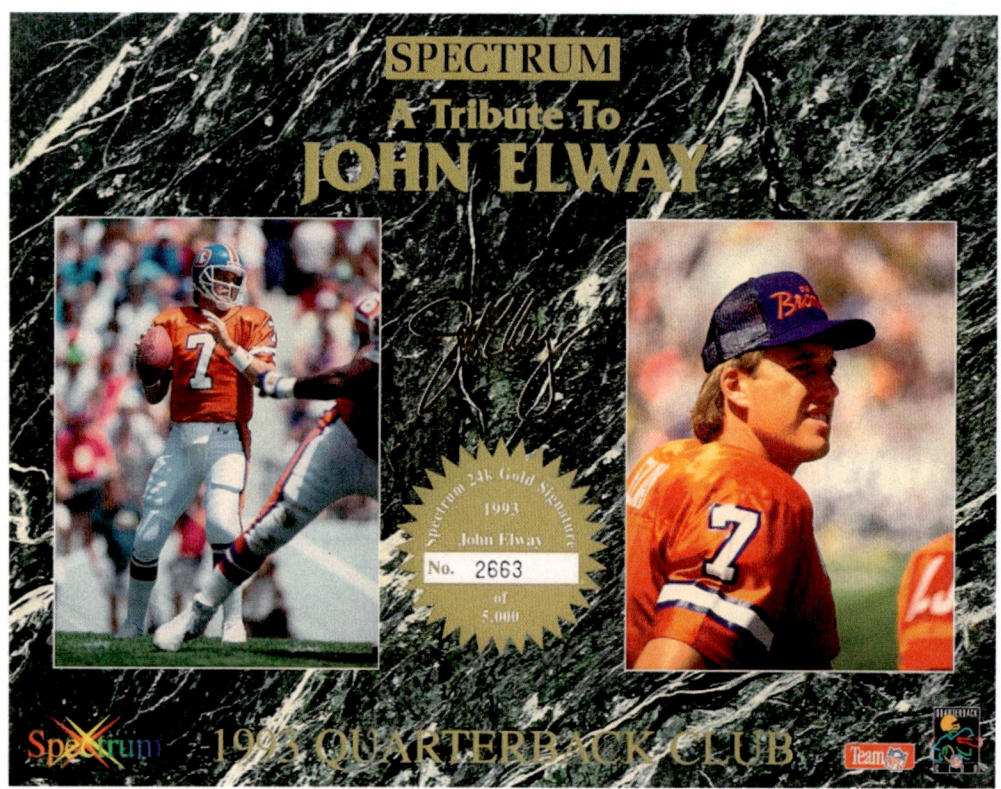

1993 Spectrum QB Club Tribute Sheet #3 24K Autograph

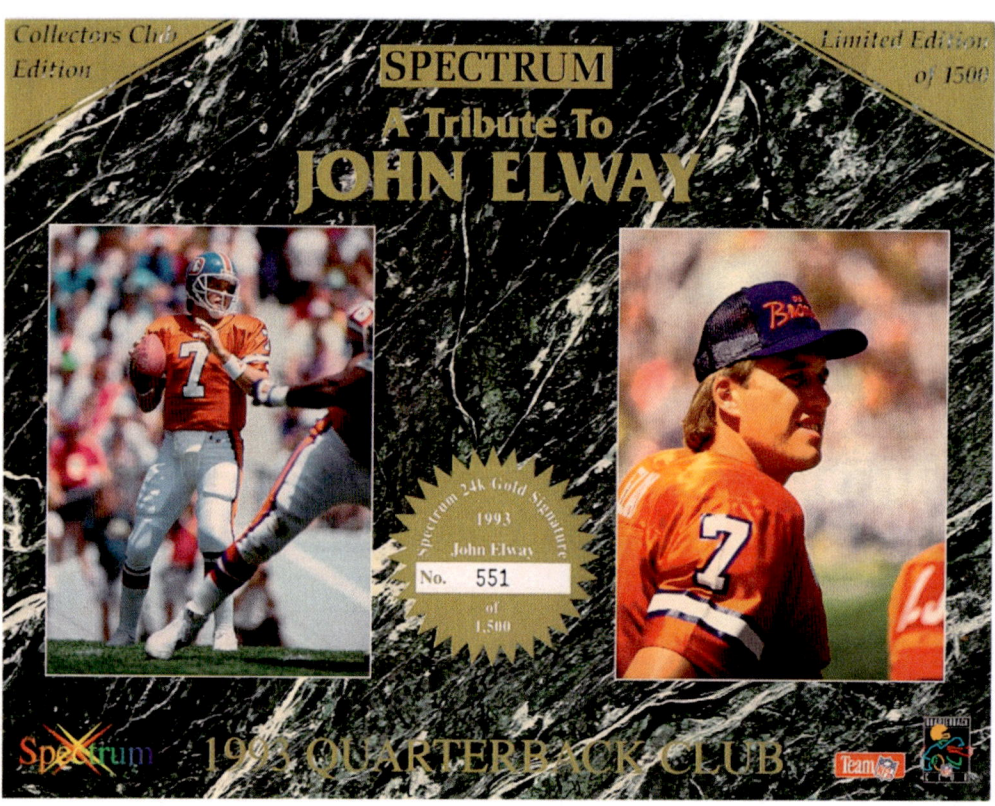

1993 Spectrum QB Club Tribute Sheet #3 Collectors Club Edition

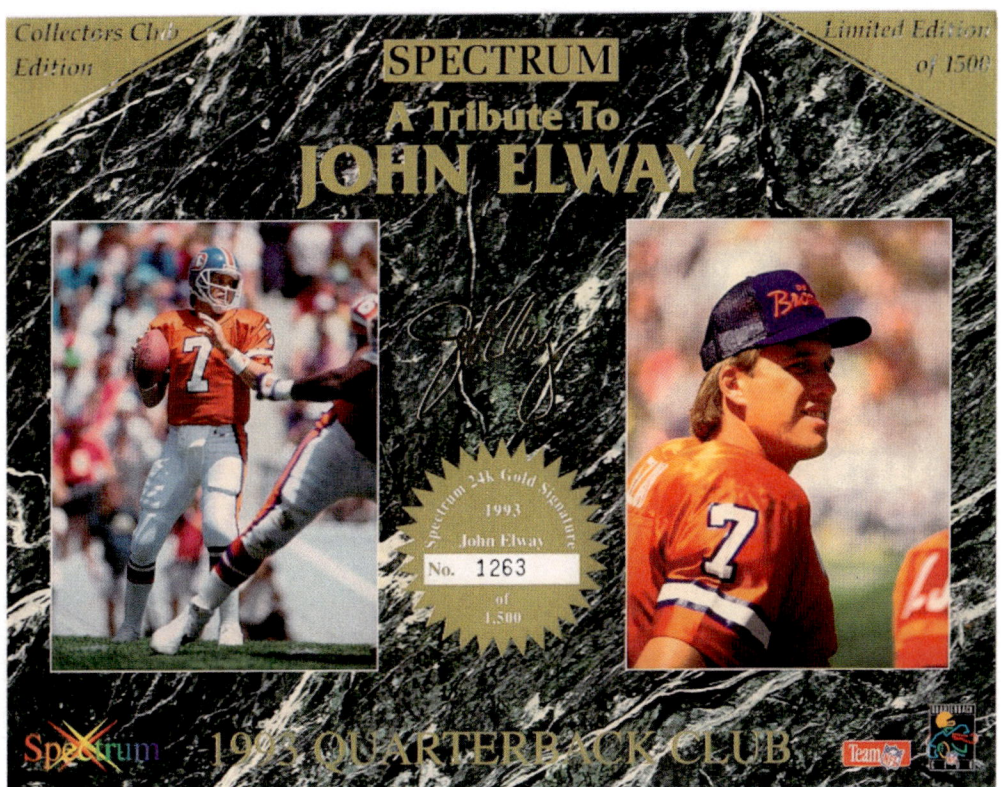

1993 Spectrum QB Club Tribute Sheet #3 Collectors Club Edition 24K Auto

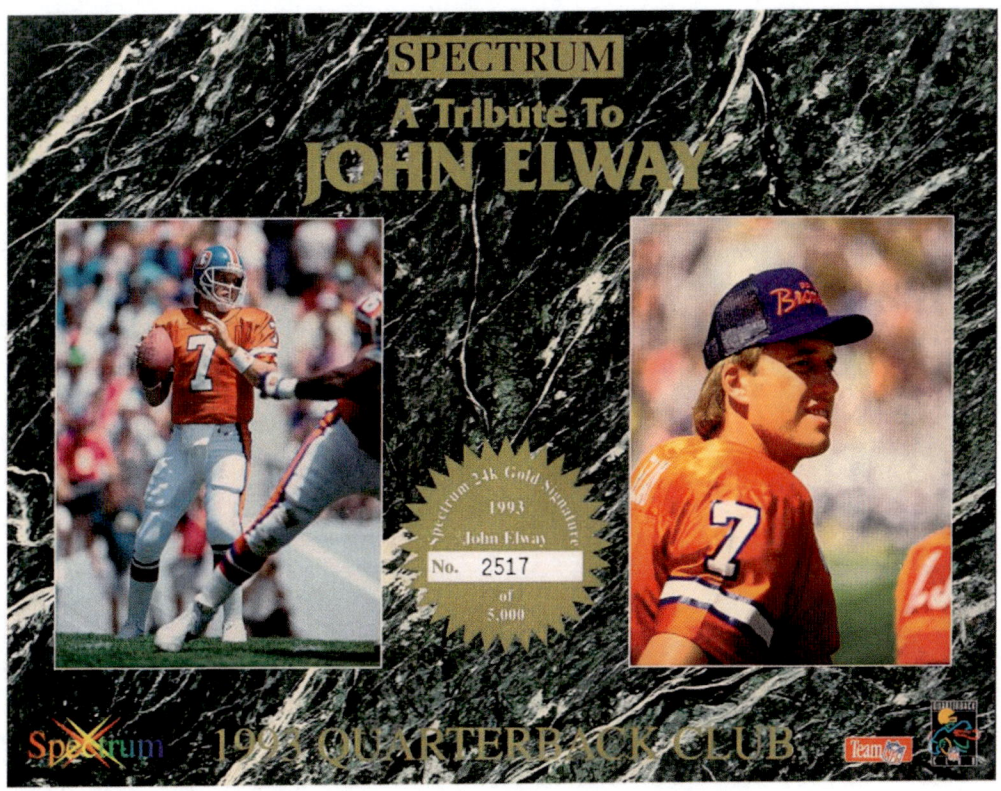

1993 Spectrum QB Club Tribute Sheet #3

JOHN ELWAY
Denver Broncos

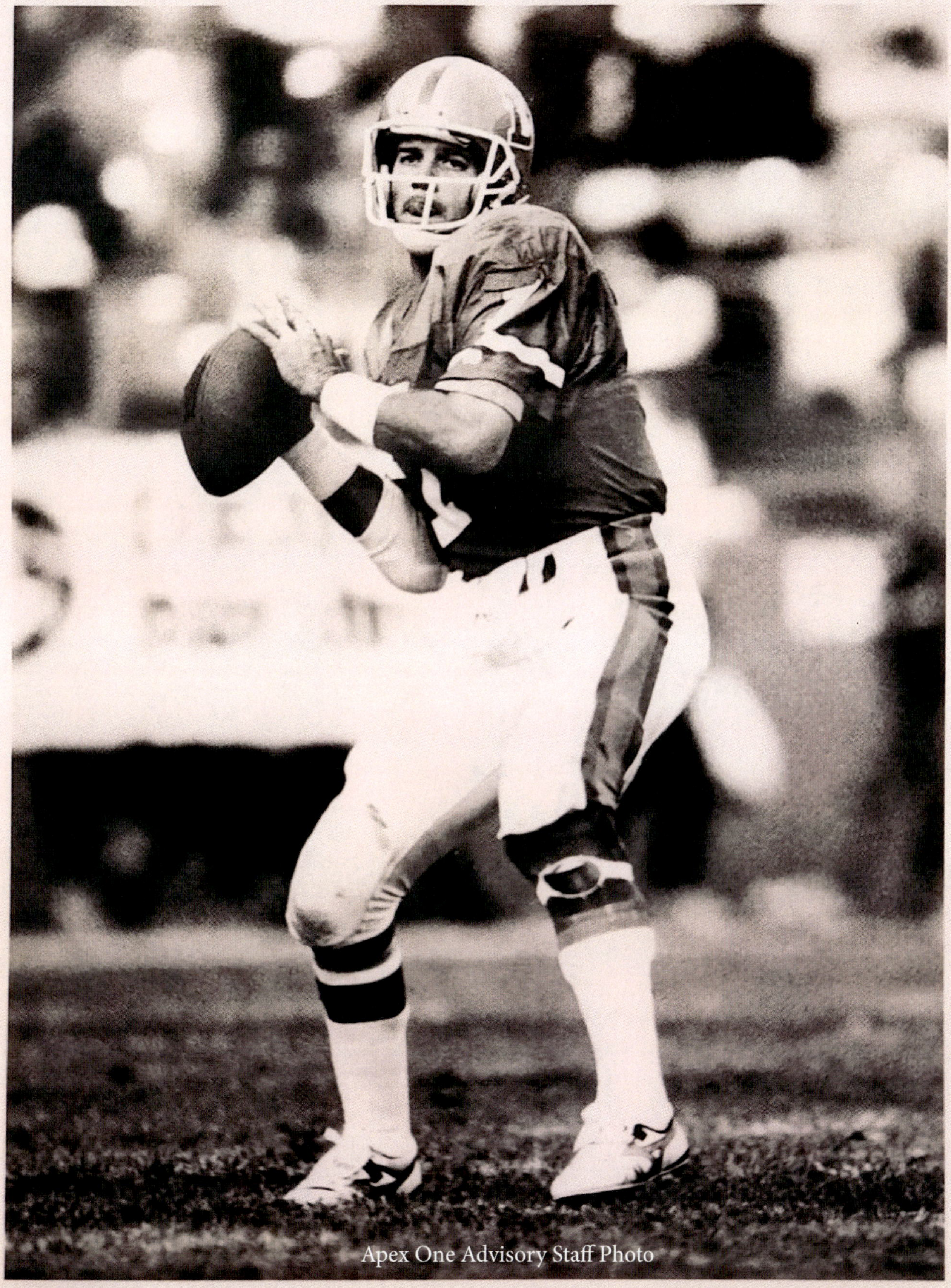

Apex One Advisory Staff Photo

JOHN ELWAY

GART SPORTS SUPERSTORE
GRAND OPENING
NOVEMBER 1993

General Mills

WHOLE GRAIN
WHEATIES ®

FREE
John Elway
POSTER
ON THIS BOX!

Collect All Four NFL Stars

The Breakfast of Champions

NET WT 12 OZ (340 grams)

1993 Wheaties Poster

JOHN ELWAY
Quarterback-Denver Broncos

General Mills

WHOLE-GRAIN FLAKES

WHOLE GRAIN
WHEATIES®
The Breakfast of Champions

COMMEMORATIVE EDITION

JOHN ELWAY

DENVER BRONCOS

NET WT 18 OZ 510 g

1994

1994 Action Packed #26

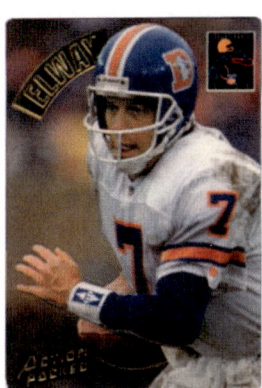

1994 Action Packed #174

The 1994 Denver Broncos finished 7-9, fourth in the AFC West. They failed to make the playoffs, and Head Coach Wade Phillips was fired.

Elway started 14 games. He had 307 completions on 494 attempts for 3490 yards, and 16 touchdowns. He added 235 rushing yards on 58 carries with 4 touchdowns. He was voted to the his sixth Pro-Bowl.

1994 Action Packed
24K Gold #G3

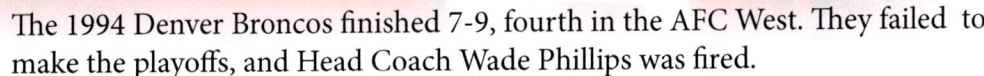

The NFL celebrated its 75th anniversary, for selected games the teams wore retro uniforms and all jerseys were adorned with this special commorative patch.

1994 Action Packed
24K Gold #G45

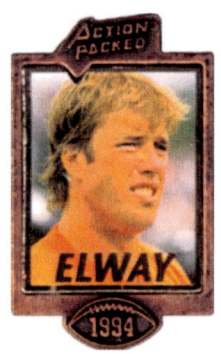

1994 Action Packed
Badge Of Honor Pin
#5

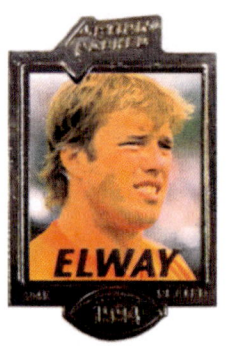

1994 Action Packed
Badge Of Honor Pin
24K Gold #5

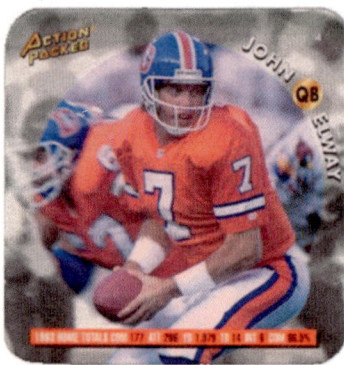

1994 Action Packed
CoStars #1

1994 Action Packed
CoStars #5

1994 Action Packed
Signature #26

1994 Action Packed
Fantasy Forecast #FF10

1994 Action Packed Mammoth #MM6

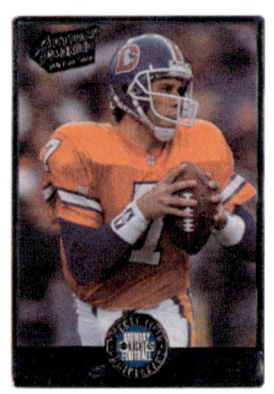

1994 Action Packed
Monday Night Football
#12

1994 Action Packed
Monday Night Football
Silver #5

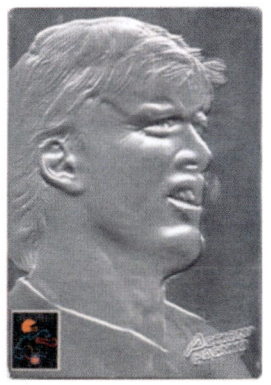

1994 Action Packed #QB3

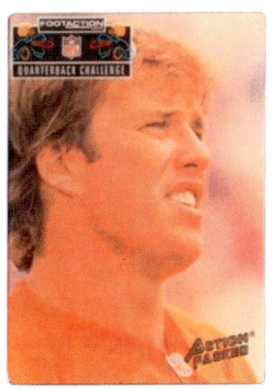

1994 Action Packed
Foot Action Quarterback
Choice FA-2

1994 Bowman #80

1994 Classic NFL
Experience #25

1994 Collector's Choice
#300

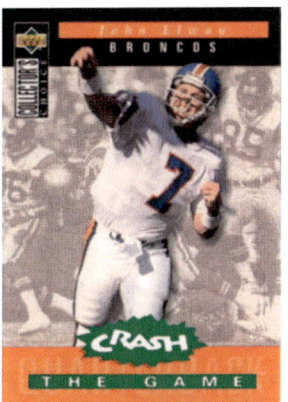

1994 Collector's Choice
Crash The Game #6
Green

1994 Collector's Choice
Crash The Game #6
Blue

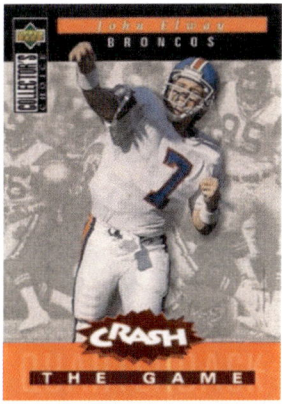

1994 Collector's Choice
Crash The Game #6
Bronze

1994 Collector's Choice
Crash The Game #6 Gold

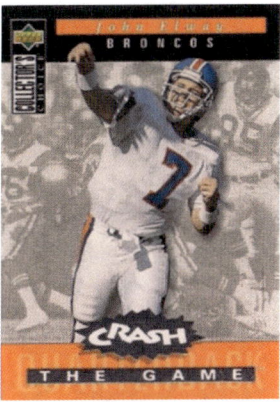

1994 Collector's Choice
Crash The Game #6 Silver

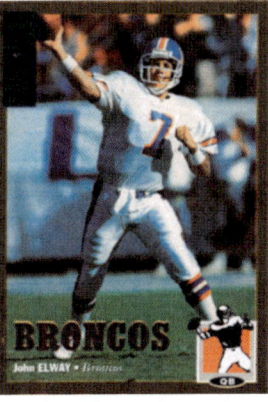

1994 Collector's Choice
Gold #300

1994 Collector's Choice
Silver #300

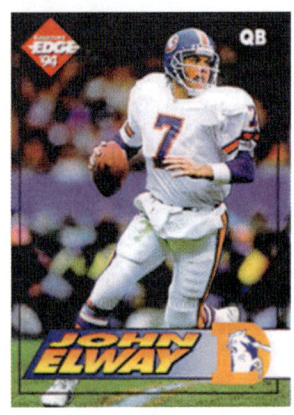

1991 Collector's Edge
#51

1994 Collector's Edge
Boss Squad #1

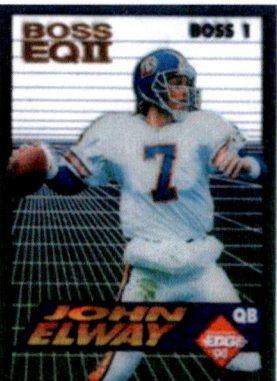

1994 Collector's Edge
Bronze Boss Squad EQII#1

1994 Collector's Edge
Boss Squad Silver #1

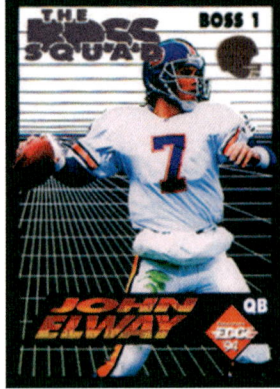

1994 Collector's Edge Boss
Squad Silver Helmet #1

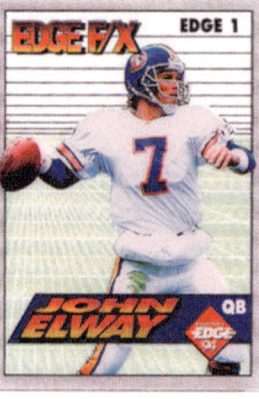

1994 Collectors Edge
FX#1

1994 Collector's Edge
FX Gold Back #1

1994 Collector's Edge
FX Gold Letters #1

1994 Collector's Edge
FX Gold Shield #1

1994 Collector's Edge
FX Red Letters #1

1994 Collector's Edge
FX Silver Back #1

1994 Collector's Edge
FX Silver Letters #1

1994 Collector's Edge
FX Silver Shield #1

1994 Collector's Edge
FX White Back

1994 Collector's Edge
FX Silver Letters Helmet #1

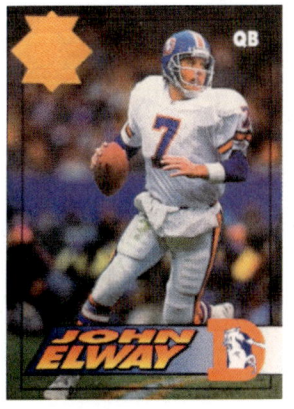

1994 Collectors Edge #51
1st Day Gold

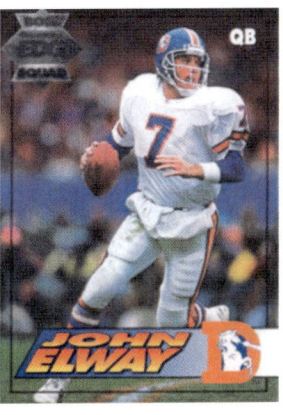

1994 Collector's Edge
FX Silver Letters #1

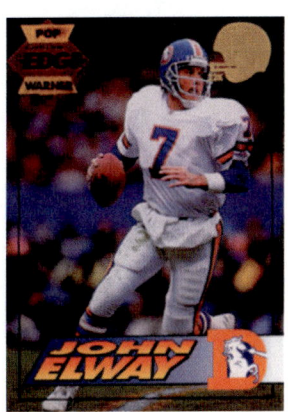

1994 Collector's Edge
FX Silver Shield #1

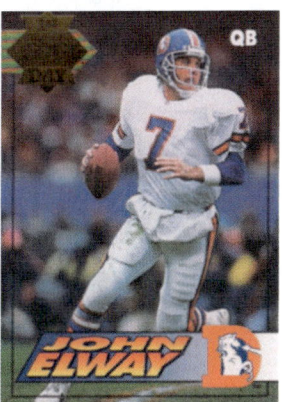

1994 Collector's Edge
FX White Back

1994 Costacos Brothers
Post Card #5

1994 Excalibur #18

1994 Excalibur 22K Gold
#13

1994 Dixon Pencil
Card Back

1994 Excalibur SL1

1994 Excalibur SL2

1994 Excalibur SL3

1994 Dixon Pencil

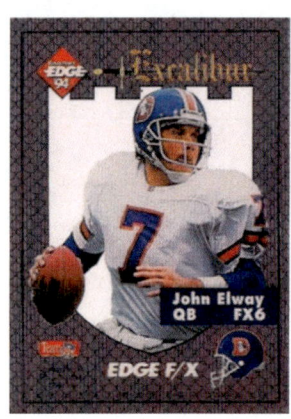

1994 Excalibur FX #6

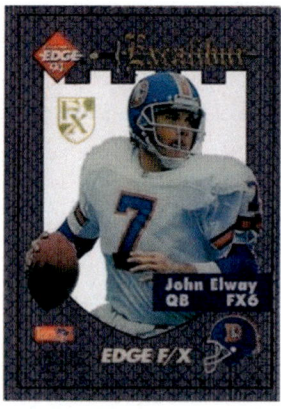

1994 Excalibur FX
Gold Shield #6

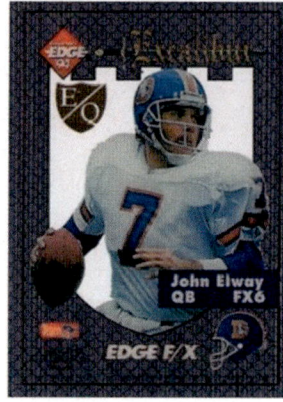

1994 Excalibur FX
Gold Shield EQ #6

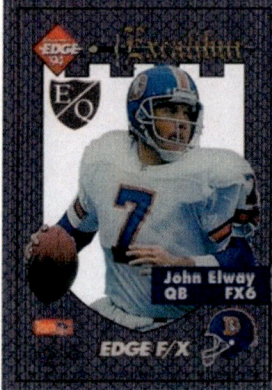

1994 Excalibur FX
Silver Shield EQ #6

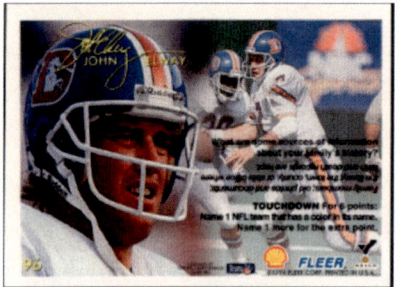

1994 FACT Fleer Shell #96

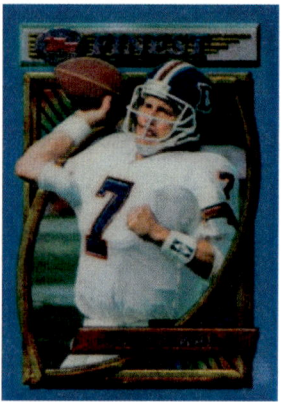

1994 Finest #119

1994 Finest Refractor
#119

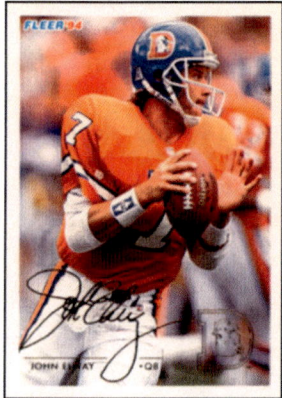

1994 Fleer #135

1994 Fleer League Leader #3

1994 Fleer Living Legends #2

1994 GameDay #118

1994 GameDay
GameBreak #4

1994 Images #15

1994 Images All-Pro
#A16

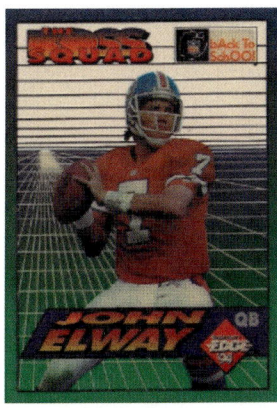

1994 NFL Porperties
Back To School #3

1994 Pacific #124

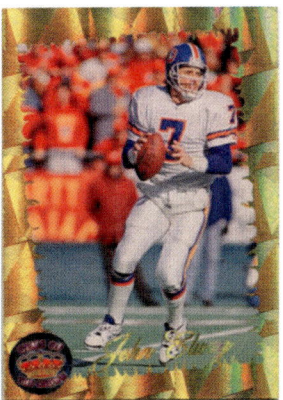

1994 Pacific Gems
of the Crown #9

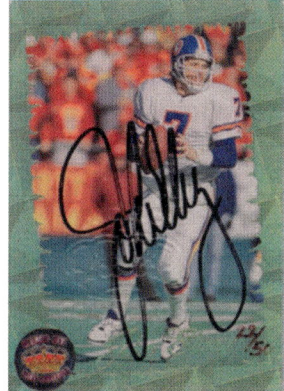

1994 Pacific Gems
of the Crown Auto #9

1994 Pacific Marquee
#10

1994 Pacific Marquee
Prism Gold #10

1994 Pacific Prism #36

1994 Pacific Prism Gold
#36

1994 Pacific Triple Folder #9

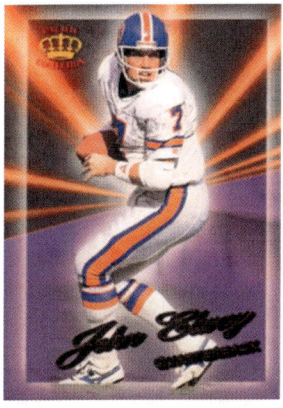

1994 Pacific Triple Folder
Rookies and Stars #RS10

1994 Pinnacle #12

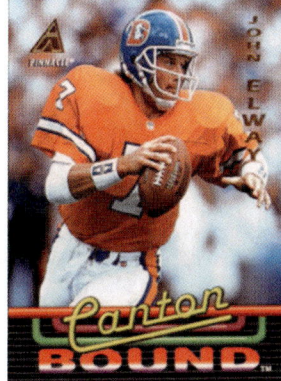

1994 Pinnacle Canton
Bound #7

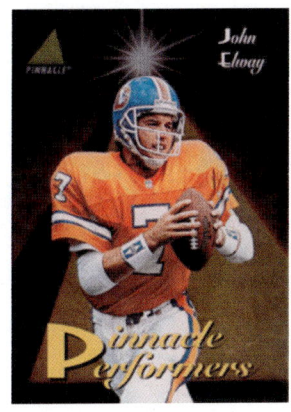

1994 Pinnacle
Performers #7

1994 Pinnacle
Trophy Collection #12

1994 Playoff #43

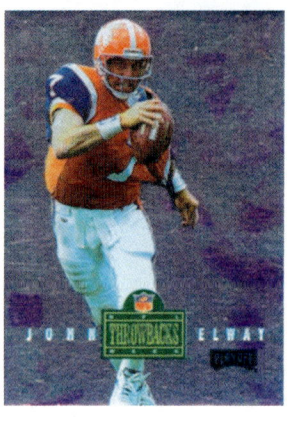

1994 Playoff Contenders #44

1994 Playoff Contenders Back to Back #BB2

1994 Playoff Contenders Throwback #9

1994 ProLine Live #34

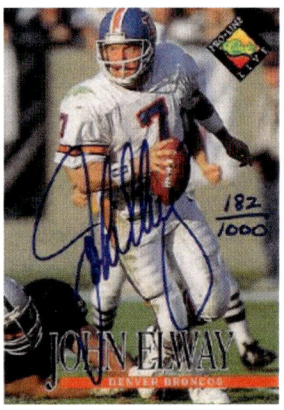

1994 ProLine Live #394

1994 ProLine Live Autograph #40

1994 ProLine Live MVP Sweepstakes #8

1994 Pro Magnet #2

1994 Pro Tag #45

1994 Reebok Calling Card

1994 Press Pass Super Bowl Photo Board #1

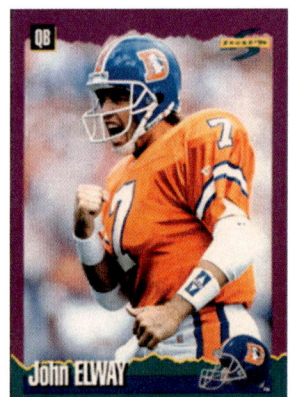

1994 Score #7

1994 Score Gold Zone #7

1994 Select #10

1994 SkyBox Impact #72

1994 SkyBox Ultimate
Impact #10

1994 SkyBox #46

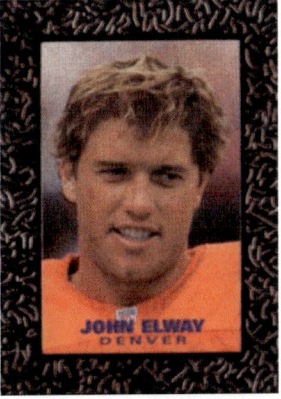

1994 SkyBox Premium
Revolution #R6

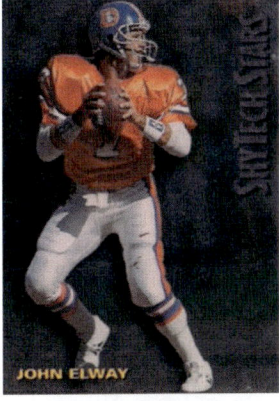

1994 SkyBox
SkyTech Star #ST4

1994 SP #80

1994 SP Die Cut #80

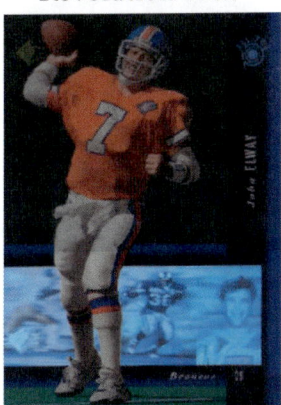

1994 SP Holoview
Pro Bowl #11

1994 SP Holoview
Pro Bowl Die Cut #11

1994 Sports Flic #28

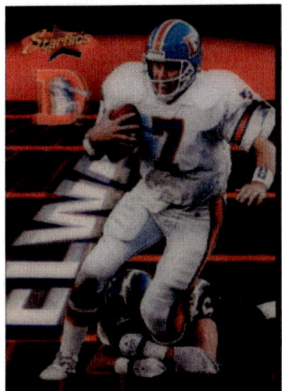

1994 Sports Flic #181

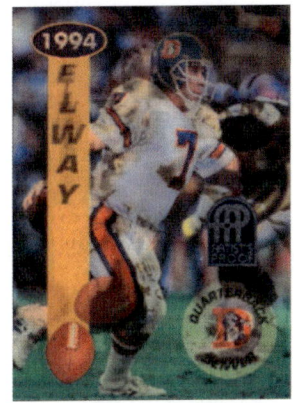

1994 Sports Flic
Artist Proof #28

1994 Sports Flic
Artists Proof #181

1994 Sports Flic
Head to Head #10

1994 Stadium Club #90

1994 Stadium Club #558

1994 Stadium Club
Bowman's Best #BK8

1994 Stadium Club
Bowman's Best
Refractor #BK8

1994 Stadium Club
First Day Production #90

1994 Stadium Club
First Day Production #558

1994 Stadium Club
Member's Only #42

1994 Stadium Club
Member's Only
Parallel #90

1994 Stadium Club
Member's Only #558

1994 Stadium Club
Member's Only Parallel
Bowman's Best #8

1994 Stadium Club Members
Only Parallel Super Team #8

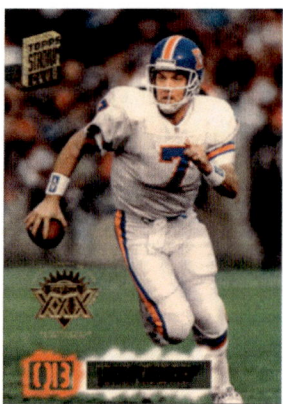

1994 Stadium Club
Super Bowl #90

1994 Stadium Club
Super Bowl #558

1994 Stadium Club
Super Team #ST8

1994 Stadium Club Super
Bowl Super Team #ST8

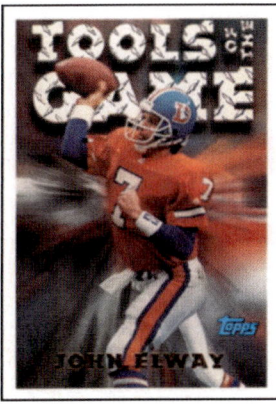

1994 Topps #196

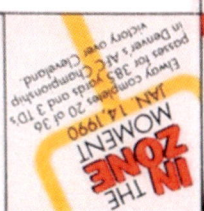

1994 Topps #540

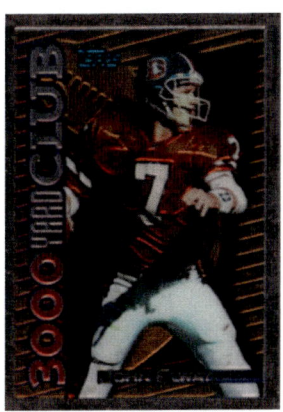

1994 Topps 1000/3000
#21

1994 Tony's Pizza
Quareterback Cube #3

October 17, 1994

One of the greatest games in the history of Monday Night Football. Elway scores on a 4-yard run to give the Broncos a 28-24 lead with 1:29 remaining. On the final drive, Joe Montana goes 7/8 for 75 yards and hits Willie Davis for a 5-yard touchdown with 0:08 remaining for a 31-28 Kansas City win.

1994 Topps Special
Effects #196

1994 Topps Special
Effects #540

1994 Ultra Achievement Award Jumbo #2

1996 Ultra #86

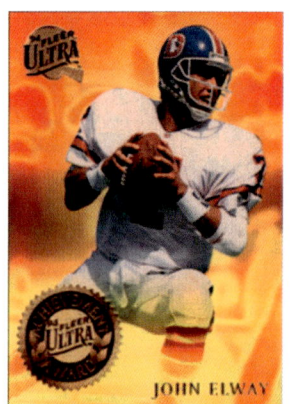

1994 Ultra Achievement
Award #2

1994 Ultra Flair
Hot Numbers #4

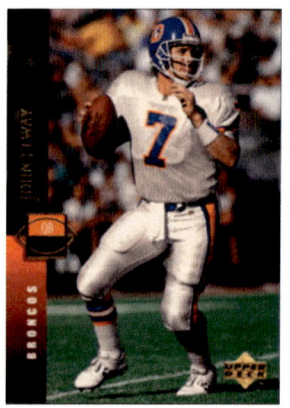

1994 Upper Deck #218

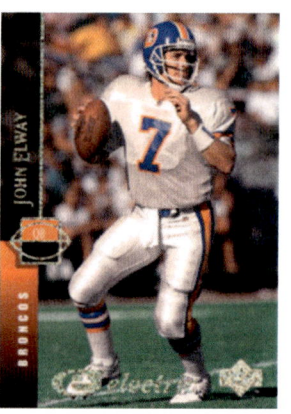

1994 Upper Deck
Electric Gold #218

1994 Upper Deck
Electric Silver #218

1994 Upper Deck Pro Bowl #12

1994 Upper Deck Pro Bowl Sample #3

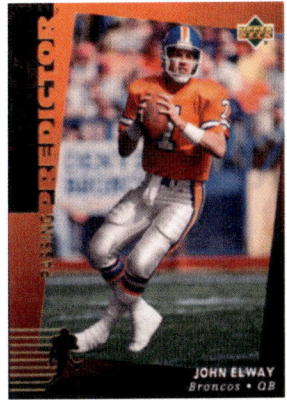

1994 Upper Deck
Predictor League
Leader #RP3

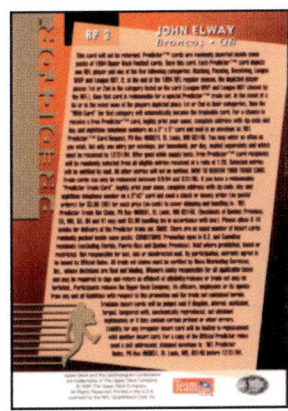

Reverse

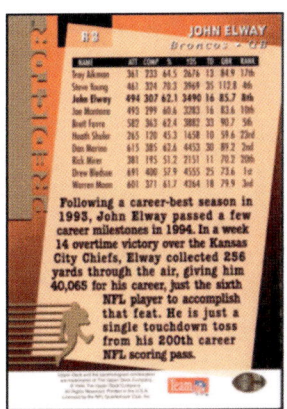

1994 Upper Deck Predictor
League Leader Prizes #R3

1994 Committee of 101 - 1987

1994 Committee of 101 - 1993

October 30, 1994.

A 26-14 victory over Cleveland, Elway completed 30/41 passes for 349 yards, and 2 touchdowns. He was named NFL Player of the Week.

John Elway

In 1993, Denver Bronco quarterback John Elway led the NFL with 551 attempts, 348 completions and 4,030 passing yards.

1994 Sports Heros Feats and Facts Poster

1995

The 1995 Denver Broncos were 8-8 under new Head Coach Mike Shannahan. They finished fourth in the AFC West, and failed to qualify for the playoffs.

Elway started all 16 games, completed 316/542 passes for 3970 yards, and 26 touchdowns. He added 176 rushing yards on 41 carries, with 1 touchdown.

1995 Action Packed #23

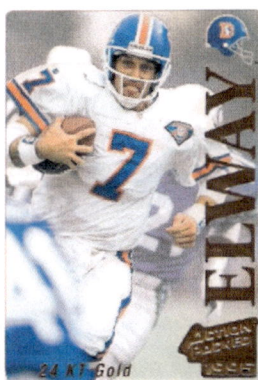

1995 Action Packed 24KG #8

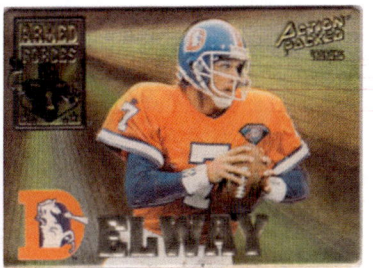

1995 Action Packed
Armed Forced #AF9

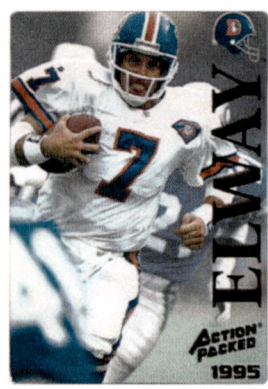

1995 Action Packed
#23

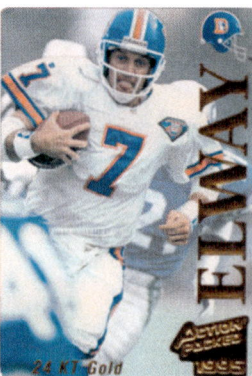

1993 Action Packed
24K #8G

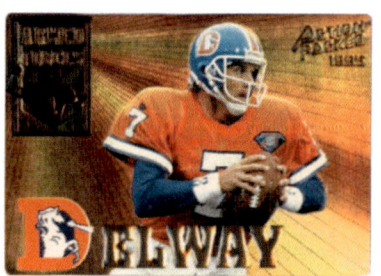

1995 Action Packed
Armed Forces #AF9

1995 Action Packed
Armed Forces Braille
#AF9

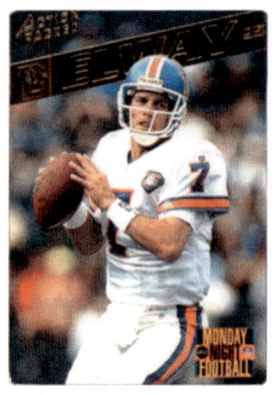

1995 Action Packed
Monday Night Football
#58

1995 Action Packed
Monday Night Football
#108

1995 Action Packed
Monday Night Football
24K Gold #8

1995 Action Packed
Monday Night Football
High Lights #58

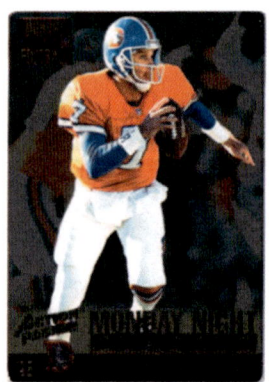

1995 Action Packed
Monday Night
Football High
Lights #108

1995 Action Packed
Night Flights
24K #5

1995 Action Packed
Monday Night
Football Reverse
Angle #7

1995 Action Packed
Quick Silver #14

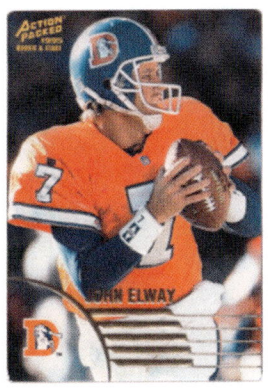

1995 Action Packed
Rookies and Stars #14

1995 Action Packed
Rookies and Stars
24K Gold #8

1995 Action Packed
Rookies and Stars
Closing Seconds #9

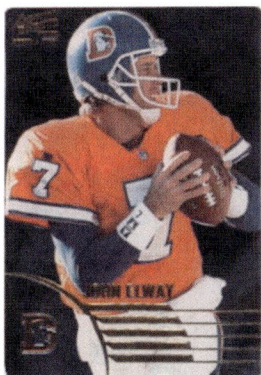

1995 Action Packed
Rookies and Stars
Stargazers #14

1995 Bowman #160

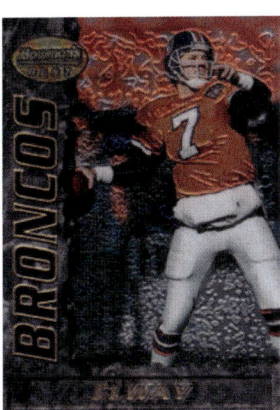

1995 Bowman's Best #V90

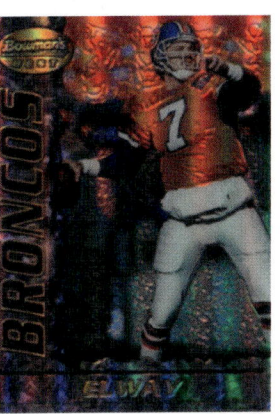

1995 Bowman's Best
Refractor #V90

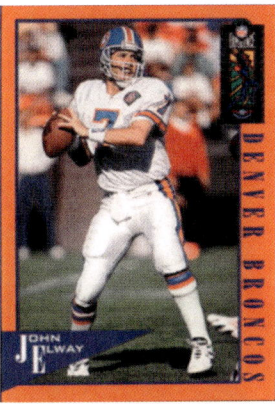

1995 Classic NFL
Experience #30

1995 Classic NFL
Experience Gold #30

1995 Classic NFL
Experience
Super Bowl Game #4

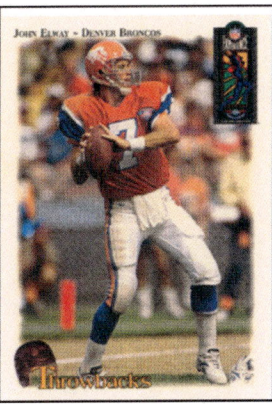

1995 Classic NFL
Experience Throwback
#18

September 10, 1995

A 31-21 loss to Dallas, Elway finds Anthony Miller for a second quarter, 11-yard, touchdown. It is the 200th touchdown pass of his career. Elway completed 11/24 passes for 252 yards, and 2 touchdowns in the loss

1995 Cleo Valentines

1995 Collectors Choice
#88

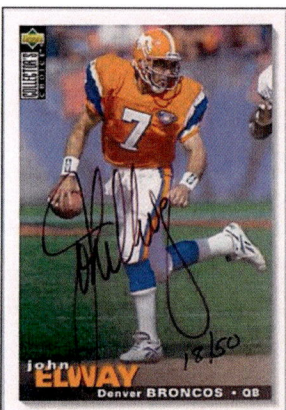

1995 Collectors Choice
Auto #88

September 17, 1995

As time expired, Elway connected with Rod Smith for a 43-yard touchdown. It was a last second 38-31 Denver win. He completed 30/47 passes for 327 yards, and two touchdowns, and was named the NFL Player of the Week.

1995 Collectors Choice
Crash The Game #C2A

1995 Collectors Choice
Crash The Game #C2B

1995 Collectors Choice
Crash The Game #C2C

1995 Collectors Choice
Crash The Game Gold
Redemption #C2

1995 Collectors Choice
Crash The Game
Touchdown
Redmeption #C2

1995 Collectors Choice
Crash The Game Silver
Redemption #C2

1995 Collectors Choice
Crash The Game
Touchdown
Redemption #C2

1995 Collectors Choice
Crash The Game Gold
#C2A

1995 Collectors Choice
Crash The Game Gold
#C2B

1995 Collectors Choice
Crash The Game Gold
#C2C

1995 Collectors Choice
Players Club #88

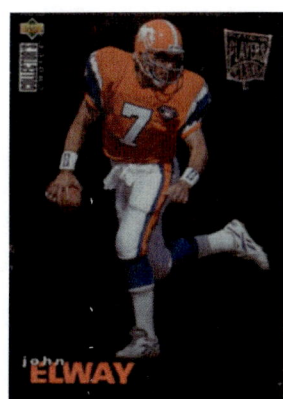

1995 Collectors Choice
Players Club Platinum
#88

1995 Collectors Choice
Update #U67

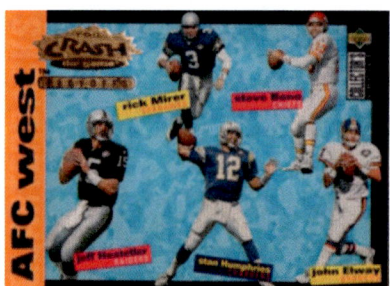

1995 Collectors Choice
Crash The Playoffs Gold #CP3

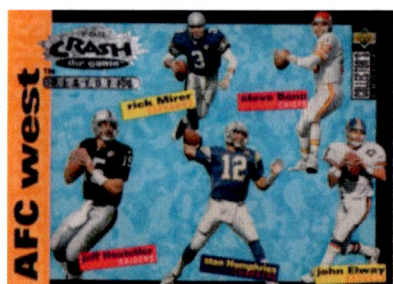

1995 Collectors Choice
Crash The Playoffs #CP3

1995 Collectors Choice
Update Gold #U67

1995 Collectors Choice
Update Stickems #26

1995 Collector Choice
Update Silver #U67

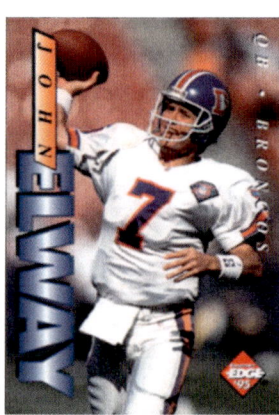

1995 Collectors Edge #59

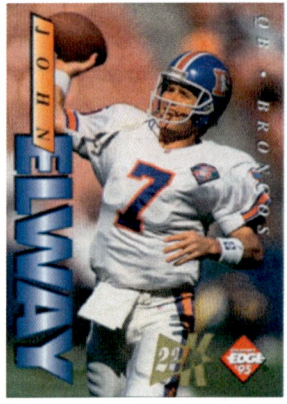

1995 Collectors Edge
22K Gold #59

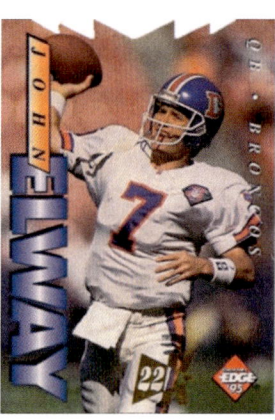

1995 Collectors Edge
22K Gold Die Cut #59

1995 Collectors Edge
Black Lable #59

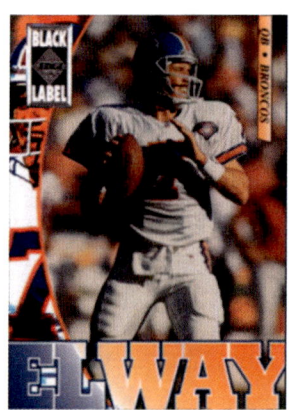

1995 Collectors Edge
Black Lable Silver #59

1995 Collectors Edge
Black Lable Quantom
Motion #5

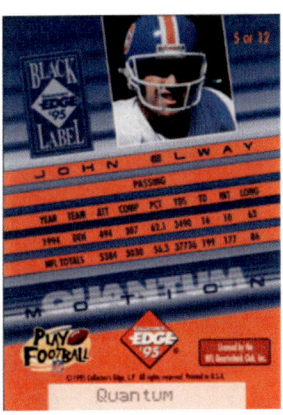

1995 Collectors Edge
Black Lable Quantum
Motion Promo #5

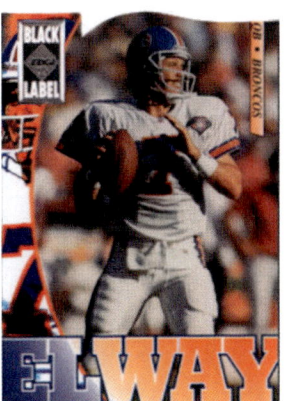

1995 Collectors Edge
Black Lable Silver
Die Cut #58

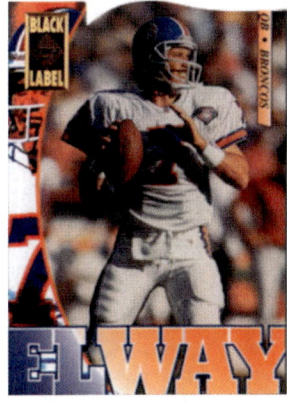

1995 Collectors Edge
Black Lable Die Cut #58

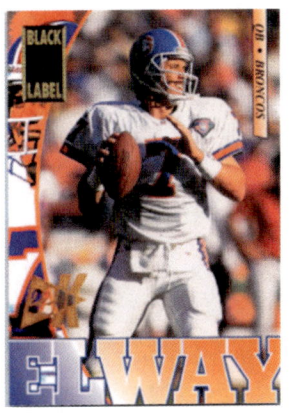

1995 Collectors Edge
Black Label
22K Gold #59

1995 Collectors Edge
Die Cut #59

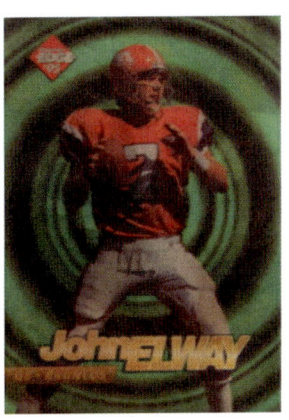

1995 Collectors Edge
Edge Tech #5

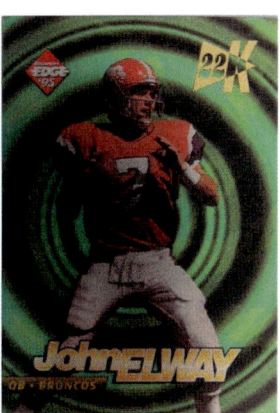

1995 Collectors Edge
Edge Tech 22K gold #5

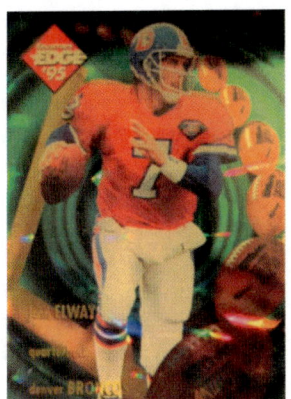

1995 Collectors Edge
Edge Tech Black Label #5

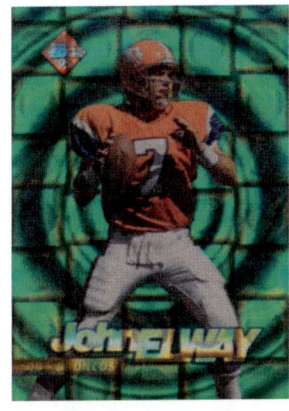

1995 Collectors Edge
Edge Tech Circular
Prism #5

1995 Collectors Edge
Edge Tech
Quantom #5

1995 Edge Tech
Quantom Die Cut #5

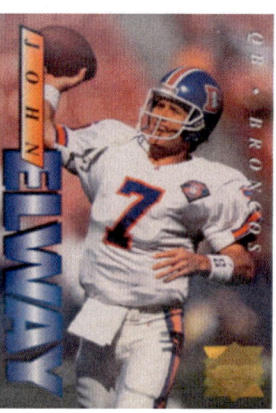

1995 Edge Tech
Gold Logo #59

1995 Edge Tech
Instant Replay #9

1995 Edge Tech
Instant Replay Prism #9

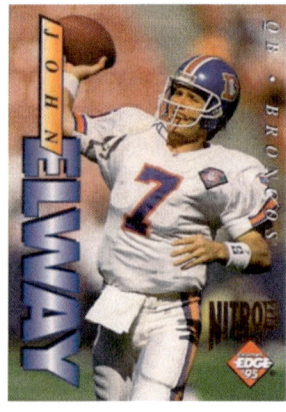

1995 Edge Tech
Nitro 22K Gold #59

1995 Crown Royale #1300

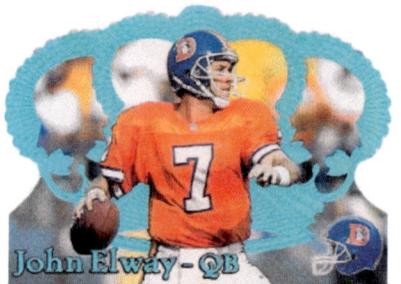

1995 Crown Royale
Blue Holofoil #130

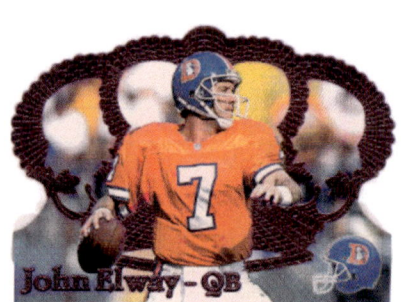

1995 Crown Royale
Copper #130

1995 Crown Royal
Pro Bowl Die Cut
#PB13

1995 Crown Royale
Pride of the NFL
#PN9

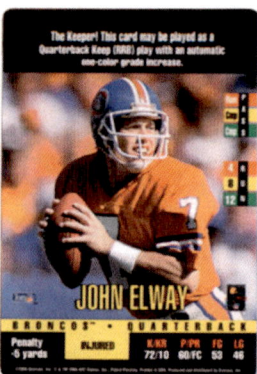

1995 Donruss Red
Zone #87

1995 Excalibur #21

1995 Excalibur 22K
#3 Sword

1995 Excalibur 22K
Gold Shield Gold
Prism #3 Sword

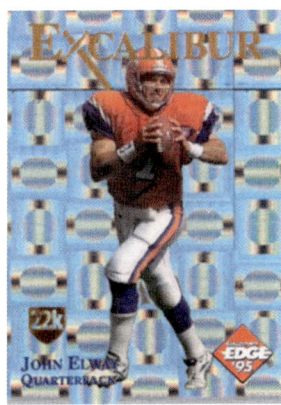

1995 Excalibur 22K
Gold Shield Silver
Prism #3 Sword

1995 Excalibur 22K
Prism Insert #3 Sword

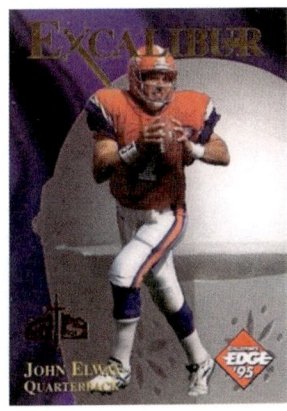

1995 Excalibur 22K
Sword and Stone
Bronze #KG3

1995 Excalibur 22K
Sword and Stone
Diamond #KG3

1995 Excalibur 22K
Sword and Stone
Gold #KG3

1995 Excalibur 22K
Sword and Stone
Silver #KG3

1995 Excalibur
Die Cut #21

1995 Excalibur
Die Cut Sword and
Stone Bronze #21

1995 Excalibur
Die Cut Sword
and Stone Diamond
#21

1995 Excalibur
Die Cut Sword
and Stone Gold
#21

1995 Excalibur
Die Cut Sword
and Stone Silver
#21

1995 Excalibur
Edge Tech Sword
and Stone #ET7

1995 Excalibur
Edge Tech Sword
and Stone Bronze
#ET7

1995 Excalibur
Edge Tech Sword
and Stone Diamond
#ET7

1995 Excalibur
Edge Tech Sword
and Stone Gold
#ET7

1995 Excalibur
Edge Tech Sword
and Stone Silver
#ET7

1995 Excalibur Sword
and Stone Bronze #21

1995 Excalibur Sword
and Stone Diamond #21

1995 Excalibur Sword
and Stone Gold #21

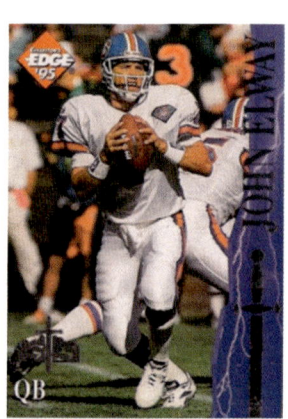

1995 Excalibur Sword
and Stone Silver #21

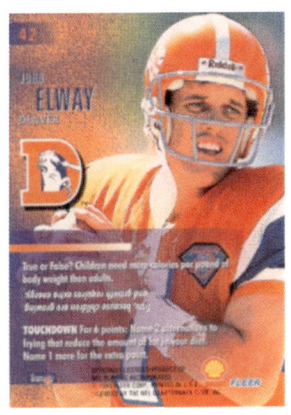

1995 FACT Fleer Shell #42

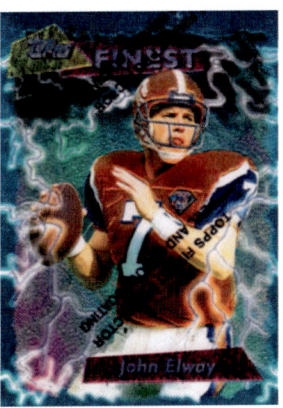

1995 Finest #220

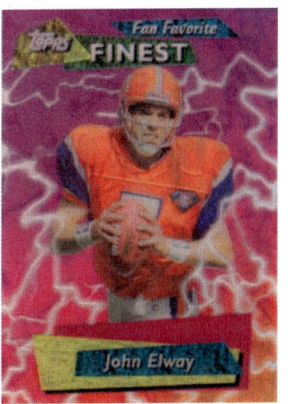

1995 Finest Fan
Favorites #FF13

1995 Finest Landmark #9

1995 Finest Landmark
Bronze #9

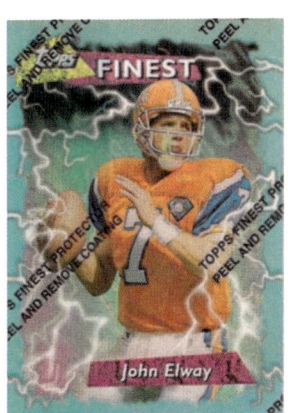

1995 Topps Finest
Refractor #220

1995 Flair #61

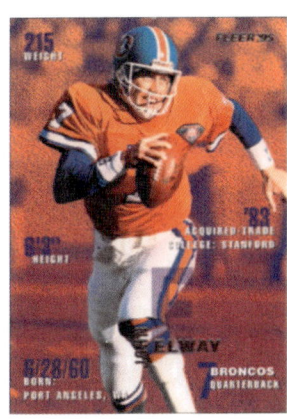

1995 Fleer #110

1995 Images Live Focused #F7

1995 Images Limited #5

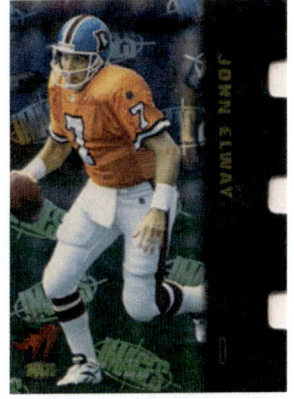

1995 Images Limited
Die Cut #DC5

1995 Images Limited Focused #F7

1995 Images Limited
Icons #6

1995 Images Limited
Live #5

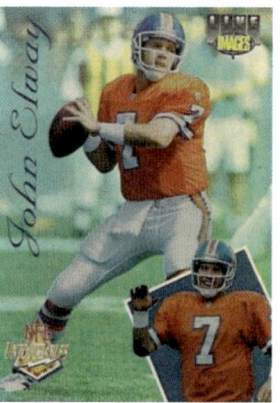

1995 Images Live
Untouchables #U6

1995 Metal #57

1995 Metal
Gold Blaster #5

1995 Metal Silver
Foil #13

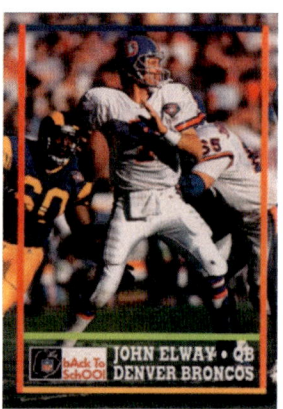

1995 NFL Properties
Back To School #2

1995 NFL Properties
Santa #1

1995 NFL Properties
South Florida Card Show

1995 NFL Properties
Show Redemption #6B

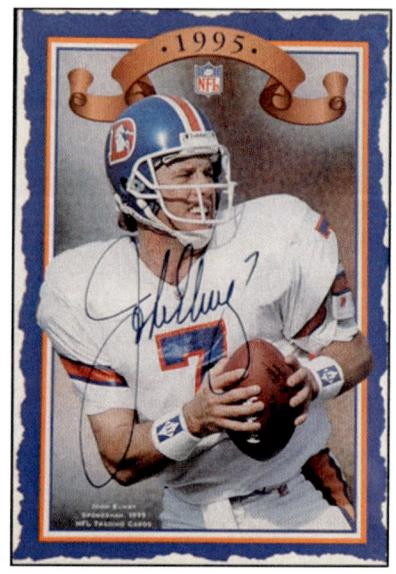

1995 NFL Properties
Show Redemption Auto #6B

1995 Pacific #286

1995 Pacific Blue #286

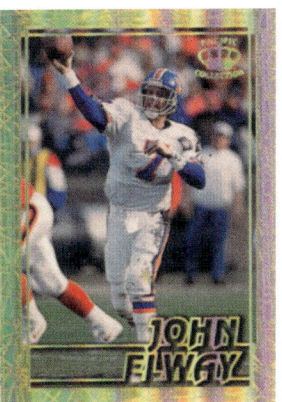

1995 Pacific Gems
of the Crown #GC9

1995 Pacific Gold
Crown Die Cuts
#DC5

1995 Pacific Gold Crown
Die Cuts Flat Gold #DC5

1995 Pacific Gridiron #84

1995 Pacific Gridiron
Copper #84

1995 Pacific Gridiron
Gold #84

1995 Pacific Gridiron
Platinum #84

1995 Pacific Gridiron
Red #84

1995 Pacific Prism #23

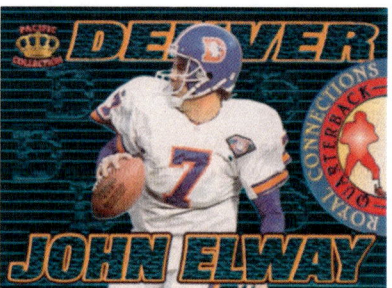

1995 Pacific Prism
Connections #4A

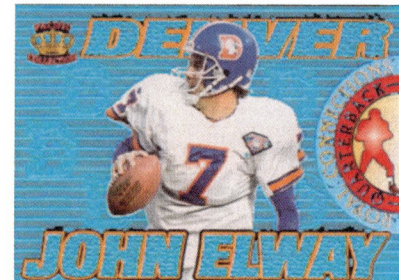

1995 Pacific Prism
Connections
Blue Holofoil #4A

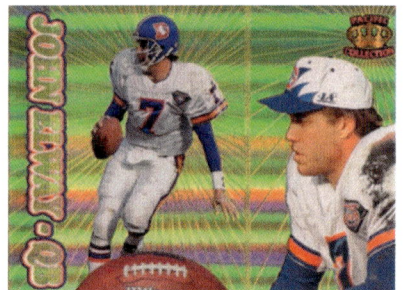

1995 Pacific Prism
Connections
Blue Holofoil #4A

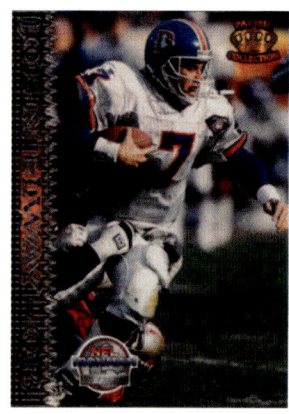

1995 Pacific Platinum #286

1995 Pacific Triple Folder #36

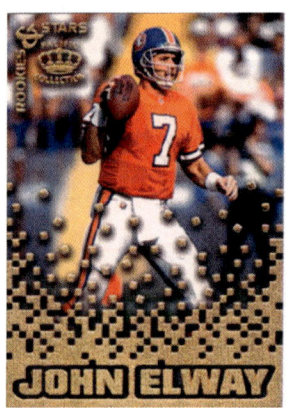

1995 Pacific Triple
Folders Rookies and
Stars #13

1995 Pacific Triple
Folders Rookies and
Stars Blue #13

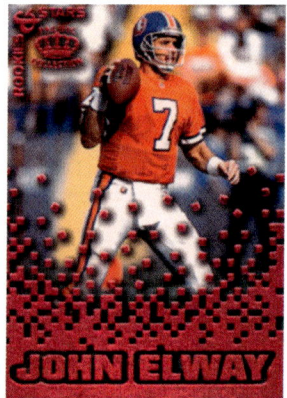

1995 Pacific Triple
Folders Rookies and
Stars Raspberry #13

1995 Pacific Triple
Folders Rookies and
Stars Silver #13

1995 Pacific Triple
Folder Big Gun #BG4

1995 Pacific Triple
Folder Crystalline #CR5

1995 Pacific Triple
Folder Careers #C3

1995 Pacific Triple
Folder Teams #12

1995 Pinnacle #32

1995 Pinnacle #198

1995 Pinnalce #246

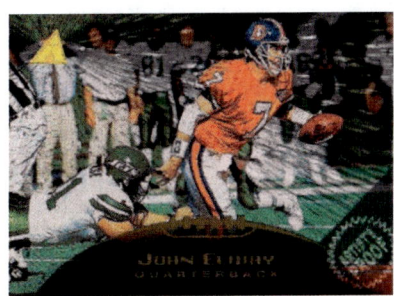

1995 Pinnacle Artist Proof #32

1995 Pinnacle Artist
Proof #198

1995 Pinnacle Artist
Proof #246

1995 Pinnacle Black
and Blue #9

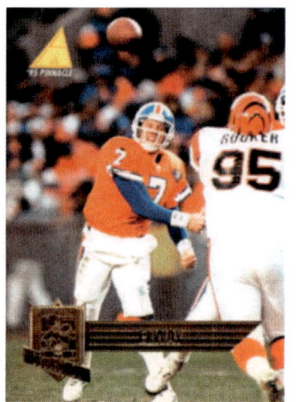

1995 Pinnacle Club #64

1995 Pinnacle Club #65

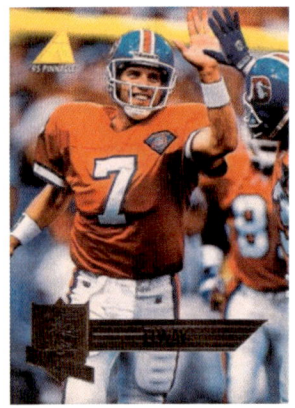

1995 Pinnacle Club #66

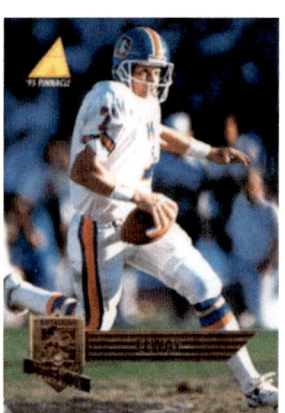

1995 Pinnacle Club #67

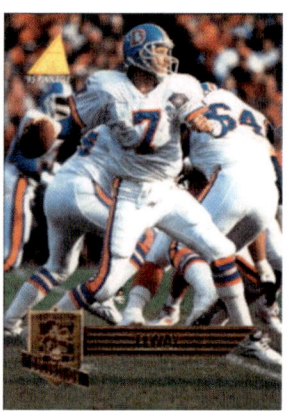

1995 Pinnacle Club #68

1995 Pinnacle Club #69

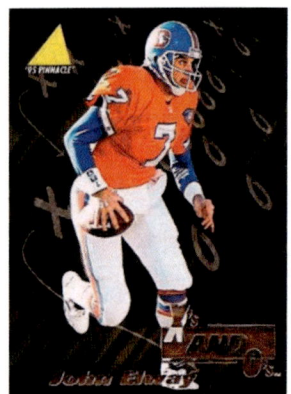

1995 Pinnacle Club #70

1995 Pinnacle Club #70

1995 Pinnacle Club #72

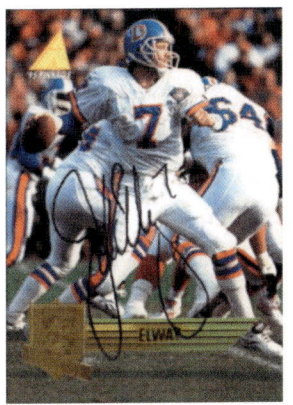

1995 Pinnacle Club
Collection #AU68

1995 Pinnacle Club
Arial Assault #AA14

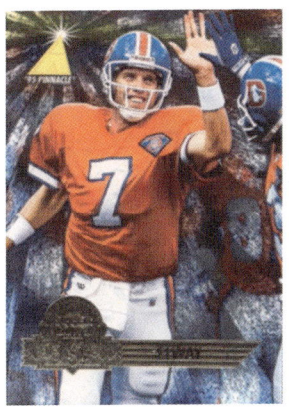

1995 Pinnacle Card
Show #5

1995 Pinnacle Arms
Race #3

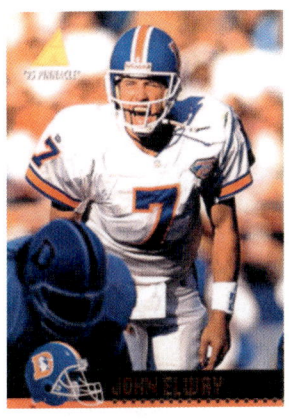

1995 Pinnacel Dial
Corporation #DC7

1995 Pinnacle
Showcase #9

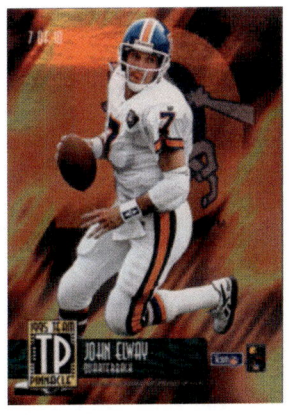

1995 Pinnacle
Team Pinnacle #7

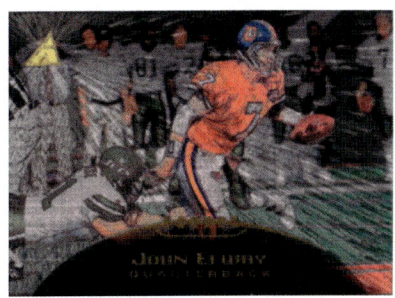

1995 Pinnacle Trophy
Collection #32

1995 Pinnacle Trophy
Collection #198

1995 Pinnacle Trophy
Collection #246

1995 Playoff Absolute #1

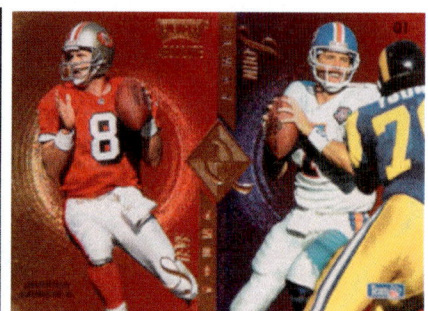

1995 Playoff Absolute
Die Cut Helmet #5

1995 Playoff Absolute Quad
Series #Q1

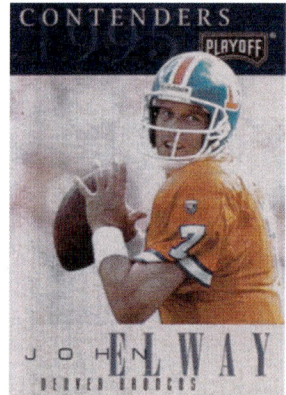

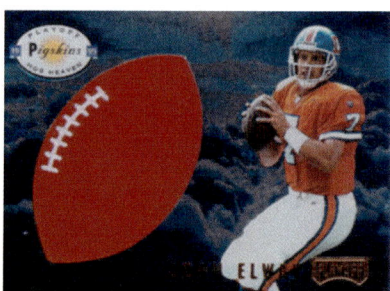

1995 Playoff
Contenders #7

1995 Playoff Contenders
Back To Back #7

1995 Playoff Contenders
Hog Heaven #8

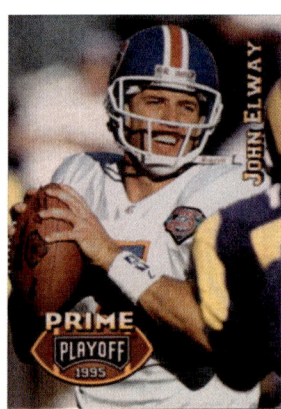

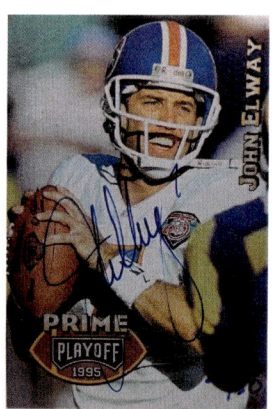

1995 Playoff Prime #1

1995 Playoff Prime
Auto #1

1995 Playoff Prime
Mini #1

1995 ProLine #236

1995 ProLine
Autograph #35

1995 ProLine Game
Breakers #GB7

1995 ProLine Game
Breakers Printers
Proof #GB7

1995 ProLine Grand
Gainers #18

1995 ProLine Game of the
Week #H2

1995 ProLine Game of the
Week #V2

1995 ProLine Game of the
Week Redemption #2

1995 ProLine Impact #6

1995 ProLine Impact Gold #6

1995 ProLine National
Silver #236

1995 ProLine MVP
Redemption #12

1995 ProLine MVP
Redemption/200 #12

1995 ProLine Pogs/Caps #C7

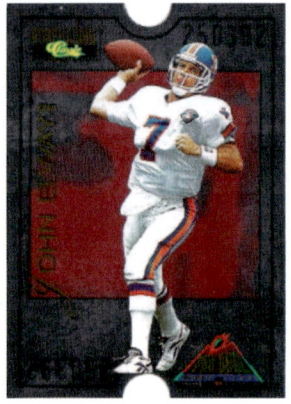

1995 ProLine
Pro Bowl #PB9

1995 ProLine
Precision Cuts #P2

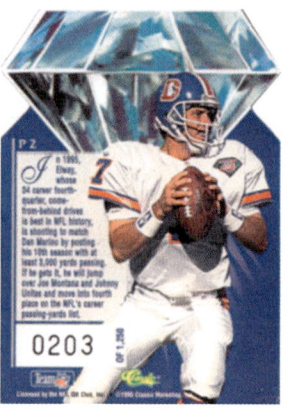

Reverse

1995 ProLine Precision
Cuts Sample

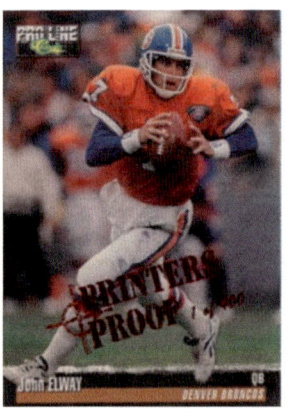

1995 ProLine Printers
Proof #236

1995 ProLine Printers
Proof Silver /175 #36

1995 ProLine
Silver #236

1995 ProLine
Series 2 #13

1995 ProLine Series 2
Printers Proof #13

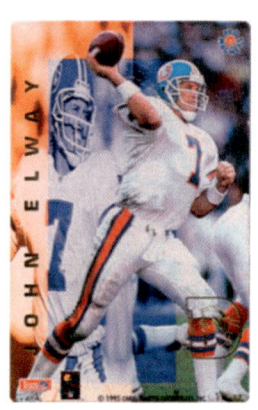

1995 Pro Magnets #37

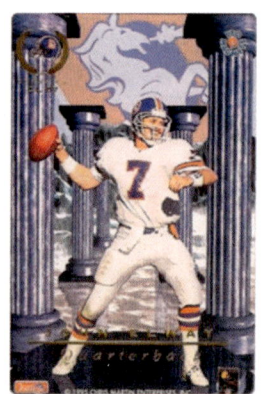

1995 Pro Magnets
Classic #CL7

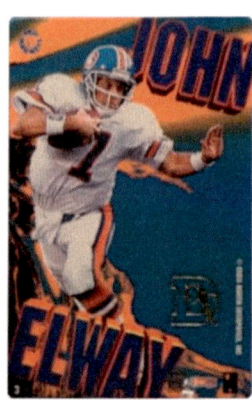

1995 Pro Magnets
In The Zone #3

1995 Pro Magnets
Super Hero Jumbo #2

1995 Pro Stamps #66

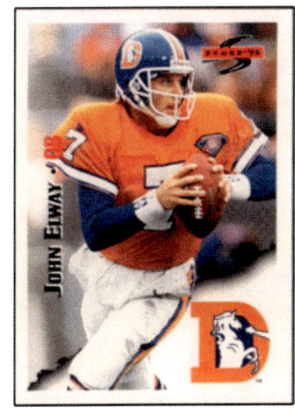

1995 Score #32

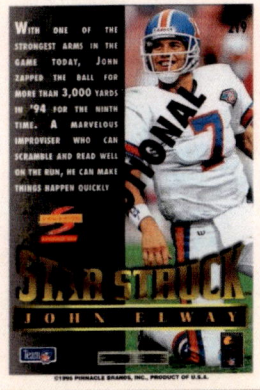

1995 Score #219

1995 Score Reverse
#219 Promo

1995 Score Dream
Team #DT10

November 5, 1995

A 38-6 victory over Arizona, Elway completed 16/21 passes for 256 and 3 touchdowns,
in doing so, he becomes the 7th player in league history to pass for 40,000 yards.

1995 Score #235

1995 Score Reverse #235

1995 Score Reverse #235 Promo

1995 Score Offense
Inc #12

1995 Score Promo #32

1995 Score Pass Time #PT6

1995 Score Pin Card #13

1995 Score Lapel Pin

1995 Score Red Siege #32

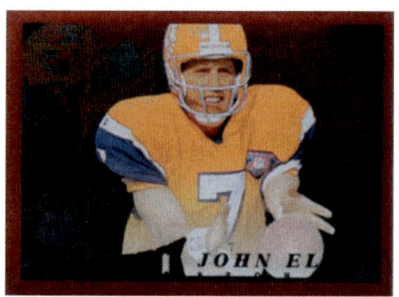

1995 Score Red Siege #219

1995 Score Red Seige #235

1995 Score Red Siege
Artist Proof #235

1995 Score Red Siege
Artist Proof #32

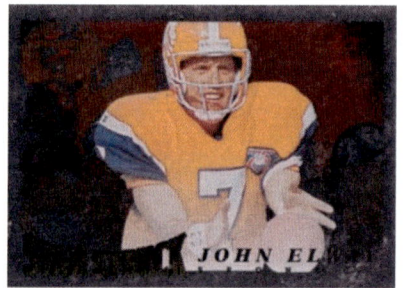

1995 Score Red Siege
Artist Proof #219

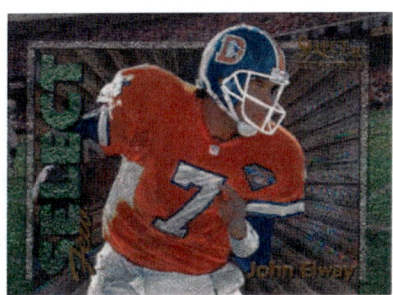

1995 Select Certified #46   1995 Select Certified #2   1995 Select Certified
Mirror Gold #46

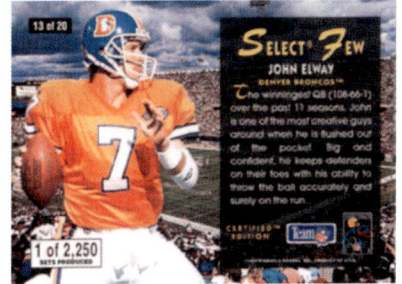

1995 Select Certified
Select Few 1/2290 #13

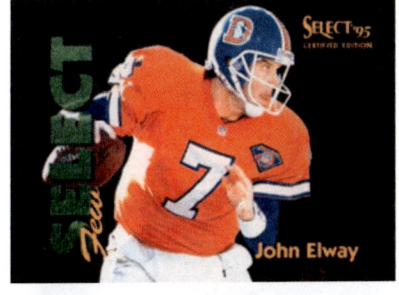

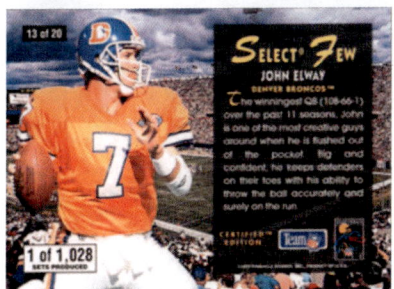

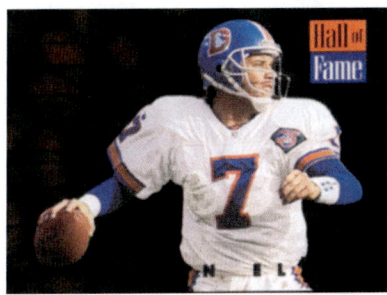

1995 Select Certified   1995 SkyBox Impact #42   1995 SkyBox Impact Future
Select Few 1/1028 #13   Hall of Famer #HF4

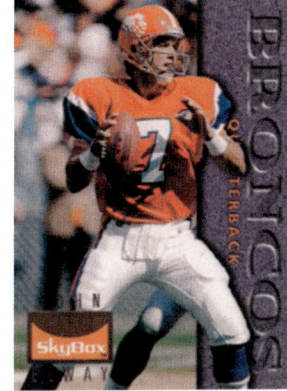

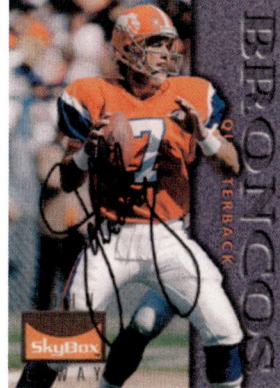

1995 SkyBox Impact   1995 SkyBox   1995 SkyBox Premium #154   1995 SkyBox Premium
Prime Time   Premium #36   Autograph #36
Promo #IP24

1995 SkyBox Premium
Pay Dirt #8

1995 SkyBox Premium
Pay Dirt Blue #8

1995 SkyBox Premium
Pay Dirt Green #8

1995 SkyBox Premium
Pay Dirt Purple #8

1995 SkyBox Premium
Pay Dirt Red #8

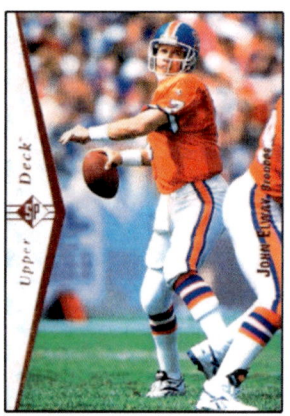

1995 SP #134

1995 SP All-Pro #7

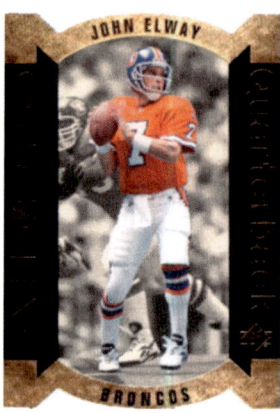

1995 SP All-Pro Gold #7

1995 SP Championship
#99

1995 SP Championship
Die Cut #99

1995 SP Championship
Playoff Showcase #PS18

1995 SP Championship
Playoff Showcase
Die Cut #PS18

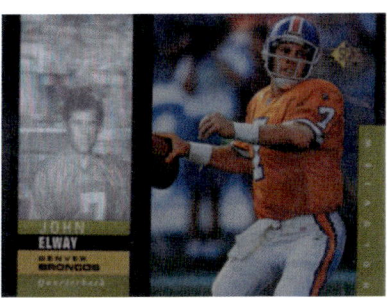

1995 SP Holoview #14

1995 SP Holoview Die Cut #14

1995 Sport Flix #22

1995 Sport Flix #156

1995 Sport Flix #171

1995 Sport Flix
Artist Proof #22

1995 Sport Flix
Artist Proof #156

1995 Sport Flix
Artist Proof #171

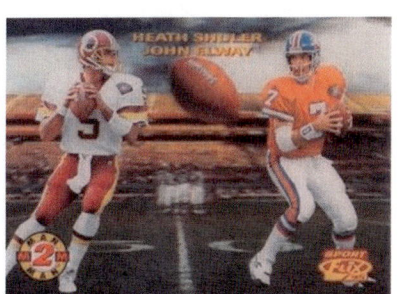

1995 Sport Flix
Man to Man #6

1995 Sport Flix
Pro Motion #PM5

1995 Stadium Club #189

1995 Stadium Club #260

1995 Stadium Club
Diffraction #189

1995 Stadium Club
Ground Atack #G4

1995 Stadium Club
MVP #5

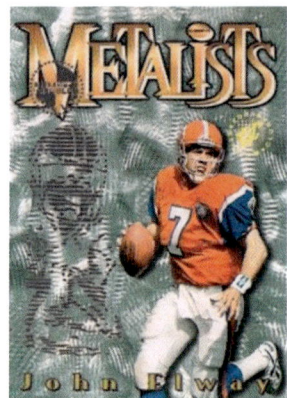

1995 Stadium Club
Metalists #M3

1995 Stadium Club
Members Only 50 #9

1995 Stadium Club
Members Only #189

1995 Stadium Club
Members Only #260

1995 Stadium Club
Members Only
Diffraction #189

1995 Stadium Club
Members Only
Ground Attack #G4
Reverse

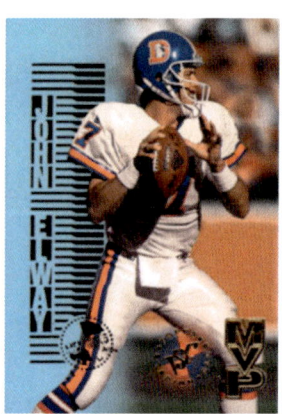

1995 Stadium Club
Members Only
MVP #5

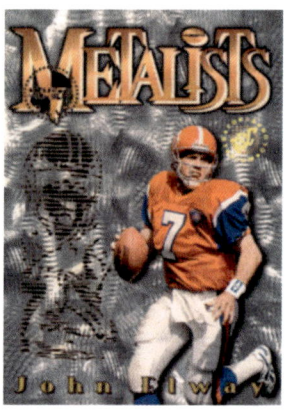

1995 Stadium Club
Members Only
Metalists #M3

1995 Stadium Club
Members Only
Nightmares #30

1995 Stadium Club
Members Only
Power Surge #P7

1995 Stadium Club
Nightmares #30

1995 Stadium Club
Power Surge #P7

1995 Summit #16

1995 Summit #190

1995 Summit #195

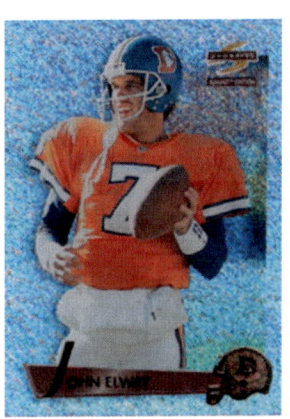

1995 Summit
Ground Zero #16

1995 Summit
Ground Zero #190

1995 Summit
Ground Zero #195

1995 Topps #37

1995 Topps #400

1995 Topps 1000/3000
Boosters #37

1995 Topps Air Raid #6

1995 Topps Factory
Jaguars #37

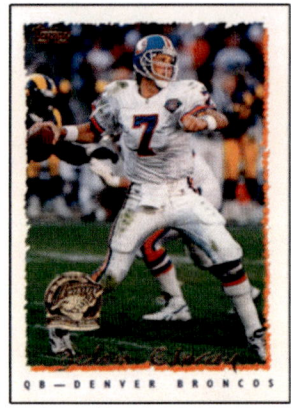

1995 Topps Factory
Jaguars #400

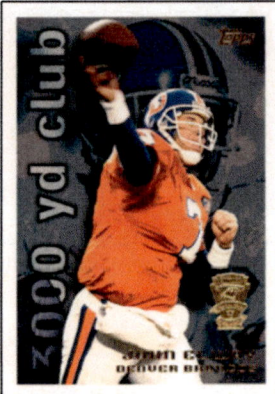

1995 Topps Factory
Panthers #37

1995 Topps Factory
Panthers #400

1995 Topps Finest
Booster #B182

1995 Topps Finest
Booster Refractor
#B182

1995 Topps Mystery
Finest #7

1995 Topps Mystery
Finest Refractor #7

1995 Ultra #91

1995 Ultra #486

1995 Ultra Gold
Medalion #91

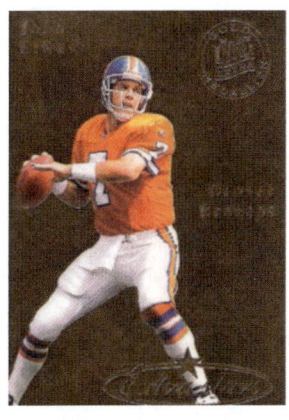

1995 Ultra Gold
Medalion #486

1995 Ultra Ultrabilities #6

1995 Upper Deck #82

1995 Upper Deck
Electric Gold #82

1995 Upper Deck
Electric Silver #82

1995 Upper Deck
Predictor League
Leader #RP5

1995 Upper Deck
Predictor League
Leader Prizes #RP5

1995 Upper Deck
Pro Bowl #20

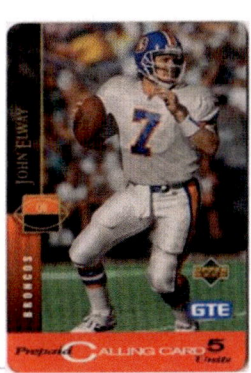

1995 Upper Deck
Phone Card #5

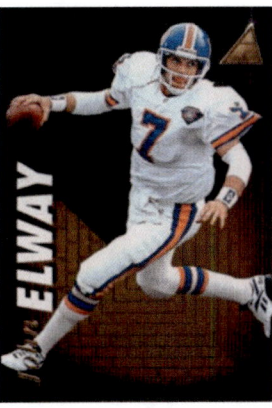

1995 Zenith #Z14

1995 Zenith
Z-Team #ZT7

December 24, 1995

A 31-28 victory over the Los Angeles Raiders, Elway completed 24/41 passes
for 320 yards, and 2 touchdowns. He was named NFL Player of the Week.

1996

At 13-3, the 1996 Denver Broncos were first in the AFC West, and tied with the Green Bay Packers for the best record in the League. By wrapping up the division early, they had homefield advantage for the playoffs, were able to rest their starters at the end of the season. They faced the Jacksonville Jaguars in the divisional round. After their long layoff, the Broncos were flat, played with no sense of urgency, and were ultimately upset 30-27.

Elway started 15 games, completed 287/466 passes, for 3328 yards, and 26 touchdowns. He added 249 yards on 50 carries, with four touchdowns. He was selected to his seventh Pro-Bowl.

1996 Pocket Schedule

1996 Action Packed #61

1996 Action Packed
24K Gold #13

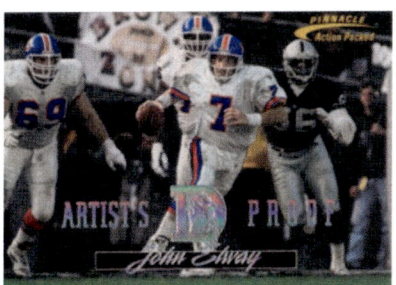

1996 Action Packed
Artist Proof #61

Action Packed Scuplter's
Proof #61

1996 Bowmans Best
#115

1996 Bowmans Best
Atomic Refractor #115

1996 Bowmans Best
Cuts #7

1996 Bowmans Best
Cuts Atomic Refractor #7

1996 Bowmans Best
Cuts Refractor #7

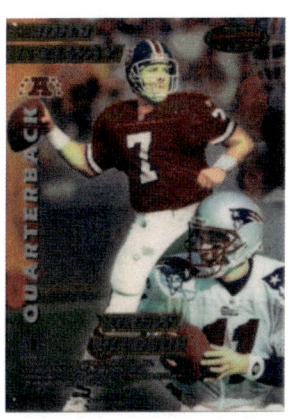

1996 Bowmans Best
Mirror Image #2

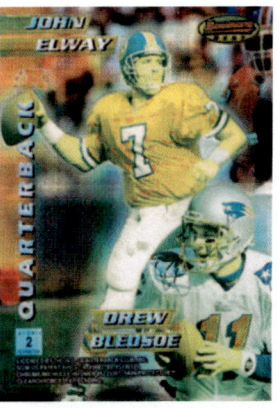

1996 Bowmans Best
Mirror Image Atomic
Refractor #2

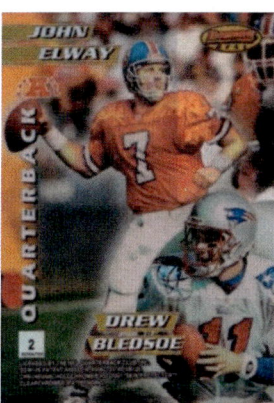

1996 Bowmans Best
Mirror Image
Refractor #2

Sports Illustrated Presents

Pro Football '96

Scouting Reports
For Every NFL Team

Peter King Picks 'Em:
The Top 25 Emerging Stars

Pro Football's Biggest Myths
Debunked by Dr. Z

Mile-High Hopes

John Elway looks to lead the Broncos back to the top

1996 Bravo Magazine Germany

1996 Bowmans Best Refractor #115

1996 Bowmans Best Super Bowl #115

1996 Collectors Edge Presidents Reserve #254

1996 Collectors Edge Presidents Reserve Air Force One #22

Reverse

1996 Collectors Edge Presidents Reserve Air Force One CS #22

1996 Collectors Edge Presidents Reserve Air Force One #22 Jumbo

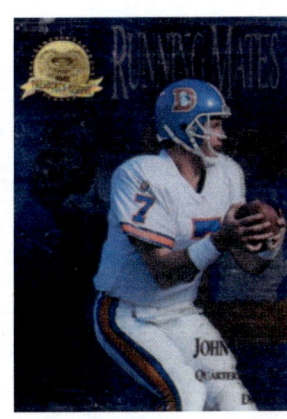
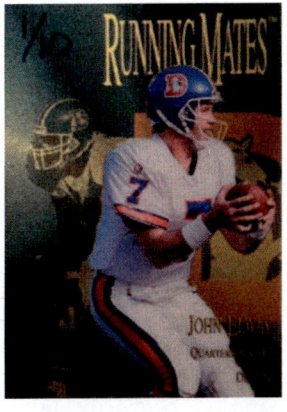

1996 Collectors Edge President's Reserve Honor Guard #HG16

1996 Collectors Edge Presidents Reserve Running Mates #RM13

1996 Collectors Edge Presidents Reserve Running Mates Gold #RM13

Reverse

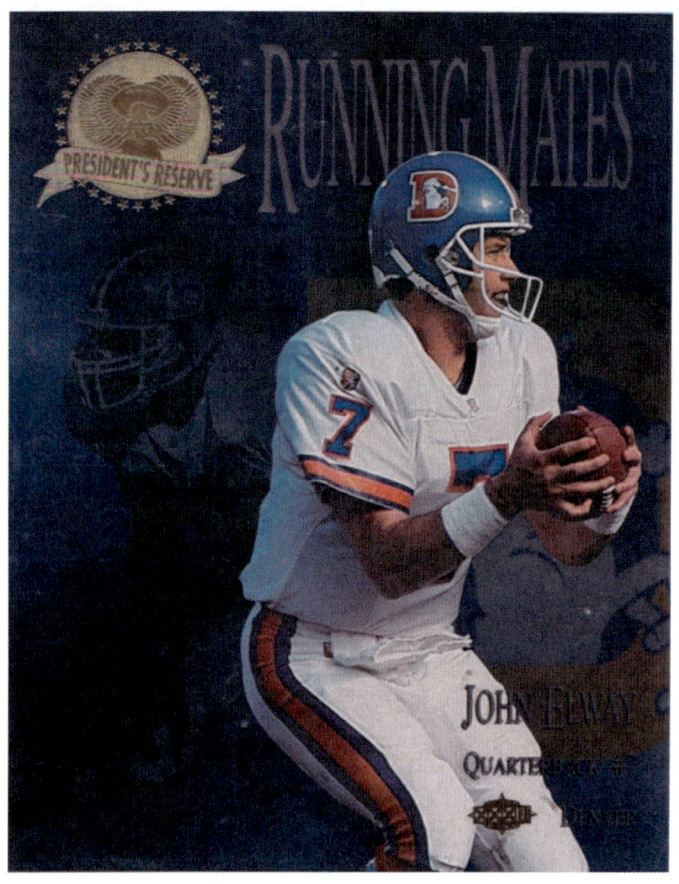

1996 Collectors Edge Presidents
Reserve Running Mates Jumbo #RM3

1996 Collectors Edge Presidents Reserve
Running Mates Gold Jumbo #RM3

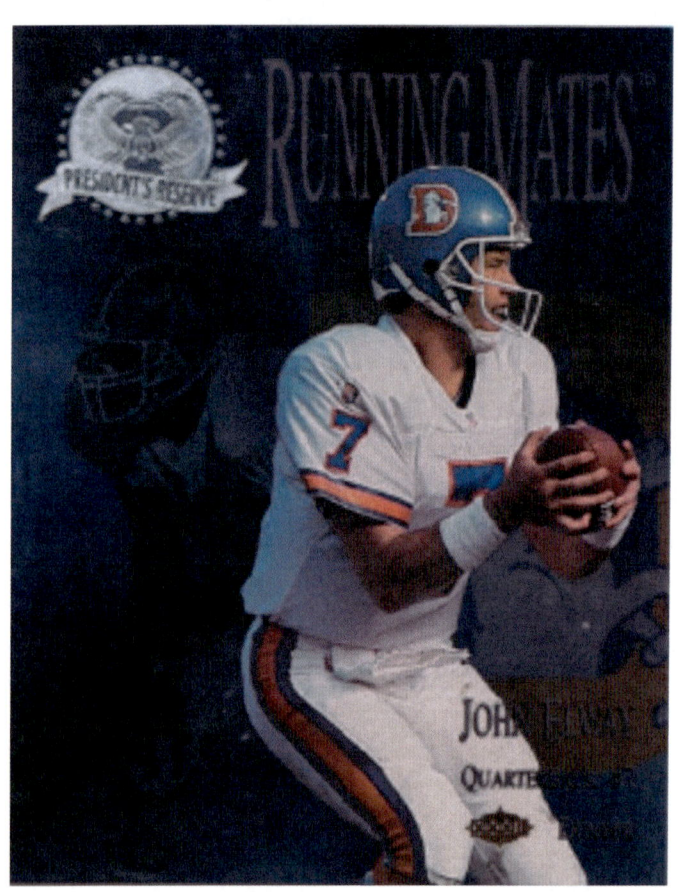

1996 Collectors Edge Presidents Reserve
Running Mates Jumbo SIlver #RM3

1996 Classic NFL
Experience #20

1996 Classic NFL
Experience Printers
Proof #20

1996 Classic
NFL Experience
Sculpted #S7

1996 Classic
NFL Experience
Super Bowl Gold #20

1996 Classic
NFL Experience
Super Bowl Game #A1

1996 Classic
NFL Experience
Super Bowl Red #20

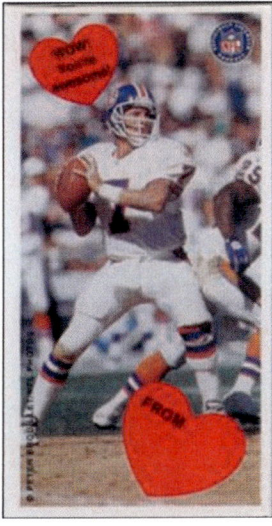

1996 Cleo
Quarterback Club
Valentine #4

1996 Collectors Choice #55

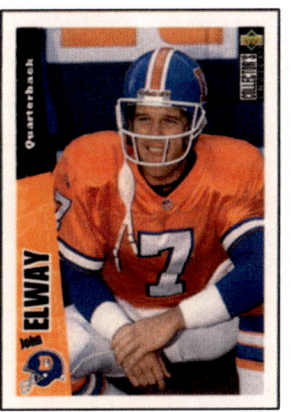

1996 Colletors Choice #11

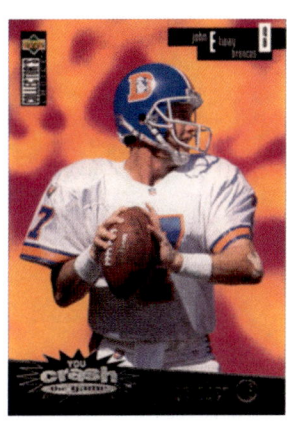

1996 Collectors
Choice Crash
The Game #CG2A

1996 Collectors
Choice Crash
The Game #CG2B

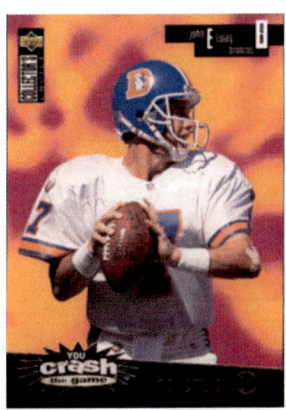

1996 Collectors
Choice Crash
The Game #CG2C

1996 Collectors
Choice Crash
The Game Gold
#CG2A

1996 Collectors
Choice Crash
The Game Gold
#CG2B

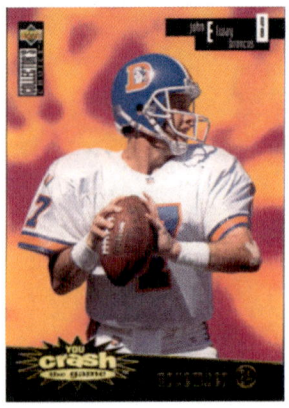

1996 Collectors Choice
Crash The Game Gold
#CG2C

1996 Collectors Choice
Crash The Game Gold
Redemption #2

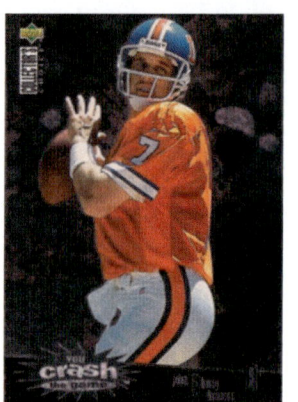

1996 Collectors Choice
Crash The Game Silver
Redemption #2

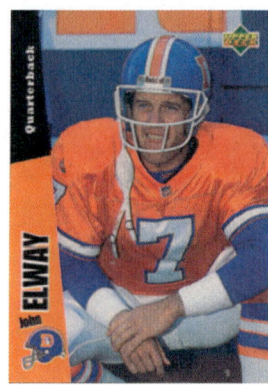

1996 Collectors Choice
Folz Vending Mini #11

1996 Collectors Choice
MVP #M13

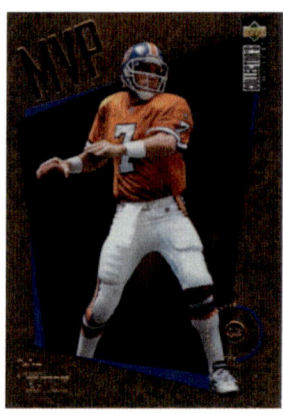

1996 Collectors Choice
MVP Gold #M13

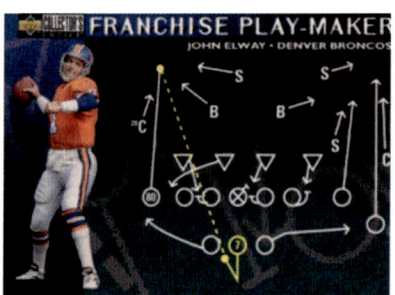

1996 Collectors Choice Update #U68

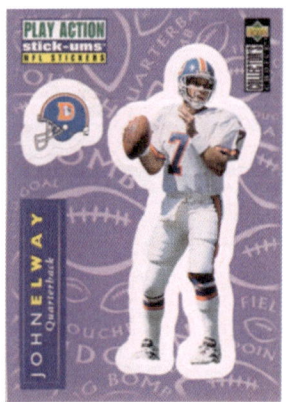

1996 Collectors Choice
Update Stick-Ums #S7

1996 Collectors Choice
Update Stick-Ums
Mystery Base Card #B9

1996 Collectors Choice
Update You Make The
Play #Y25

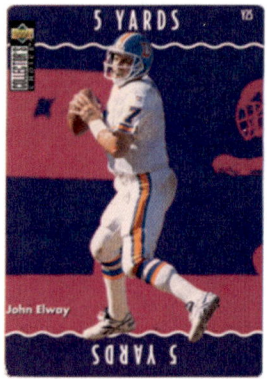

1996 Collectors Choice
Update You Make The
Play #Y70

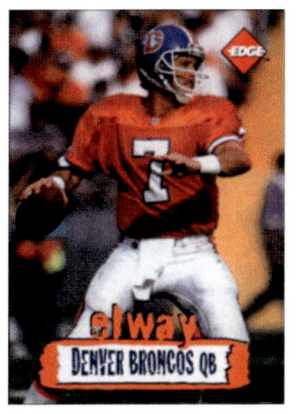

1996 Collectors Edge #67

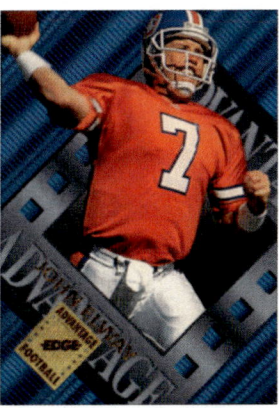

1996 Collectors
Edge Advantage #8

1996 Collectors
Edge Advantage
Crystal Cuts #CC11

1996 Collectors
Edge Advantage
Crystal Cuts
Silver #CC11

1996 Collectors
Edge Advantage
Game Ball #G6

1996 Collectors
Edge Advantage
Perfect Play Foils #8

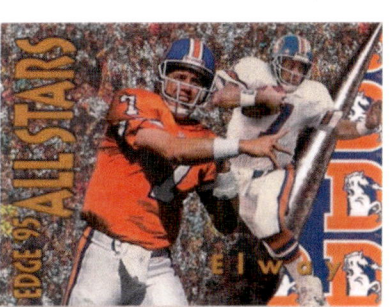

1996 Collectors Edge
All-Stars #4

1996 Collectors Edge
Advantage Role
Models #RM1

1996 Collectors
Edge Advantage
Super Bowl
Game Ball #SB5

1996 Collectors
Edge Die Cut #67

1996 Collectors
Edge Holofoil #67

1996 Collectors Edge
Protoges #4

1996 Collectors
Edge Quantom
Motion #8

1996 Collectors Edge
Quantom Motion Foil
#8

1996 Collectors Edge
Ripped #4

1996 Collectors Edge
Ripped Die Cut #4

1996 Costacos Poster Sample

1996 Crown Royal #77

1996 Crown Royal Blue #77

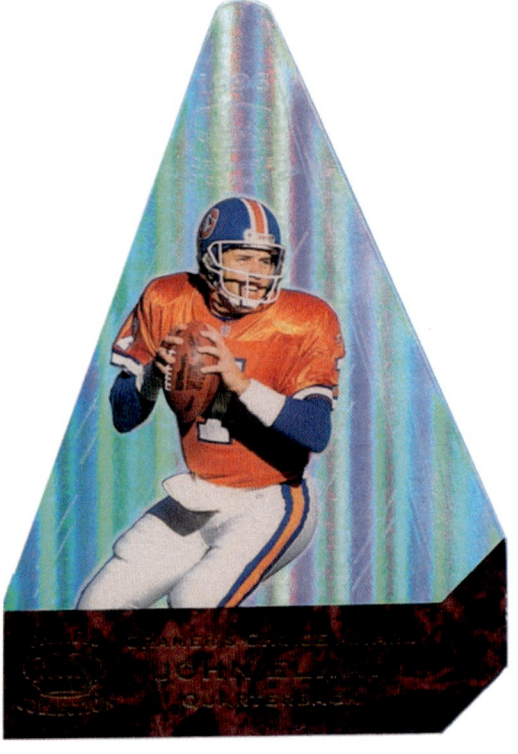

1996 Crown Royal Cramers
Choice Jumbo #1

1996 Crown Royal
Field Force #8

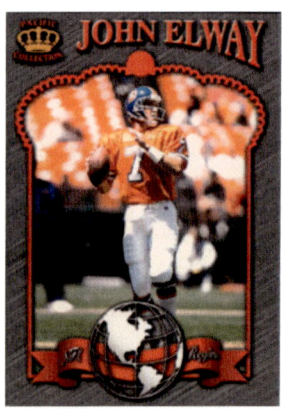

1996 Crown Royal
NFL Regime #10

1996 Crown Royal Silver #77

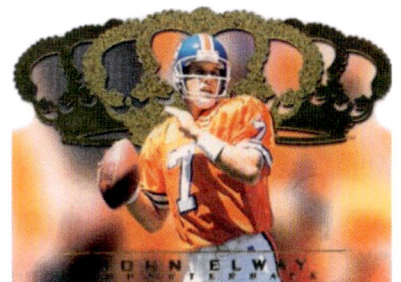

1996 Crown Royal
Triple Crown Diecut #2

1996 Donruss #173

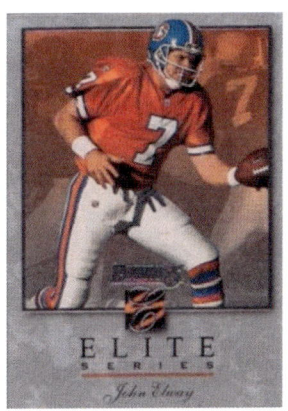

1996 Donruss Elite
#10

1996 Donruss Elite
Gold #10

1996 Donruss
Hit List #20

1996 Donruss
Press Proof #173

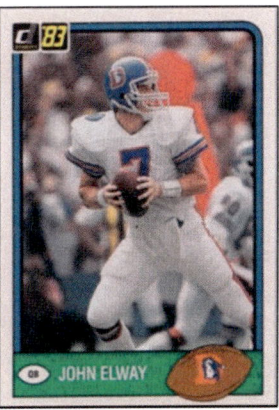

1996 Donruss
What If #10

1996 Donruss
Will To Win #10

1996 FACT Fleer Shell #74

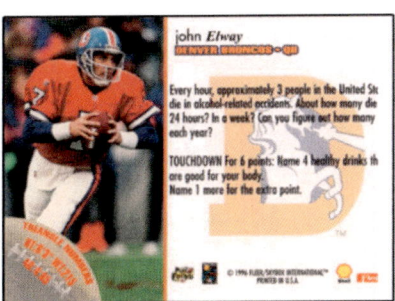

Reverse

1996 Finest #G230

1996 Finest #S310

1996 Finest
Refractor #G230

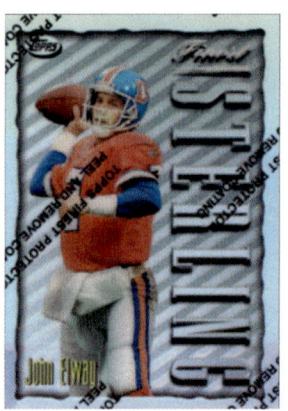

1996 Finest
Refractor #S310

1996 Finest Pro Bowl Jumbo #17

1996 Fleer #40

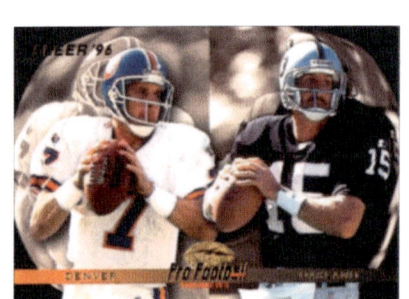

1996 Fleer #191

1996 Flickball #98

1996 Hills Back To School

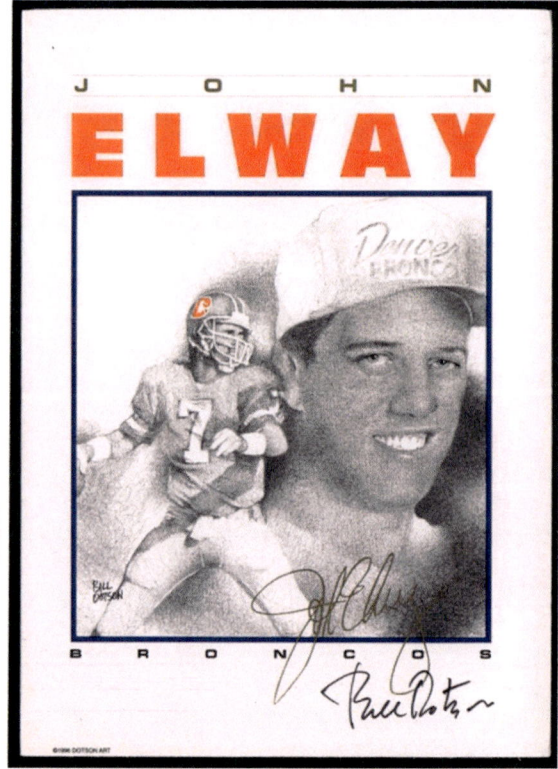

1996 Dotsun Post Card

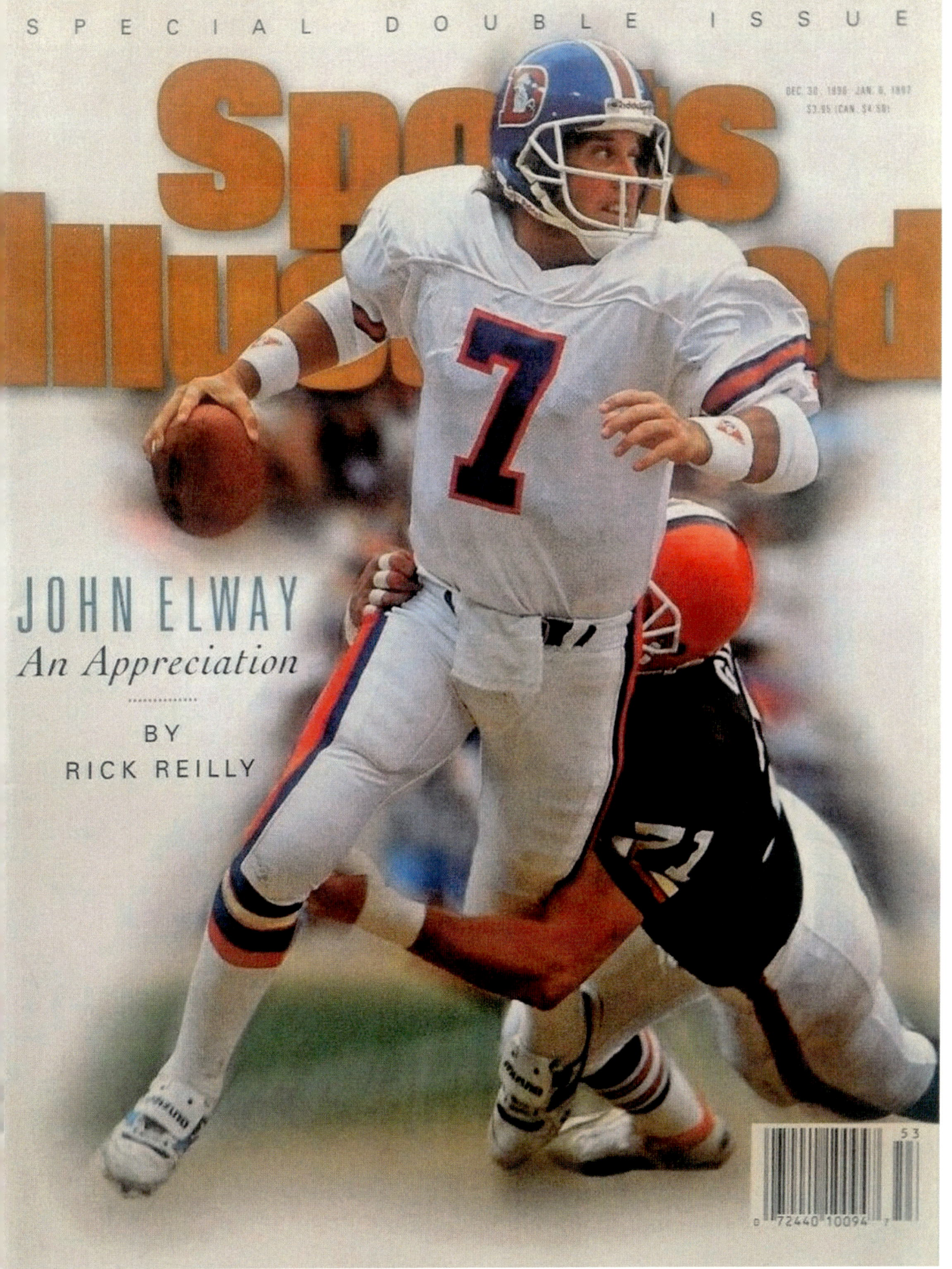

Sports Illustrated

DEC. 30, 1996 · JAN. 6, 1997
$3.95 (CAN. $4.50)

JOHN ELWAY
An Appreciation

BY
RICK REILLY

1996 Laser View
Inscriptions #6

1996 Laser View
Inscriptions #6

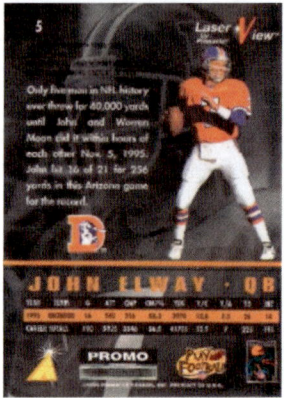

1996 Laser View
Promo #5

1996 Laser View
Eye on the Prize #7

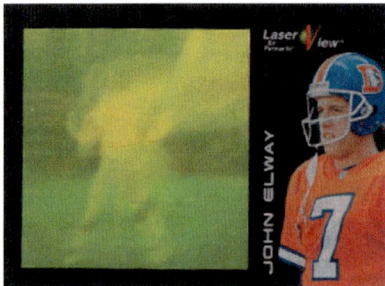

1996 Laser View Gold #5

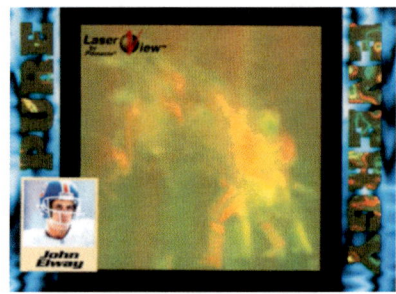

1996 Laser View Gold #32

1996 Laser View
Inscriptions #6

1996 Leaf #109

1996 Leaf #109

1996 Leaf American
All Stars Gold #18

1996 Leaf Collectors
Edition #109

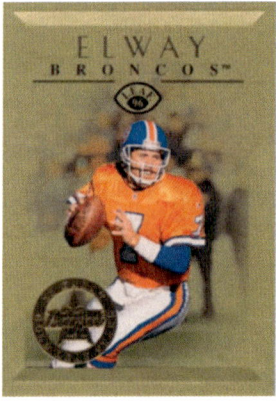

1996 Leaf Gold
Leaf Stars #15

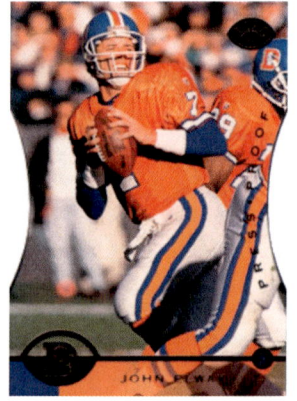

1996 Leaf Press
Proof #109

1996 Leaf Red #109

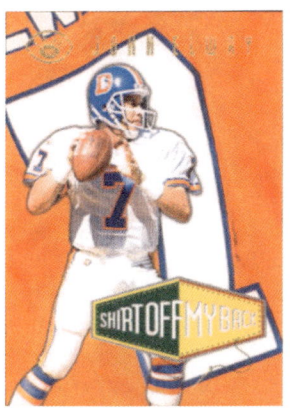

1996 Leaf Shirt
Off My Back #7

1996 Leaf Statistical
Standouts #1

1996 Metal #35

1996 Metal Platinum
Portraits #3

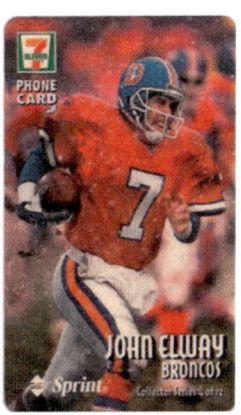

1996 Leaf Precious
Metal #35

1996 Motion Vision #12

1996 Motion Vision #19

1996 NFL Properties
7-11 #1

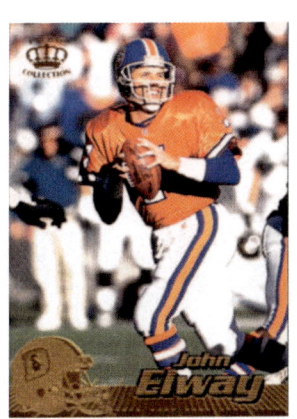

1996 NFL Properties
Back to School #2

1996 Pacific #128

1996 Pacific Blue #128

1996 Pacific Bomb Squad #2

When I was young I loved to collect football cards.

I still have around 23,862 in my closet. And every night before I went to bed, I'd pick one card and study all that player's stats real hard. So that maybe when I fell asleep I could dream I was him.

Now I'm on a football card. I guess you could say My dreams came true. Think I'll ever collect your card?

Reach for the stars.
Reach for football cards.

1996 Pacific Card
Supials #11

1996 Card Supials
Small #11

1996 Pacific Cramers Choice #CC2

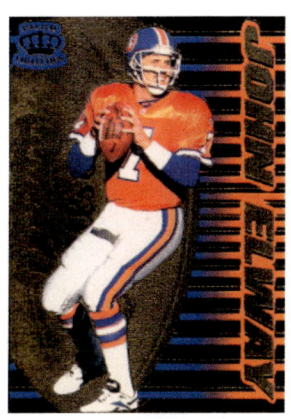
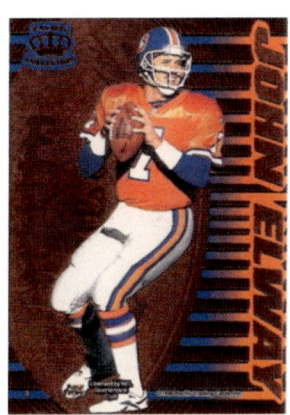

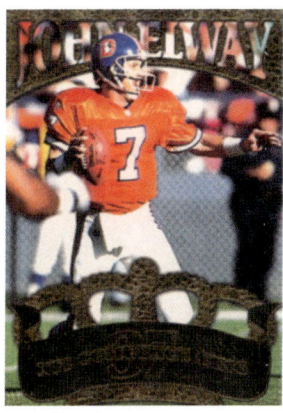

1996 Pacific
Dynagon #41

Pacific Dynagon
Tandems#3

1996 Pacific Dynagon
Dynamic Duos #DD18

1996 Pacific Dynagon
Kings Of The NFL #K9

1996 Pacific Gridiron #36

1996 Pacific Gridiron Bronze #36

1996 Pacific Gridiron Gems #GG13

1996 Pacific Gems of the Crown #15

1996 Pacific Gridiron Gold #36

1996 Pacific Gridiron Gold
Crown Die Cuts #6

1996 Pacific Gridiron
Gold Crown Die Cut
#GC12

1996 Pacific Gridiron Platinum #36

1996 Pacific Gold Crown
Die Cuts Platinum #6

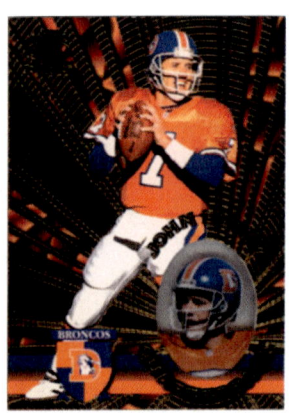

1996 Pacific Invincible
#42

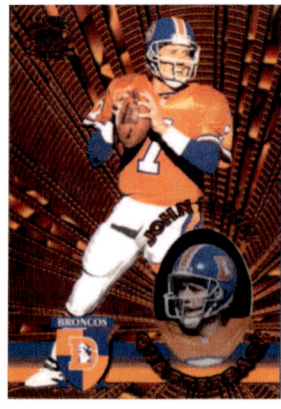

1996 Pacific Invincible
Bronze #42

1996 Pacific Invincible
Kick Started Die Cut
#KS4

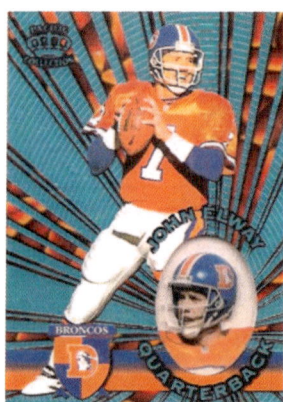

1996 Pacific Invincible
Platinum Blue #42

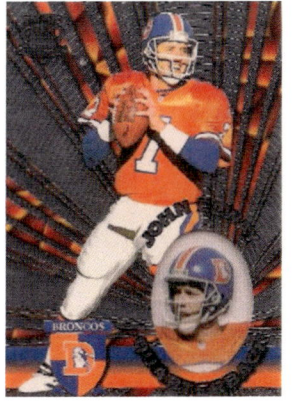

1996 Pacific Invincible
Silver #42

1996 Pacific Invincible
Smash Mouth #49

1996 Pacific Litho
Cell #30

1996 Pacific Litho
Cell Bronze #30

1996 Pacific Litho Cell
Feature Performers
#FP6

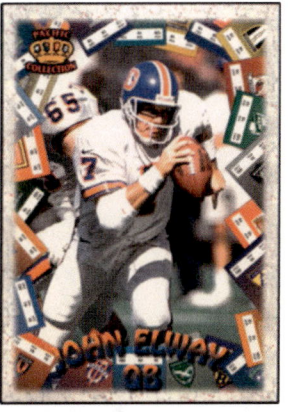

1996 Pacific Litho Cells
Game Time #GT70

1996 Pacific Litho
Cell Litho Proof #10

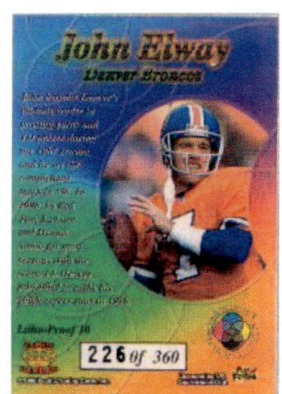

1996 Pacific Litho Cell
Litho Proof Certified #10

1996 Pacific Litho Cell
Moments In Time #8

1996 Pacific Litho
Cell Silver #30

1996 Pacific Power
Core #PC6

1996 Pacific Red #128

1996 Pacific Silver #128

1996 Pacific
The Zone #8

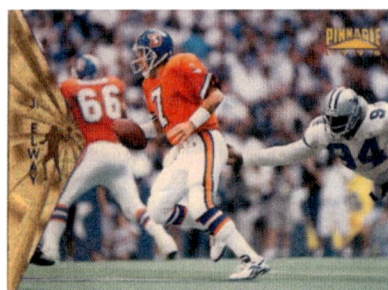
1996 Pinnacle #67

1996 Pinnacle Artist Proof #67

1996 Pinnacle
Bimbo Bread #5

1996 Pinnacle Black
And Blue #9

1996 Pinnacle Foil #67

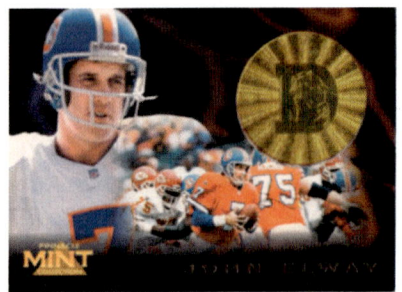
1996 Pinnacle Mint #2

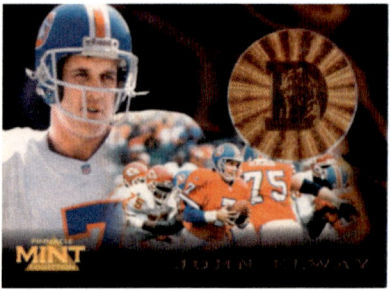
1996 Pinnacle Mint Bronze #2

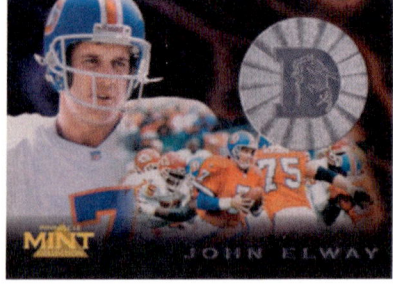
1996 Pinnacle Mint Silver #2

1996 Pinnacle Mint
Coins Brass #2

1996 Pinnacle Mint
Coins Gold #2

1996 Pinnacle Mint
Coins Nickel #2

1996 Pinnacle Mint
Coins Silver #2

1996 Pinnacle Premium Stock #67

1996 Pinnacle
Super Bowl Card Show #5

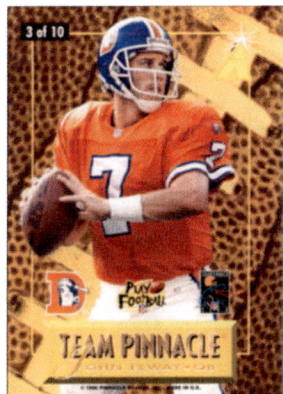

1996 Pinnacle
Team Pinnacle #3

1996 Pinnacle Trophy
Collection #67

1996 Playoff Absolute #103

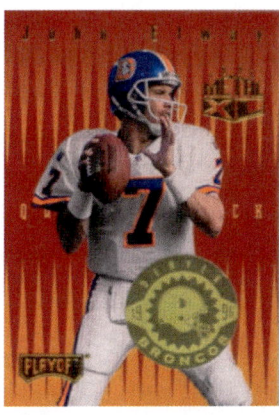

1996 Playoff Absolute
Metal XL #20

1996 Palyoff Absolute
Quad Series #9

1996 Playoff Absolute
Xtreme Team #8

1996 Playoff Contenders
Air Command #5

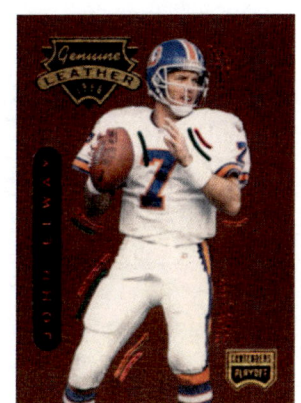

1996 Playoff Contenders
Leather #7

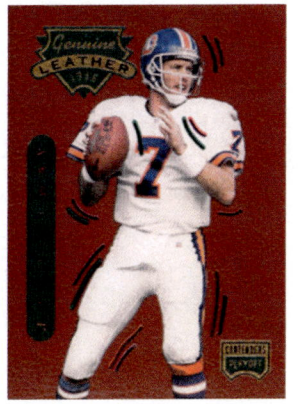

1996 Playoff Contenders
Leather Accent #7

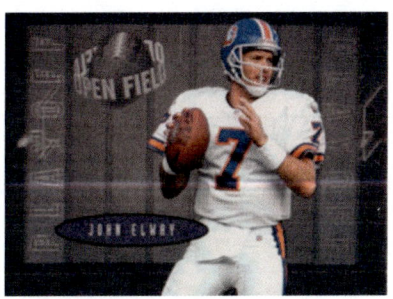

1996 Playoff Contenders
Open Field Foil #7

1996 Playoff Contenders
Open Field Hologram #7

1996 Playoff Contenders
Pennants #7

1996 Playoff Illusions
#74

1996 Playoff Illusions
Optical Illusion #5

1996 Playoff Illusions
Spectralusion Dominion
#74

1996 Playoff Illusions
Spectralusion Elite #74

1996 Playoff Illusions
XXI #74

1996 Playoff Illusions
XXXI Spectralusion
#74

1996 Playoff Leather
Bound #2

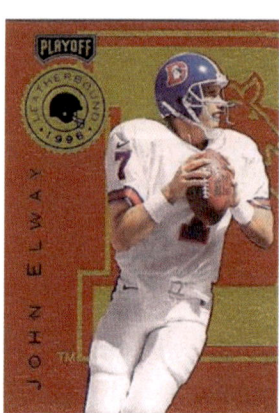

1996 Playoff Leather
Bound Gold #2

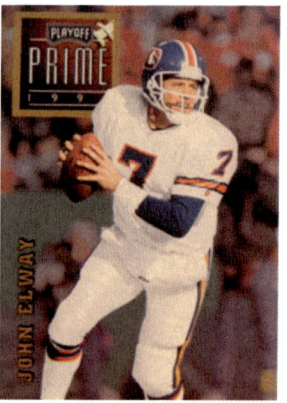

1996 Playoff Prime
#162

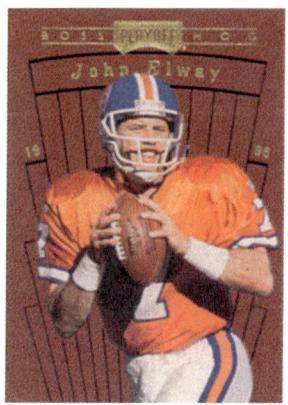

1996 Playoff Prime
Boss Hogs #16

1996 Playoff
X&O #162

1996 Playoff Trophy
Contenders #7

1996 Playoff Trophy
Contenders Mini
Back-to-Back #42

1996 Playoff Trophy
Contenders Playoff
Zone #3

1996 Pro Cube #3

1996 Pro Line #3

1996 Pro Line Anaheim
National Convention #3

1996 Pro Line
Printers Proof #3

1996 Pro Line DC3 #9

1996 Pro Line
Headliners #3

1996 Pro Line
Intense #86

1996 Pro Line
Intense Double
Intensity #86

1996 Pro Line
Intense-Determined #9

1996 ProLine
Phone Cards
$10.00

1996 Pro Line
Phone Cards
$25.00 Die Cut

1996 Pro Line
Phone Card $3

1996 Pro Line
Phone Card $5

1996 Pro Line
Phone Card Test

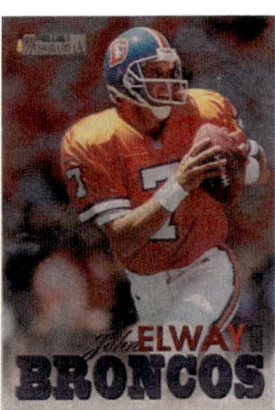

1996 Pro Line
Memorabilia #86

1996 Pro Line
Memorabilia
Stretch Drive #DS8

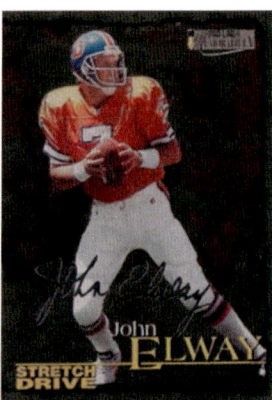

1996 Pro Line
Memorabilia
Stretch Drive Silver
Signature #DS8

1996 Pro Line
National #3

1996 Pro Line
Printers Proof #3

1996 Pro Line
Rivalries #R5

1996 Pro Magnets #72

1996 Pro Magnets
12 #2

1996 Pro Magnets
Die Cut #4

1996 Pro Stamp
#63

1996 Score #59

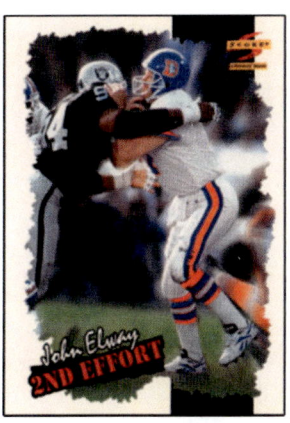

1996 Score #246

1996 Score #271

1996 Score #275

1996 Score
Artist Proof #59

1996 Score
Artist Proof #246

1996 Score
Artist Proof #271

1996 Score
Artist Proof #275

1996 Score Board
NFL Laser #18

1996 Score Board
Laser Images #19

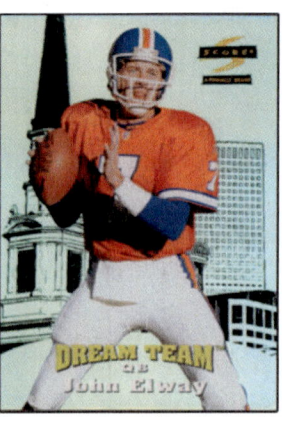

1996 Score Dream
Team #4

1996 Score Field
Force #59

1996 Score Field
Force #246

1996 Score Field
Force #271

1996 Score Field
Force #275

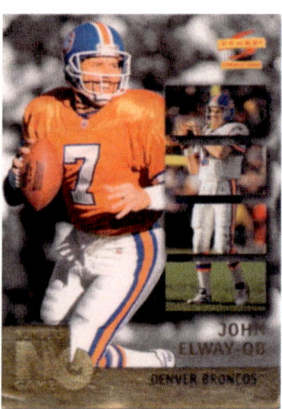

1996 Score
Numbers Game #4

1996 Score Settle
The Score #16

1996 Score Settle
The Score #17

1996 Score Settle
The Score #18

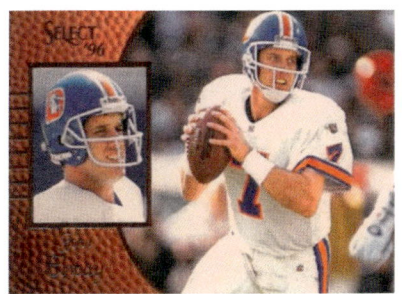

1996 Select #40

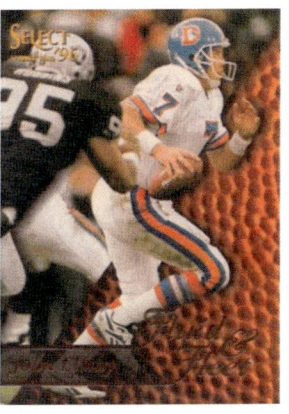

1996 Select #183

1996 Select #200

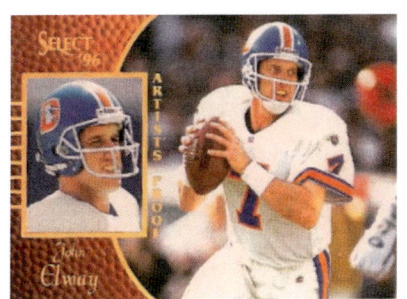

1996 Select
Artist Proof #40

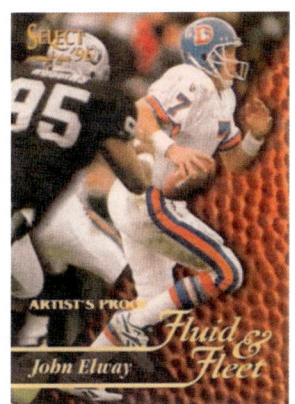

1996 Select
Artist Proof #183

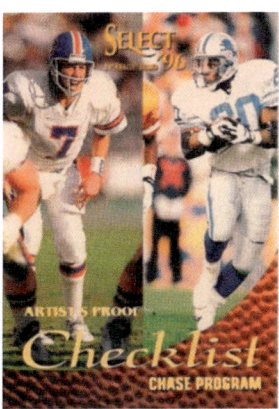

1996 Select
Artist Proof #200

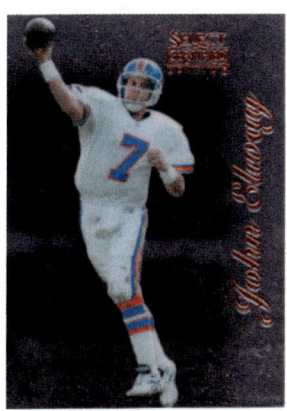

1996 Select
Certified #69

1996 Select
Certified #121

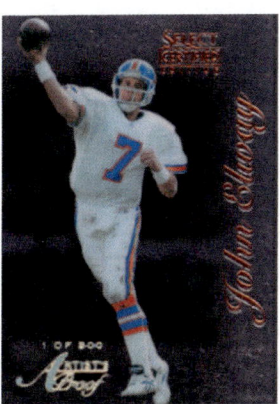

1996 Select Certified
Artist Proof #69

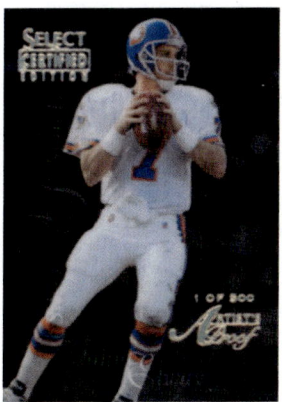

1996 Select Certified
Artist Proof #121

1996 Select
Certified Blue #69

1996 Select
Certified Blue #121

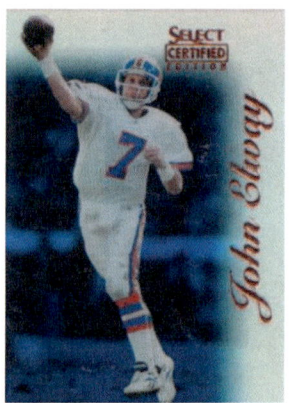

1996 Select Certified
Mirror Blue #69

1996 Select Certified
Mirror Blue #121

1996 Select Certified
Mirror Gold #69

1996 Select Certified
Mirror Gold #121

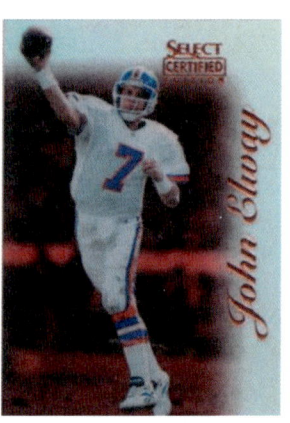

1996 Select Certified
Mirror Red #69

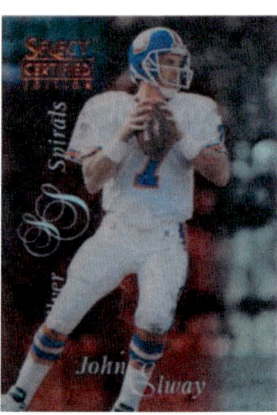

1996 Select Certified
Mirror Red #121

1996 Select Certified
Premium Stock
Mirror Red #69

1996 Select Certified
Premium Stock
Mirror Red #121

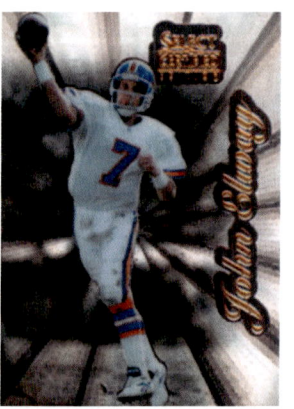

1996 Select Certified
Premium Stock #69

1996 Select Certified
Premium Stock #121

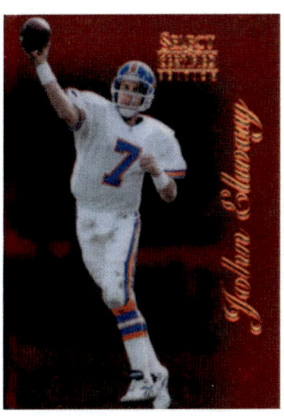

1996 Select Certified
Red #69

1996 Select Certified
Red #121

1996 Select Certified
Thumbs Up #35

1996 Select Prime
Cuts #8

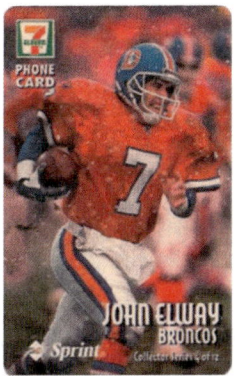

1996 Sprint 7-11
Phone Card #3

1996 Sky Box Impact
#42

1996 Sky Box Impact
Rookies #79

1996 Sky Box Rookies
Draft Board #8

1996 Sky Box Impact
Versa Team #3

1996 Sky Box
Premium #51

1996 Sky Box Premium
Close-Ups #5

1996 Sky Box Premium
Rubies #51

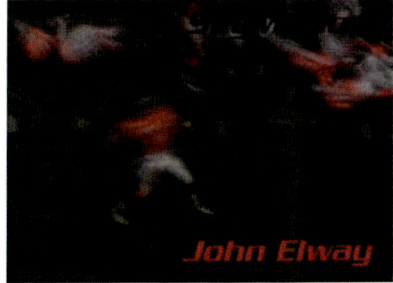

1996 Sky Box Sky Motion #15

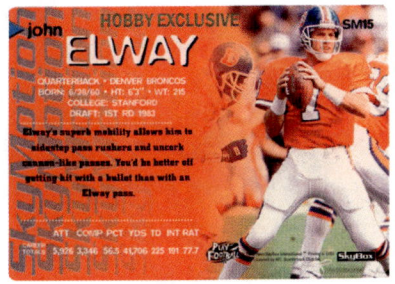

1996 Sky Box Sky Motion Gold #15

1996 SP #99

1996 SP Xplosives #X7

1996 SP Hologram #7

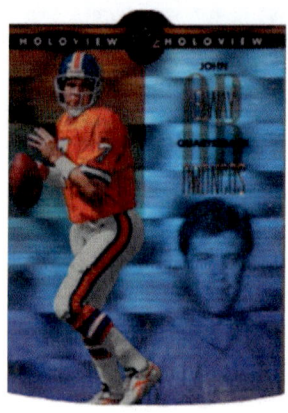

1996 SP Hologram
Die-Cut #7

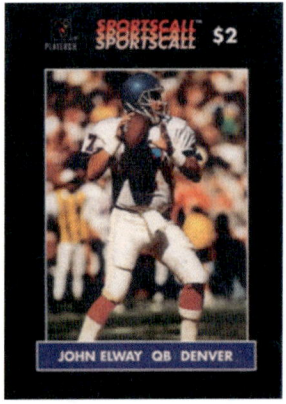

1996 Sporstcall
Phone Call #109

1996 Sports Illustrated
For Kids #437

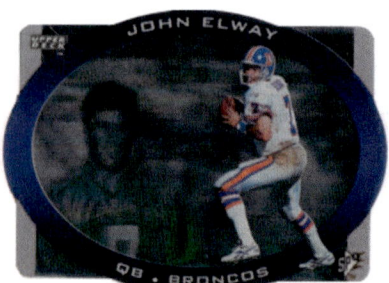

1996 SPX #15

1996 SPX Gold #15

1996 SPX Holofame #HM6

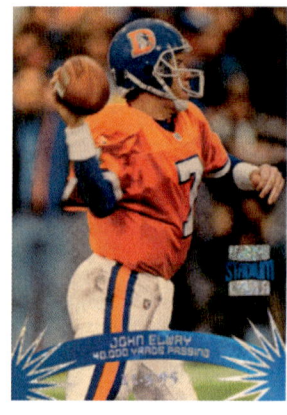

1996 Stadium Club #158

1996 Stadium Club #200

1996 Stadium Club
Dot Matrix #200

1996 Stadium Club
Members Only #158

1996 Stadium Club
Members Only #200

1996 Stadium Club
Match Proof (Rev)
#200

1996 Stadium Club
Photo Gallery #PG17

1996 Stadium Club
Sunday Night
Redemption #3B

1996 Stadium
Star Test Proof

1996 Starting Lineup

1996 Summit #58

1996 Summit #196

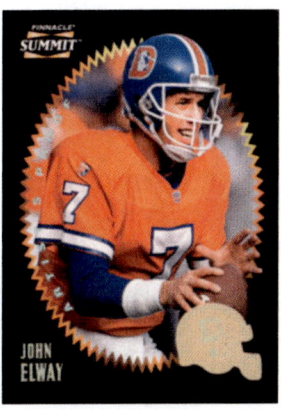

1996 Summit
Artist Proof #58

1996 Summit
Artist Proof #196

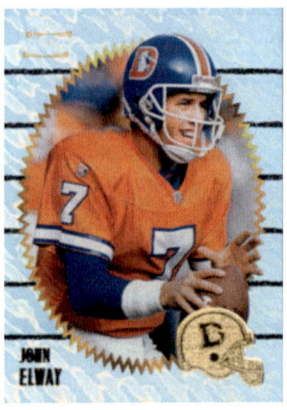

1996 Summit
Ground Zero #58

1996 Summit
Ground Zero #196

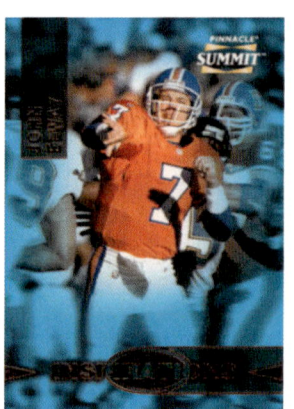

1996 Summit
Inspirations #10

1996 Summit
Premium Stock #58

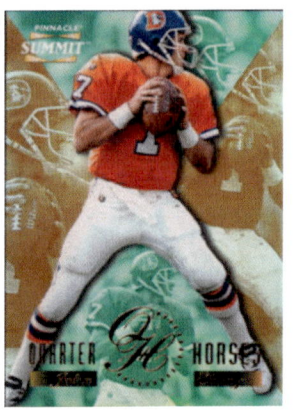

1996 Summit
Premium Stock #196

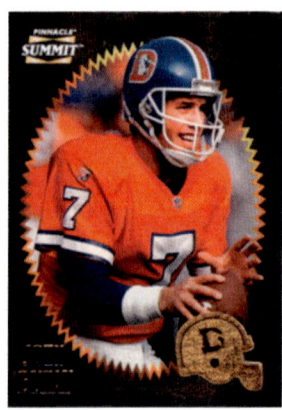

1996 Summit
Silver Foil #58

1996 Summit
Silver Foil #196

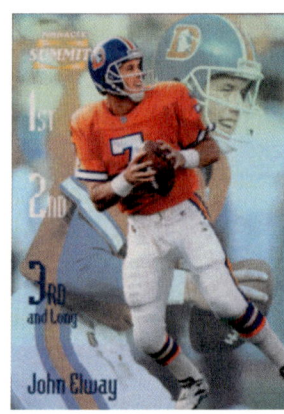

1996 Summit Third
And Long #13

Reverse

1996 Summit Third
And Long Promo #13

1996 Summit Third
And Long Mirage
Prizes #13

1996 Summit Third
And Long Mirage
Redemption #13

1996 Summit
Turf Team #14

1996 Summit
Turf Team Foil #14

1996 Tombstone Pizza
Quarterback Club
Cap #11

1996 Topps Aneheim Dual
Signature

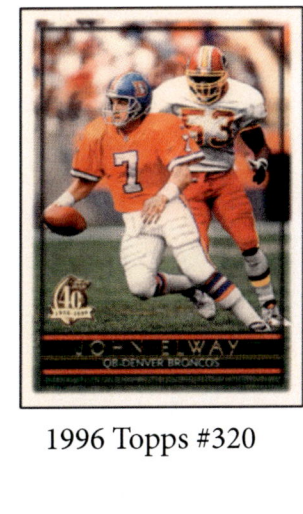

1996 Topps #320

1996 Topps #326

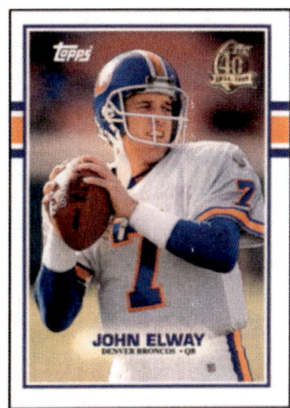

1996 Topps
40th Anniversary
Retros #34

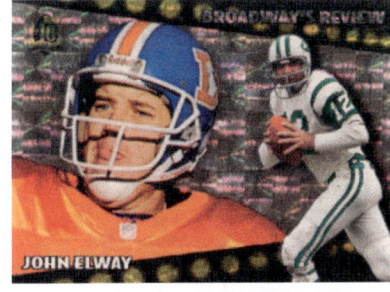

1996 Topps Broadway Reviews #BR9

December 1, 1996

A 34-7 Bronco victory over
Seattle, Elway completed 17/27 passes for 189 yards and 2 touchdowns. He added two rushes for 7 yards
and a score. It was Elway's 125th career victory putting him in first place all-time. (Fran Tarkenton 124)

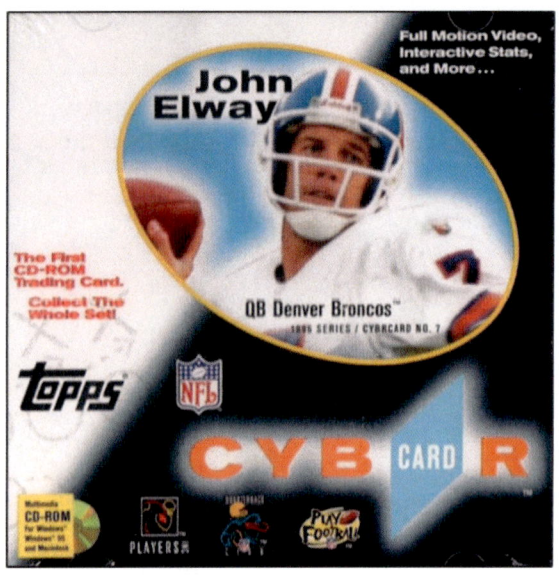

1996 Topps Cyber Disc

1996 Topps Chrome #115

1996 Topps Chrome #133

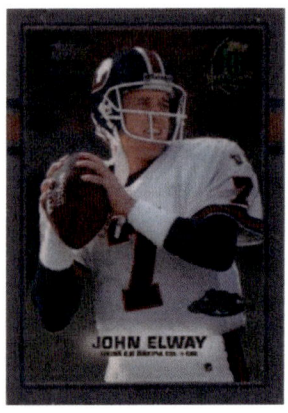

1996 Topps Chrome
40th Anniversary
Retros #34

1996 Topps Chrome
40th Anniversary
Retros Refractor #34

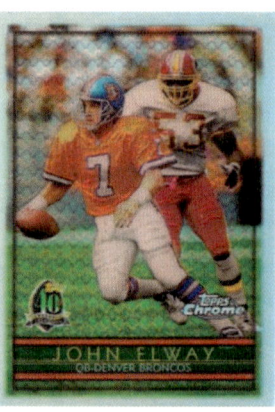

1996 Topps Chrome
Refractor #115

1996 Topps Chrome
Refractor #133

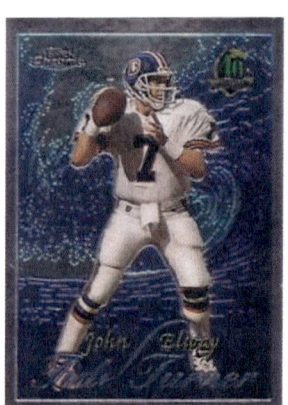

1996 Topps Chrome
Tide Turners #TT15

1996 Topps Chrome
Tide Turners Refractor
#TT15

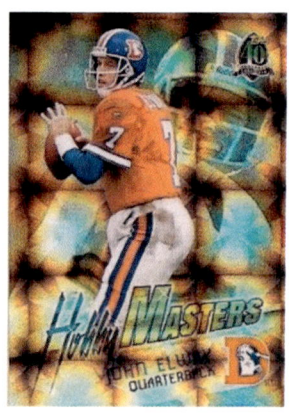

1996 Topps Hobby
Masters #MH20

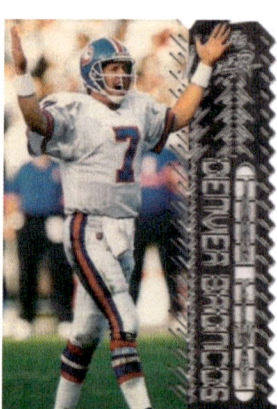

1996 Topps Lasers #65

1996 Topps Lasers
Stadium Star #65

1996 Ultra #45

1996 Ultra
Mr. Momentum #4

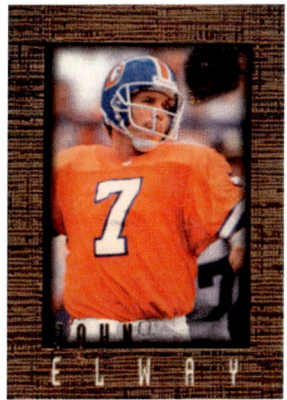

1996 Ultra
Sensations #31

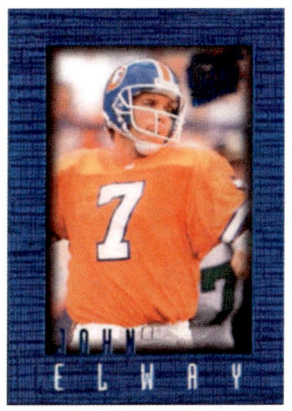

1996 Ultra Sensations
Blue #31

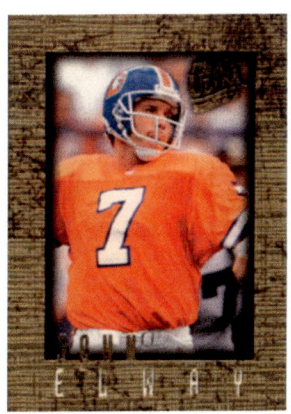

1996 Ultra Sensations
Marble Gold #31

1996 Ultra Sensations
Pewter #31

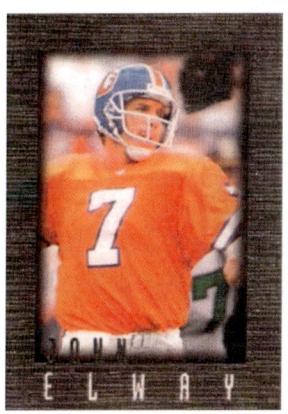

1996 Ultra Sensations
Rainbow #31

1996 Upper Deck #99

1996 Upper Deck
Hot Properties #HT7

1996 Upper Deck Hot
Properties Gold #HT7

1996 Upper Deck
Powerdeck - Predictor #PR6

1996 Upper Deck
Powerdeck - Predictor #PH6

1996 Upper Deck
Pro View #7

1996 Upper Deck
Pro View Gold #7

1996 Upper Deck
Pro View Silver
#7

1996 Upper Deck
Silver #69

1996 Upper Deck Silver
Helmet Club #AW5

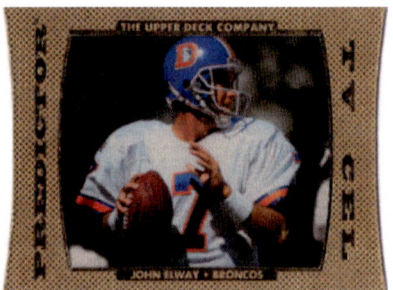

1996 Upper Deck
TV Cells #6

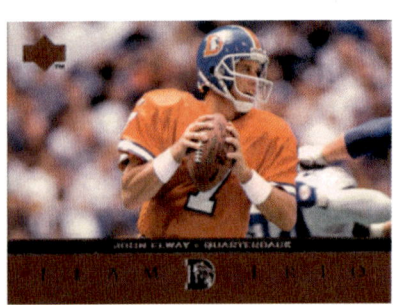

1996 Upper Deck
Team Trio #TT34

1996 Zenith #36

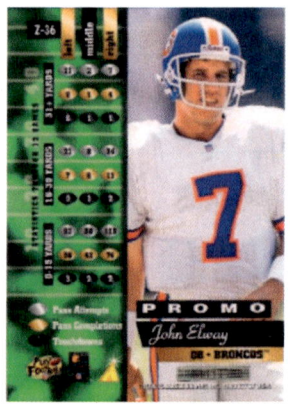

1996 Zenith Promo

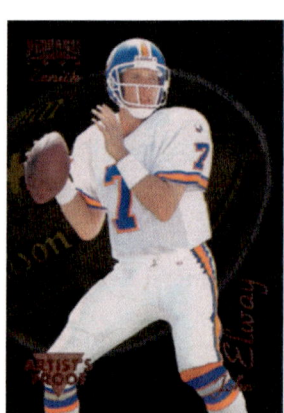

1996 Zenith
Arrtist Proof #36

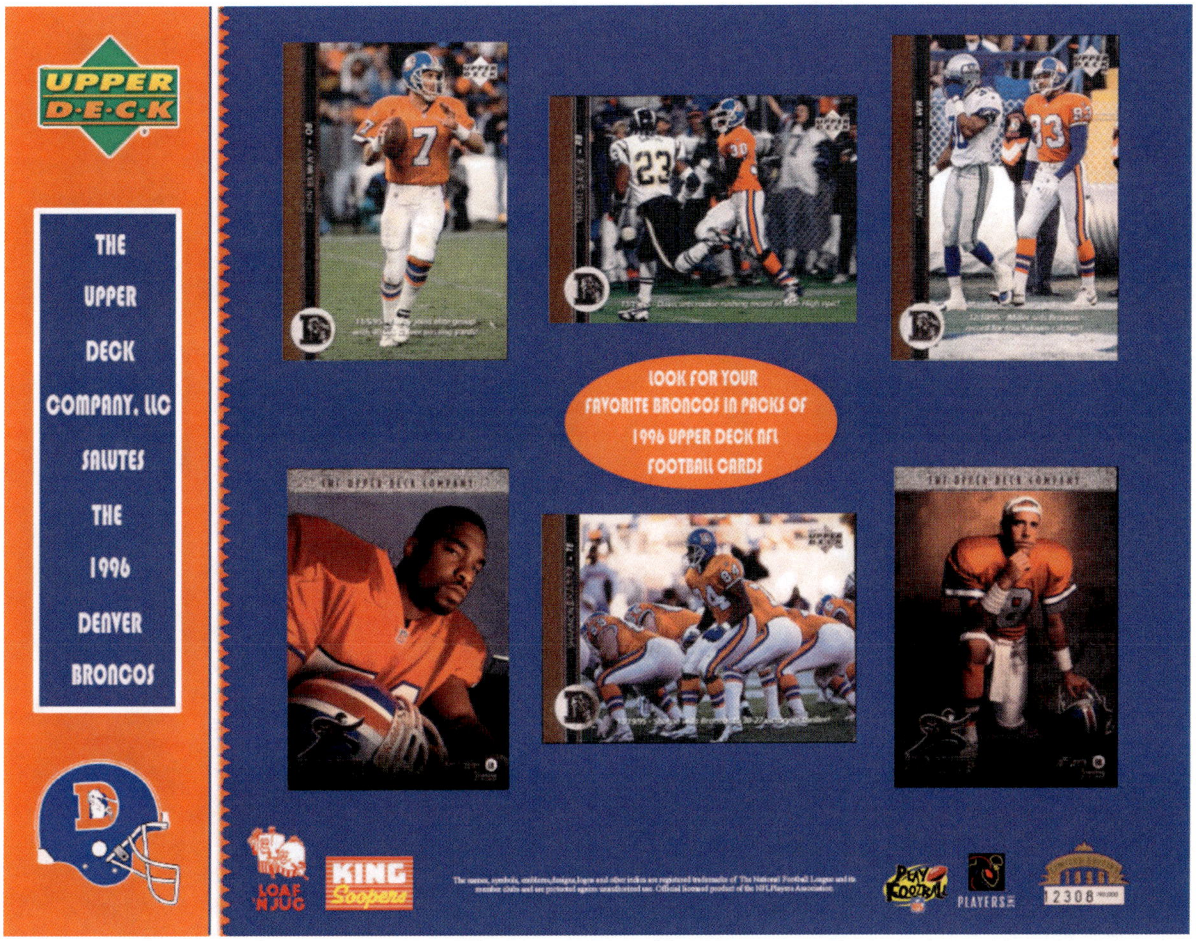

1996 Upper Deck Team Sheet

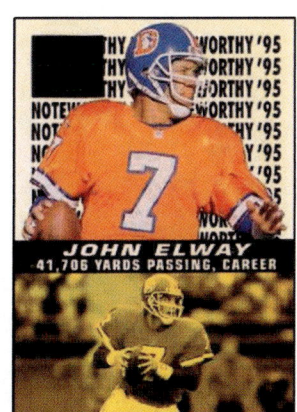

1996 Zenith
Noteworthy 95 #11

1996 Zenith Z Team #16

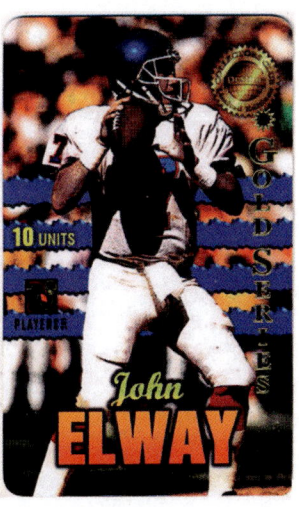

1996 Pro Football Elite
Series Men of Destiny

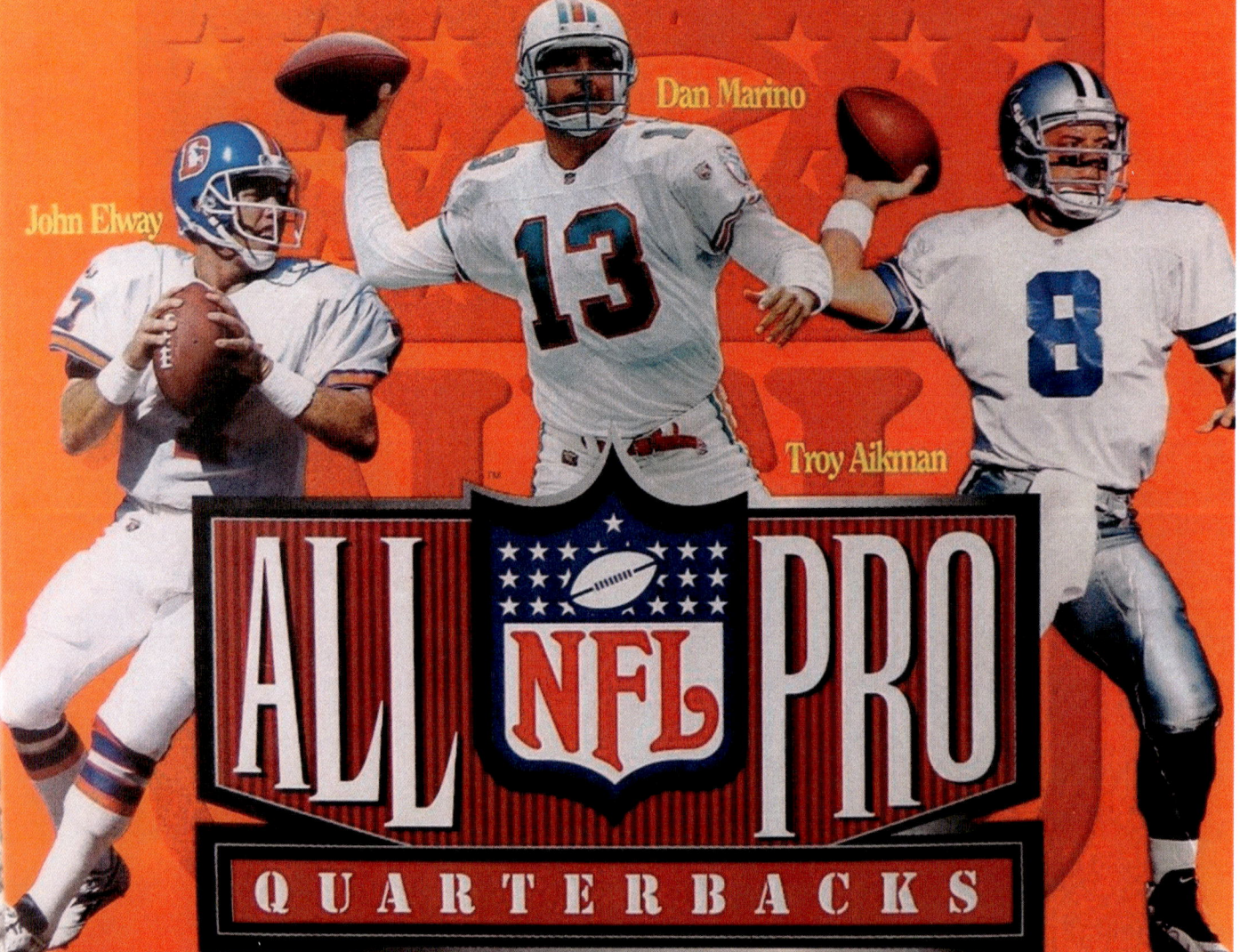

1997

The Broncos unveiled new uniforms in the spring.

They fiinished second in the AFC West with a 12-4 record. In a playoff rematch, Denver defeated Jacksonville 42-17 in the wildcard round. They went on the road to beat Kansas City at Arrowhead Stadium in the divisional round, 14-10. They then beat Pittsburgh at Three River Stadium, 24-21 for the AFC title. Super Bowl XXXII and a date with the NFL Champion Green Bay Packers was next. Denver won its first ever NFL Championship 31-24.

Elway played 16 games, completed 280/502 passes for 3635 yards, and 27 touchdowns. He added 218 rushing yards on 50 carries with one touchdown.

He was selected to his eighth Pro-Bowl.

1997 Action Packed #10

1997 Action Packed
24K Gold #10

1997 Columbia Schedule

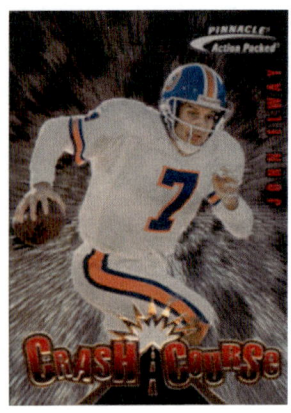

1997 Action Packed
Crash Course #6

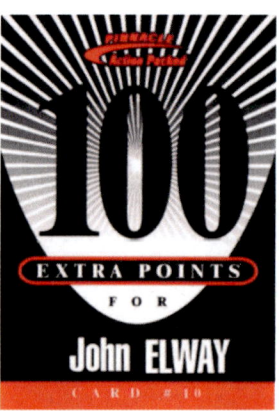

1997 Action Packed
Extra Points #10

1997 Action Packed
First Impression #10

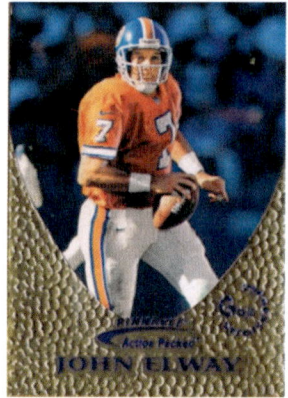

1997 Action Packed
Gold Impression #10

1997 Action Packed
Pinnacle Scoring
Core Preview #7

1997 Black Diamond
#43

1993 Black Diamond
Gold #43

1997 Black Diamond
Title Quest #8

1997 Bowmans Best #60

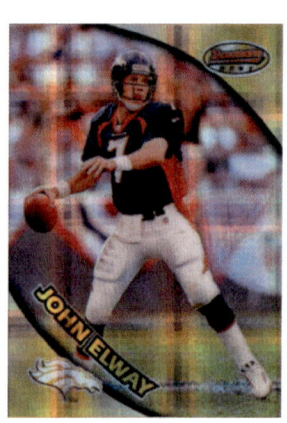

1997 Bowmans Best
Atomic Refractor #60

1997 Bowmans Best
Cuts #BC3

1997 Bowmans Best
Cuts Atomic Refractor
#BC3

1997 Bowmans Best
Cuts Refractor #BC3

1997 Bowmans Best
Mirror Image #MI1

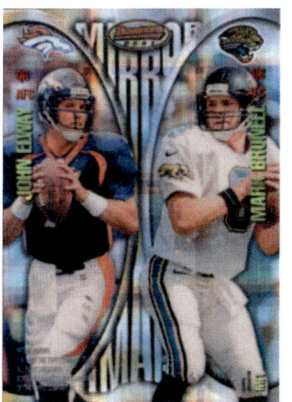

1997 Bowmans Best
Mirror Image Atomic
Refractor #MI1

1997 Bowmans Best
Mirror Image
Refractor #MI1

1997 Bowmans Best
Refractor #60

1997 Bowmans Best
Jumbo #4

1997 Bowmans Best
Jumbo Atomic Refractor #4

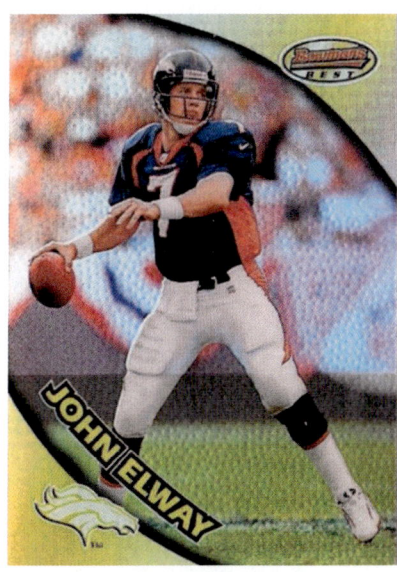

1997 Bowmans Best
Jumbo Refractor #4

1997 Bowmans Best
Jumbo Super Bowl #4

1997 Bowmans Best
Jumbo Super Bowl
Atomic Refractor #4

1997 Bowmans Best
Jumbo Super Bowl
Refractor #4

1997 Broncos Collectors
Choice #DN9

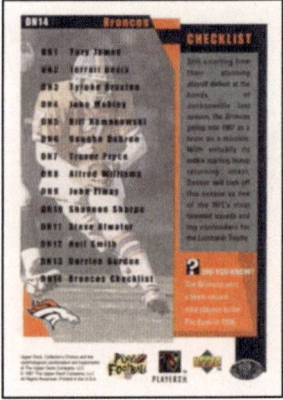

1997 Broncos Collectors
Choice #DN14

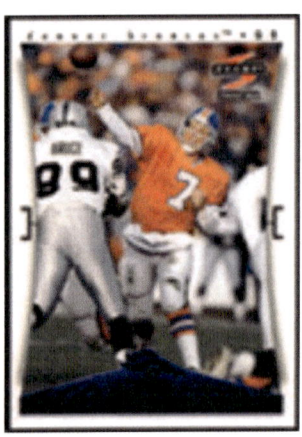

1997 Broncos Score #1

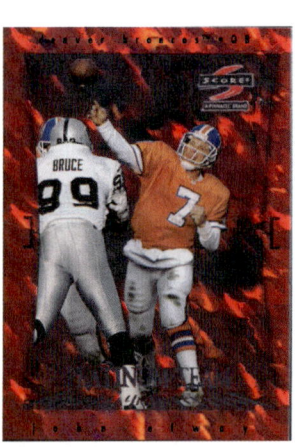

1997 Broncos Score
Platinum #1

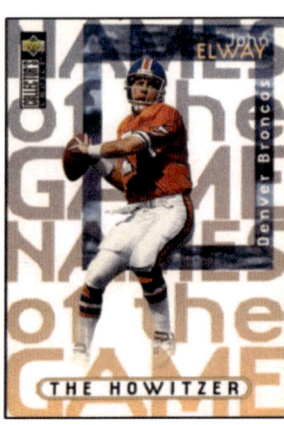

1997 Collectors
Choice #52

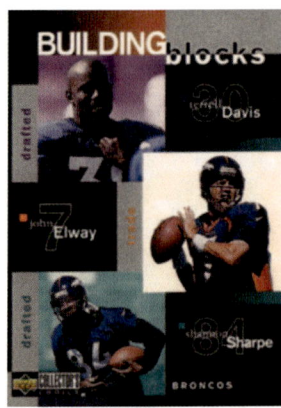

1997 Collectors
Choice #300

1997 Collectors Choice #412

1997 Collectors
Choice Crash The
Game #8A

1997 Collectors
Choice Crash The
Game #8B

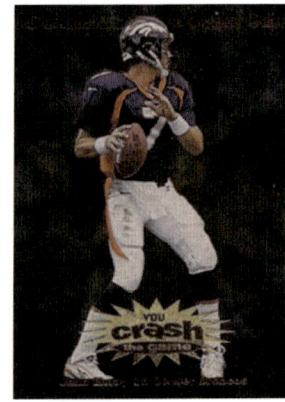

1997 Collectors Choice
Crash The Game
Redemption Prizes #CR8

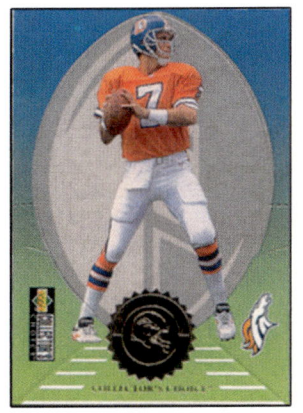

1997 Collectors Choice
Mini-Standee #ST5

1997 Collectors Choice
Star Quest #SQ83

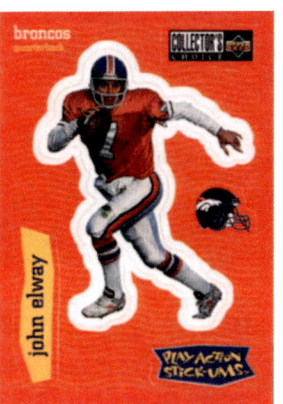

1997 Collectors Choice
Stick-Ums #S17

1997 Collectors Choice
Turf Champions #TC90

1997 Collectors Choice
Turf Champions Jumbo
#TC90

1997 Collectors Edge
Extreme #49

1997 Collectors Edge
Extreme Super Bowl
Diamond #49

1997 Collectors Edge
Extreme Finess #11

1997 Collectors Edge
Extreme Foil #P49

1997 Collectors Edge
Extreme Frontrunners
#9

1997 Collectors Edge
Extreme Force #13

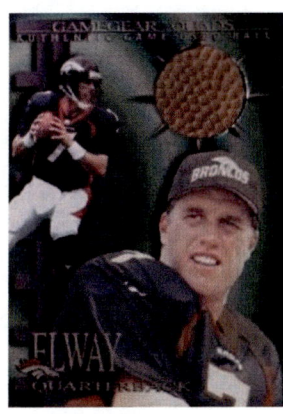

1997 Collectors Edge
Extreme Game Gear
Quads #10A

1997 Collectors Edge Extreme Game Gear Quads #10B (Jersey)

1997 Collectors Edge Extreme Game Gear Quads #10C (Pants)   1997 Costacos Poster Promo

1997 Collectors Edge Extreme Game Gear Quads #10D (Shoe)

1997 Collectors Edge
Masters #76

1997 Collectors Edge
Masters Holofoil #76

1997 Collectors Edge
Masters Nitro #76

1997 Collectors Edge
Masters Night Games #8

1997 Collectors Edge
Masters Night Games
Prisms #8

1997 Collectors Edge
Masters Playoff Game Ball #6

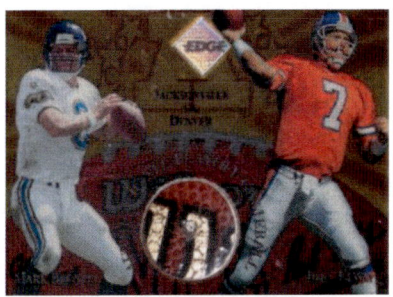

1997 Collectors Edge
Masters Playoff Game
Ball Diamond #6

1997 Collectors Edge
Masters Playoff Game
Ball Gold Logo #6

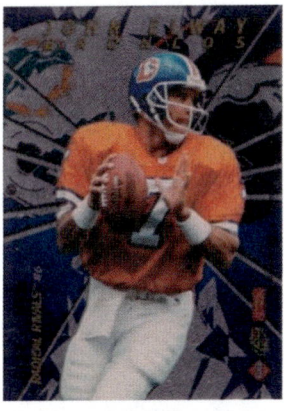

1997 Collectors Edge
Masters Radical Rivals #6

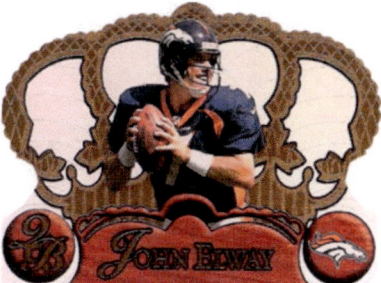

1997 Crown Royal #41

1997 Crown Royal
Blue Holofoil #41

1997 Crown Royale
Cell Fusion #5

1997 Crown Royale
Chalk Talk #5

1997 Crown Royale Cramers
Choice Jumbo #4

1997 Crown Royale
Cramers Choice Jumbo
Purple #4

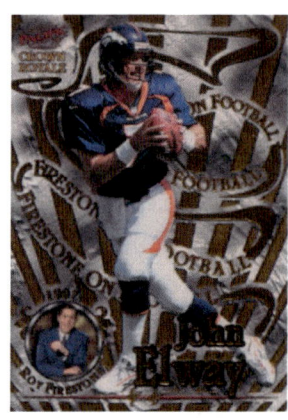

1997 Crown Royale
Firestone On Football #6

1997 Crown Royale
Gold Holofoil #41

1997 Crown Royale
Silver #41

1997 Crown Royale
Pro Bowl Die Cut #5

1997 Costacos Poster Promo

1997 Costacos Poster Promo

1997 Donruss #18

1997 Donruss Elite #13

1997 Donruss Elite
Gold #13

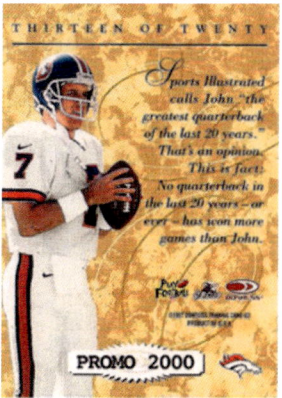

1997 Donruss Elite
Promo #13

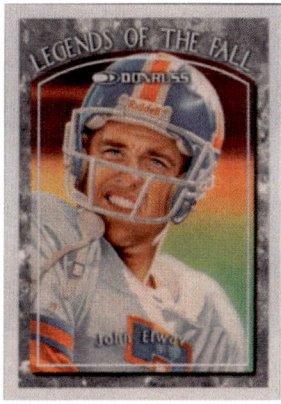

1997 Donruss Legends
of the Fall #3

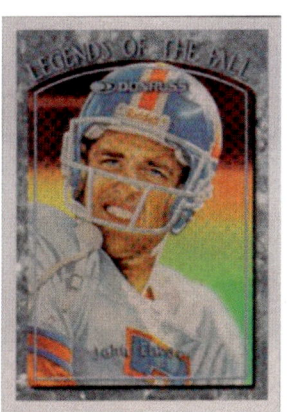

1997 Donruss Legends
of the Fall Canvas #3

 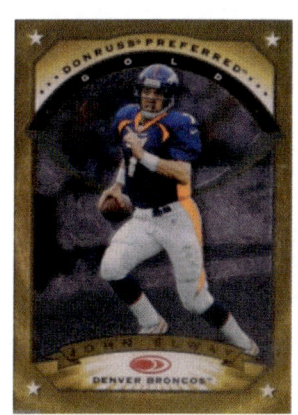

1997 Donruss Passing Grade #6

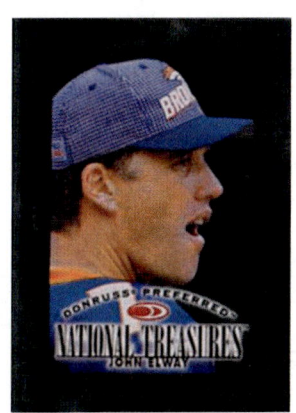

1997 Donruss Preferred #34

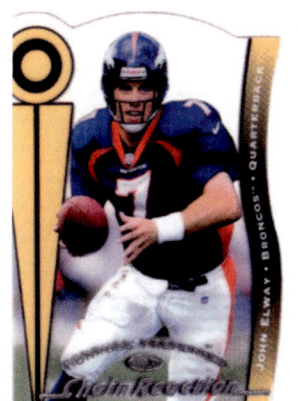

1997 Donruss Preferred
Cut to the Chase #142

1997 Donruss Preferred
Chain Reaction #5A

1997 Donruss Preferred
Cut To The Chase #34

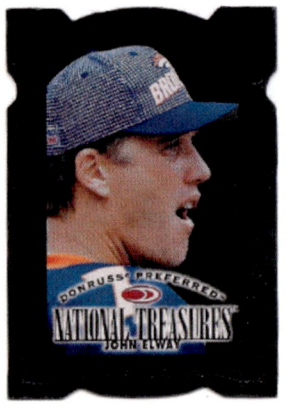

1997 Donruss Preferred
Cut To The Chase #142

1997 Donruss Preferred
Double Wide Tins #9

1997 Donruss Press Proof
Gold Die Cut #18

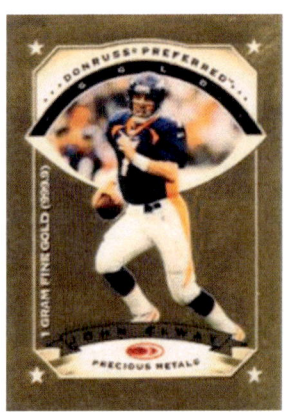

1997 Donruss Preferred
Prescious Metals #7

1997 Donruss Press
Proofs Silver #18

1997 Donruss Preferred
Stare Masters #19

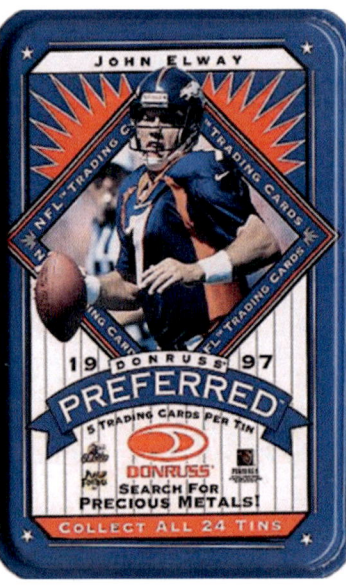

1997 Donruss Preferred
Tins #7

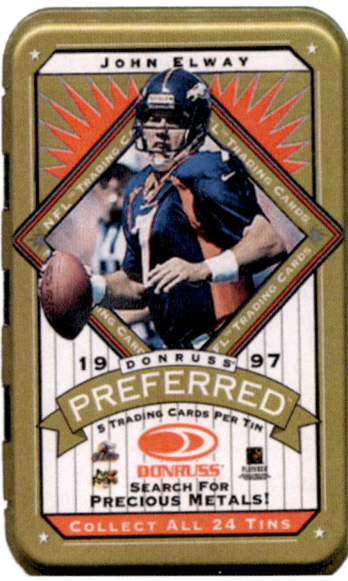

1997 Donruss Preferred
Tins Gold #7

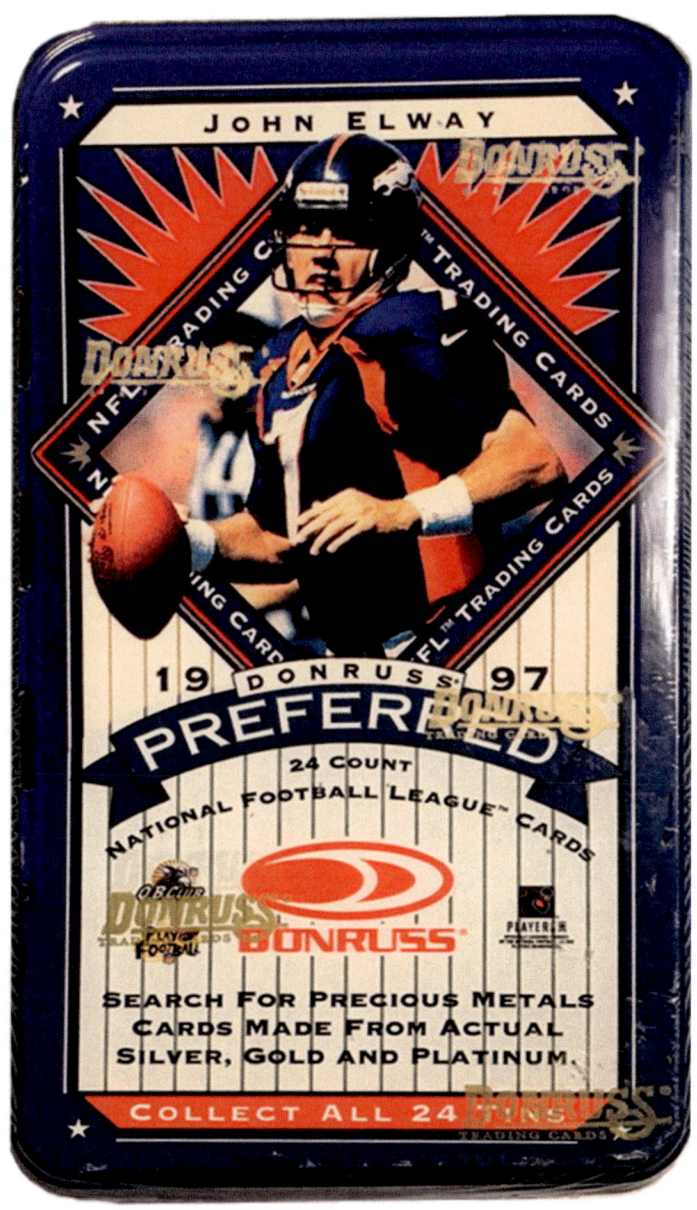

1997 Donruss Preferred
Tins Blue Box #7

1997 Donruss Preferred
Tins Gold Box #7

1997 Donruss Preferred
Tins Silver #7

1997 Donruss Preferred - Double-Wide Tins

1997 Donruss Zoning
Commission #8

1997 E-X2000 #39

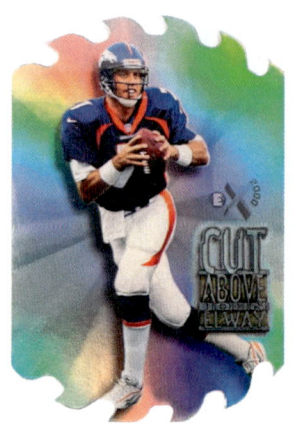

1997 E-X2000
A Cut Above #8

1997 E-X 2000
Essential Credentials #39

1997 Excalibur #39

1997 Excalibur 22K
Knights #2

1997 Excalibur 22K
Knights Black Magnum
#2

1997 Excalibur 22K
Knights Supreme Edge
#32

1997 Excalibur Game
Gear Helmets #4

1997 Excalibur
Maraduers #16

1997 Excalibur
Maraduers
Supreme Edge #16
#/50

1997 Excalibur
National #7

1997 Excalibur Non Foil
Parallel #39

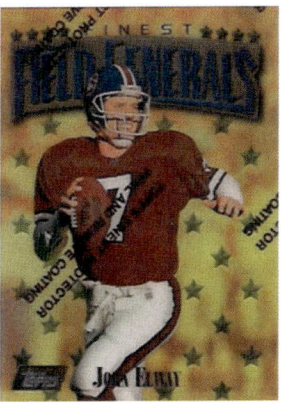

1997 Finest #170

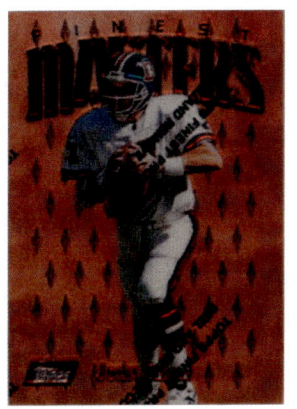

1997 Finest #210

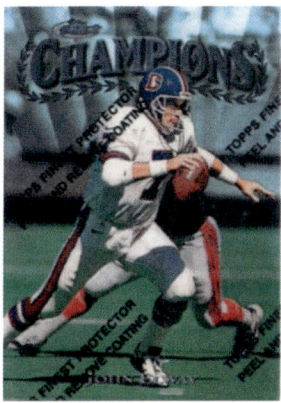

1997 Finest #300

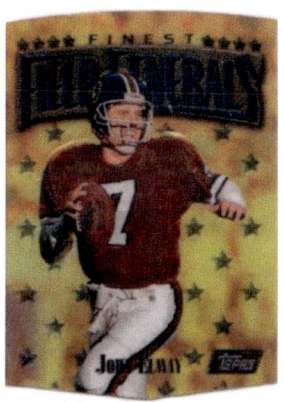

1997 Finest Embossed
#170

1997 Finest Embossed
#300

1997 Finest Embossed
Refractor #170

1997 Finest Embossed
Refractor #300

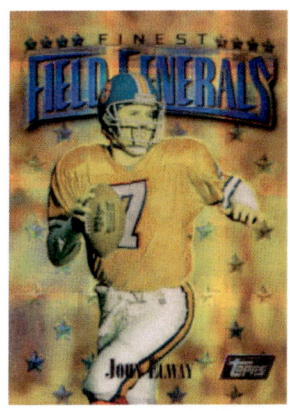

1997 Finest Refractor
#170

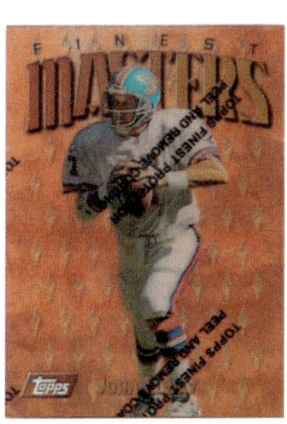

1997 Finest Refractor
#210

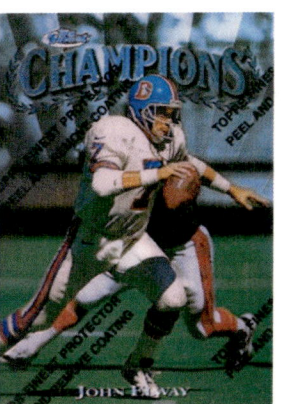

1997 Finest Refractor
#300

1997 Flair Showcase
Midas Touch #MT2

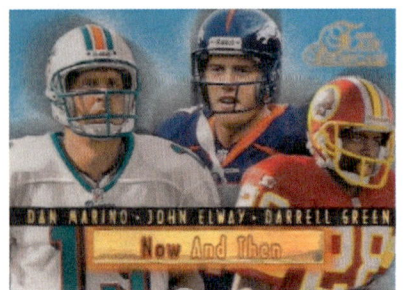

1997 Flair Showcase
Now and Then #NT1

1997 Flair Showcase
Row 0 #7

1997 Flair Showcase
Row 1 #7 Grace

1997 Flair Showcase
Row 2 #7 Style

1997 Flair Showcase
Legacy Collection #A7

1997 Flair Showcase
Legacy Collection #B7

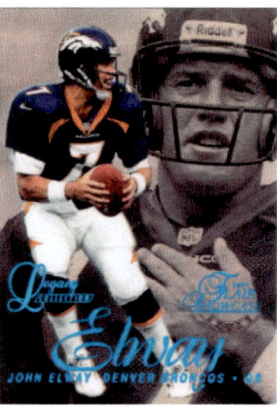

1997 Flair Showcase
Legacy Collection #C7

1997 Flair Showcase
Legacy Collection
Masterpiece #A7

1997 Flair Showcase
Legacy Collection
Masterpiece #A7

1997 Flair Showcase
Legacy Collection
Masterpiece #C7

1997 Fleer #37

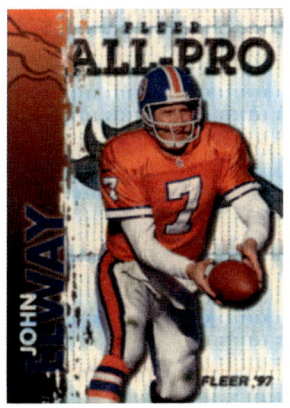

1997 Fleer All-Pros #6

1997 Fleer Crystal Silver #37

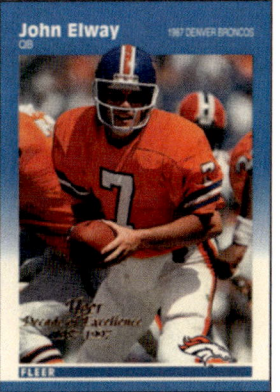

1997 Fleer Decade of Excellence #3

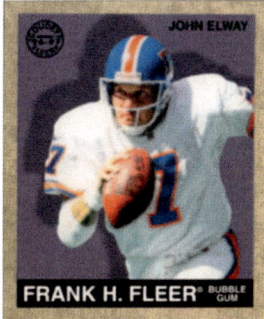

1997 Fleer Goudey #15

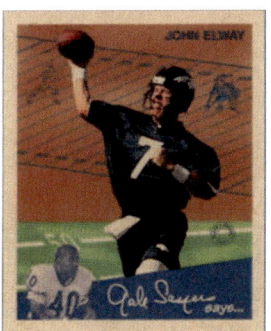

1997 Fleer Goudey II #7

1997 Fleer Goudey II Gridiron Greats #7

1997 Fleer Goudey Vintage Goudey #4

1997 Fleer Goudey Gridiron Greats #15

1997 Fleer Goudey Tittle Says #7

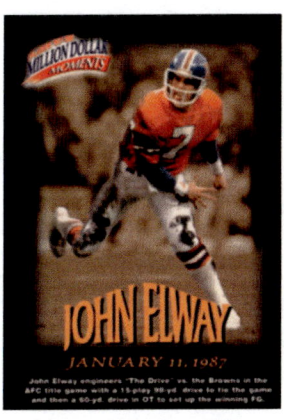

1997 Fleer Million Dollar Moments #8

1997 Fleer Thrill Seekers #4

1997 Fleer Tiffany Blue #37

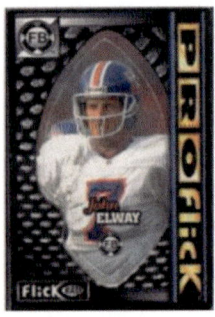

1997 FlickBall #13

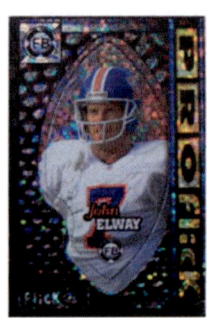

1997 FlickBall Foil #13

1997 FlickBall
Quarterback Greats #QB4

1997 FlickBall
Quarterback Club #4

1997 Leaf #9

1997 Leaf #192

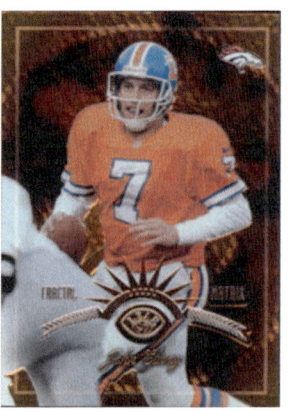

1997 Leaf Fractal
Matrix #9

1997 Leaf Fractal
Matrix #192

1997 Leaf Fractal
Matrix Die Cut #9

1997 Leaf Fractal
Matrix Die Cut #192

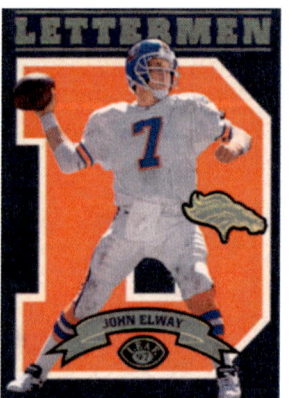

1997 Leaf Letterman #7

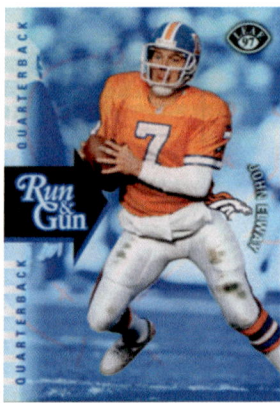

1997 Leaf Run and
Gun #3

1997 Leaf Signature #35

1997 Leaf Signature Autographs #35

1997 Leaf Signature First Down Marker #35

1997 Leaf Signature Autographs First Down Marker #35

1997 Leaf Signature
Proof #9

1997 Leaf Signature
Proof #192

1997 Metal Universe
Marvel Metals #8

1997 Metal Universe #88

1997 Metal Universe
Prescious Metals
Gems #88

1997 Metal Universe
Prescious Metals
Green Gems #88

1997 Metal Universe
Titanium #10

1997 Motion Vision #15

1997 NFL Properties
Mini Sticker

1997 Motion Vision Jumbo #SS3

1997 NFL Properties

1997 Cleo Valentines

1997 Pacific #11

1997 Pacific Big
Numbers Die Cut #6

1997 Pacific Card
Supials #8

1997 Pacific Card
Supials Small #8

1997 Pacific Copper
#117

1997 Pacific Cramers Choice #4

1997 Pacific Dynagon #43

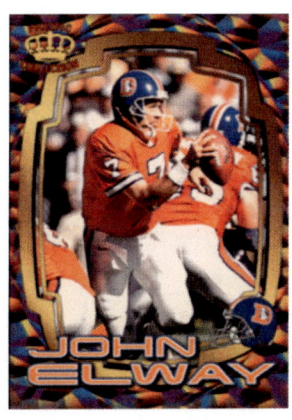

1997 Pacific Dynagon
Best Kept Secret #60

1997 Pacific Dynagon
Copper #43

1997 Pacific Dynagon
Careers #3

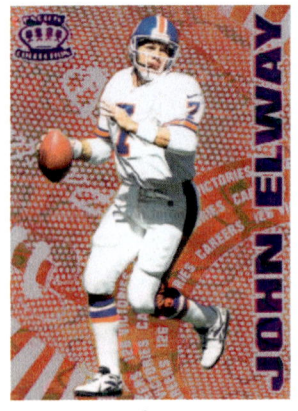

1997 Pacific Dynagon
Careers Holofoil Gold #43

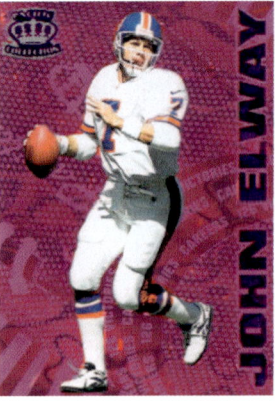

1997 Pacific Dynagon
Careers Purple #3

1997 Pacific Dynagon
Player of the Week #5

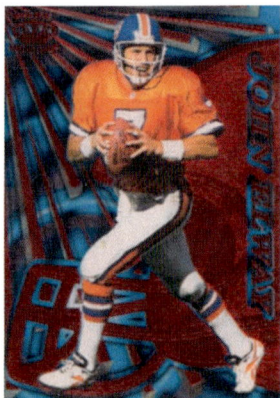

1997 Pacific Dynagon
Red #143

1997 Pacific Dynagon
Royal Connections #6A

1997 Pacific Dynagon
Silver #43

1997 Pacific Team Checklist #9

1997 Pacific Dynagon
Tandems #9

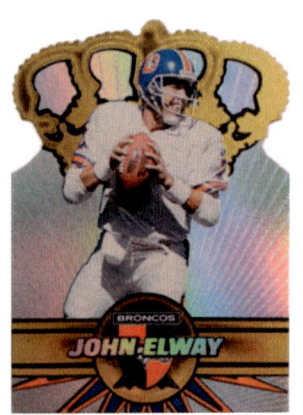

1997 Pacific Dynagon
Gold Crown Die Cuts #10

1997 Pacific Invincable
Copper #44

1997 Pacific Invincable
Copper #44

1997 Pacific Invincable
Canton, Ohio #3

1997 Pacific Invincable
Moments In Time #5

1997 Pacific Invincable
Platinum Blue #44

1997 Pacific Invincable
Pop Card #4

1997 Pacific Invincable
Pop Card Prizes #4

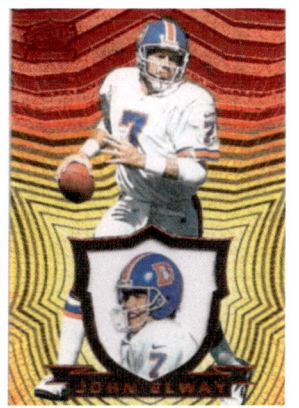

1997 Pacific Invincable
Red #44

1997 Pacific Invincable
Silver #44

1997 Pacific Invincable
Smash Mouth #7

1997 Pacific Invincable
Smash Mouth Xtra #7

1997 Pacific Philadelphia
#93

1997 Pacific Philadelphia
Copper #53

1997 Pacific Philadelphia
Gold #53

1997 Pacific Philadelphia
Heart of the Game #6

1997 Pacific Philadelphia
Milestone #6

1997 Pacific Philadelphia
Photo Engravings #8

1997 Pacific
Philadelphia
Red #53

1997 Pacific
Philadelphia
Silver #53

1997 Pacific Platinum
Blue #117

1997 Pacific Red
#117

1997 Pacific Silver
#117

1997 Pacific The
Zone #5

1997 Pinnacle #9

1997 Pinnacle #191

1997 Pinnacle #200

1997 Pinnacle Artist
Proof #P9

1997 Pinnacle Artist
Proof #P94

1997 Pinnacle Certified
#10

1997 Pinnacle Certified
Certified Team #13

1997 Pinnacle Certified
Certified Team Gold #13

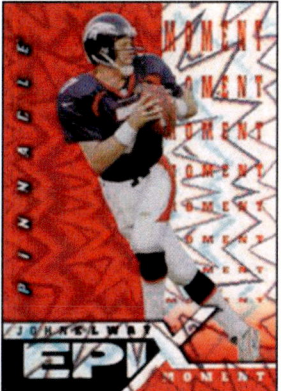

1997 Pinnacle Certified
Epix Moment #E20

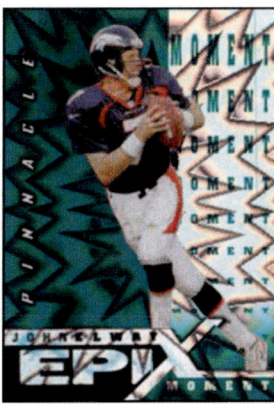

1997 Pinnacle Certified
Epix Moment Emerald #E20

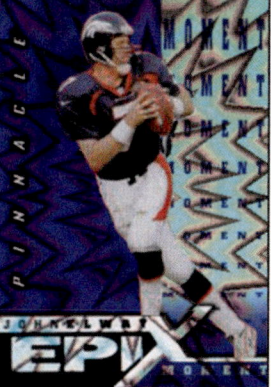

1997 Pinnacle Certified
Epix Moment Purple #E20

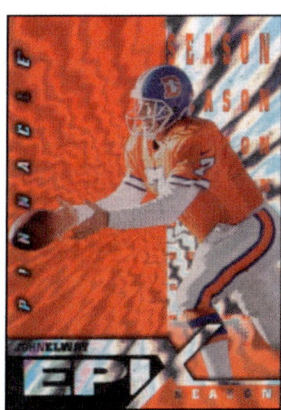

1997 Pinnacle Certified
Epix Season #E20

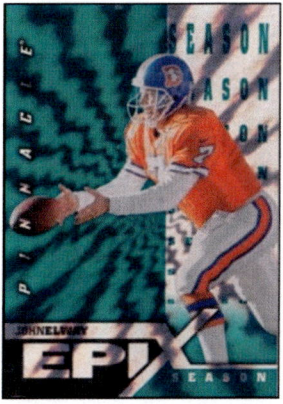

1997 Pinnacle Certified
Epix Season Emerald #E20

1997 Pinnacle Certified
Epix Season Purple #E20

1997 Pinnacle Certified
Epix Game #E20

1997 Pinnacle Certified
Epix Game Emerald #E20

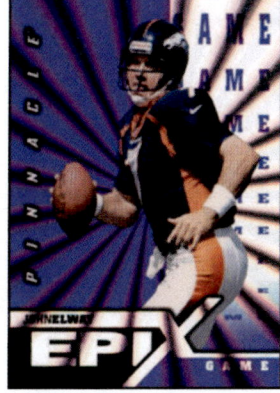

1997 Pinnacle Certified
Epix Game Purple #E20

1997 Pinnacle Certified
Mirror Blue #10

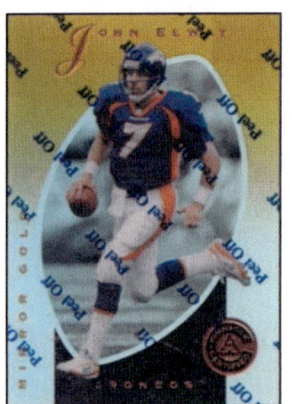

1997 Pinnacle Certified
Mirror Gold #10

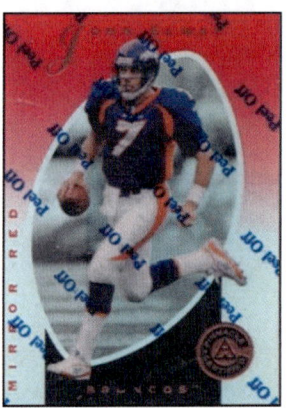

1997 Pinnacle Certified
Mirror Red #10

1997 Pinnacle Certified
Promo #10 Reverse

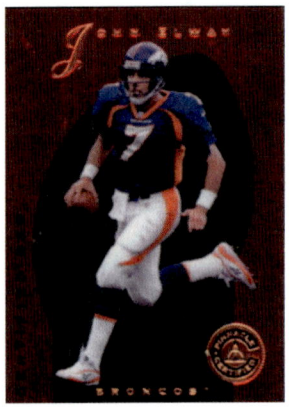

1997 Pinnacle Certified
Red #10

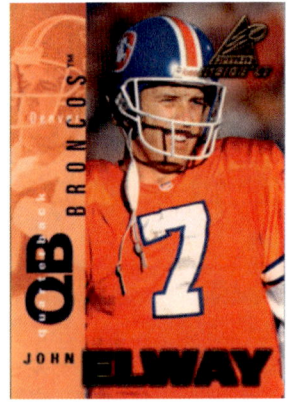

1997 Pinnacle Inside #8

1997 Pinnacle
Inscriptions #7

1997 Pinnacle
Inscriptions #35

1997 Pinnacle
Inscriptions
Artist Proof #7

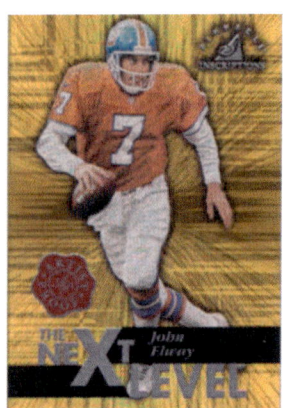

1997 Pinnacle
Inscriptions
Artist Proof #35

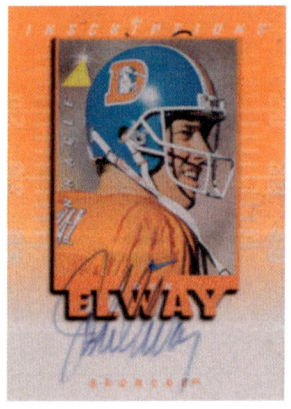

1997 Pinnacle
Inscriptions
Autographs #8

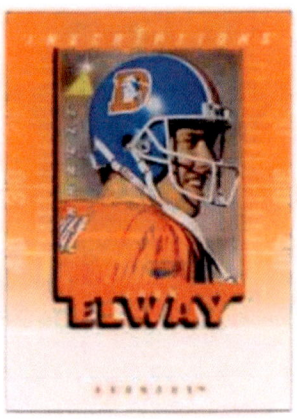

1997 Pinnacle
Inscriptions
Unlisted Non-Signed

1997 Pinnacle Inscriptions
Challenge Collection #7

1997 Pinnacle Inscriptions
Challenge Collection #35

1997 Pinnacle Inscriptions
Fourth And Goal #9

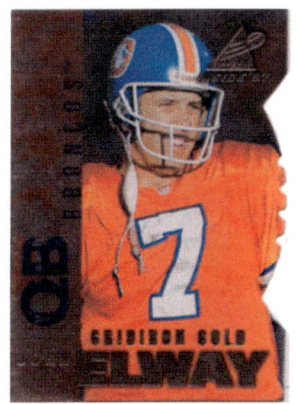

1997 Pinnacle Inscriptions
Grid Iron Gold #8

1997 Pinnacle Inscriptions
V2 #V5

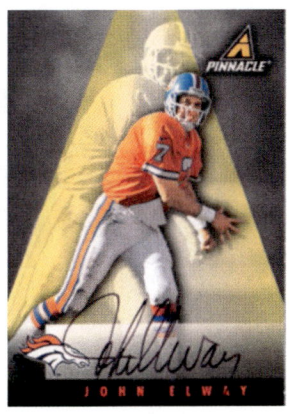

1997 Pinnacle Inside
Autographs #8

1997 Pinnacle Inside
Silver Lining #8

1997 Pinnacle Inscriptions
Inside Cans #21

1997 Pinnacle Inscriptions
Cans Gold #21

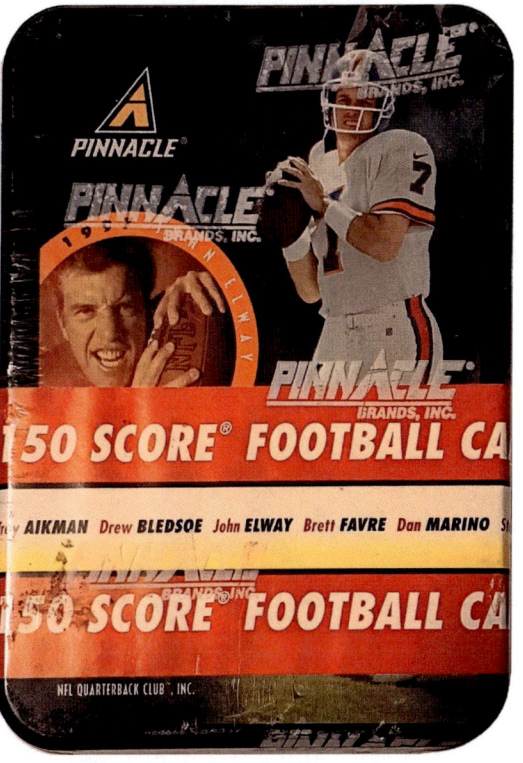

1997 Pinnacle 150 Card Tin

1997 Pinnacle Mint #9

1997 Pinnacle Mint #30

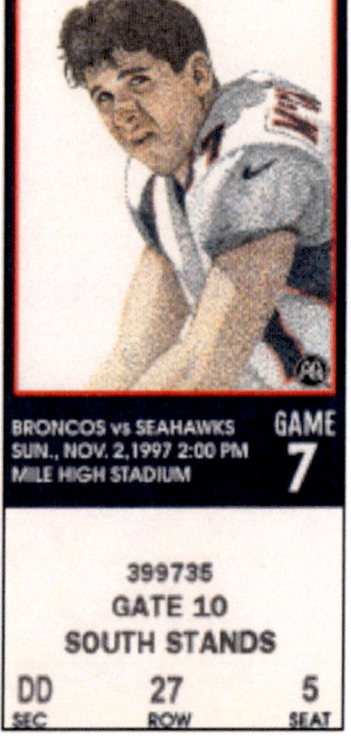

November 2, 1997

A 30-27 victory over Seattle, Elway completed 19/30 passes for 252 yards, and 2 toucdowns. He was named NFL Player of the Week.

1997 Pinnacle Mint Gold Team Pinnacle #9

1997 Pinnacle Mint Gold Team Pinnacle #30

1997 Pinnacle Mint Silver Team Pinnacle #9

1997 Pinnacle Mint Silver Team Pinnacle #30

1997 Pinnacle Mint Coins

Brass

Gold Plate

Gold Proof

Nickel

Silver Proof

Solid Silver

Solid Gold

1997 Pinnacle Power Pack
Jumbo #9

1997 Pinnacle
Press Plate #9

1997 Pinnacle
Press Plate #191

1997 Pinnacle
Press Plate #200

1997 Pinnacle
Rembrandt #3

1997 Pinnacle
Rembrandt Gold #3

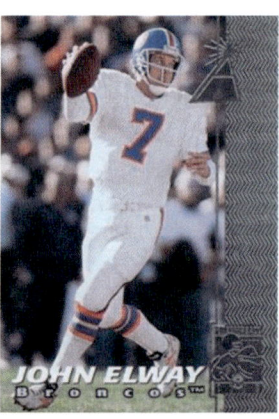

1997 Pinnacle
Rembrandt Silver #3

1997 Pinnacle
Scoring Core #17

1997 Team Pinnacle #4

1997 Pinnacle Team
Pinnacle Mirrors #4

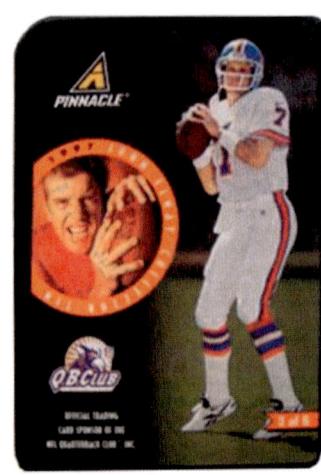

1997 Pinnacle Tins #3

1997 Pinnacle Totally
Certified Platinum Blue
#10

1997 Pinnacle Totally
Certified Platinum
Gold #10

1997 Pinnacle Totally
Certified Platinum Red
#10

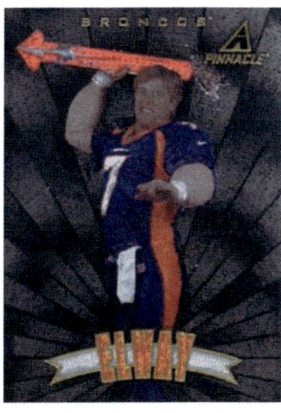

1997 Pinnacle Trophy
Collection #P9

1997 Pinnacle Trophy
Collection #P94

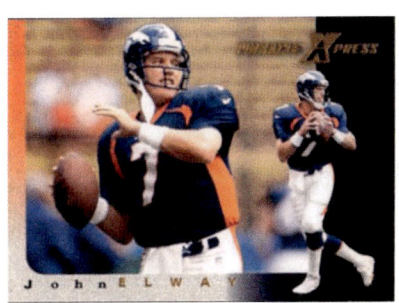

1997 Pinnacle X-Press #P4

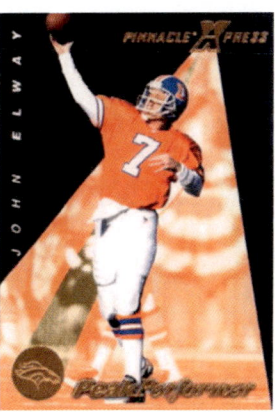

1997 Pinnacle X-Press
#P145

1997 Pinnacle X-Press
Autumn Warriors #4

1997 Pinnacle X-Press
Autumn Warriors #145

1997 Pinnacle X-Press
Bombs Away #7

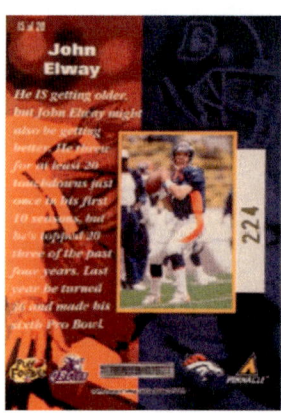

1997 Pinnacle X-Press
Divide and Conquer #15

Reverse

1997 Pinnacle X-Press
Divide and Conquer
Promo #15

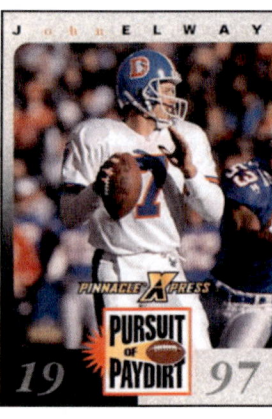

1997 Pinnacle X-Press
Metal Works #9

1997 Pinnacle X-Press
Metal Works Gold #9

1997 Pinnacle X-Press
Metal Works Silver #9

1997 Pinnacle X-Press
Persuit of Paydirt #22

1997 Playoff Absolute #200

1997 Playoff Absolute
Bronze Redemption #200

1997 Playoff Absolute Chip Shots #200

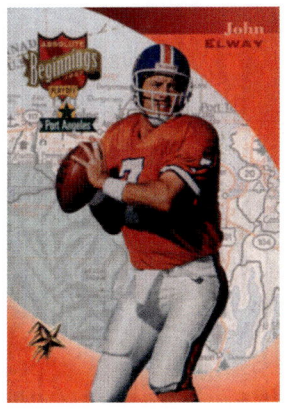

1997 Playoff Absolute
Gold Redemption #200

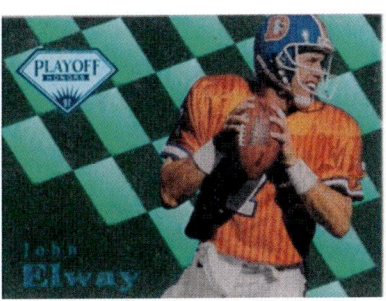

1997 Playoff Absolute
Honors #PH9

1997 Playoff Absolute
Leather Quads #6

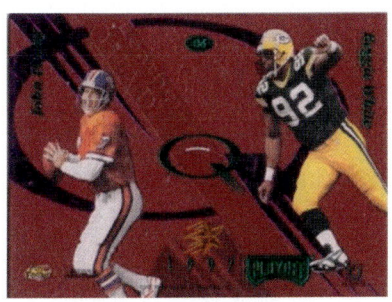

1997 Playoff Absolute Leather
Quads Gold Redemption #6

1997 Playoff Absolute
Pennants #187

1997 Playoff Absolute Pennants
Gold Redemption #187

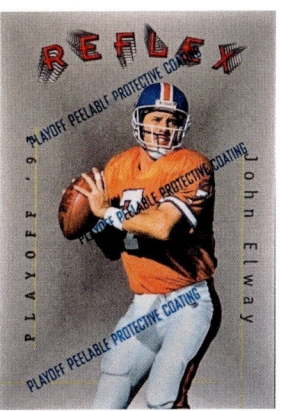

1997 Playoff Absolute
Reflex #19

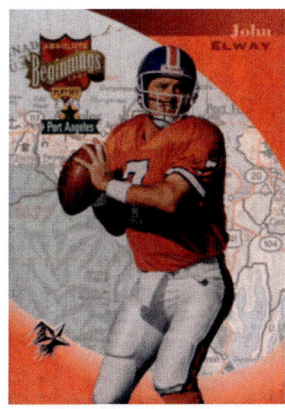

1997 Playoff Absolute
Silver Redemption #200

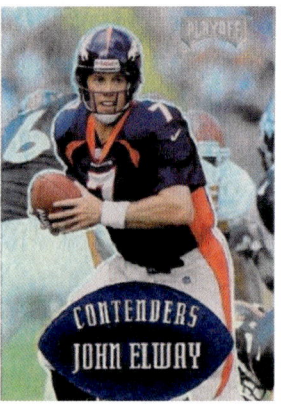

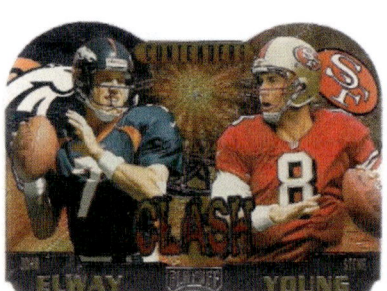

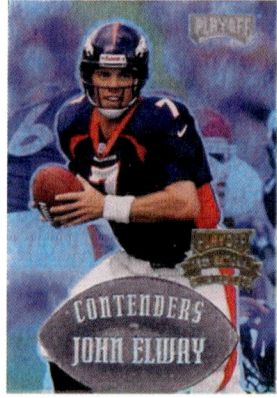

1997 Playoff
Contenders #43

1997 Playoff Contenders
Blue #43

1997 Playoff Contenders
Clash #4

1997 Playoff Contenders
National Redemption

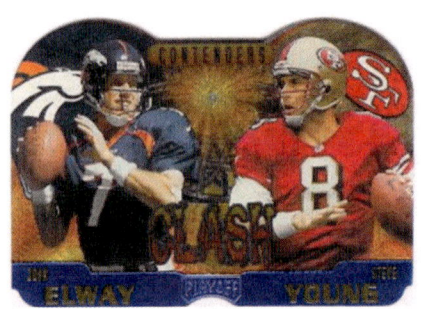

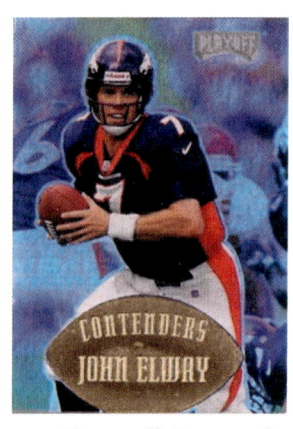

1997 Playoff Contenders
Clash Blue #4

1997 Plauyoff Contenders
Gold #43

1997 Playoff Contnders
Leather Helmet Die Cut #13

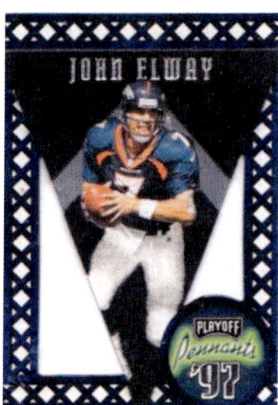

1997 Playoff Contnders
Leather Helmet Die Cut
Blue #13

1997 Playoff Contnders
Leather Helmet Die Cut
Red #13

1997 Playoff Contenders
Pennant Black #5

1997 Playoff Contenders
Pennant Blue #5

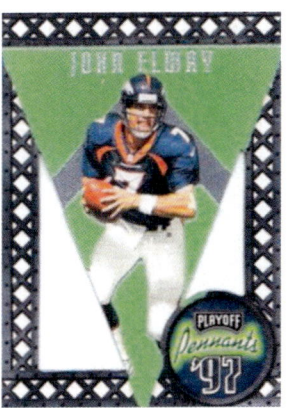

1997 Playoff Contenders
Pennant Green #5

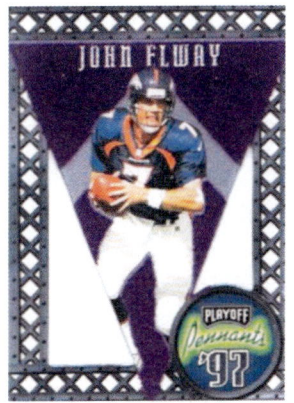

1997 Playoff Contenders
Pennant Purple #5

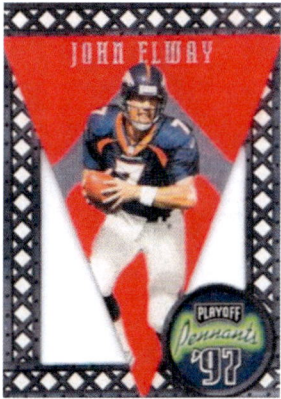

1997 Playoff Contenders
Pennant Red #5

1997 Playoff Contenders
Plaque #27

1997 Playoff Contenders
Plaque Blue #27

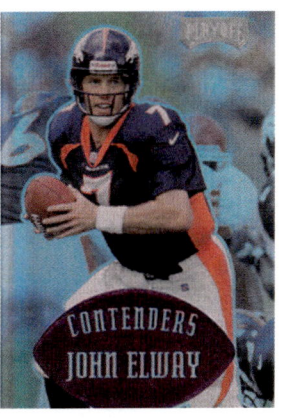

1997 Playoff Contenders
Red #43

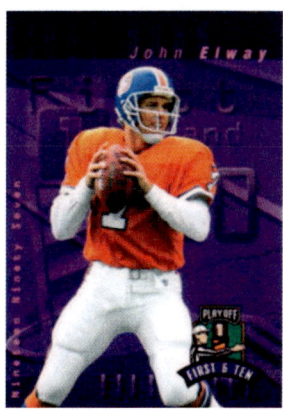

1997 Playoff
First and Ten #200

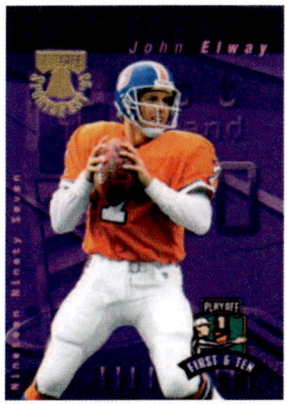

1997 Playoff
First and Ten
Sportsfest Promo

1997 Playoff
First and Ten
Hot Persuit #19

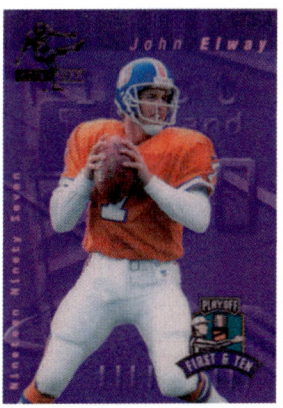

1997 Playoff
First and Ten
Kickoff #200

1997 Playoff
First and Ten
Kickoff Sportsfest
Promo #200

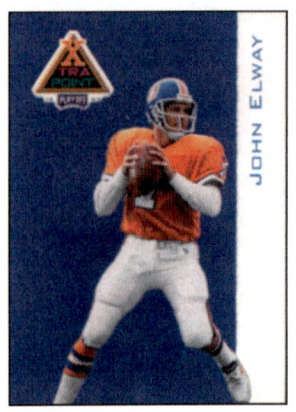

1997 Playoff First and Ten X-Tra Point Blue #XP5

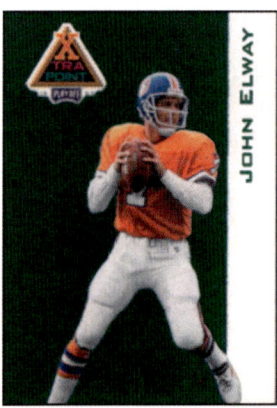

1997 Playoff First and Ten X-Tra Point Green #XP5

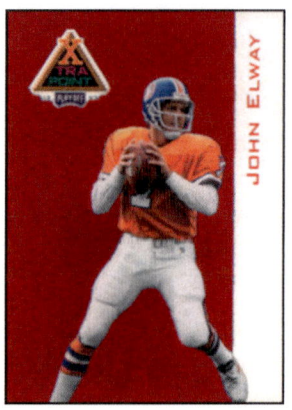

1997 Playoff First and Ten X-Tra Point Red #XP5

1997 Playoff First and Ten X-Tra Point Yellow #XP5

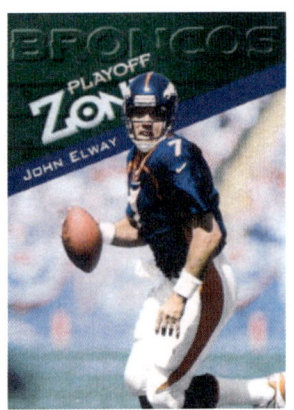

1997 Playoff Zone #110

1997 Playoff Zone Close Ups #7

1997 Playoff Zone Close Ups Gold #7

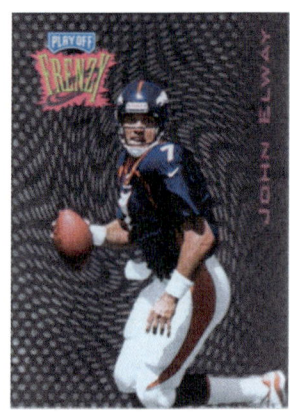

1997 Playoff Zone Frenzy #5

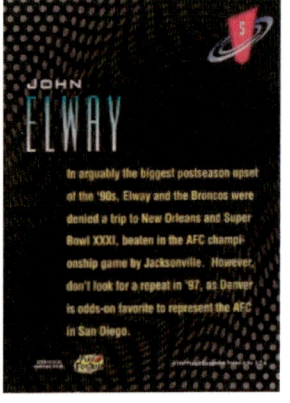

Reverse

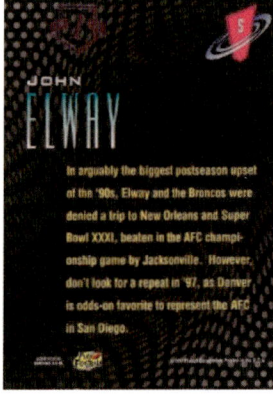

1997 Playoff Zone Frenzy Gold #110

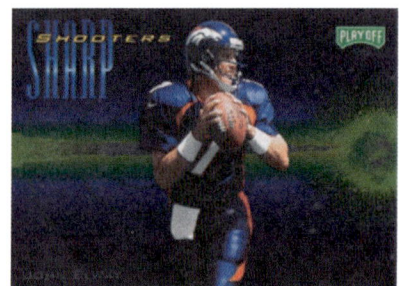

1997 Playoff Zone Sharpshooter #3

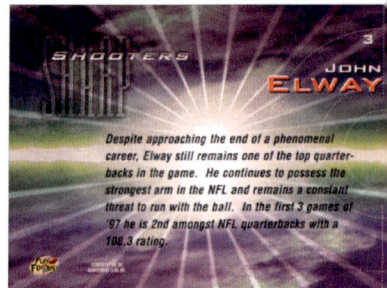

Reverse

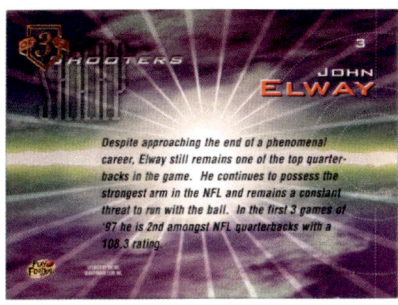

1997 Playoff Zone Sharpshooter
Gold #3

1997 Playoff Zone Sharpshooter
Red #3

1997 Pro Line #79

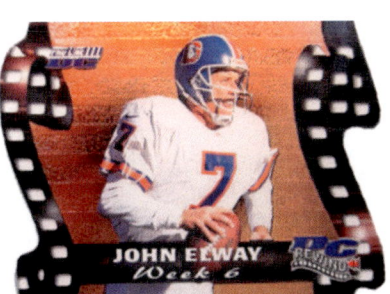

1997 Pro Line DC3 #66

1997 Pro Line DC3 #73

1997 Pro Line DC3 #95

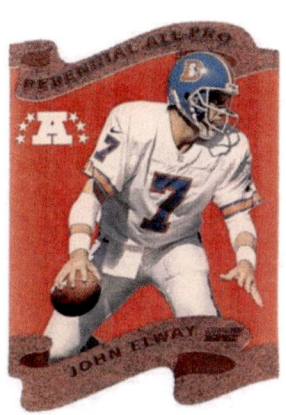

1997 Pro Line
DC All-Pros #11

1997 Pro Line
DC3 Road To The
Super Bowl #SB21

1997 Pro Line
Memorabilia #13

1997 Pro Line
Memorabilia Signature
Series #13

1997 Pro Line
Rivalries #RV1

1997 Revolution #42

1997 Revolution Air
Mail Die Cuts #10

1997 Revolution
Copper #42

1997 Revolution
Platinum Blue #42

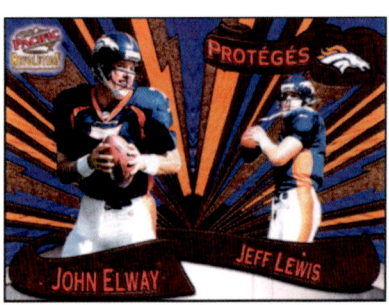

1997 Revolution Protoges #6

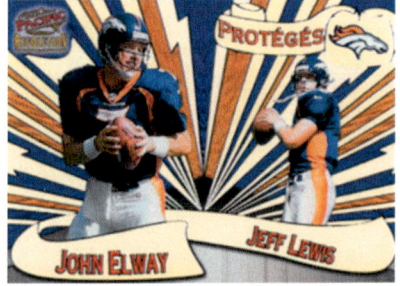

1997 Revolution Protoges
Silver #6

1997 Revolution Red #42

1997 Revolution Ring
Bearers #2

1997 Revolution
Silver #42

1997 Revolution Silk #7

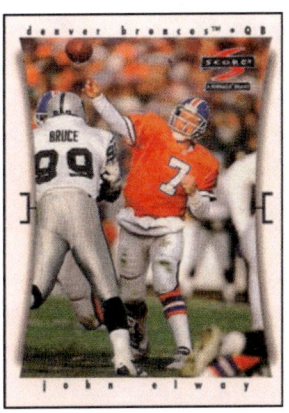

1997 Score #1

1997 Score #312

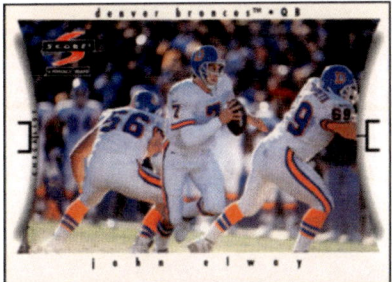

1997 Score #329

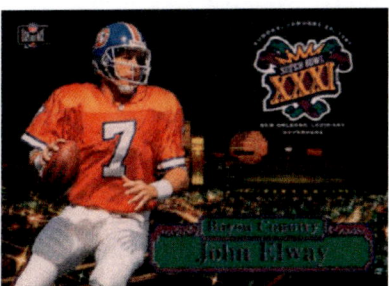

1997 Score Board NFL
Experience Bayou
Country #BC7

1997 Score Board NFL
Experience Season's
Heroes #SH18

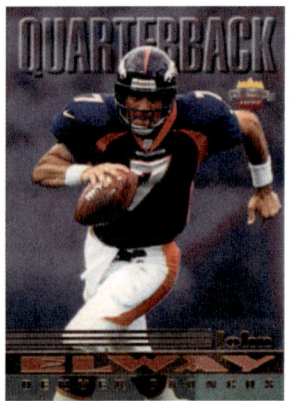

1997 Score Board Playbook
By The Numbers #QB7

1997 Score Board Playbook
By The Numbers Magnified
Gold #QB7

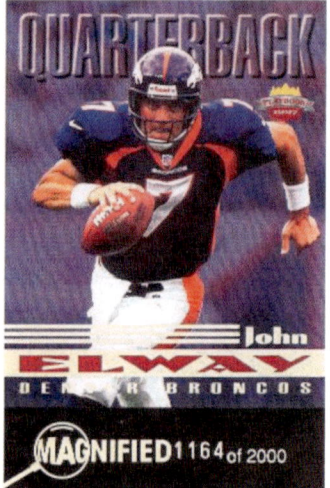

1997 Score Board Playbook
By The Numbers Magnified
Silver #QB7

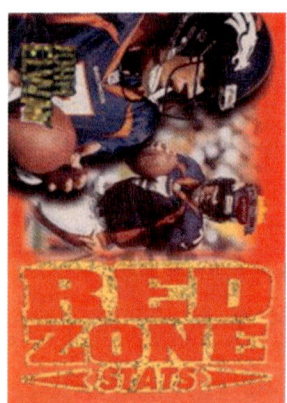

1997 Score Board
Playbook By The
Numbers Red Zone
Stats #RZ5

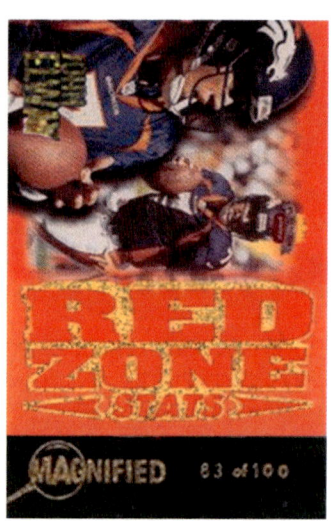

1997 Score Board Playbook
By The Numbers Red Zone
Stats Magnified Gold #RZ5

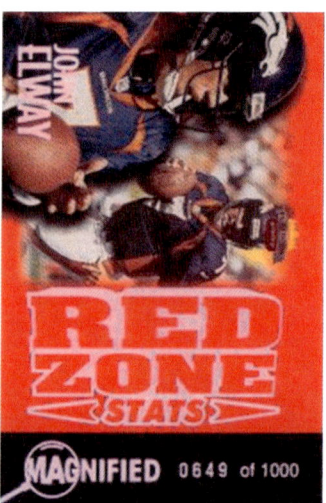

1997 Score Board Playbook
By The Numbers Red Zone
Stats Magnified Silver #RZ5

1997 Score Board Playbook
By The Numbers Standout
Numbers #SN7

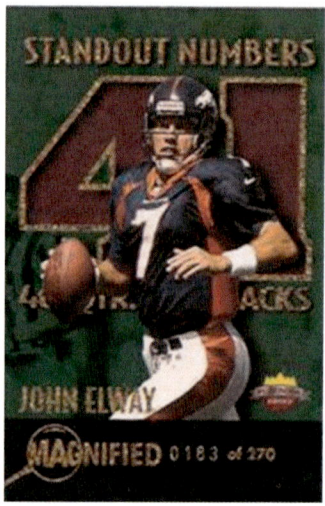

1997 Score Board Playbook
By The Numbers Standout
Numbers Magnified Gold
#SN7

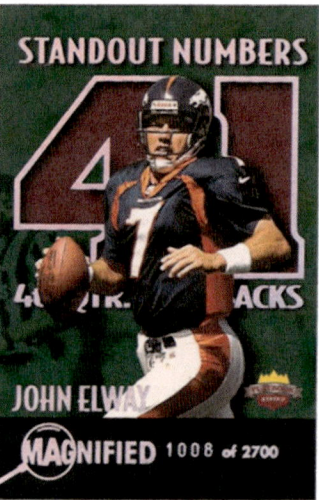

1997 Score Board Playbook
By The Numbers Standout
Numbers Magnified Silver
#SN7

1997 Score Board NFL
Experience Season's
Heros #SH18

1997 Score Board
Playbook Mirror
Image #8

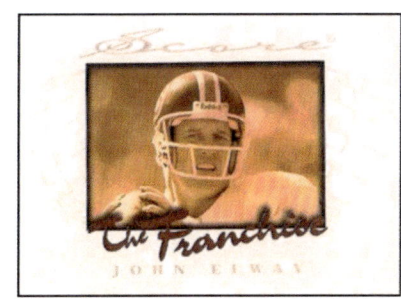

1997 Score Franchise #8

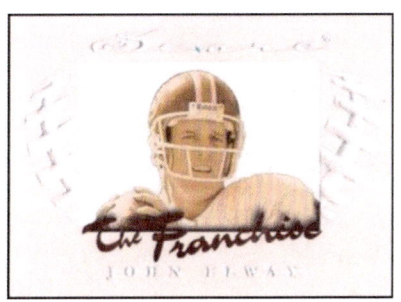

1997 Score Franchise Enchanted #8

1997 Score Hobby
Reserve #1

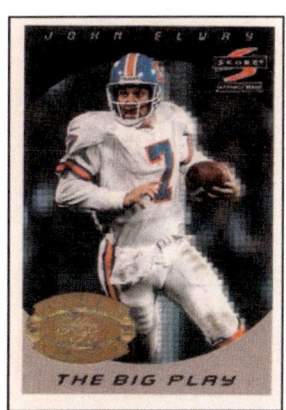

1997 Score Hobby
Reserve #312

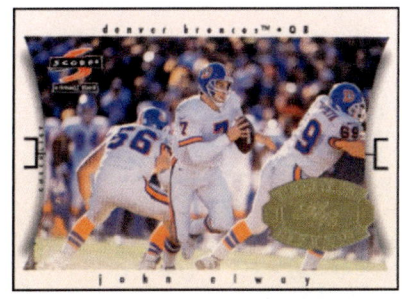

1997 Score Hobby
Reserve #329

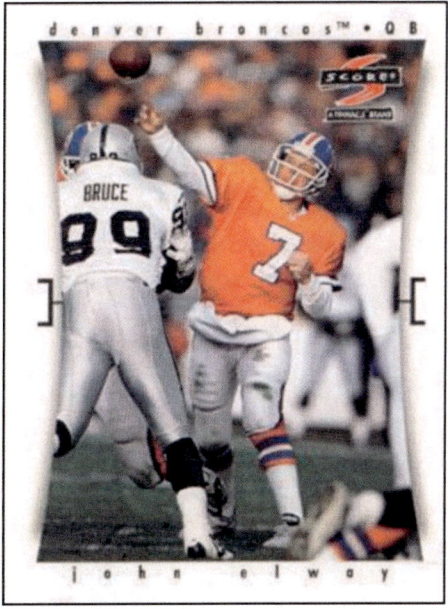

1997 Score Jumbo #1

1997 Score Unlisted
(Mastercut?) #312

1997 Score Premier
Club #1

1997 Score Premier
Club #312

1997 Score Premier
Club #329

1997 Score Reserve
Collection #1

1997 Score Reserve
Collection #312

1997 Score Reserve
Collection #329

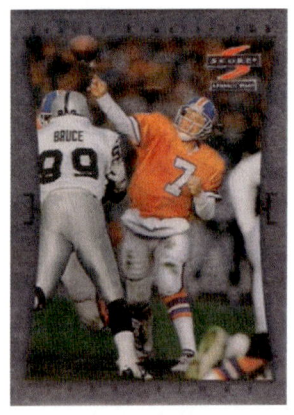

1997 Score Showcase #1

1997 Score Showcase #312

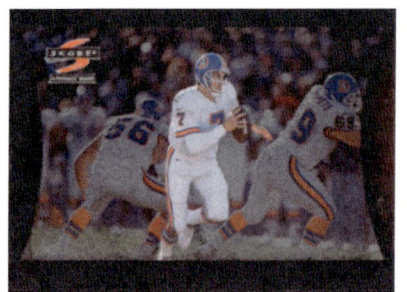

1997 Score Showcase #329

1997 Score Showcase
Artist Proof #1

1997 Score Showcase
Artist Proof #312

1997 Score Showcase
Artist Proof #329

1997 Sprint Heroes Of
The Game Phone Card

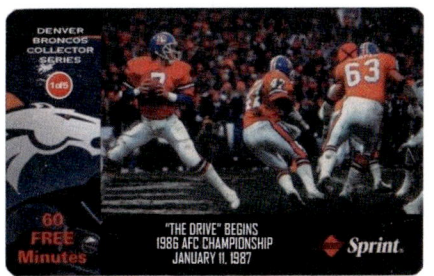

1997 Sprint Phone Card

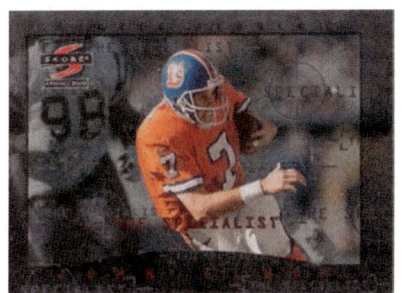

1997 Score Specialist #5

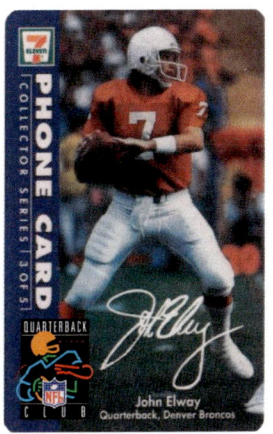

1997 Seven - Eleven
Phone Card

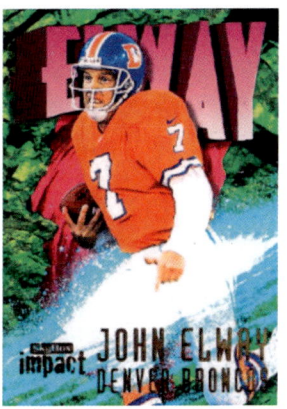

1997 SkyBox Impact #7

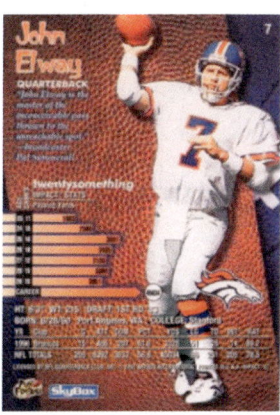

Reverse

1997 SkyBox Impact
Rave #7

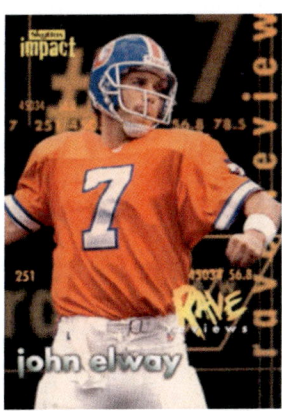

1997 SkyBox Impact
Rave Reviews #2

1997 SkyBox Impact
Total Impact #6

1997 SkyBox
Previews #98

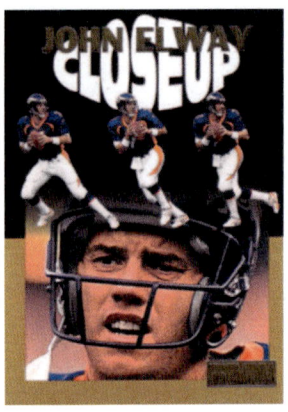

1998 SkyBox Premium
Close Ups #8

1997 SkyBox Premium
Inside The Numbers #98
Reverse

1997 SkyBox Premium
Players #15

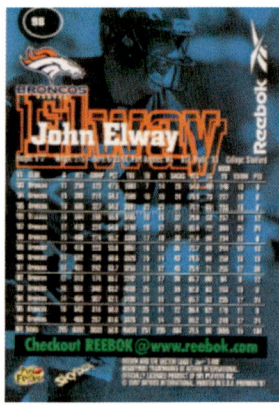

1997 SkyBox Premium
Reebok Green #98
Reverse

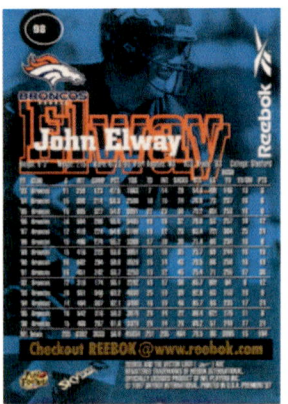

1997 SkyBox Premium
Reebok Gold #98
Reverse

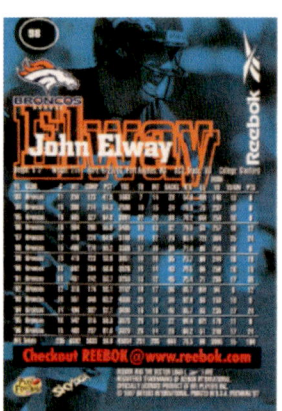

1997 SkyBox Premium
Reebok Red #98
Reverse

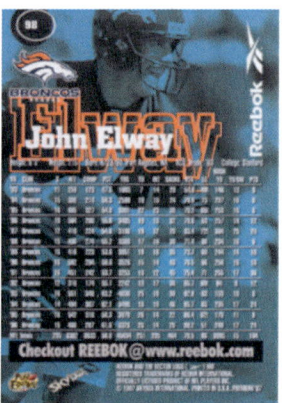

1997 SkyBox Premium
Reebok Silver #98
Reverse

1997 SkyBox Premium
Rubies #98

1997 SP Authentic #76

1997 SP Authentic
Profiles #P37

1997 SP Authentic
Profiles Die Cut#P37

Reverse

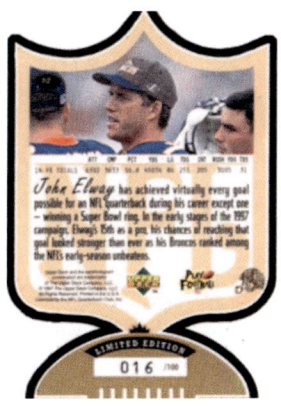

1997 SP Authentic
Profiles Die Cuts 100 #37
#/100 Reverse

1997 SPX #23

1997 SPX Gold #23

1997 Staduim Club #70

1997 Stadium Club
Pro Bowl #70

1997 Stadium Club
Aerial Assault #AA5

1997 Stadium Club
First Day #70

1997 Stadium Club
Members Only #50

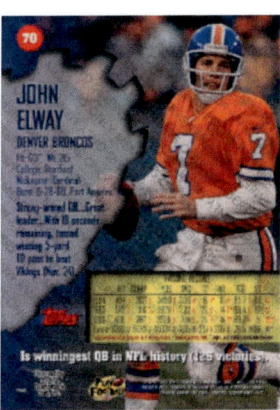

1997 Stadium Club
Members Only
Parallel #70
Reverse

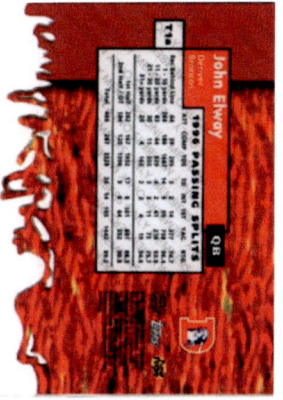

1997 Stadium Club
Members Only
Parallel #TIA2
Reverse

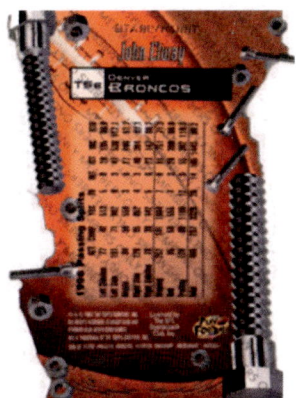

1997 Stadium Club
Members Only
Parallel #T5B
Reverse

1997 Stadium Club
Members Only
Parallel #AA5

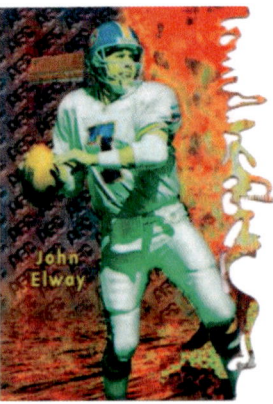

1997 Stadium Club
Triumverate Atomic
Refractor #T5B

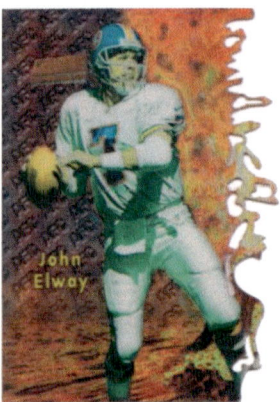

1997 Stadium Club
Triumverate Refractor
#T5B

1997 Stadium Club
Triumverate II
#T1A

1997 Stadium Club
Triumverate Atomic
Refractor II #T1A

1997 Stadium Club
Triumverate II
Refractor #T1A

1997 Starline Poster Sample

1997 Starting Line Up

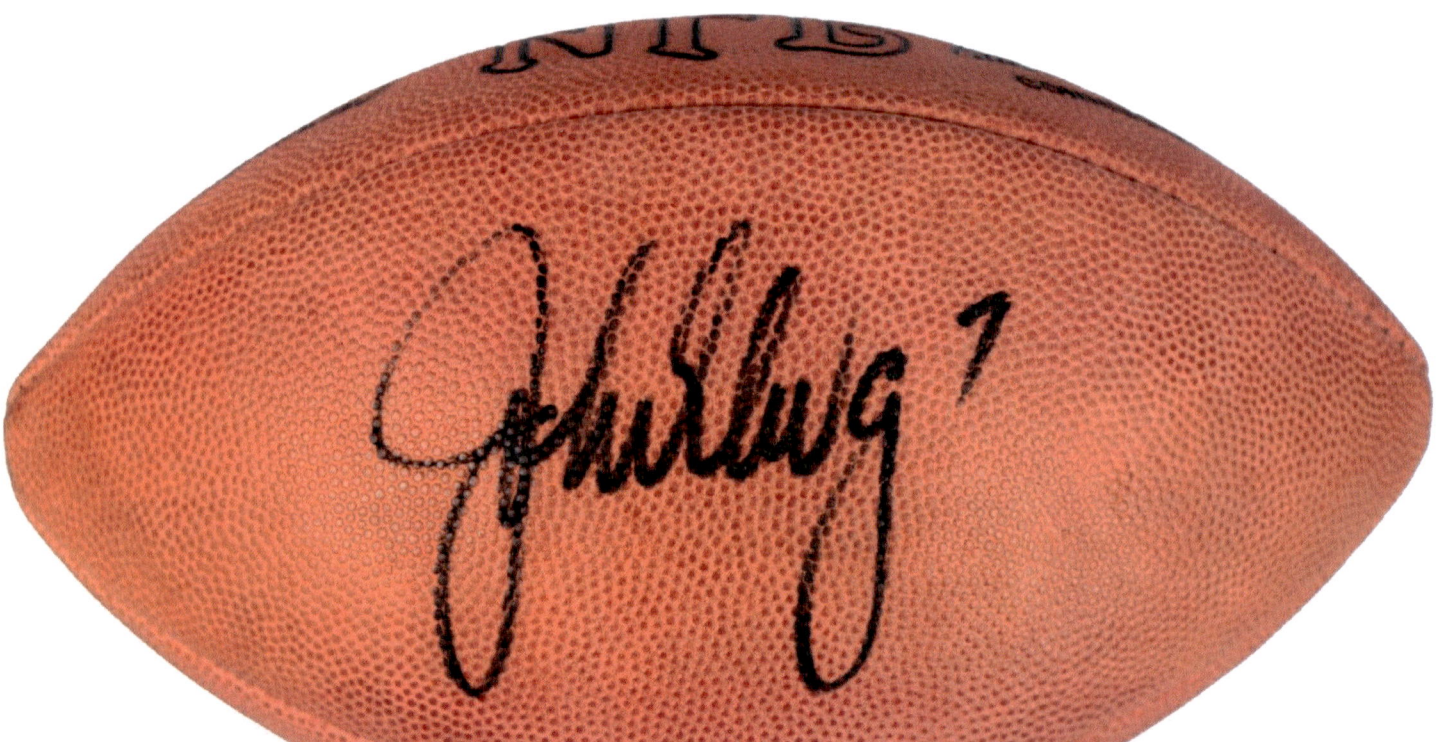

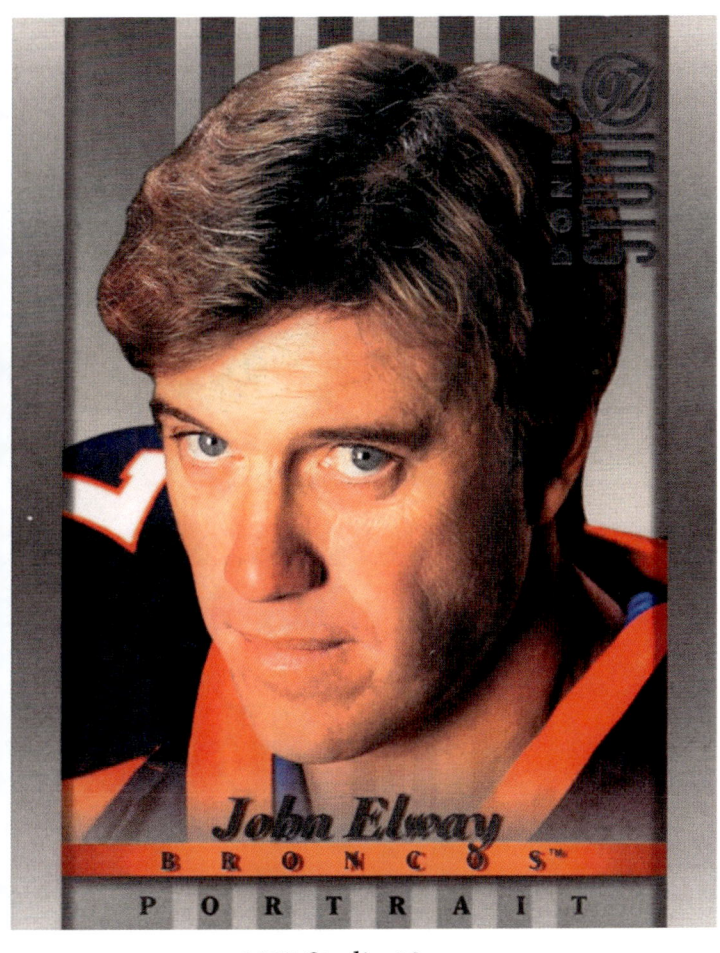

1997 Studio #8

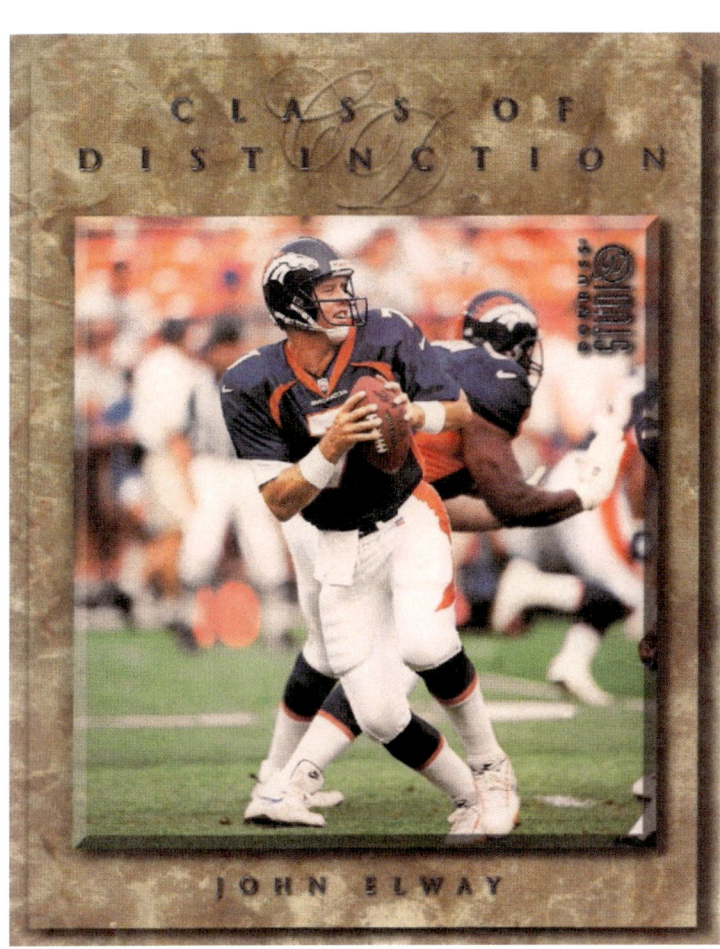

1997 Studio Class of Distinction #29

1997 Studio Class of Distinction
Portrait Proof Silver #29

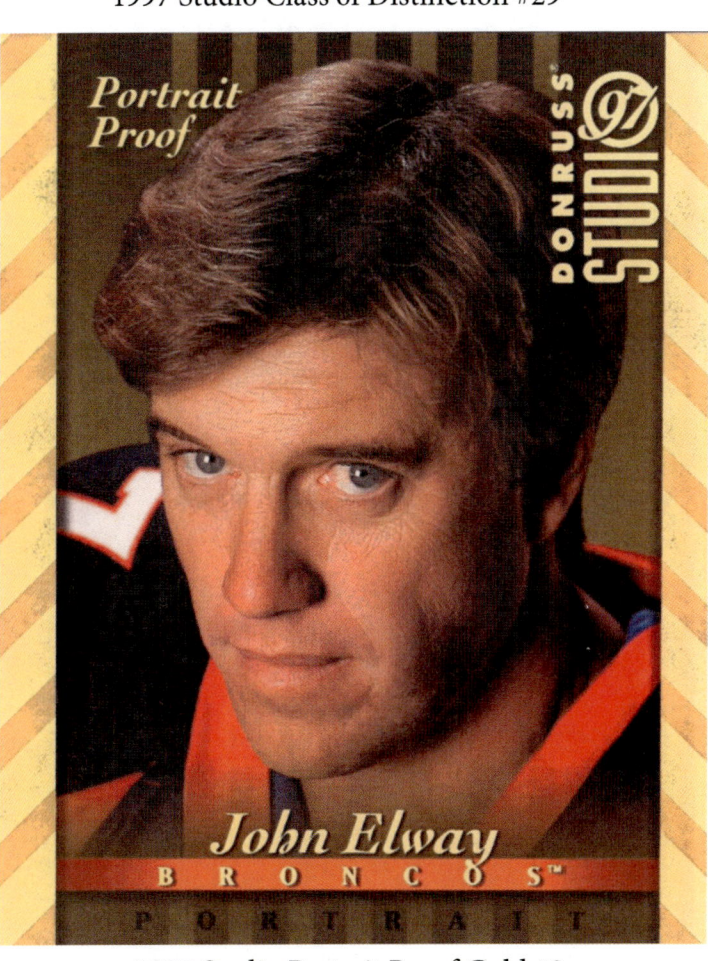

1997 Studio Portrait Proof Gold #8

1997 Studio Portrait Proof Silver #8

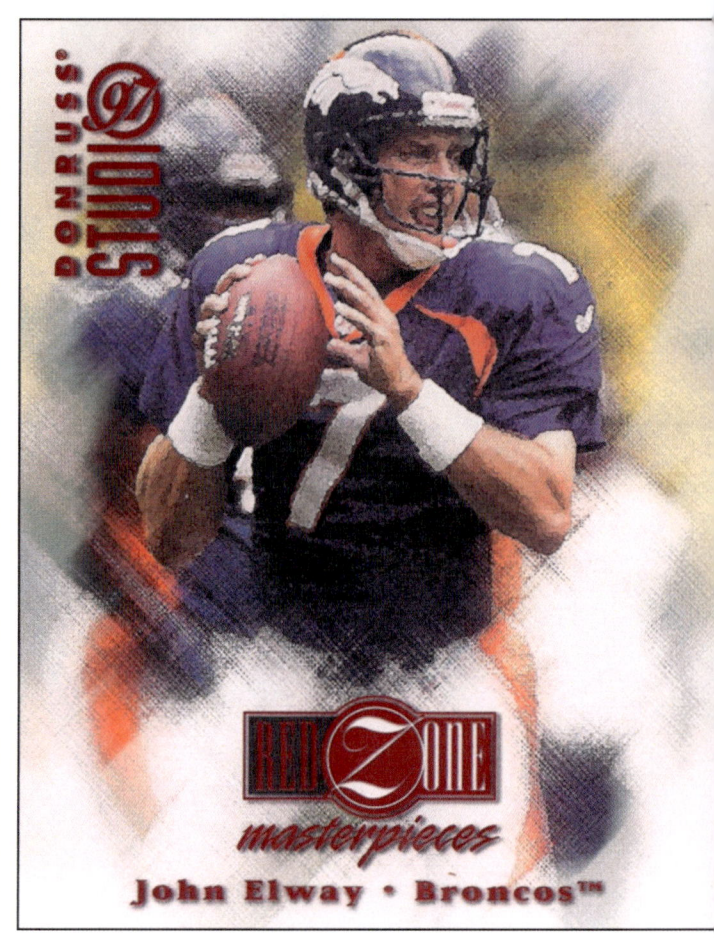

1997 Studio Red Zone Masterpiece #8

1997 Studio Stained Glass Stars #8 Reverse Promo

1997 Studio Stained Glass Stars #8

1997 Studio Stained Glass Stars #8 Reverse

1997 Topps #200

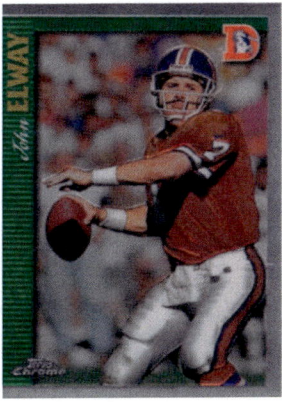

1997 Topps Chrome #200

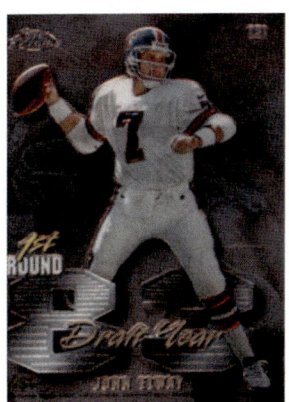

1997 Topps Chrome Draft Year #DR1

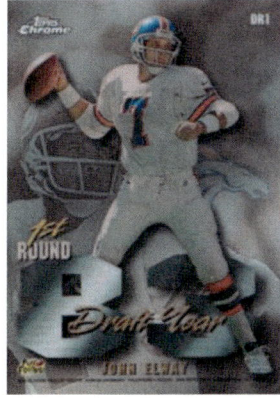

1997 Topps Chrome Draft Year Refractor #DR1

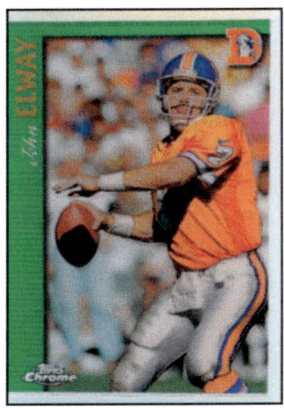

1997 Topps Chrome Refractor #200

1997 Topps Gallery #75

1997 Topps Gallery Critics Choice #CC5

1997 Topps Gallery Gallery of Heros #GH17

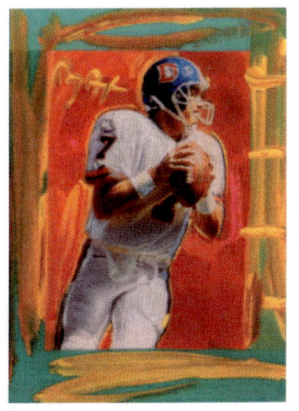

1997 Topps Gallery Peter Max Serigraph #PM4

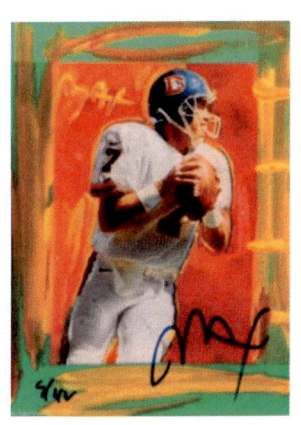

1997 Topps Gallery Peter Max Serigraph Signature #PM4

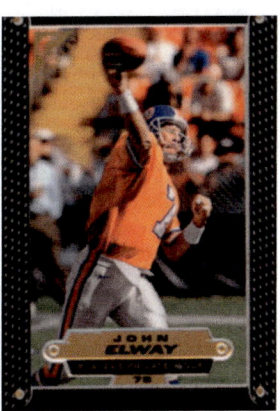

1997 Topps Gallery Players Private Issue #75

1997 Topps Hall Bound #HB9

1997 Topps High
Octane #HO11

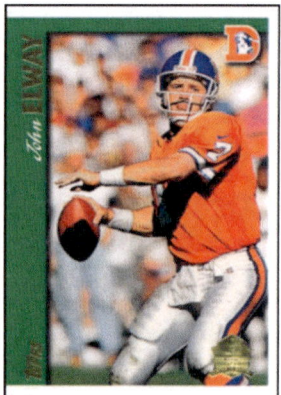

1997 Topps Minted
In Canton #200

1997 Topps Mystery
Finest Bronze #M10

1997 Topps Mystery
Finest Bronze Refractor
#M10

1997 Topps Mystery
Finest Gold #M10

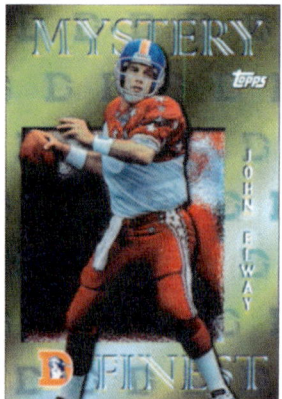

1997 Topps Mystery
Finest Gold Refractor
#M10

1997 Topps Mystery
Finest Silver #M10

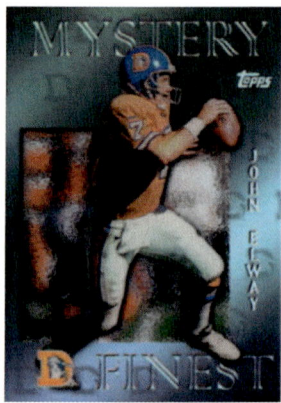

1997 Topps Mystery
Finest Silver Refractor
#M10

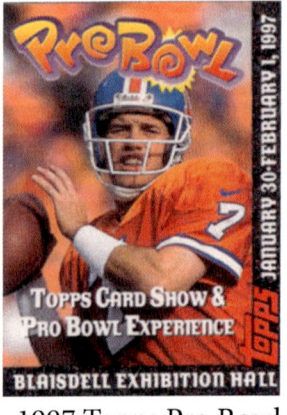

1997 Topps Pro Bowl
Card Show

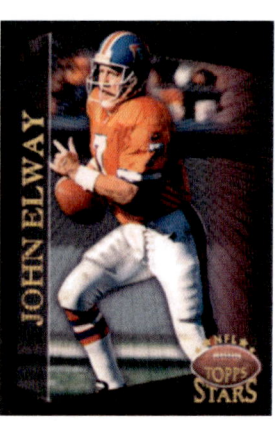

1997 Topps Stars #7

1997 Topps Stars
Foil #7

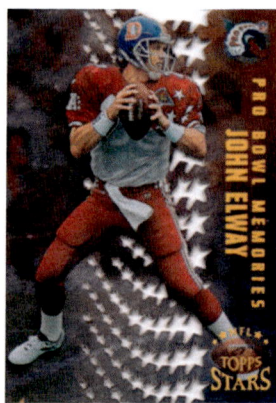

1997 Topps Pro Bowl
Memories #PBM6

1997 UD3 #44

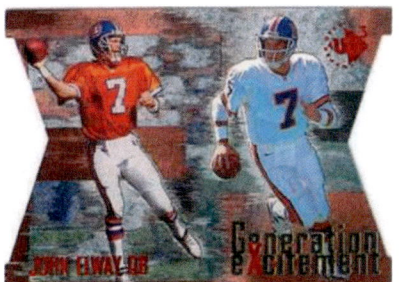

1997 UD3 Generation
Excitement #GE4

1997 Ultra #50

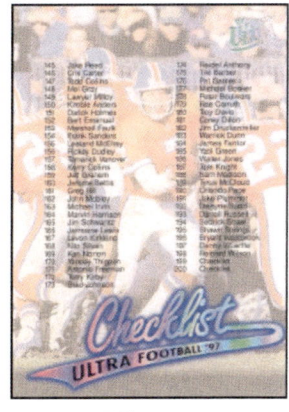

1997 Ultra #200

1997 Ultra #334

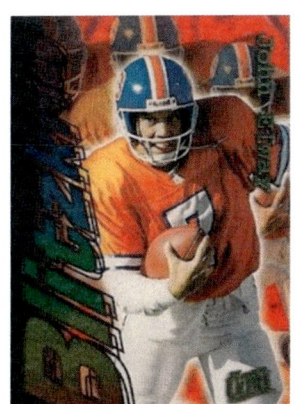

1997 Ultra Blitzkrieg
#15

1997 Ultra Blitzkreig
Die Cut #15

1997 Ultra Comeback
Kids 34

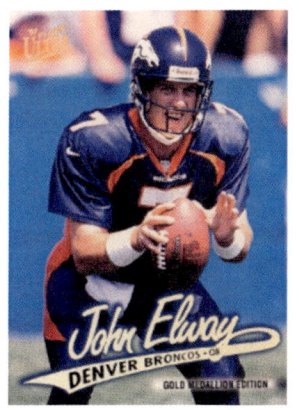

1997 Ultra Gold
Medallion #50

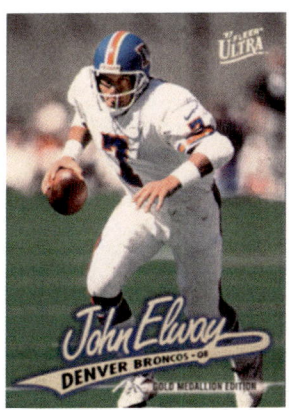

1997 Ultra Gold
Medallion #334

1997 Ultra
Main Event #5

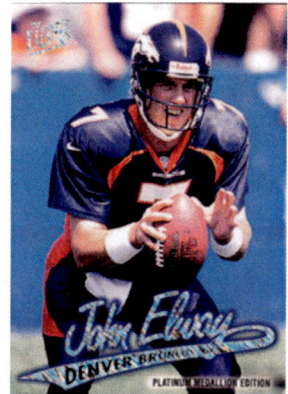

1997 Ultra Platinum
Medallion #50

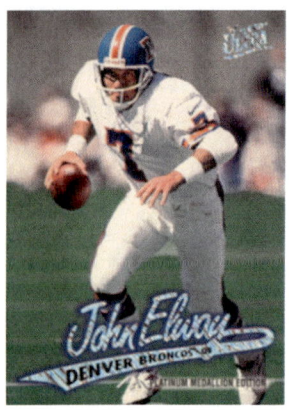

1997 Ultra Platinum
Medallion #334

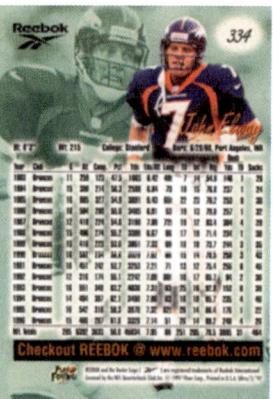

1997 Ultra Reebok
#334 Reverse

1997 Ultra Reebok
Gold #334 Reverse

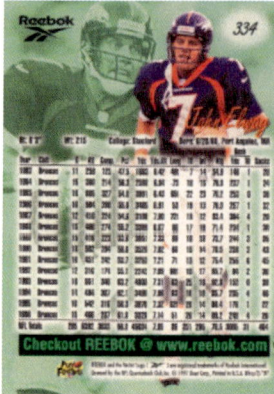

1997 Ultra Reebok
Green #334 Reverse

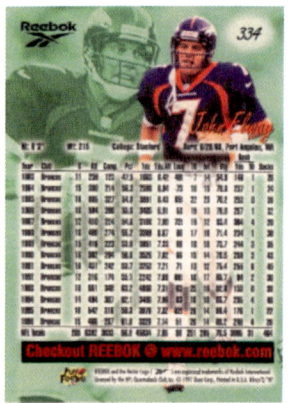

1997 Ultra Reebok
Red #334 Reverse

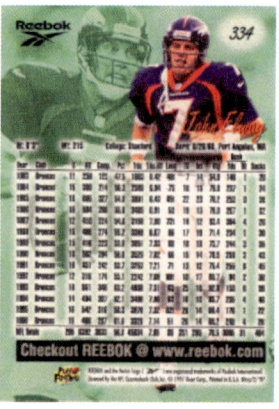

1997 Ultra Reebok
Silver #334 Reverse

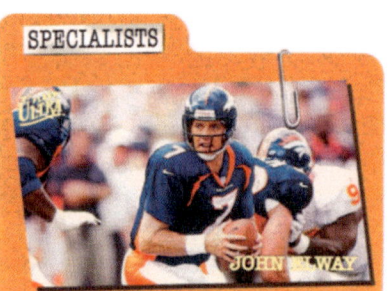

1997 Ultra Specialists #15

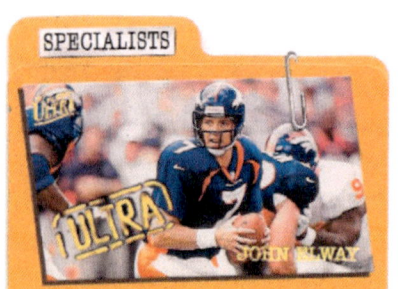

1997 Ultra Specialists Ultra #15

1997 Ultra Sunday
School #5

1997 Upper Deck #34

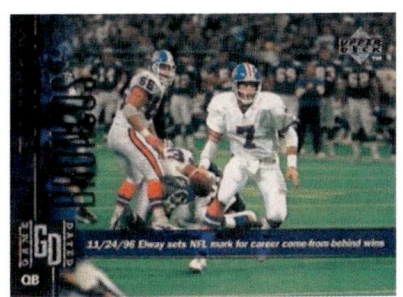

1997 Upper Deck #81

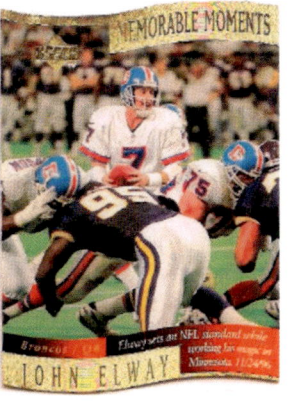

1997 Upper Deck Game
Dated Moments Foils #7

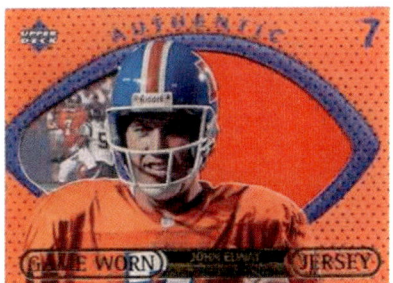

1997 Upper Deck
Game jersey #GJ7

1997 Upper Deck
Star Attractions #SA3

1997 Upper Deck
Star Attractions
Gold #SA3

1997 Upper Deck Star
Crossed #SC11

1997 Upper Deck
Team Mates #TN17

1997 Zenith #48

1997 Zenith #136

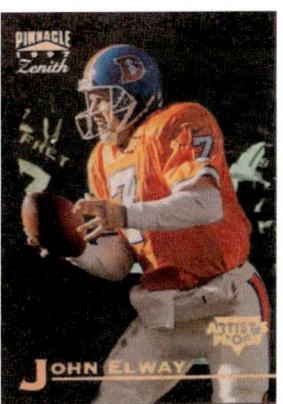

1997 Zenith
Artist Proof #48

1997 Zenith Artist
Proof #136

1997 Zenith V2-V2

1997 Zenith Z-Team #ZT4

1997 Zenith Z-Team
Mirror Gold #ZT4

January 11, 1998
AFC Championship
A 24-21 win over the Pittsburgh Steelers, Elway completed 18/31 passes for 210 yards and 2 touchdowns.

J 38 05 05
GATE SECTION ROW SEAT
FIELD

SUPER BOWL XXXII

SAN DIEGO

AFC-NFC WORLD CHAMPIONSHIP GAME
SUNDAY, JANUARY 25, 1998
QUALCOMM STADIUM, SAN DIEGO

$275 ALL TAXES INCLUDED
GATES OPEN AT NOON

SUPER BOWL XXXII
SUNDAY, JANUARY 25, 1998 · 3:00 P.M.
QUALCOMM STADIUM, SAN DIEGO
$275 ALL TAXES INCLUDED
FIELD

GATE SECTION ROW SEAT
J 38 05 05

January 25, 1998
Super Bowl XXXII
A 31-24 victory for Denver,
Elway was 12/22 for 123 yards, and had 17 yards rushing
with one touchdown.

1997 World Championship Ring

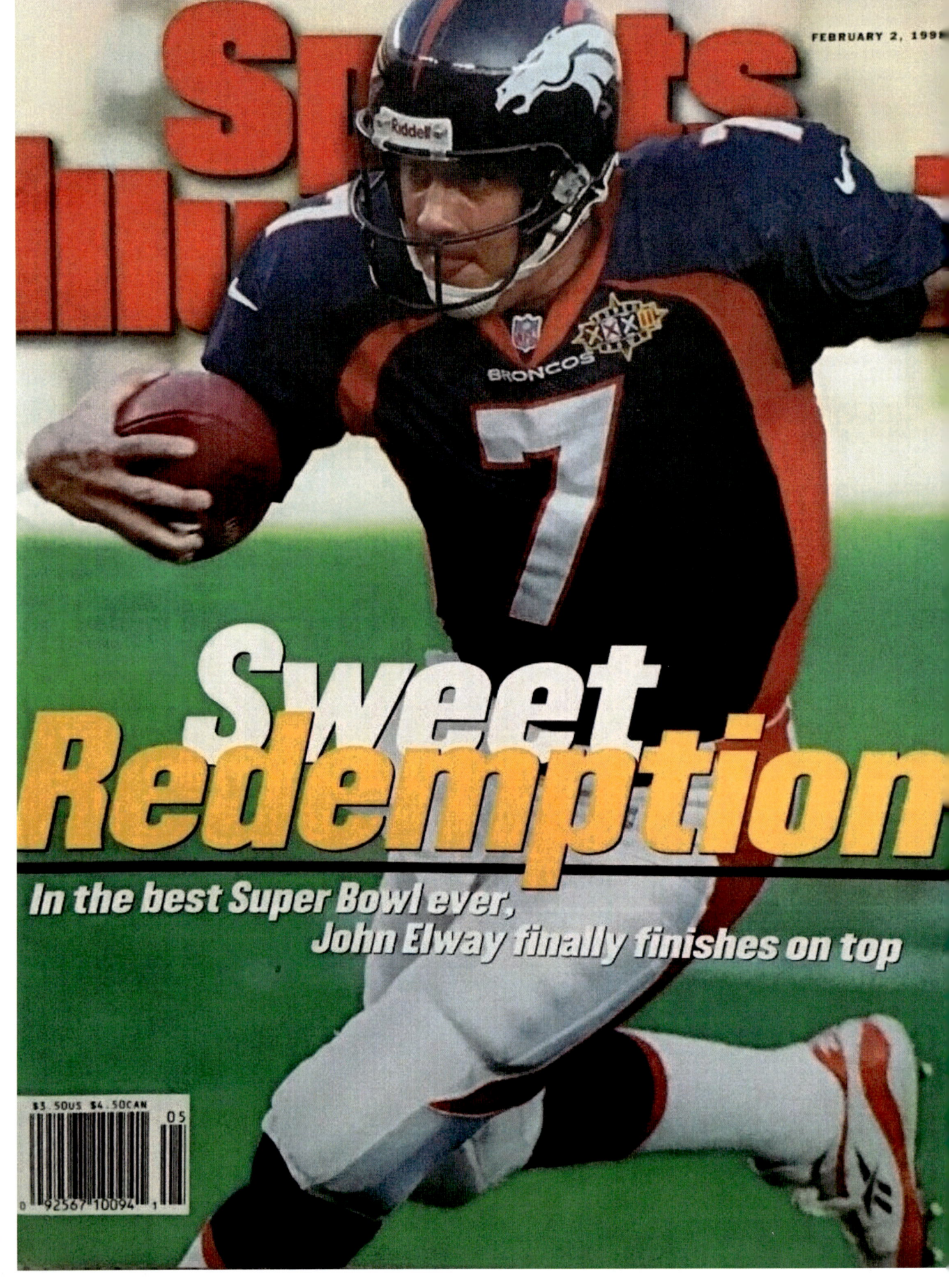

FEBRUARY 2, 1998

Sports Illustrated

Sweet Redemption

In the best Super Bowl ever, John Elway finally finishes on top

Sports Illustrated

PRESENTS

SUPER BOWL CHAMPIONS

THE 1997 DENVER BRONCOS

$5.95US

85

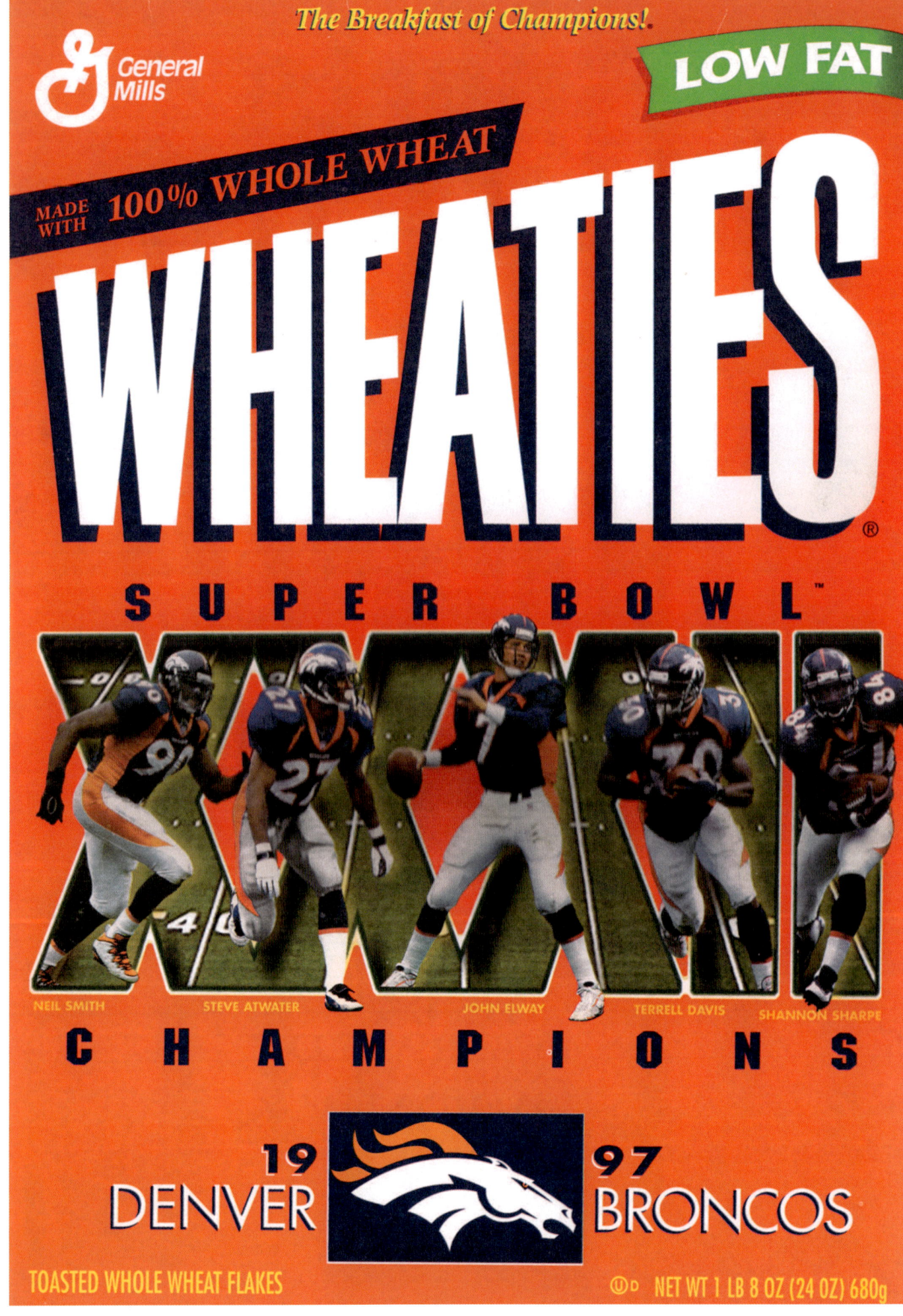

1998 Japanese Magazine Pull-Out

1998

The defending champion Broncos started the season on a 13 game win streak. Consecutive losses in weeks 15 and 16 were the only blemishes on the season. Denver was 14-2, and first in the AFC West. They cruised through the playoffs with a 38-3 victory over the Miami Dolphins in the divisional round, a 23-10 win over the New York Jets in the AFC Championship, and a 34-19 win over the NFC Champion Atlanta Falcons (coached by Dan Reeves) in Super Bowl XXXIII.

Elway would start 12 games missing four due to injury. He completed 210/356 passes for 2806 yards, and 22 touchdowns. His 300th career touchdown pass came in the season finale against Seattle. He added 97 yards rushing on 34 carries with a touchdown. He was named to his ninth Pro Bowl.

Super Bowl XXXII Champions

1998 Sprint Schedule

1998 Aurora #46

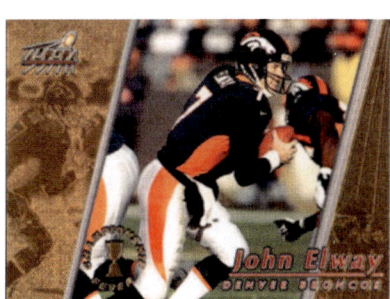

1998 Aurora Championship
Fever #14

1998 Nike Broncos Merchandise
Pocket Schedule

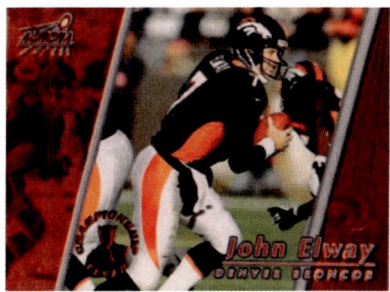

1998 Aurora Championship
Fever Copper #14

Sports Illustrated

Can Denver Win 'Em All?

Believe It!

$2.95 US/$3.95 CAN

48 >

0 724454 6

NOVEMBER 30, 1998

ww.cnnsi.com

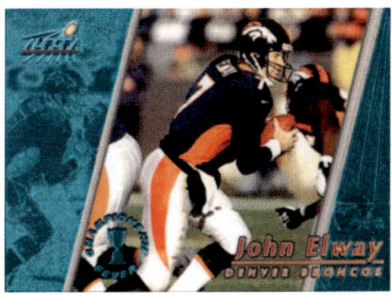

1998 Aurora Championship
Fever Platinum Blue #14

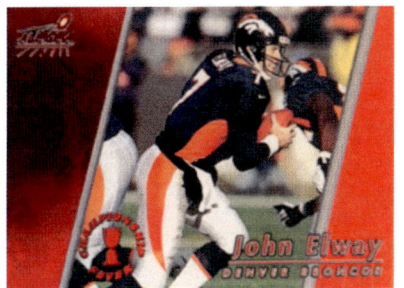

1998 Aurora Championship
Fever Red #14

1998 Aurora Championship
Fever Silver #14

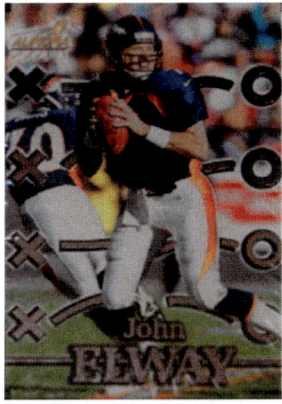

1998 Aurora Cube #5

1998 Aurora Face
Mask Cell Fusion #5

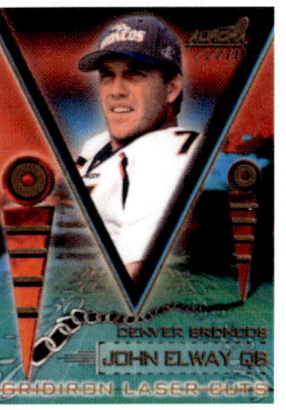

1998 Aurora Grid Iron
Laser Cut #6

1998 Aurora
NFL Command #2

1998 Black Diamond
#143

1998 Black Diamond
Double #143

1998 Black Diamond
Platinum Cut #PC7

1998 Black Diamond
Platinum Cut Double
#PC7

1998 Black Diamond Platinum Cut Quadruple Horizontal #PC7

1998 Black Diamond Platinum Cut Quadruple Vertical #PC7

1998 Black Diamond Platinum Cut Triple #PC7

1998 Black Diamond Quadruple #143

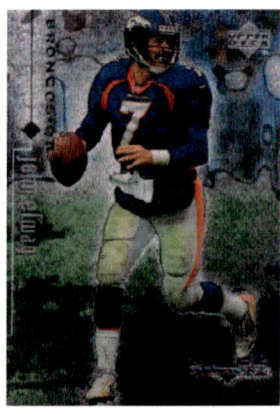
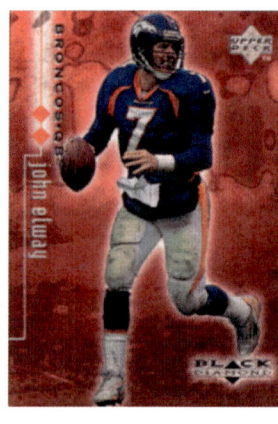
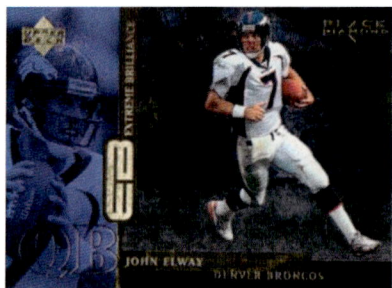

1998 Black Diamond Rookies #25

1998 Black Diamond Rookies Double #25

1998 Black Diamond Rookies Extreme Brilliance #B8

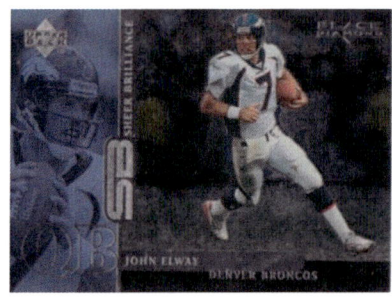
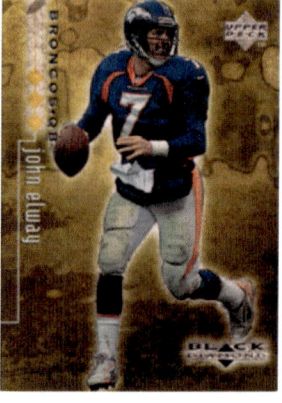

1998 Black Diamond Rookies Quadruple #25

1998 Black Diamond Rookies Sheer Brilliance #B8

1998 Black Diamond Rookies Triple #25

1998 Black Diamond Rookies White Onyx #ON7

1998 Black Diamond
Triple #143

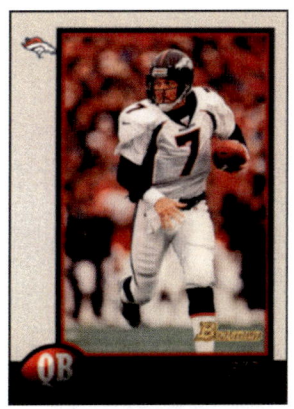

1998 Bowman #100

1998 Bowman Best #50

1998 Bowman Best
Atomic Refractor #50

1998 Bowmans Best
Mirror Image Fusion
#MI7

1998 Bowmand Best
Mirror Image Fusion
Atomic Refractor #MI7

1998 Bowmand Best
Mirror Image Fusion
Refractor #MI7

1998 Bowmans Best
Refractor #50

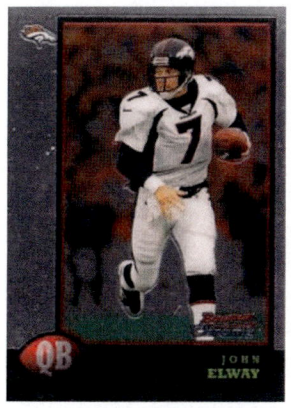

1998 Bowman Chrome
#100

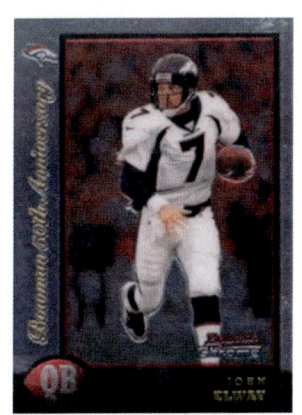

1998 Bowman Chrome
Golden Anniversary #100

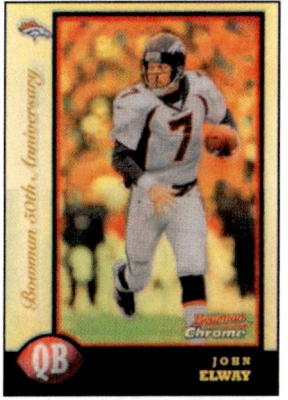

1998 Bowman Chrome
Golden Anniversary
Refractor #100

1998 Bowman
Chrome Interstate #100

1998 Bowman Chrome
Interstate Refractor #100

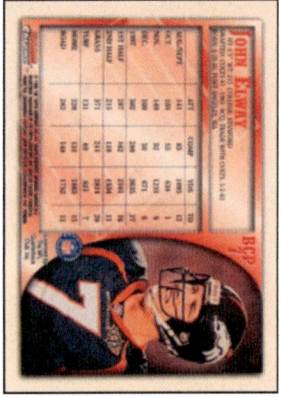

1998 Bowman Chrome
Preview #BCP7 Reverse

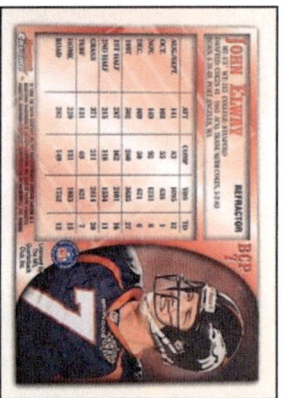

1998 Bowman Chrome
Preview Refractor
#BCP7 Reverse

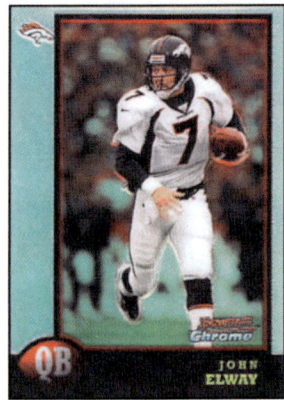

1998 Bowman Chrome
Refractor #100

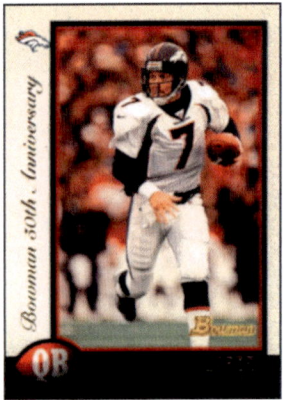

1998 Bowman Golden
Anniversary #100

1998 Bowman
Interstate #100

1998 Collectors Edge
Advantage #50

1998 Collectors Edge
Advantage 50 Point #50

1998 Collectors Edge
Advantage Gold #50

1998 Collectors Edge
Advantage Printers
Plate

1998 Collectors Edge
Advantage Livin Large
#5

1998 Collectors Edge
Advantage Livin Large
Holofoil #5

JOHN ELWAY

QUARTERBACK
DENVER BRONCOS

1998 Brenner Football

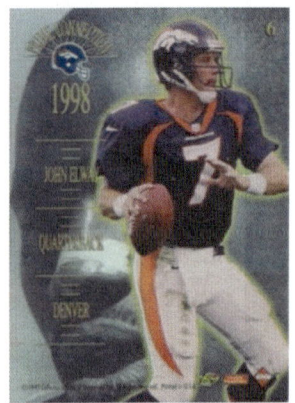

1998 Collectors Edge
Advantage Prime
Connections #6

1998 Collectors Edge
Advantage Personal
Victory #1

Reverse/Media Sample

1998 Collectors Edge
Shockwave #SW7

1998 Collectors Edge
Advantage Silver #50

1998 Collectors Edge
First Place #70

1998 Collectors Edge
First Place 50 Point #70

1998 Collectors Edge
First Place 50 Point
Silver #70

1998 Collectors Edge
First Place Gold
One-Of-One #70

1998 Collectors Edge
First Place Record
Setters #70

1998 Collectors Edge
First Place Record
Setters Gold #70

1998 Collectors Edge
First Place
Successors #9

1998 Collectors Edge
First Place Triumph
#10

1998 Collectors Edge
First Place Triple
Threat #34

1998 Collectors Edge
Masters #53

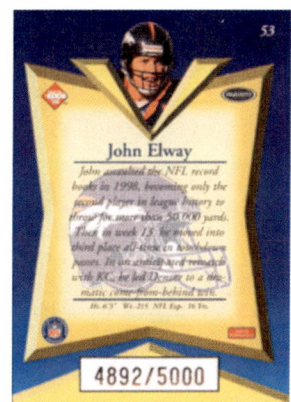

Reverse #/5000

1998 Collectors Edge
Masters #176

Reverse #/5000

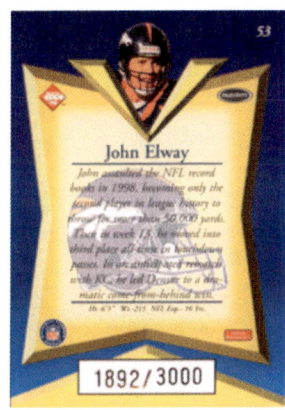

1998 Collectors Edge
Masters 50 Point #53
Reverse

1998 Collectors Edge
Masters 50 Point #176
Reverse #/3000

1998 Collectors Edge
Masters 50 Point
Gold #53

Reverse #/150

1998 Collectors Edge
Masters 50 Point
Gold #176

Reverse #/150

1998 Collectors Edge
Masters Gold
Redemption 100 #53
Reverse #/100

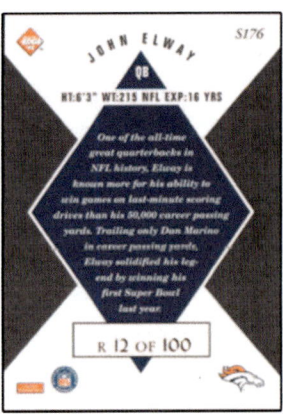

1998 Collectors Edge
Masters Gold
Redemption 100 #176
Reverse #/100

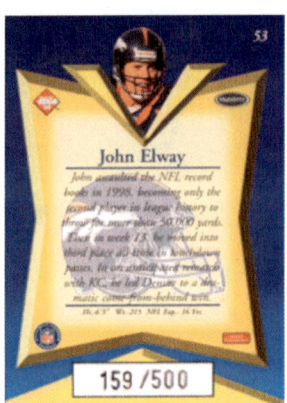

1998 Collectors Edge
Masters Gold
Redemption #53
Reverse #/500

1998 Collectors Edge
Masters Gold
Redemption #176
Reverse #500

1998 Collectors Edge
Masters Hologold #53

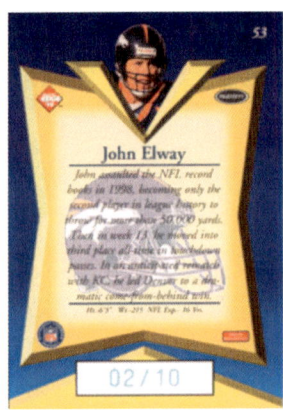

Reverse #/10

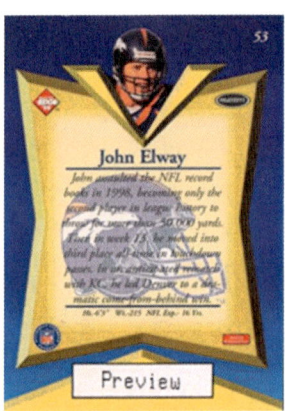

1998 Collector's Edge
Masters Hologram
Preview Reverse

1998 Collectors Edge
Masters Hologold
#176

1998 Collectors Edge
Masters Legends
#ML9

1998 Collectors Edge
Masters Main Event #9

1998 Collectors Edge
Masters Sentinels #S1

1998 Collectors Edge
Master Super Master
#SM2

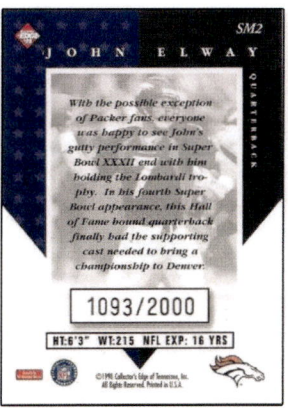

Reverse #/2000

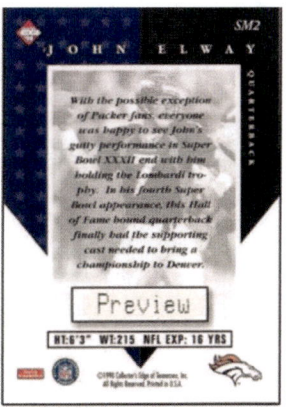

Preview Reverse

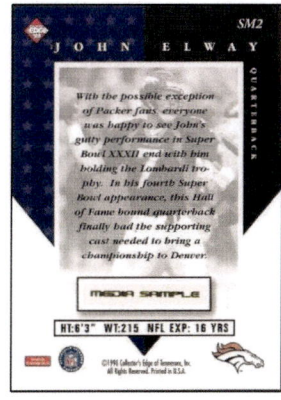

Media Sample Reverse

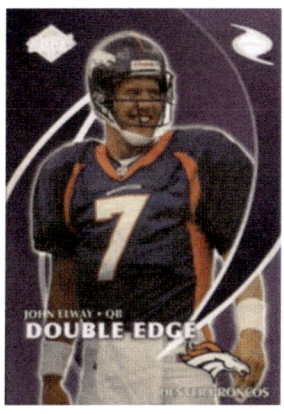

1998 Collectors Edge
Odyssey Double Edge
#8A

1998 Collectors Edge
Odyssey Double Edge
#8B

1998 Collectors Edge
Odyssey Game Ball
Redemption #6t

1998 Collectors Edge
Odyssey #42

1998 Collectors Edge
Odyssey #163

1998 Collectors Edge
Odyssey #207

1998 Collectors Edge
Odyssey #235

1998 Collectors Edge
Odyssey Level 1
Galvanized #42

1998 Collectors Edge
Odyssey Level 1
Galvanized #163

1998 Collectors Edge
Odyssey Level 1
Galvanized #207

1998 Collectors Edge
Odyssey Level 1
Galvanized #235

1998 Collectors Edge
Odyssey Level 2
Hologold #42

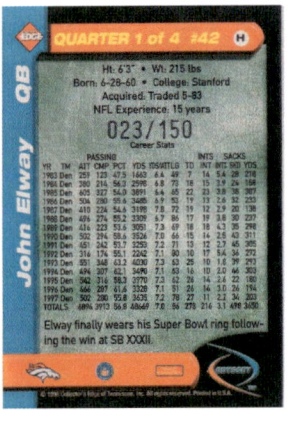

Reverse #150

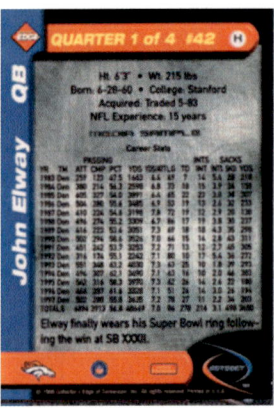

Media Sample Reverse

1998 Collectors Edge
Odyssey Level 2
Hologold #163

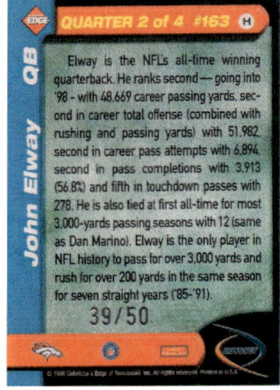

Reverse #/50

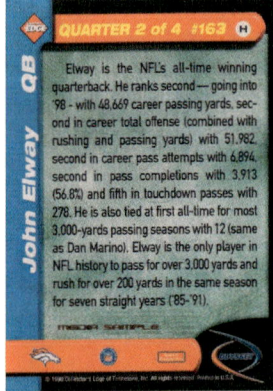

Media Sample

1998 Collectors Edge
Odyssey Level 2
Hologold #207

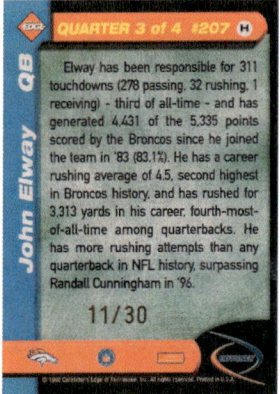

Reverse #/30

1998 Collectors Edge
Odyssey Level 2
Hologold #235

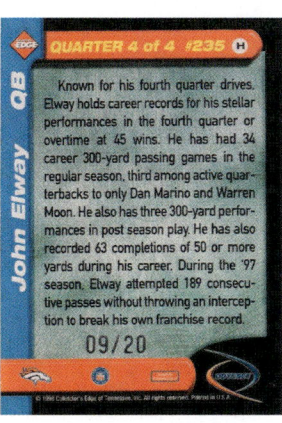

Reverse #/20

1998 Collectors Edge
Odyssey Leading Edge #7

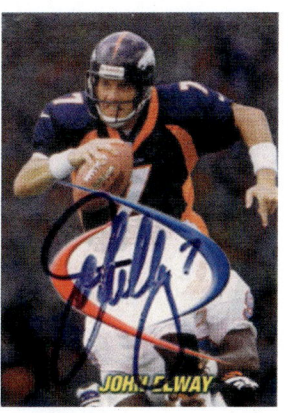

1998 Collectors Edge
Odyssey Prodigies #11

1998 Collectors Edge
Odyssey Prodigies Red #11

1998 Collectors Edge
Odyssey Preview 3Q
#207

1998 Collectors Edge
Odyssey Preview 3Q
#235

No Official Listing

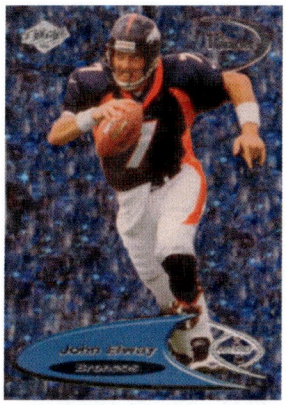

1998 Collectors Edge
Odyssey Single
Edge #42

1998 Collectors Edge
Odyssey Single
Edge #163

1998 Collectors Edge
Odyssey Single
Edge #207

1998 Collectors Edge
Odyssey Single
Edge #235

1998 Collectors Edge
Odyssey Super Limited
Edge #3

1998 Collectors Edge
Spectrum #6

1998 Collectors Edge
Spectrum Proof #6

No Official Listing

1998 Collectors Edge
Super Bowl XXXII #1

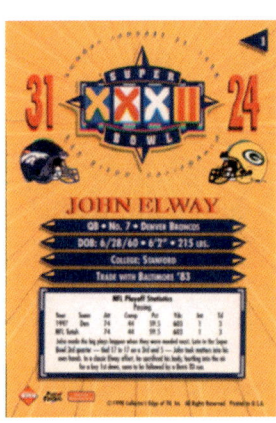

Reverse #1

1998 Collectors Edge
Super Bowl XXXII
#1 Unlisted Parallel

1998 Collectors Edge
Super Bowl XXXII
Silver #1

50 Point Gold
Stamped # B1

Reverse B#1

1998 Collectors Edge
Super Bowl XXXII
Unlisted Parallel

Reverse

1998 Collectors Edge
Masterpiece Personal Collection

1998 Collectors Edge
Super Bowl Card Show #6

Reverse

1998 Collectors Edge
Super Bowl Card
Show Gold Foil #6

Reverse #/1000

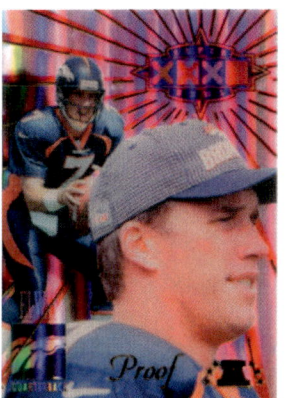

1998 Collectors Edge
Super Bowl Card
Show Proof #6

Reverse #/500

1998 Collectors Edge
Supreme Seasons
Review #49

1998 Collectors Edge
Supreme Seasons
Review Gold Ingot
#49

1998 Collectors Edge
Supreme Seasons
Review Marker #5

1998 Collectors Edge
Supreme Seasons
Review Marker
Preview #5

1998 Collectors Edge
Supreme Seasons
Review T3 #6

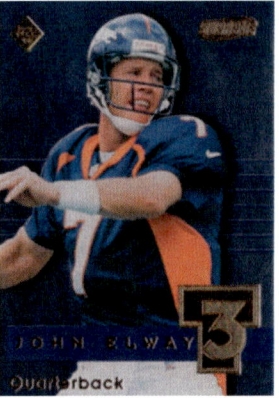

1998 Collectors Edge
Supreme Seasons
Review T3 #5

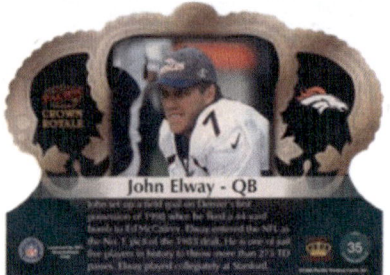

1998 Crown Royale #35 Reverse

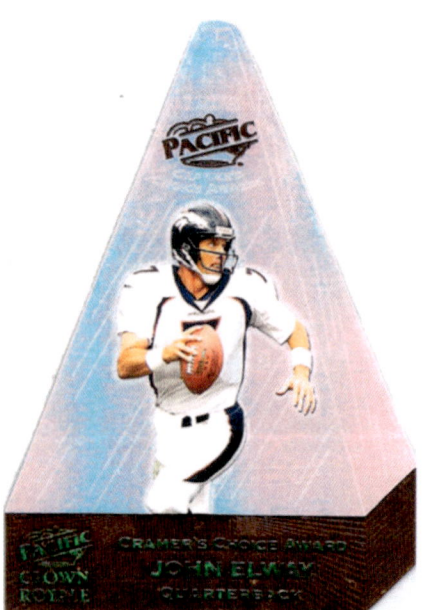

1998 Crown Royale
Cramers Choice
Jumbo #2

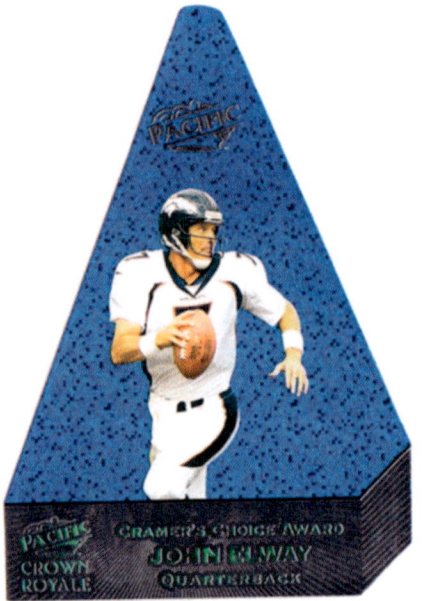

1998 Crown Royale
Cramers Choice
Jumbo Dark Blue #2

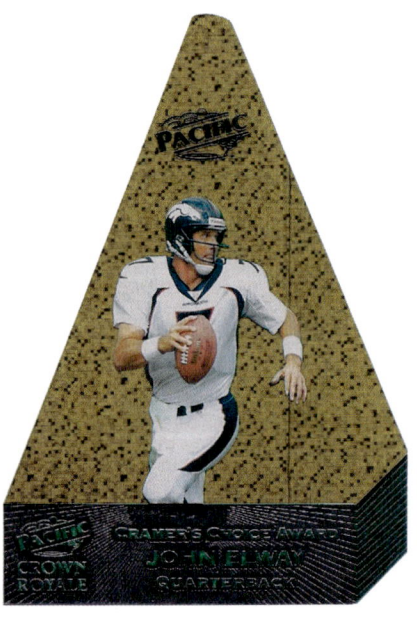

1998 Crown Royale
Cramers Choice
Jumbo Gold #2

1998 Crown Royale
Cramers Choice
Jumbo Green #2

1998 Crown Royale
Cramers Choice
Jumbo Light Blue #2

1998 Crown Royale
Cramers Choice
Jumbo Purple #2

1998 Crown Royale
Cramers Choice
Jumbo Red #2

1998 Crown Royale
Living Legends #4

1998 Crown Royale
Limited Series #35
Reverse

1998 Crown Royale
Master Performers #5

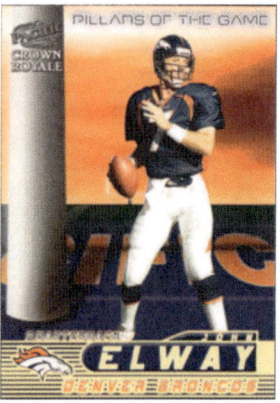

1998 Crown Royale
Pillars Of The Game
#6

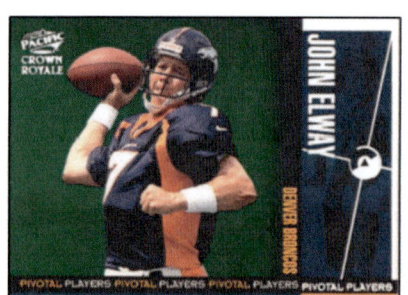

1998 Crown Royale
Pivitol Players #8

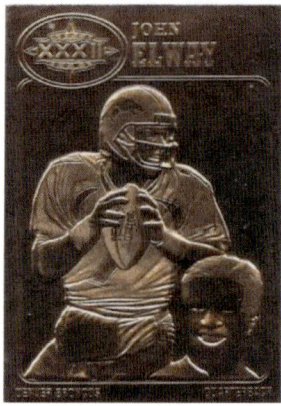

1998 Danbury Mint #11

1998 E-X 2001 #10

1998 E-X 2001
Essentials Credentials
Future #10

1998 E-X 2001
Essentials Credentials
Now #10

1998 E-X 2001
Helmet Heros #9

1998 Finest #1

1998 Finest Protector #1

1998 Finest Mystery
Finest 1 #M11

1998 Finest Mystery
Finest 1 #M11 Reverse

1998 Finest Mystery
Finest 1 #M12

1998 Finest Mystery
Finest 1 #M13

1998 Finest Mystery
Finest 1 #M14

1998 Finest Mystery
Finest 1 Refractor M11

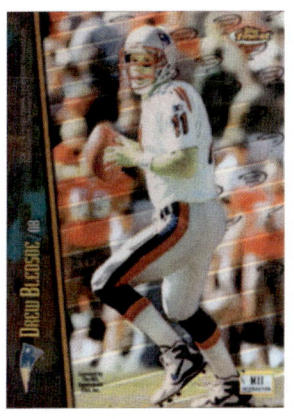

1998 Finest Mystery
Finest 1 Refractor
Reverse #M11

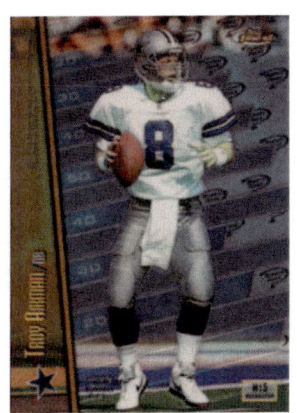

1998 Finest Mystery
Finest 1 Refractor
#M12

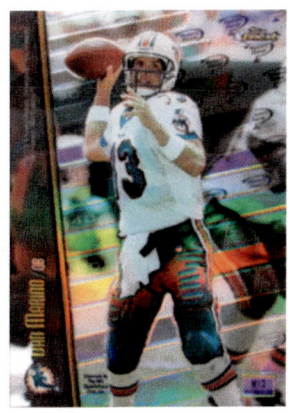

1998 Finest Mystery
Finest 1 Refractor
#M13

1998 Finest Mystery
Finest 1 Refractor
#M14

1998 Finest Mystery
Finest 2 #M13

1998 Finest Mystery
Finest 2 #M13

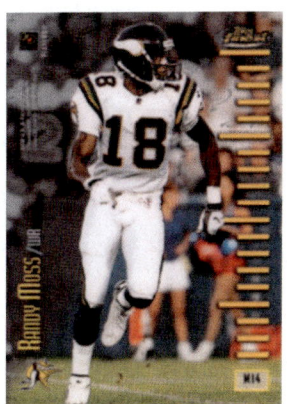

1998 Finest Mystery
Finest 2 #M14

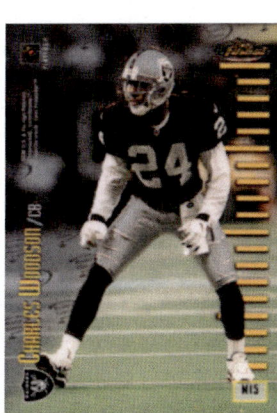

1998 Finest Mystery
Finest 2 #M15

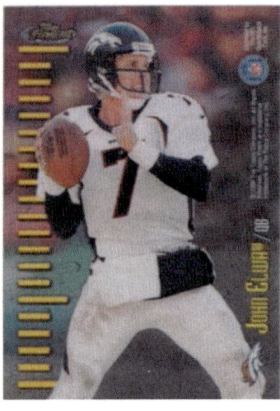
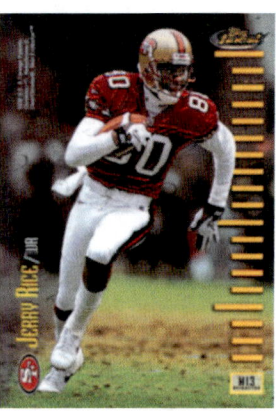
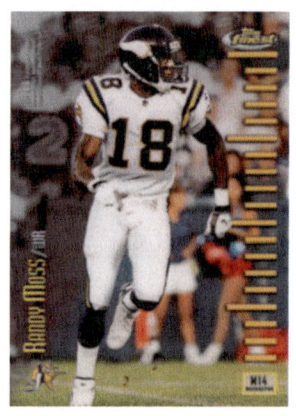
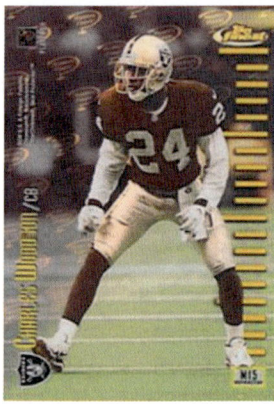

1998 Finest Mystery Finest Refractor M13

1998 Finest Mystery Finest Refractor M13

1998 Finest Mystery Finest Refractor #M14

1998 Finest Mystery Finest Refractor #M15

1998 Finest Jumbo #1

1998 Finest Refractor Jumbo #1

1998 Finest No Protector Jumbo #1

1998 Finest No Protector Jumbo Refractor #1

1998 Finest Pro Bowl Jumbo #1

1998 Finest Pro Bowl Jumbo Refractor #1

1998 Finest Super Bowl
Jumbo #1

1998 Finest Super Bowl
Jumbo Refractor #1

1998 Flair Showcase
Legacy Collection Masterpiece
Row 0 #7

1998 Flair Showcase Row 0 #7

1998 Flair Showcase Legacy
Row 0 #7

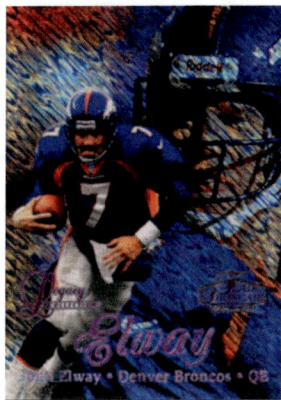

1998 Flair Showcase
Legacy Collection
Masterpiece Row 1 #7

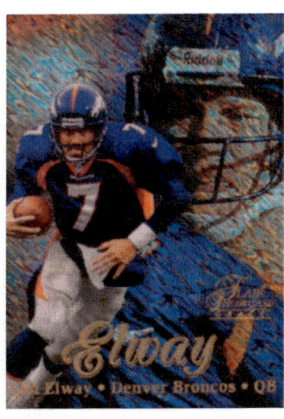

1998 Flair Showcase
Row 1 #7

1998 Flair Showcase
Legacy Row 1 #7

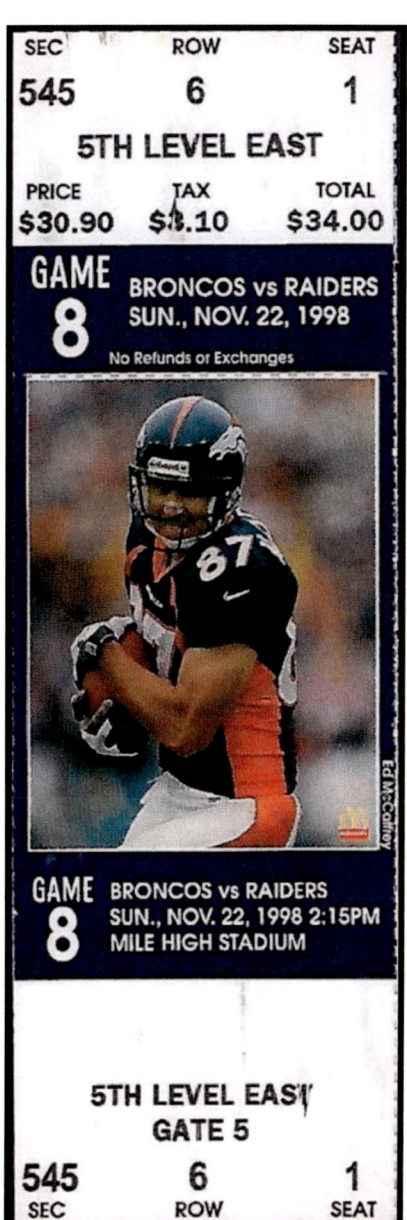

November 22, 1998

a 40-14 victory over the Los
Angeles Raiders, Elway completed 17/25 passes for 197
yards and 3 touchdowns.

On a 10 yard pass to Willie
Green, Elway becomes the
second player in NFL history
(Dan Marino) to pass for more
than 50,000 yards.

1998 Flair Showcase
Legacy Collection
Masterpiece Row 2 #7

1998 Flair Showcase
Row 2 #7

1998 Flair Showcase
Legacy Row 2 #7

1998 Flair Showcase
Legacy Collection
Masterpiece Row 3 #7

1998 Flair Showcase
Row 3 #7

1998 Flair Showcase
Legacy Row 3 #7

1998 Finest Stadium Stars
Jumbo #SS20

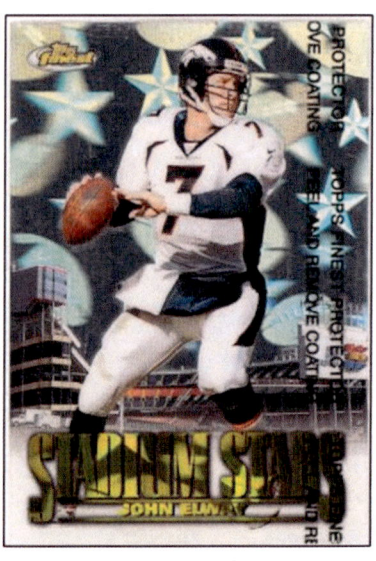

1998 Finest Stadium Stars
Jumbo Refractor #SS20

1998 Finest Finest Moment
Jumbo #

1998 Fleer Tradition
Big Numbers

Reverse

1998 Fleer Brilliants #1

1998 Fleer Brilliants
24K Gold #1

1998 Fleer Brilliants
Blue #1

1998 Fleer Brilliants
Gold #1

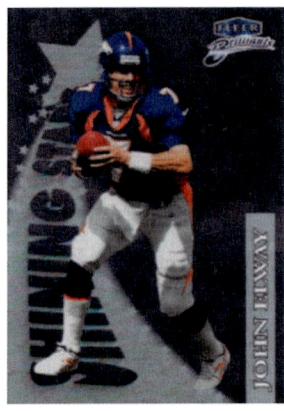

1998 Fleer Brilliants
Shining Star #13

1998 Fleer Brilliants
Shining Star Pulsars #12

1998 Fleer Tradition #3

1998 Fleer Tradition
Heritage #3

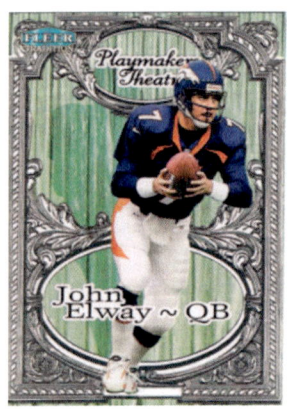

1998 Fleer Playmakers
Theatre #PT4

1998 Leaf Rookies and
Stars #120

1998 Leaf Rookies and
Stars #249

1998 Leaf Rookies and
Stars Crusade Green #9

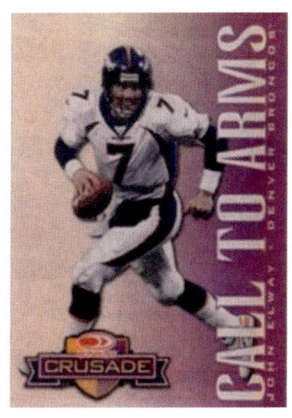
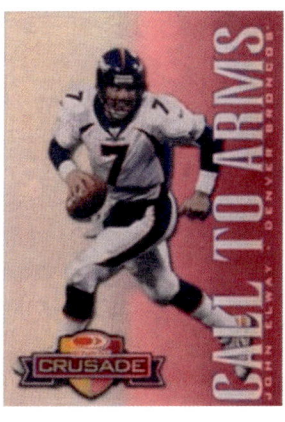
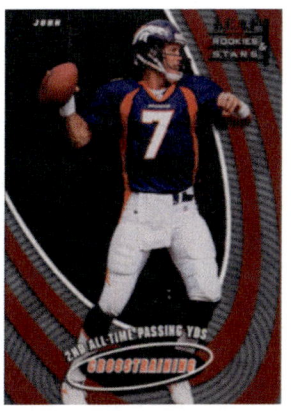
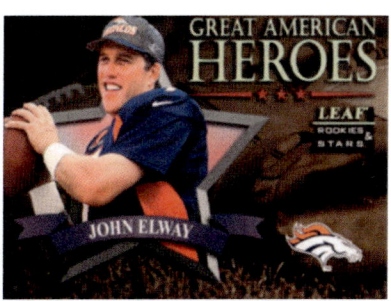

1998 Leaf Rookies and Stars Crusade Purple #9

1998 Leaf Rookies and Stars Crusade Red #9

1998 Leaf Rookies and Stars Cross Training #4

1998 Leaf Rookies and Stars Great American Heros #9

1998 Leaf Rookies and Stars Greatest Hits #3

1998 Leaf Rookies and Stars Longevity #120

1998 Leaf Rookies and Stars Longevity #249

1998 Leaf Rookie and Stars Longevity Holofoil #120

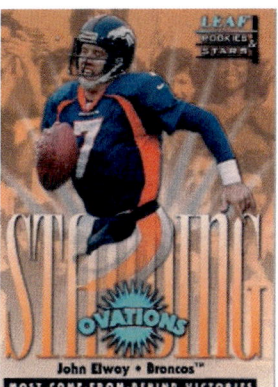

1998 Leaf Rookies and Stars Longevity Holofoil #249

1998 Leaf Rookies and Stars MVP Contenders #7

1998 Leaf Rookies and Stars Standing Ovation #9

1998 Leaf Rookies and Stars Standing Ovation Promo #9 Reverse

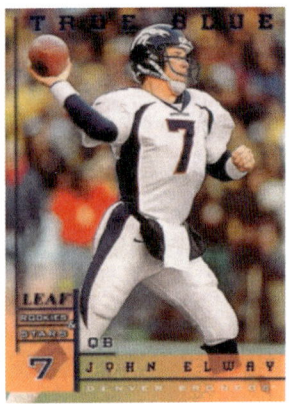

1998 Leaf Rookies and Stars True Blue #120

1998 Leaf Rookies and Stars True Blue #249

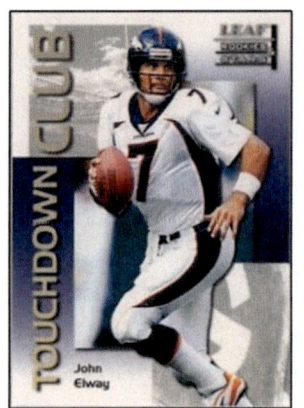

1998 Leaf Rookies and Stars Touchdown Club #18

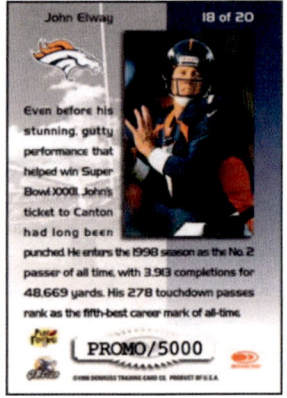

1998 Leaf Rookies and Stars Touchdown Club #18 Promo Reverse

1998 Leaf Rookies and Stars Ticket Masters #7

1998 Leaf Rookies and Stars Ticket Masters Die Cut #7

1998 Metal Universe #7

1998 Metal Universe Pecious Gems #7

1998 Metal Universe Precious Metal Gems Masterpiece

1998 Metal Universe Decided Edge Insert #3

1998 Metal Universe Decided Edge #3

1998 Metal Universe E-X 2001 Previews #4

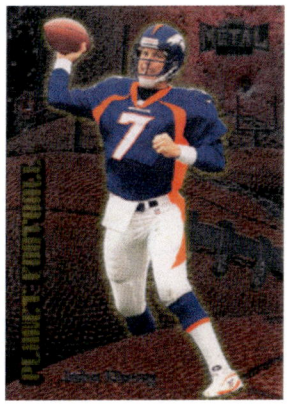

1998 Metal Universe
Planet Football #5

1998 Metal Universe
Precious Metal Gems #7

1998 Pacific #126

1998 Pacific Cramers
Choice #2

1998 Pacific Dynagon
Turf #5

1998 Pacific Dynagon
Titanium Turf #5

1998 Pacific Gold
Crown Die Cuts #9

1998 Pacific Omega #68

1998 Pacific Omega
EO Portraits #6

1998 Pacific Omega
EO Portraits
Laser Cut #6

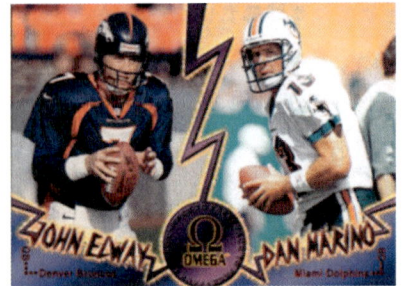

1998 Pacific Omega
Face to Face #3

1998 Pacific Omega
Online #8

1998 Pacific Omega Prisms #6

1998 Pacific Platinum
Blue #126

1998 Pacific Red #126

1998 Pacific Team Checklist #9

1998 Pacific Timelines #5

1998 Paramount #67

1998 Paramount
Copper #67

1998 Paramount
Kings of the NFL #6

1998 Paramount Kings
of the NFL Proof #6

1998 Paramount
National Promo
Embossed #67

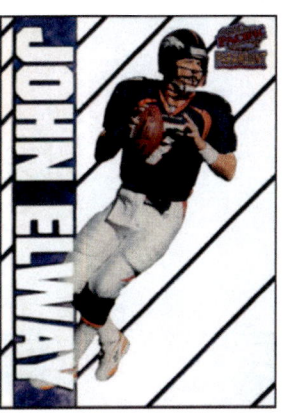

1998 Paramount
Personal Best #10

1998 Paramount
Platinum Blue #67

1998 Paramount Pro
Bowl Die Cuts #2

1998 Paramount Red #67

1998 Paramount Silver
#67

1998 Paramount
Super Bowl XXXII #2

1998 Paramount
Super Bowl XXXII #3

1998 Pinnacle
Inscriptions
Pen Pals #4

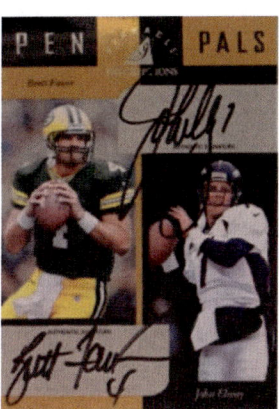

1998 Pinnacle
Inscriptions
Pen Pals #5

1998 Pinnacle
Inscriptions
Pen Pals #6

1998 Pinnacle Inscriptions
Autograph NNO

1998 Pinnacle Inscriptions
Promo #33

1998 Pinnacle Inscriptions
#33

1998 Pinnacle Baseball
All-Star Fan Fest

1998 Pinnacle Inside
Conference Clash
Test Issue #AFC 5

1998 Pinnacle
Inside Behind The
Numbers #3

1998 Pinnacle Inside
Stand Up Guys
#10AB Promo

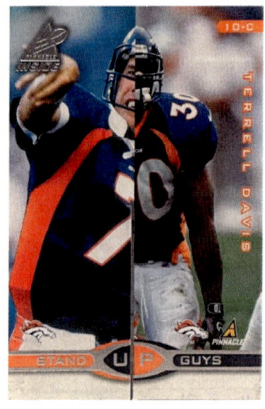

1998 Pinnacle Inside
Stand Up Guys
#9CD Promo

1998 Pinnacle Inside Stand Up Guys Promo

1998 Pinnacle Mint
Coins Brass #1

1998 Pinnacle Mint
Coins Nickel #1

1998 Pinnacle Mint
Team Pinnacle
Unissued Proof

1998 Pinnacle Mint #1

1998 Pinnacle Mint
#34

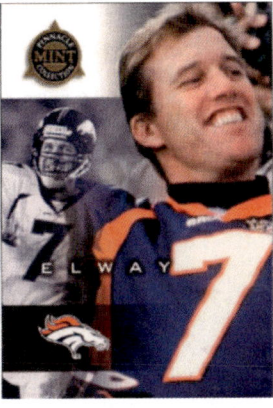

1998 Pinnacle Mint
#67

1998 Pinnacle Mint
Gold #1

1998 Pinnacle Mint
Gold #34

1998 Pinnacle Mint
Gold #67

1998 Pinnacle Mint
Gems #8

1998 Pinnacle Mint
Impeccable Promo #1

1998 Pinnacle Mint
Impeccable #1

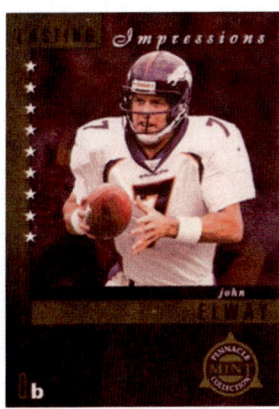

1998 Pimmacle Mint
Lasting Impressions #2

1998 Pinnacle Mint
Minted Moments #3

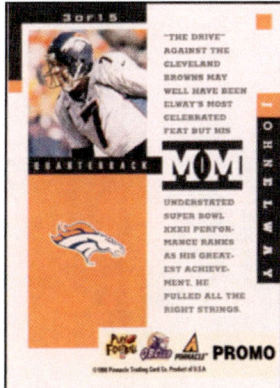

1998 Pinnacle Mint
Minted Moments Promo
#3

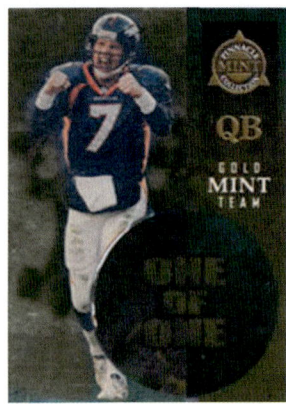

1998 Pinnacle Mint
One-of-One #1

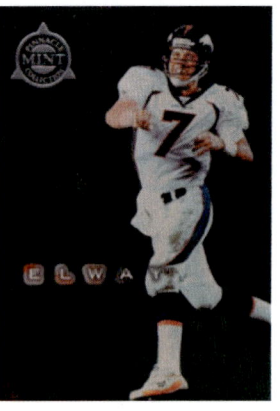

1998 Pinnacle Mint
One-of-One #34

1998 Pinnacle Mint
One-of-One #67

1998 Pinnacle Mint
Silver #1

1998 Pinnacle Mint
Silver #34

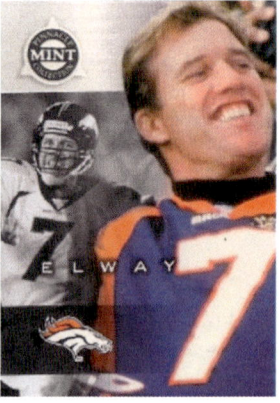

1998 Pinnacle Mint
Silver #67

1998 Pinnacle Mint
Team Pinnacle Points 1 #4

1998 Pinnacle Mint
Team Pinnacle Points 5 #4

1998 Pinnacle Mint
Team Pinnacle Points 10 #4

1998 Pinnacle Team
Pinnacle Promo

1998 Pinnacle Plus
Sunday's Best Promo #2

1998 Playoff Absolute
7-11 #1

1998 Playoff Absolute
Hobby #1

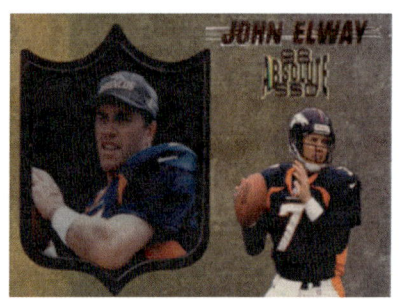

1998 Playoff Absolute
Hobby Gold #1

1998 Playoff Absolute
Hobby Silver #1

1998 Playoff Absolute
Honors #PH13

1998 Playoff Absolute Platinum
Quads #1

1998 Playoff Absolute
Retail #1

1998 Playoff Absolute
Retail Green #1

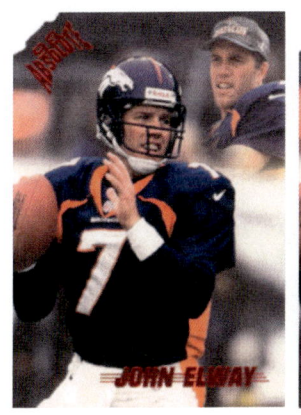

1998 Playoff Absolute
Retail Red #1

No Official Listing

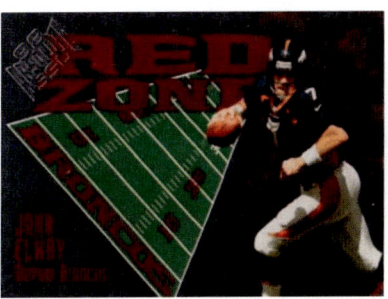

1998 Playoff Absolute
Red Zone #7

1998 Playoff Absolute
Red Zone Die Cuts #7

1998 Playoff Absolute
Shields #7

1998 Playoff Absolute
Shields Die Cut #7

1998 Playoff Absolute
Statistically Speaking #7

1998 Playoff Absolute
Statistically Speaking
Die Cut #7

1998 Playoff Absolute
Tandems #2A

1998 Playoff Contenders
Leather #23

1998 Playoff Contenders
Leather Gold #23

1998 Playoff Contenders
Leather Red #23

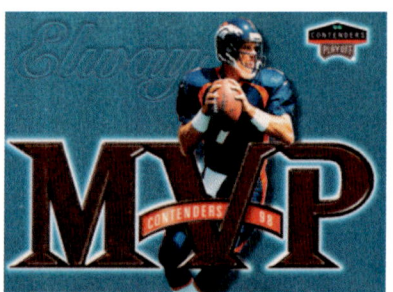

1998 Playoff Contenders
Leather Registered
Exchange #23

1998 Playoff Contenders
MVP Contenders #7

1998 Playoff Contenders Pennants #26

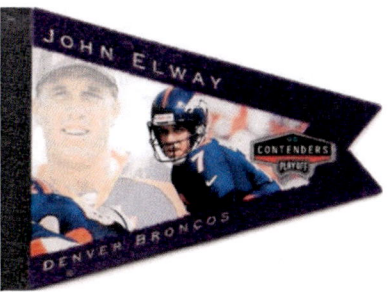

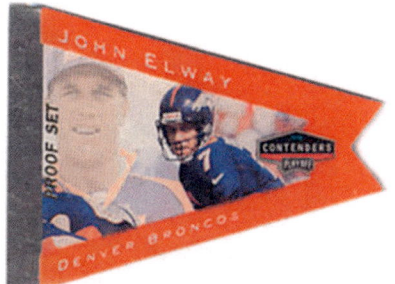

1998 Playoff Contenders
Pennants Proof #26

1998 Playoff Contenders
Pennants Gold #26

1998 Playoff Contenders
Pennants Red #26

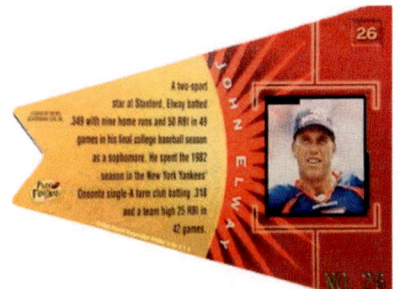

1998 Playoff Contenders
Pennants Registered
Exchange #26

1998 Playoff Contenders
Super Bowl Leather #2

1998 Playoff Contenders
Ticket #24

1998 Playoff Contenders
Ticket Gold #24

1998 Playoff Contenders
Ticket Red #24

1998 Playoff Contenders
Ticket Proof #24

1998 Playoff Contenders
Ticket Registered
Exchange #24

1998 Playoff Contenders
Ticket Super Bowl Miami
#24

1998 Playoff Momentum
7-11 NNO Ismail Reverse

1998 Playoff Contenders
Touchdown Tandems #24

1998 Playoff Momentum
Class Reunion Quads #1

1998 Playoff Momentum Class
Reunion Quads Jumbo #1

1998 Playoff Momentum
Class Reunion Tandems #1

1998 Playoff Momentum
End Zone Express #8

1998 Playoff Momentum End
Zone Express Non Die Cut #8

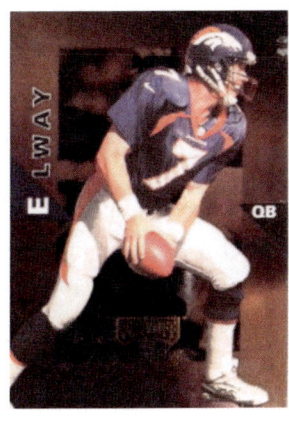

1998 Playoff Momentum
Hobby #70

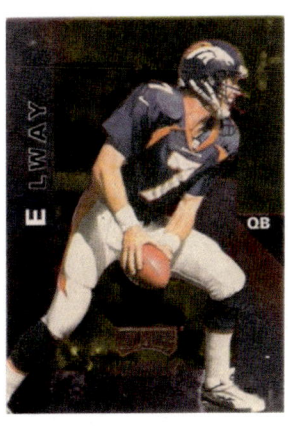

1998 Playoff Momentum
Hobby Gold #70

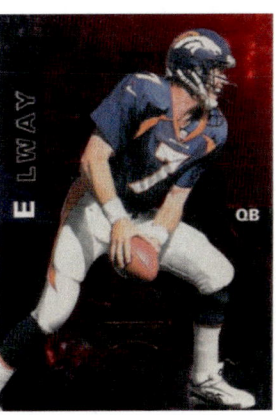

1998 Playoff Momentum
Hobby Red #70

1998 Playoff Momentum
Headliners #7

1998 Playoff Momentum
Headliners Gold #7

1998 Playoff Momentum
Headliners Gold
Replacement #7

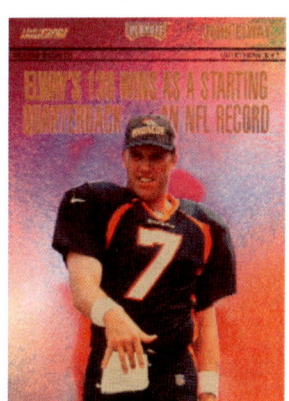

1998 Playoff Momentum
Headliners Red #7

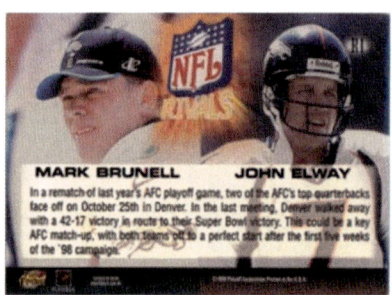

1998 Playoff Momentum
NFL Rivals #1

Reverse

1998 Playoff Momentum
Rivals Silver #R1

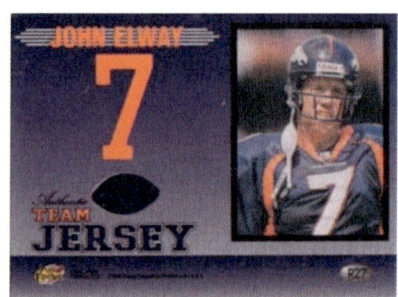

1998 Playoff Momentum
Retail #66

1998 Playoff Momentum
Retail Red #66

1998 Playoff Momentum
Team Jerseys #27

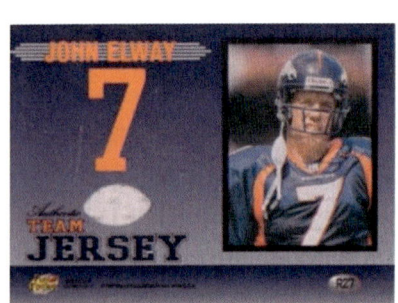

1998 Playoff Momentum
Team Jerseys Away #27

1998 Playoff Momentum
Team Threads Away #27

1998 Playoff Momentum
Team Threads Home #27

1998 Playoff Prestige
7-11 #1

1998 Playoff Prestige
Alma Mater #17

1998 Playoff Prestige
Alma Mater Blue #17

1998 Playoff Prestige
Winning Preformer #6

1998 Playoff Prestige
Winning Preformer Blue
#6

1998 Playoff Prestige
Best Of The NFL #6

1998 Playoff Prestige
Best Of The NFL
Non Die Cut #6

1998 Playoff Prestige
Checklist #9

1998 Playoff Prestige
Checklist Gold #9

1998 Playoff Prestige
Hobby #1

1998 Playoff Prestige
Hobby Gold #1

1998 Playoff Prestige
Hobby Red #1

1998 Playoff Prestige
Inside The Numbers #18

1998 Playoff Prestige
National Promo

1998 Playoff Prestige
National Promo

1998 Playoff Prestige
National Promo

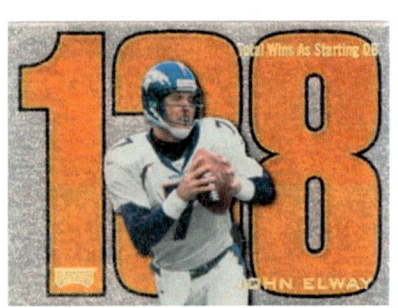

1998 Playoff Prestige Inside The
Numbers Non Die Cut #18

1998 Playoff Prestige
Retail #1

1998 Playoff Prestige
Retail Green #1

1998 Playoff Prestige
Retail Red #1

1998 Pro Line DC3
#59

1998 Pro Line DC3
Clear Cuts #1

1998 Pro Line DC 3
Gold #59

1998 Pro Line DC3
Perfect Cut #59

1998 Pro Line DC3 Perfect
Cut X-tra Effort #12

1998 Pro Line DC3 Perfect Cut
Clear Cut #1

1998 Pro Line DC3 Extra
Effort #12

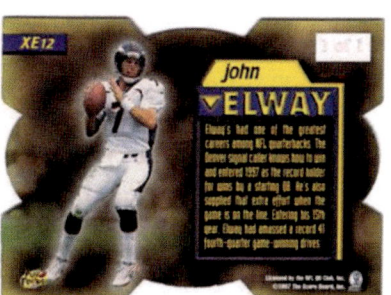

Reverse 1/1

1998 Pro Magnets #8

1998 Pro Stamp #2

1998 Revolution #37

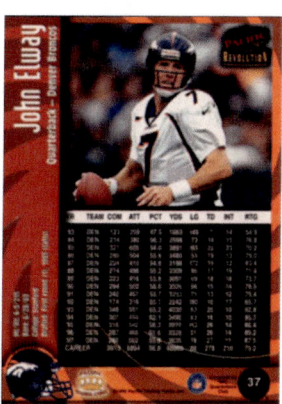

Reverse

1998 Revolution Icons #3

1998 Revolution Prime
Time Performenrs #7

1998 Revolution Rookies and Stars #7

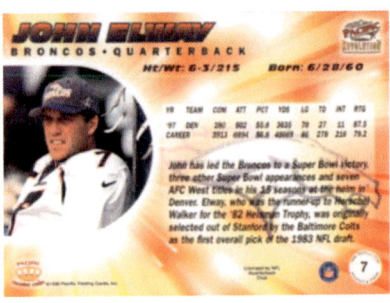

Reverse

1998 Revolution Rookies and Stars Gold #7

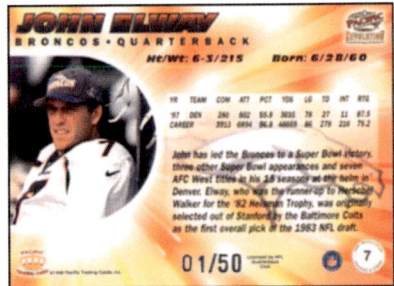

Reverse #/50

December 6, 1998

In a 35-31 victory over Kansas City, Elway completed 22/32 passes for 400 yards, and 2 touchdowns. He was named NFL Player of the Week.

1998 Revolution Shadows #37

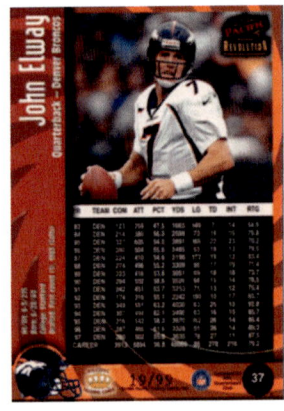

Reverse #/99

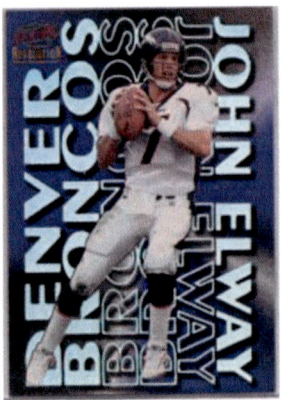

1998 Revolution Showstoppers #9

1998 Revolution Showstoppers Red #9

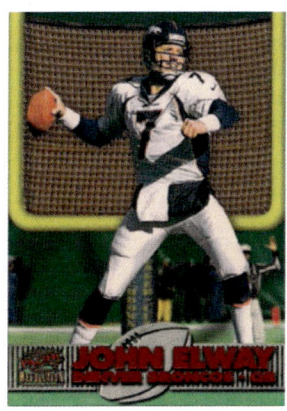

1998 Revolution
Touchdown #6

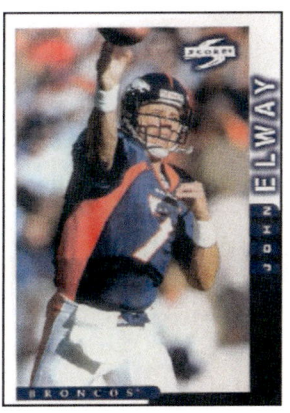

1998 Score #1

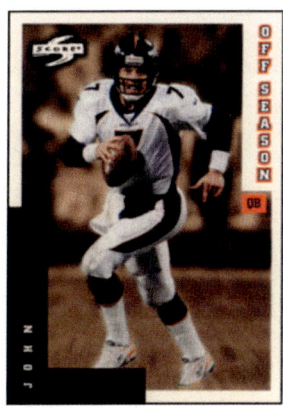

1998 Score #253

1998 Score Board Super Bowl XXXII

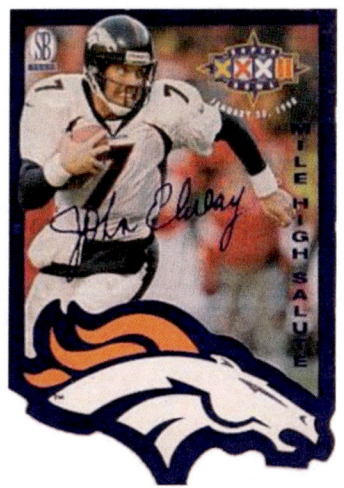

1998 Score Board
Super Bowl XXXII

1998 Score Board Jumbo #JE7

1998 Score Complete
Players #2A

1998 Score Complete
Players #2B

1998 Score Complete
Players #2C

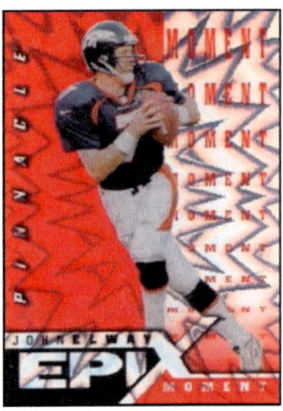

1998 Score Epix #E20

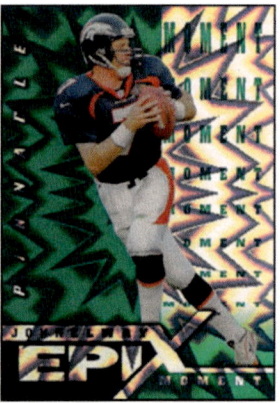

1998 Score Epix
Emerald #E20

1998 Score Epix
Hobby #13

1998 Score Epix
Hobby Emerald #13

1998 Score Epix
Hobby Purple #13

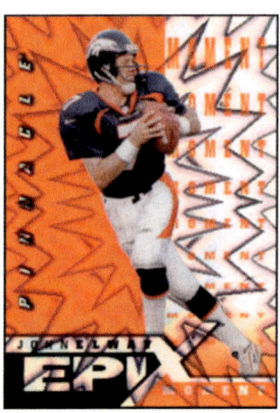

1998 Score Epix
Orange #E20

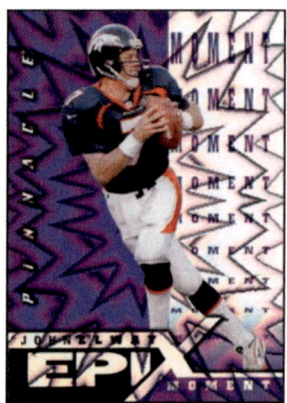

1998 Score Epix
Purple #E20

1998 Score Showcase
#PP143

1998 Score Showcase
Artist Proof #PP1

1998 Score Showcase
One-of-One #PP143

1998 Score Star Salute #14

Reverse

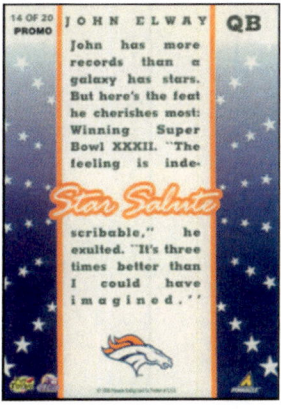

1998 Score Star Salute
Promo #14 Reverse

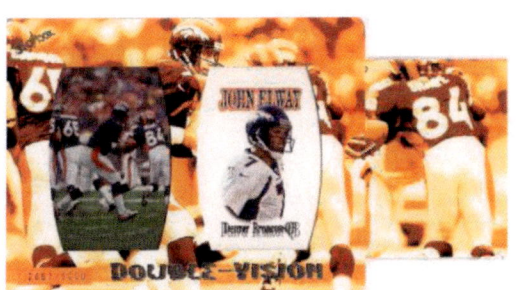

1998 Sky Box Double Vision #2

1998 Sky Box Double Vision #24

1998 SkyBox
Premium #1

1998 SkyBox
Premium #196

1998 SkyBox
Premium #208

1998 SkyBox
Premium #210

1998 SkyBox Premium
Intimidation nation #7N

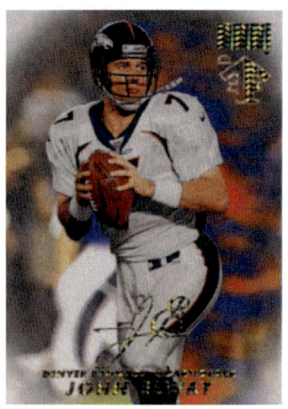

1998 SkyBox Premium
Fleet Farms #1

1998 SkyBox Premium
Fleet Farms #196

1998 SkyBox Premium
Fleet Farms #208

1998 SkyBox Premium
Fleet Farms #210

1998 SkyBox Premium
Rap Show #1

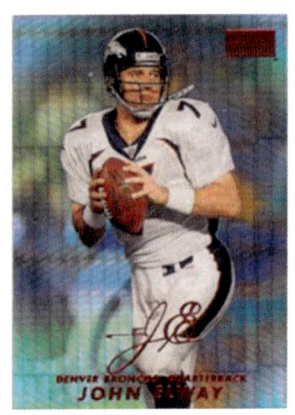

1998 SkyBox Premium
Rubies #1

1998 SkyBox Premium
Rubies #196

1998 SkyBox Premium
Rubies #208

1998 SkyBox Premium
Rubies #210

1998 SkyBox Thunder
#211

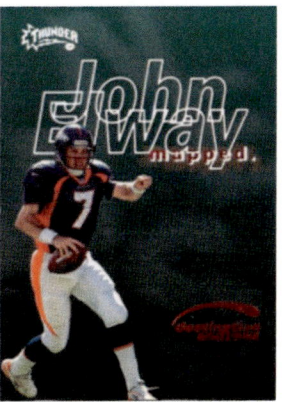

1998 SkyBox Thunder
Destination End Zone
#DE6

1998 SkyBox Thunder
Quick Strike #2QS

1998 SkyBox Thunder
Rave #211

1998 SkyBox Thunder
Super Rave #211

1998 SP Authentic
#31

1998 SP Authentic #66

1998 SP Authentic
Die Cut #31

1998 SP Authentic
Die Cut #66

1998 SP Authentic
Maximum Impact
#SE7

1998 SP Authentic
Maximum Impact
Die Cut #SE7

1998 SP Authentic
Special Forces #S12

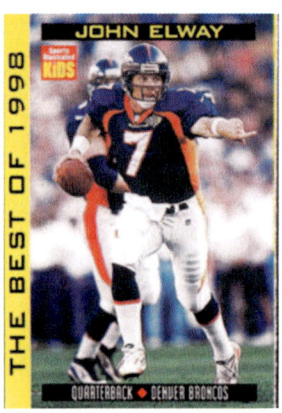

1998 Sports Illustrated
For Kids

1998 SPX #14

1998 SPX Bronze #14

1998 SPX Finite #25

1998 SPX Finite #97

1998 SPX FInite #177

1998 SPX Finite #281

1998 SPX Finite #341

1998 SPX Finite Radiance #25

1998 SPX Finite
Radiance #97

1998 SPX Finite
Radiance #177

1998 SPX Finite
Radiance #281

1998 SPX Finite
Spectrum #25

1998 SPX Finite
Spectrum #97

1998 SPX Finite
Spectrum #177

1998 SPX Finite
Radiance #281

1998 SPX Finite
Spectrum #341

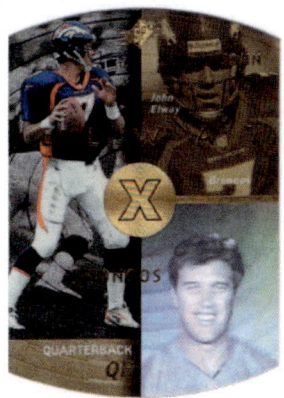

1998 SPX Gold #14

1998 SPX Grand
Finale #14

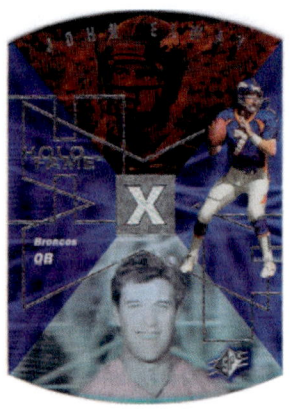

1998 SPX Hall of Fame
#HF13

1998 SPX Silver #14

1998 SPX Steel #14

1998 Stadium Club #100

1998 Stadium Club Chrome #100

1998 Stadium Club Chrome Jumbo #SSC1

1998 Stadium Club Chrome Jumbo
Refractor #SCC1

1998 Stadium Club Chrome
Refractor #SCC1

1998 Stadium Club
Double Threat #DT5

1998 Stadium Club
First Day #100

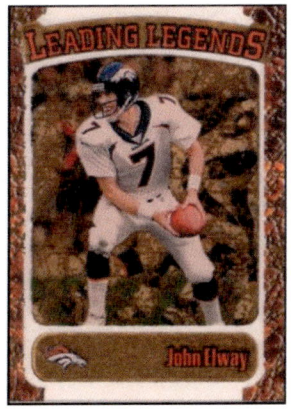

1998 Stadium Club
Leading Legends #1

1998 Stadium Club
One-of-a-Kind #100

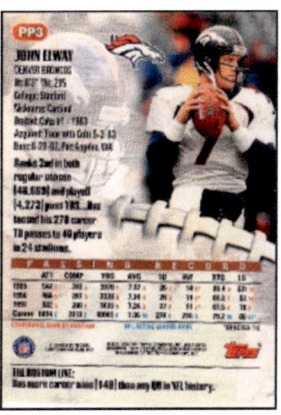

1998 Stadium Club
Promo #3 Reverse

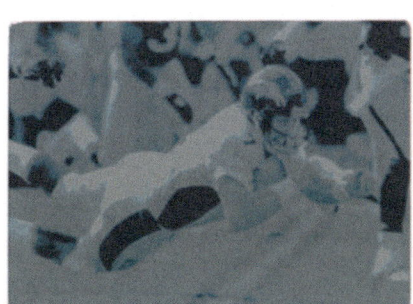

1998 Stadium Club
Printing Plate #100

1998 Stadium Club
Triumverate Luminous
#T1B

1998 Stadium Club
Triumverate
Illuminator #T1B

1998 Stadium Club
Triumverate
Luminescent #T1B

1998 Starting Lineup

1998 Starting Lineup
Classic Combos

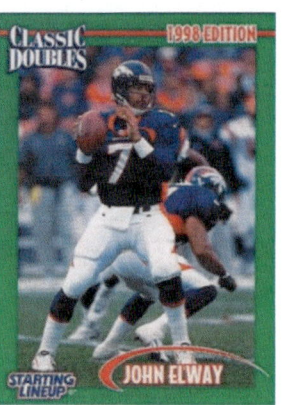

1998 Starting Lineup
Classic Combos

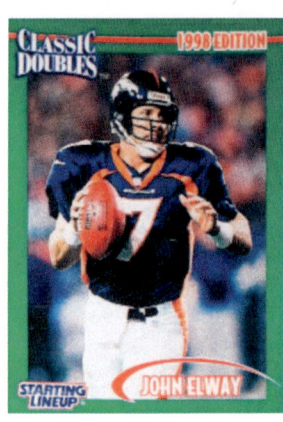

1998 Topps #300

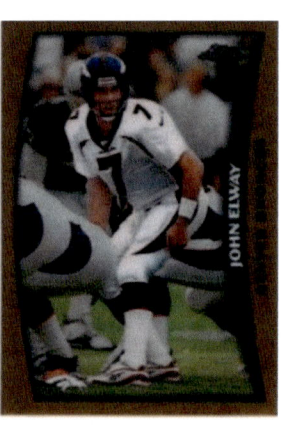

1998 Topps Action
Flats Kick Off Edition
#K3

1998 Topps Chrome
#300

Measures Of Greatness

1998 Topps Chrome
Measure Of Greatness
#MG1

1998 Topps Chrome
Measure Of Greatness
Refractor #MG1

1998 Topps Chrome
Refractor #300

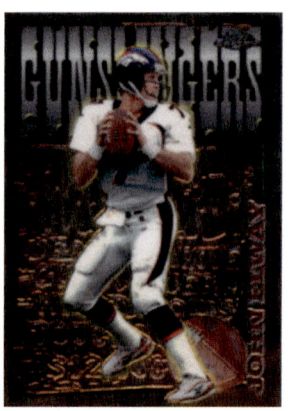

1998 Topps Chrome
Seasons Best #10

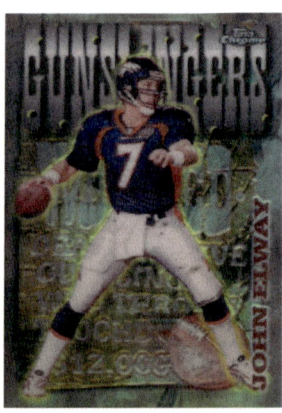

1998 Topps Chrome
Seasons Best #30

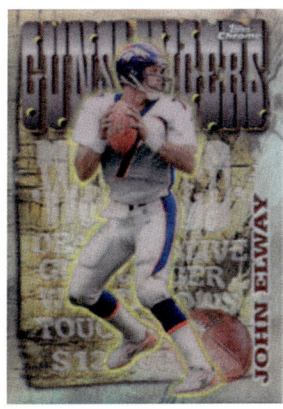

1998 Topps Chrome
Seasons Best Refractor
#10

1998 Topps Chrome
Seasons Best Refractor
#30

1998 Topps Gold Label
Class 1 #1

1998 Topps Gold Label
Class 1 Black #1

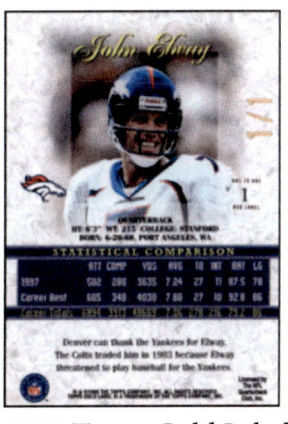

1998 Topps Gold Label
Class 1 Red One to One
#1 (1/1) Reverse

1998 Topps Gold Label
Class 1 Red #1

1998 Topps Gold Label
Class 2 #1

1998 Topps Gold Label
Class 2 Black #1

1998 Topps Gold Label
Class 2 Red #1

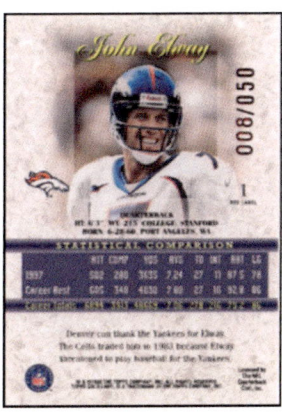

1998 Topps Gold Label
Class 2 Red One to
One #1 (#/50) Reverse

1998 Topps Gold
Label Class 3 #1

1998 Topps Gold Label
Class 3 Black #1

1998 Topps Gold Label
Class 3 One To One #1
(1/1) Reverse

1998 Topps Gold Label
Class 3 Red #1

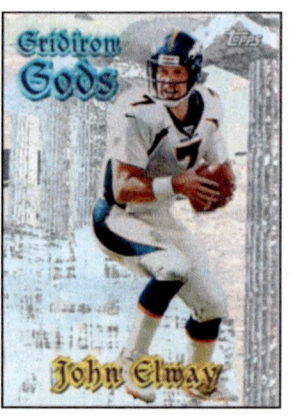

1998 Topps Gridiron
Gods #GI5

1998 Topps Measures
Of Greatness #MG1

1998 Topps Mystery
Finest #M8

1998 Topps Mystery
Finest Refractor #M8

1998 Topps Season
Best #10

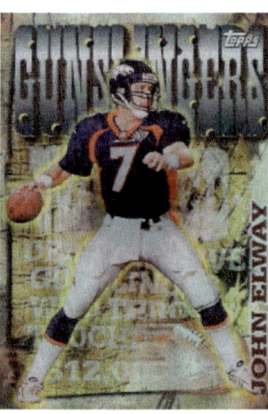

1998 Topps Seasons
Best #30

1998 Topps Season
Opener #143

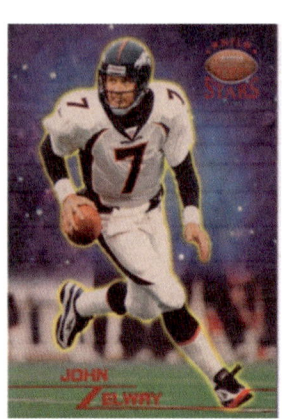

1998 Topps Stars #1

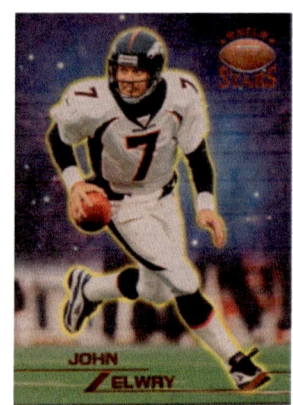

1998 Topps Stars
Bronze #1

1998 Topps Star
Galaxy #G8

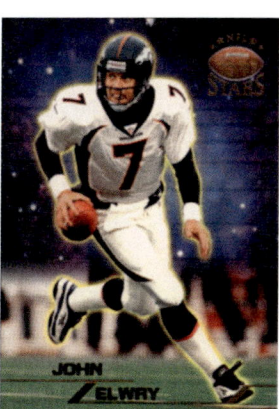

1998 Topps Star Galaxy
Gold #G8

Reverse #/50

1998 Topps Stars Galaxy
Gold Refractor #8

1998 Topps Star
Gold #1

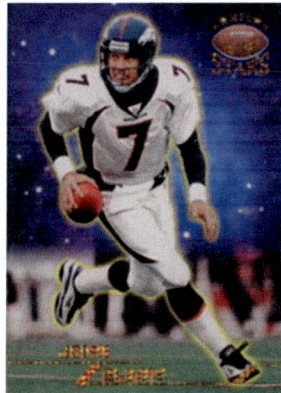
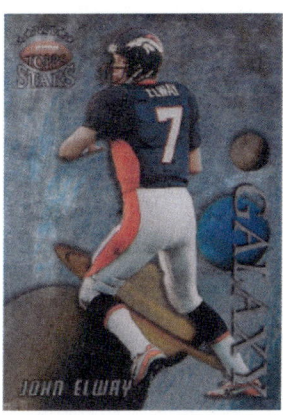
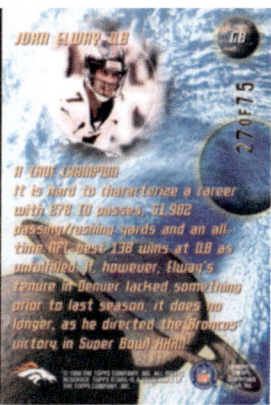

1998 Topps Star
Gold Rainbow #1

1998 Topps Star
Galaxy Silver #G8

Reverse #/15

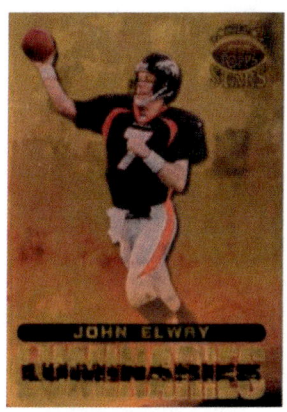
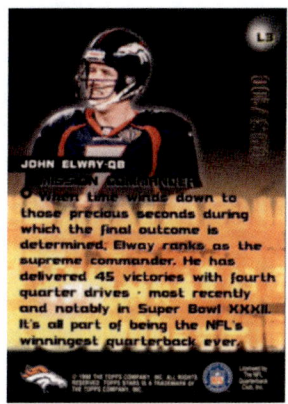
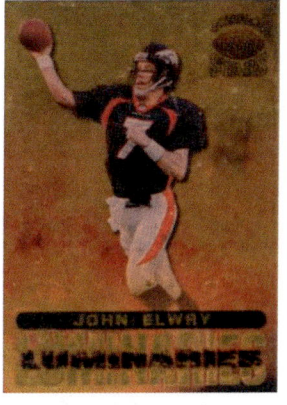

1998 Topps Stars
Luminaries #L3

Reverse #/100

1998 Topps Star
Luminaries Gold #L3

Reverse #/75

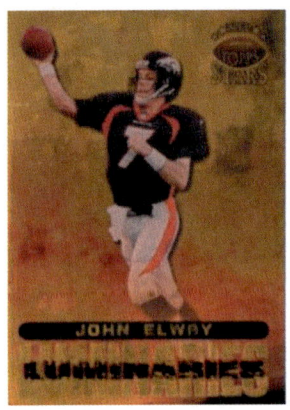

1998 Topps Star Luminaries
Gold Rainbow #L3

Reverse #/5

1998 Topps Star
Silver #1

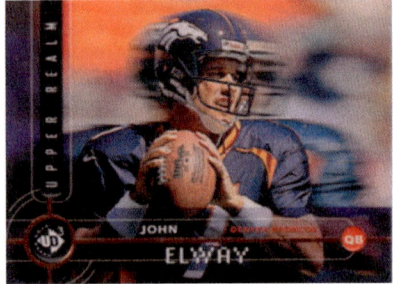
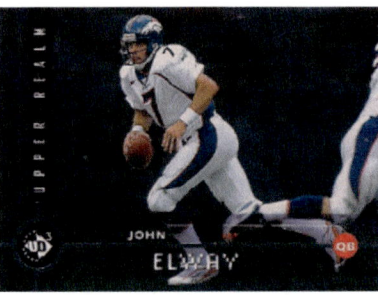

1998 UD3 #67
Upper Realm Rainbow

1998 UD3 #157
Upper Realm Light FX

1998 UD3 #247
Upper Realm Rainbow

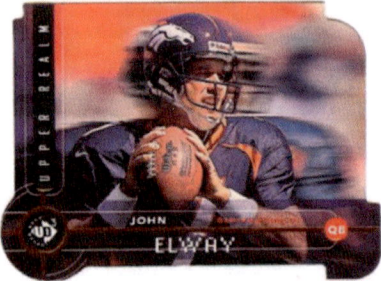
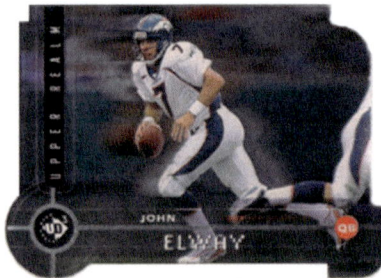

1998 UD3 Die Cut #67
Embossed

1998 UD3 Die Cut #157

1998 UD3 Die CUt #247
Rainbow

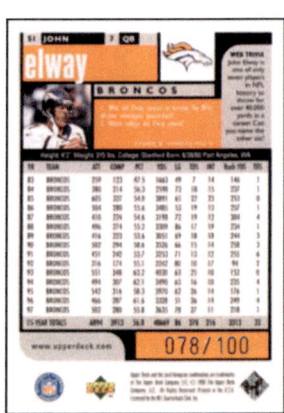

1998 UD Choice #51

1998 UD Choice
Choice Reserve #51

1998 UD Choice Jumbo #51

1998 UD Choice Prime
Choice Reserve #51
#/100 Reverse

1998 UD Choice
Starquest #7

1998 UD Choice
Starquest Gold #7

1998 UD Choice
Starquest Green #7

1998 UD Choice
Starquest Red #7

1998 UD Choice
Starquest Rookie
Blue #7

1998 UD Choice
Starquest Rookie
Gold #7

1998 UD Choice
Starquest Rookie
Green #7

1998 UD Choice
Starquest Rookie
Red #

1998 Ultra #134

1998 Ultra #200

1998 Ultra #376

1998 Ultra Canton
Classics #3

1998 Ultra Exclamation
Points #3

1998 Ultra Gold
Medallion #134G

1998 Ultra Gold
Medallion #200G

1998 Ultra Gold
Medallion #376G

1998 Ultra Masterpiece
#134

1998 Ultra Masterpiece
#200

1998 Ultra Masterpiece
#376

1998 Ultra Platinum
Medallion #134P
#/98 Reverse

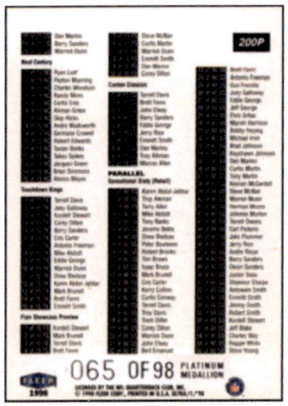

1998 Ultra Platinum
Medallion #200P
#/98 Reverse

1998 Ultra Platinum
Medallion #376P
#/98 Reverse

1998 Ultra Rush Hour #2

1998 Ultra Sensational
Sixty #21

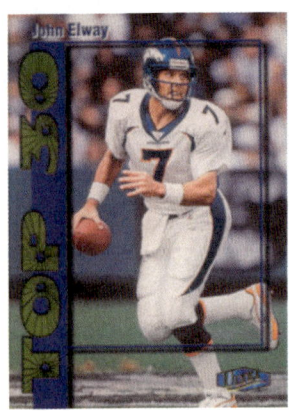

1998 Ultra Top 30 #12

1998 Upper Deck #97

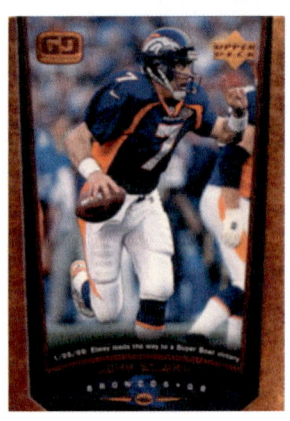

1998 Upper Deck
Bronze #97

1998 Upper Deck
Gold #97

1998 Upper Deck
Constant Threat #CT7

1998 Upper Deck
Constant Threat
Die Cut Silver #CT7

1998 Upper Deck
Constant Threat
Die Cut Silver #CT7

1998 Upper Deck
Encore FX #62

1998 Upper Deck Encore
Constant Threat #CT6

1998 Upper Deck
Encore Driving
Forces #F8

1998 Upper Deck
Encore Driving
Forces FX #F8

1998 Upper Deck Encore
Milestones #62

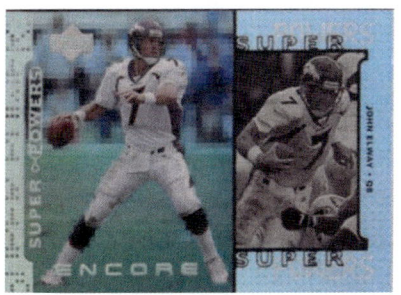

1998 Upper Deck Encore
Super Powers #S4

1998 Upper Deck
Game Jersey #GJ14

December 27, 1998

Elway completed 26/36 passes for 338 yards, and 4 touchdowns.

On his fourth touchdown, a 1-yard pass to Shannon Sharpe, Elway becomes the third player (Fran Tarkenton, Dan Marino) in NFL history with 300 career touchdown passes.

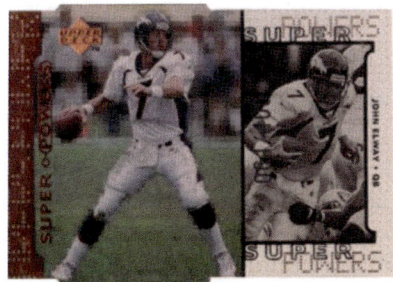

1998 Upper Deck Gold #97

1998 Upper Deck
Super Powers #S7

1998 Upper Deck
Super Powers Bronze Die
Cut #S7

1998 Upper Deck
Super Powers Silver #S7

1998 Upper Deck Super
Powers Silver Die Cut #S7

1998 Upper Deck Super
Powers Gold #S7

1998 Upper Deck Super Powers
Gold Die Cut #S7

1998 Upper Deck Uncataloged

January 17, 1999
AFC Championship
Denver 23 - NY Jets 10
Elway was 13/34 for 173 yards, and
a touchdown.

1998 "Got Milk?" Post Card

Elway earned MVP honors in Super Bowl XXXIII. He completed 18/29 passes for 336 yards, and a touchdown. He added a 3-yard touchdown run in the fourth quarter to seal the victory.

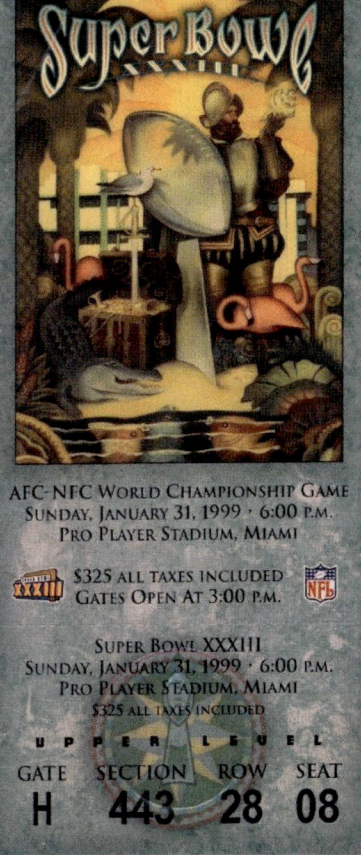

1998 World Championship Ring

January 31, 1999
Super Bowl XXXIII
Denver 34 - Atlanta 19

The Only Thing That Tastes Better Is Victory.

MILK

Where's *your* mustache?™

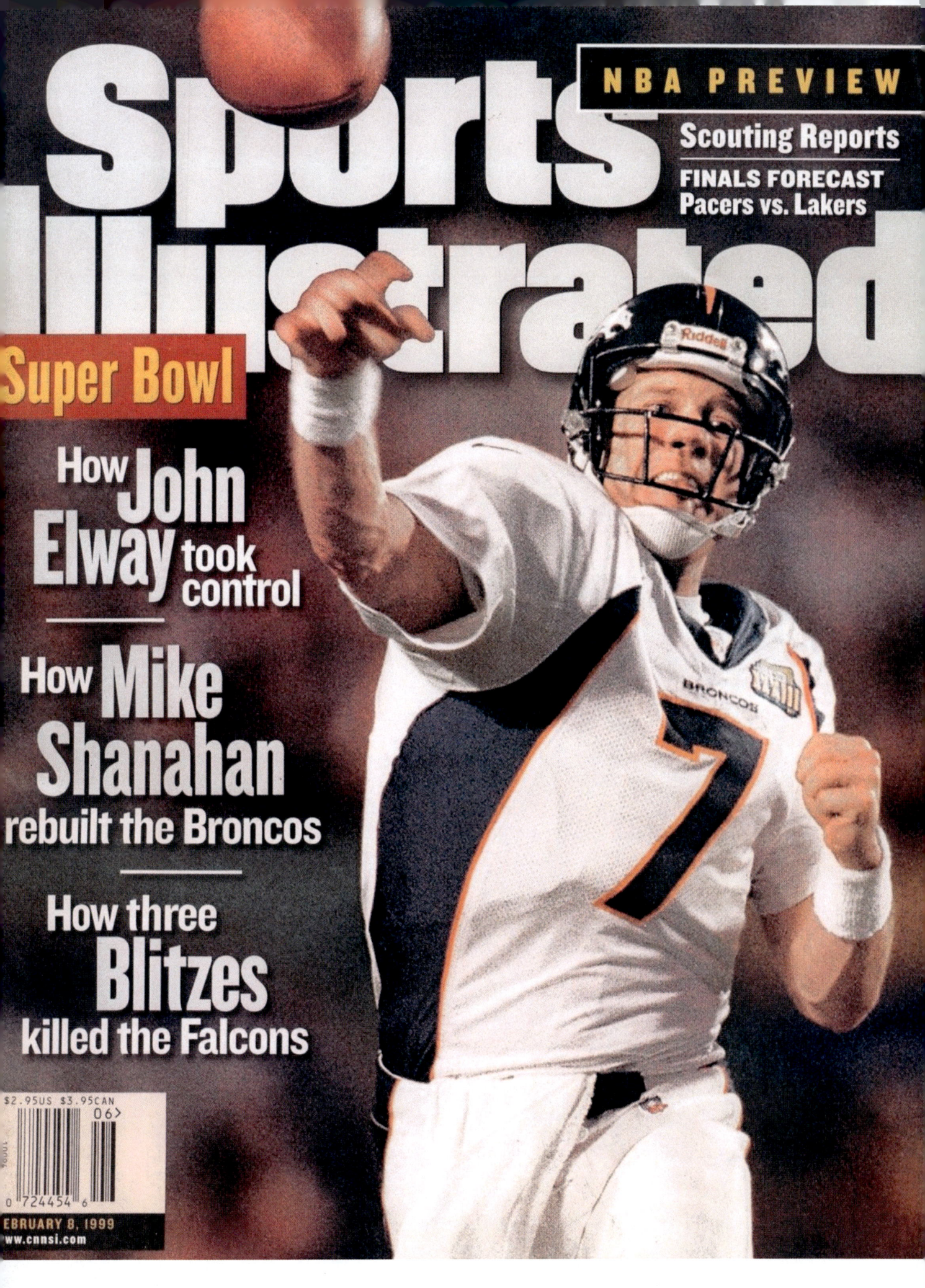

Sports Illustrated

$2.95US $3.95CAN

06>

0 724454 6

EBRUARY 8, 1999

ww.cnnsi.com

NBA PREVIEW

Scouting Reports

FINALS FORECAST
Pacers vs. Lakers

Super Bowl

How **John Elway** took control

How **Mike Shanahan** rebuilt the Broncos

How three **Blitzes** killed the Falcons

Sports Illustrated
PRESENTS

1998 DENVER BRONCOS
CHAMPS AGAIN!

ELWAY
A TRIBUTE

2/10/99 • DISPLAY UNTIL 5/10/99

Denver Broncos 1999 Pro Bowl Selctions

Back Row: Mark Schlereth, Tony Jones, Ed McCaffery, Tom Nalen
Front Row: John Elway, Bill Romanowski, Steve Atwater, Jason Elam.

February 7, 1999
Selected to his ninth Pro Bowl, a 23-10 win for the AFC, Elway played the opening series, and completed 4/5 passes. His final play as a professional was a 3-yard touchdown pass to fullback Sam Gash of the New England Patriots.

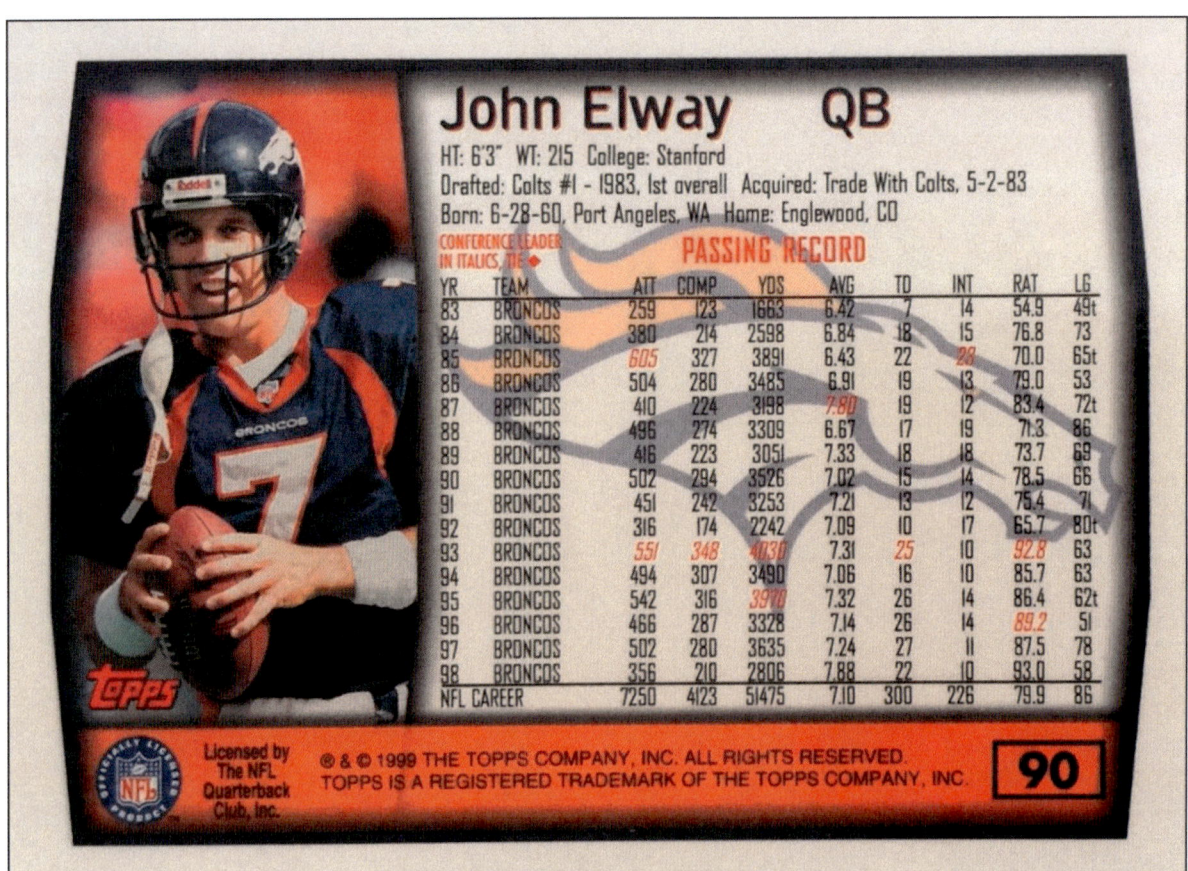

1999 Topps #90

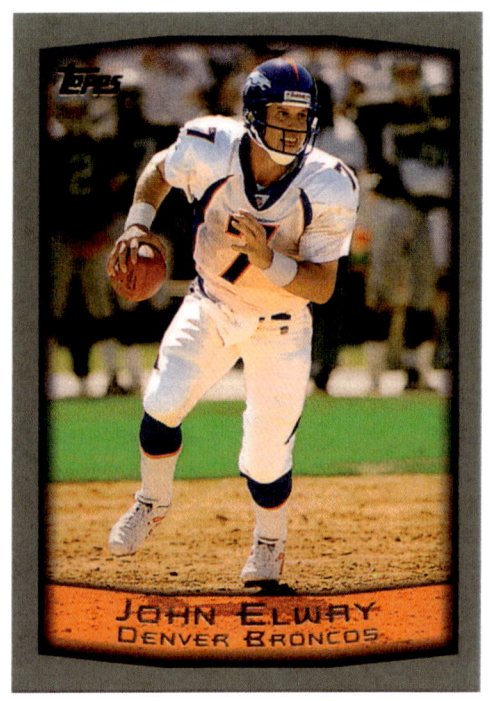

May 2, 1999

John Elway "graduated" from Pro Football, and announced his retirement fom the NFL. He left the game with more wins, 148, than any quarterback in history. Additionally his 51,475 passing yards placed him second all-time, and his 300 touchdowns placed him third. He also rushed for 3347 yards and 33 touchdowns.

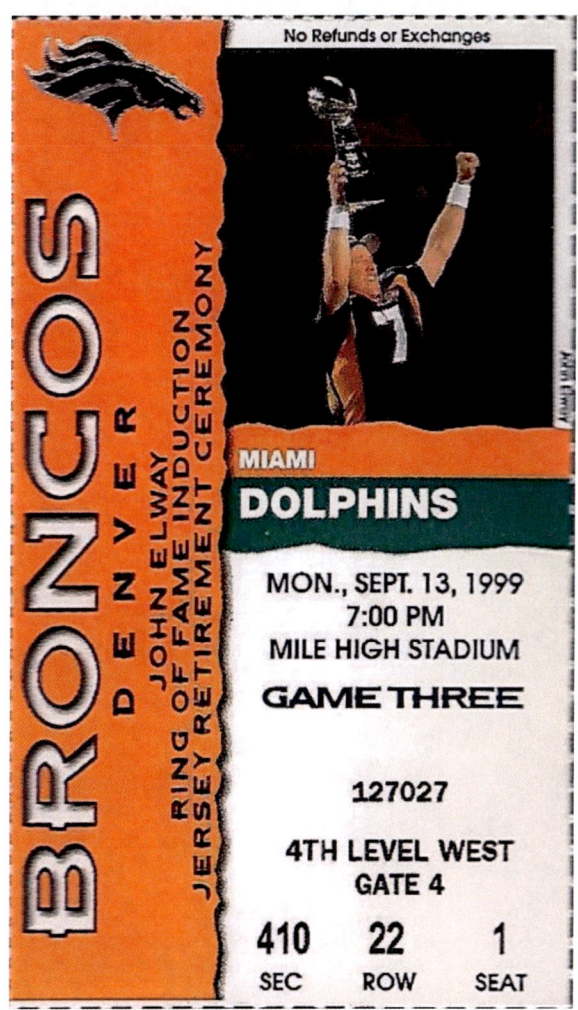

September 13, 1999
At halftime during the Monday, September 13,
1999 game against Miami, Denver retired John
Elway's number. No other Denver Broncos
player will ever wear #7 again,

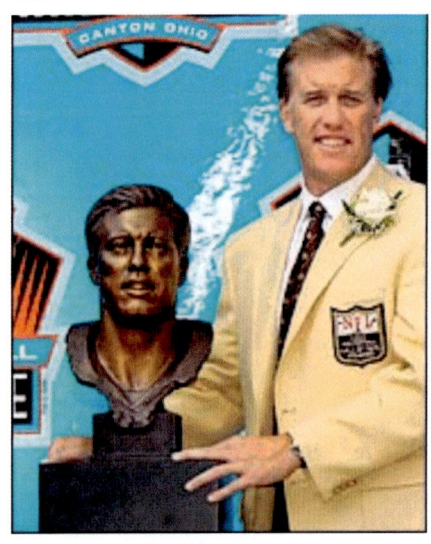

John Elway's HOF Ring

August 8, 2004

Elway along with Bob Brown, Carl Eller, and Barry Sanders is enshrined into the Professional
Football Hall of Fame.

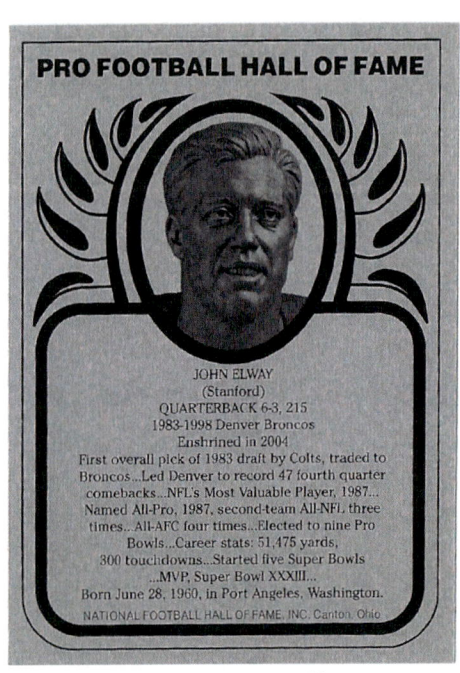

2004 HOF Metallic

2004 Topps Hall of Fame Class
#HOFJE

2004 Goal Line Art #224

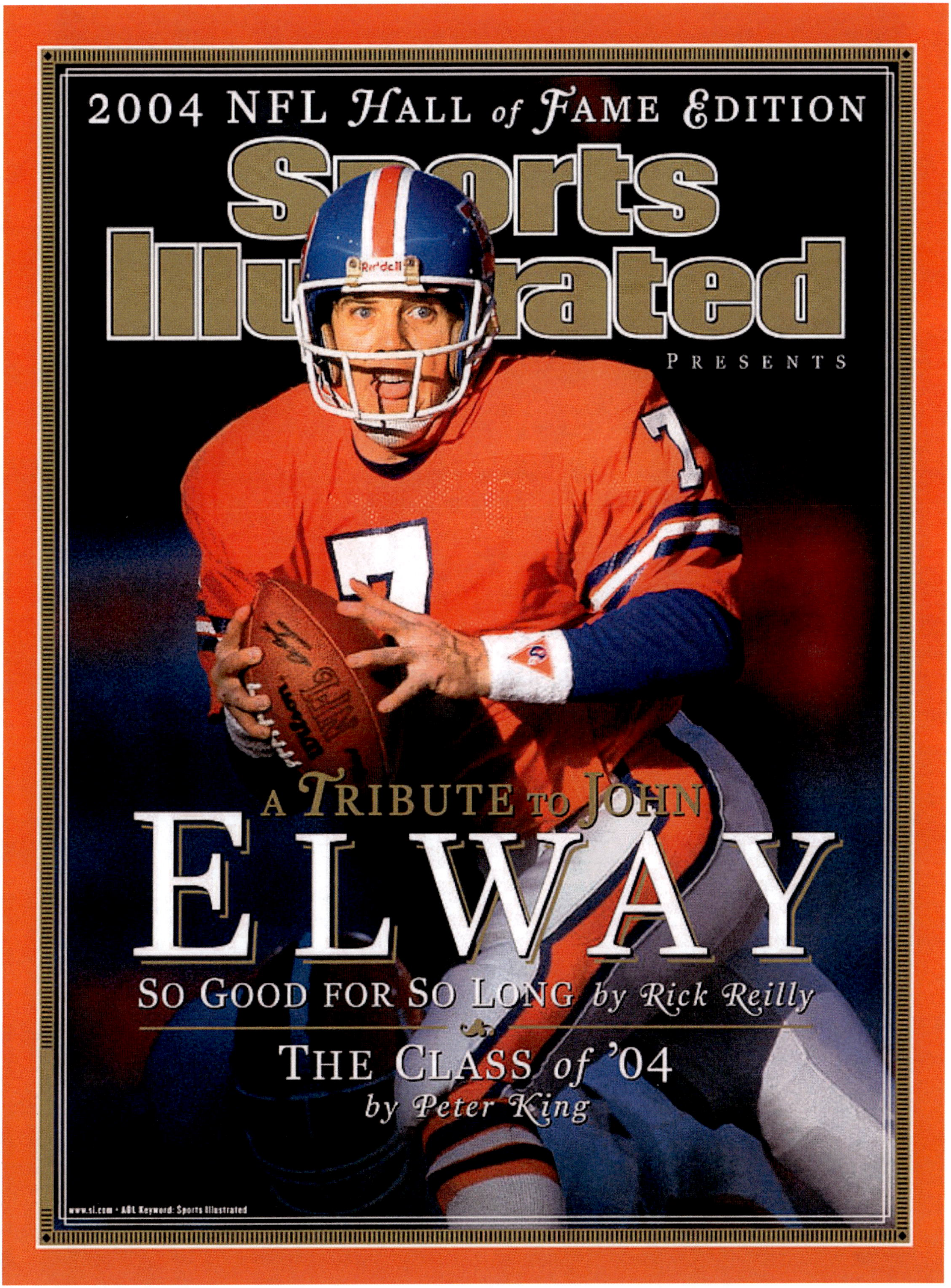

2004 NFL HALL of FAME EDITION
Sports Illustrated
PRESENTS
A TRIBUTE TO JOHN
ELWAY
SO GOOD FOR SO LONG by Rick Reilly
THE CLASS of '04
by Peter King
www.si.com • AOL Keyword: Sports Illustrated

November 7, 2013
At halftime during the Thursday Night Game against Oregon, Stanford retired Elway's jersey.

The quarterback sack becme an official statistic in 1982. During his career, Elway was sacked 516 times, most in the history of the NFL. Derrick Thomas of the Kansas City Chiefs is credited with 26 sacks against Elway.

Elway appeared on Thomas' card 3 times, and appeared on Greg Towsend's card 4 times.

'The Boz' failed to record a sack against Elway.

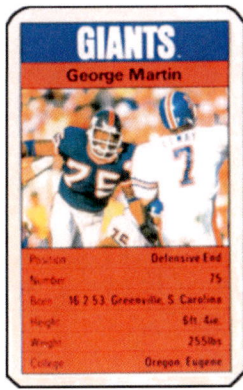

1987 Ace Fact
George Martin

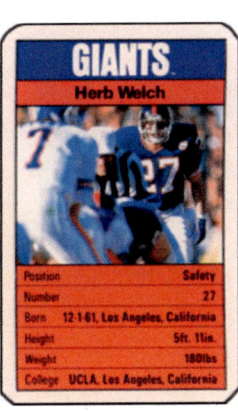

1987 Ace Fact
Herb Welch

1987 Atlanta Falcons
Pocket Schedule

1987 Fleer #85

1988 Ace Fact
Stacey Toran

1989 Pro Set #463
Greg Townsend

1988 Smokey Raiders
Greg Townsend

1990 Topps #172
Clay Matthews

1990 Pro Set #549
Lionel Washington

1990 Pro Set Super Bowl
#95 Charles Haley

1991 Pro Set #527
Jon Hand

1992 Diamond Sticker
Howie Long #42

1992 Fleer #204
Greg Townsend

1992 Pro Line Profiles
#460 Lawrence Taylor

1992 Pro Set #139
James Jones

1992 Pro Set #203
Neil Smith

1992 Pro Set Power #193
Greg Townsend

1992 Score #409
Jacob Green

1993 Pinnacle #293
Neil Smith

1993 Pinnacle
Team Pinnacle #10
Derrick Thomas

1993 Pro Set #200
Neil Smith

1993 Stadium Club
Members Only #358
Anthony Pleasant

1993 Ultra #205
Dan Saleaumua

1993 Upper Deck #193
Clay Matthews

1993 Upper Deck #265
Clyde Simmons

1994 Classic #22
Michael Dean Perry

1994 Classic #57
Steve Emtman

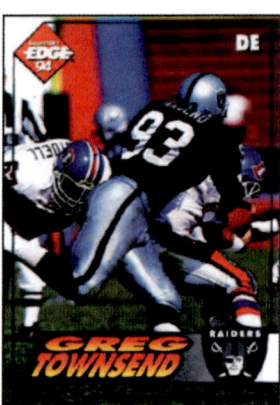

1994 Collectors Edge
#98 Greg Townsend

1994 Collectors Choice
#77 John Randle

1994 Collectors Edge
#180 Leslie O'Neil

1994 Fleer #245
Anthony Smith

1994 Pinnacle #224
Anthony Pleasant

1994 Select #87
Leslie O'Neal

1995 Collectors Choice
#246 Bryant Young

1995 Sky Box Impact
#128 Junior Seau

1995 Stadium Club #132
Robert Blackmon

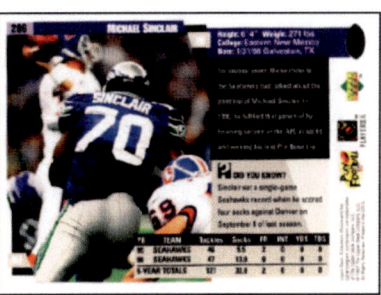

1996 Collectors Choice #286
Michael Sinclair

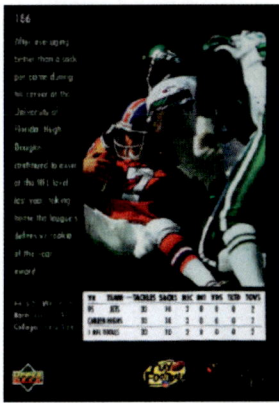

1996 SP #186
Hugh Douglas

1997 Pacific Philadelphia
#166 Shawn Lee

1997 Stadium Club
Never Compromise
#NC 30 Derrick Thomas

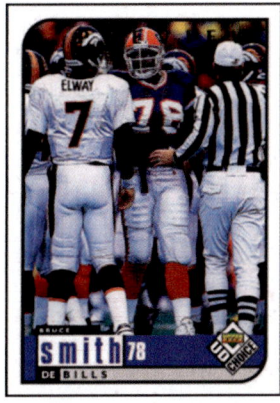

1998 Collectors Choice
#22 Bruce Smith

1998 Stadium Club #46
Derrick Thomas

A LITTLE HELP FROM MY FRIENDS

Terrell Davis, John Elway, Howard Griffith.

A big THANK YOU to Glenn Geiger, Todd Chesley, Alan Ugai, Jeff Nelson, John Harding, Brett Raitz, Jerry Parsons, John Miller, John Spano, Mike Blaisdell, Robert Tucker, Karey Lavin, and Jean Walton. This guide would not have been possible without their contributions.

Also, thank you Marshall Fogel for your expetise, patience, and access to you vast collection.

The John Elway cards listed below appear on various checklists, however, I can not verify a single example of any player.

1995 Collectors Edge
Edge Tech Black Label 22K #5

1998 Black Diamond
Rookies Black Onyx #ON7

1997 Studio Portrait
4x6 Postcard #8

1998 Playoff Absolute
SSD Heros Red #7

1997 Studio Portrait
4x6 Postcard #29

1998 Playoff Absolute
SSD Heros #7

Photo/Illustration Credits

All collectibles are meant for public consumption. All images are sourced from private collections which were obtained by collectors through private transactions, sports memorabilia stores, and auction houses. Images contained herein are used with their owner's permission. Though considered a collectible, an exhaustive search was conducted, and the original source, aucion house, and or photographers were credited where applicable. In many cases, type IV photos and reproductions are readily available through online retailers. Any omission is unintentional.

Contact us at firstandgoalpublishing@gmail.com regarding newly discovered (1983-1998) cards, uncredited photos, or those attributed in error, as future editions will be updated.

Cover- Unknown: Iconic Auctions Fall
  2014 Lot #545
6 San Jose Sports Authority
6 Ebay:Fartheroffthewall
7 *Life* October 1979
8 John Rogers Archive TSN Collection
 -Auction
10 David Madison/Getty Images
11 Unknown
14 YouTube
15 David Madison/Getty Images
16 George Gojkovich/Getty Images
17 Steiner Sports
18-19 *Playboy* August 1981
20 Unknown
21 San Jose Sports Authority
22 *ESPN The Magzine* 4/6/04
28 David Madison
29 Robert Stinnett/*Oakland Tribune,*
  Associated Press
30 Unknown
31 Bettmann
34 John Kelly/Getty Images
36 Unknown Pin Interest
39 Unknown
41 Unknown
43 Unknown
51 Unknown
52 Sports Team History
53 Unknown
55 Unknown

65 George Gojkovich/Getty Images
66 Bob Martin /Allsport
68 Manny Rubio-*USA TODAY* Sports
70 Unknown
78 Unknown
84 Michael Madrid / *USA TODAY NETWORK*
86 Focus on Sport/Getty Images
88 Ron Vesely/Getty Images
94 George Rose/Getty Images
101 George Tiedemann/*Sports Illustrated* via
  Getty Images (Set Number: X42343)
102 Ebay: MapleCityGraphics
114 Tim DeFrisco/Allsport/Getty Images
120 YouTube
133 DenverBroncos.com Eric Lars Bakke
147 Ron Vesely/Getty Images
176 RVR Photos / USA Today Sports Images
211 Unknown
262 Unknown
263 John W. McDonough /*Sports Illustrated* via
  Getty Images (Set Number: X54346 TK3 R6F13)
267 David Stluka
329 Stephen Jaffe/AFP Getty Images
335 ESPN.com Sept 14, 1999 -Associated Press
336 Ebay: joemoe84
338 Nhat V. Meyer/Bay Area News Group/MCT/
  Sipa USA
339 George Rose/Getty Images
344 Fanatics Authentic
351 Al Beto/Getty Images, Tim Clary AFP, Getty
  Images, Todd Rosenberg Associated Press

This guide is intended for research and educational purposes. It is not affiliated with or endorsed by any public or private high school, college, university, professional league, team, players union, or individual.

"I look at my career and its still hard for me to believe the way things turned out, and how things happened. I've been so blessed."
John Elway

FIRST & GOAL PUBLISHING